SHELLEY AT WORK

Oxford University Press, Ely House, London W. 1

GLASGOW NEW YORK TORONTO MELBOURNE WELLINGTON
CAPE TOWN SALISBURY IBADAN NAIROBI LUSAKA ADDIS ABABA
BOMBAY CALCUTTA MADRAS KARACHI LAHORE DACCA
KUALA LUMPUR HONG KONG TOKYO

I

a. *The Boat, the Dome, the Isle, the Eye of Creative Imagination*

b. '*The mind ... a wilderness of intricate paths ...*
a labyrinth.' '*Truth as fair as Ariadne*'

NEVILLE ROGERS

Shelley at Work

A CRITICAL INQUIRY

SECOND EDITION

OXFORD
AT THE CLARENDON PRESS
1967

© *Oxford University Press 1967*

PRINTED IN GREAT BRITAIN

TO
DOROTHY AND NORMAN
KILGOUR

PREFACE TO THE SECOND EDITION

IN preparing my revised edition of this book I have tried to avoid unnecessary expansion, both on the principle of μέγα βιβλίον μέγα κακόν and because additions might obstruct rather than assist its original purpose, which was to attempt an analysis of Shelley's thought-patterns based on an investigation of his working methods. My chief changes and additions, made necessary by the results of recent study, are the rewriting of the final pages of Chapters 11 and 16, and the insertion at the ends of Chapters 4, 5, 8, 13, and 15 of notes on neglected points arising out of them. It is my hope that, in Chapter 16, I may have come yet a little closer than others towards an understanding of 'The Triumph of Life'. Quotations from Shelley's letters have now been given in the fine new text of Professor Frederick L. Jones, in place of that of the 'Julian Edition', now outdated. Page references to Thomas Hutchinson's Oxford *Shelley* have been adapted to the reprint now current. In quotations from *The Esdaile Poems* my makeshift text of 1956 has been replaced by that of my new Oxford edition.

The preparation of my first edition was complicated not only by the difficulty of the material but by pressing problems of time and circumstance. I am grateful to my readers for their forbearance with the errors which inevitably crept in, and which I have now done my best to remove. Among those who have taken great trouble to suggest corrections, while encouraging me with evidence that their significance was not considerable, I am particularly grateful to Mr. G. M. Matthews who, by his keen deciphering of the words 'as fair as', in the quotation on p. 17, has added another touch of strength to Shelley's equation of 'truth' with 'Ariadne'. About certain points which trouble others I remain untroubled: for instance, I may or may not be wrong about the sex of the figure in Plate 1 (*b*), but what really matters, from the point of view of Shelley's 'mystery' (see p. 249), is the unimportance of this point: the quotation on p. 231 provides his own perspective. A number of my readers, including students both graduate and undergraduate, have wished me to add a chapter concerning the troubles of a few 'critics' who complain that Shelley has been 'reduced' to a Platonist, or who refer to the 'thesis' of Shelley's Platonism. But if—as that 'reduced' would seem to imply and the complainants otherwise to make plain— it is now possible to acquire a doctorate in English studies without acquiring an apprehension of what Platonism means, that, surely, is an educational problem and one far too big for reduction to the dimensions of a modest investigation concerning a particular poet. And since, today, the συνετοί for whom Shelley wrote are, I am sure, far more numerous among his readers than he could ever have hoped, I do not think that his ghost will rebuke me if I add nothing to the account of my working methods given on pp. x–xi, and if I leave to Plato himself (see pp. 148–9) the last word about those who, reared among theses, and an attendant system of rewards, can see in terms of theses alone.

I have to thank Professors Edmund Blunden, Frederick L. Jones, and J. A. Notopoulos for much patient help, both in cor- respondence and in conversation. Mr. Desmond King-Hele has given me, very kindly, some useful points about Shelley's scientific interests, and I owe to the late Donna Nerina Medici di Mari- gnano, great-granddaughter of Shelley's Vincent Novello, the discovery of Shelley's echo from Petrarch on p. 342, n. 1. In revis- ing Chapter 16 I have owed much to Mr. G. M. Matthews, Mr. Donald H. Reiman, and Professor A. M. D. Hughes for their able studies which have cleared so much of the ground. Mr. Robert Woodings, of the University of East Anglia, who has made a specialized study of the text of 'Charles I' and of Shelley's re- searches into the historical background, has sent me some kindly criticism of my remarks on the poem on p. 275: such expansion and qualification as they may call for can be left, I think, for his important forthcoming publication. Mr. William J. McTaggart and Mr. David R. Pichaske, graduate students of Ohio University, have saved me much time and labour by their energetic co-opera- tion in this revision. Not least am I indebted to Dr. R. W. Hunt, Keeper of Western Manuscripts at the Bodleian Library, and to his assistants Miss Crum and Miss de la Mare who have given generously of their expertise and their time to the checking of quotations from Shelley's manuscripts.

NEVILLE ROGERS

Ohio University, Athens, Ohio
March 1966

PREFACE TO THE FIRST EDITION

THE occasion for this book arose out of the gift of manuscripts made to the Bodleian Library in 1946 by the late Sir John Shelley-Rolls.[1] With the addition of these manuscripts to those presented in 1893 by Lady Shelley, two-thirds, roughly speaking, of the family papers inherited from Shelley and Mary—the famous 'Boscombe Collection' of the nineteenth century—came together again in the Bodleian, and since then Lord Abinger, owner of the remaining third, has permitted microfilms of it to be deposited there too. When the award of a Leverhulme Fellowship brought me temporary freedom to explore the unrivalled and unprecedented opportunities thus offered for research it was for a while difficult to decide what form of publication, first of all, would make the most advantageous use of such an enormous wealth of material. A further problem arose from the fact that the most precious part of the treasure was a buried treasure, tantalizingly lurking among the uncatalogued and hitherto uncataloguable mysteries of Shelley's notebooks. My decision was dictated in the end partly by limitations of personal time and circumstance and partly by what, as research proceeded, seemed to be demanded more and more insistently by the material itself—it was to postpone both the formal cataloguing of the notebooks and the overdue revision of the 'Oxford Shelley' while attempting something which, it happened, I had long believed to be an outstanding need among Shelley studies: a new examination and analysis of the poet's reading and thought in relation to his composition.

What Shelley's poetry requires above everything else is to be understood and judged by the ideas by which it is animated. That this has been done too seldom is because, owing to the complexity of his mind and his elaborate system of symbolism which he did not live to illuminate as he had intended in a series of metaphysical essays, it becomes difficult, very frequently, for his reader to discover what his ideas are. This is true not only of his detractors, who so often condemned him uncomprehendingly,

[1] See 'The Shelley-Rolls Gift to the Bodleian', *Times Literary Supplement*, 27 July, 3 Aug., and 10 Aug., 1951.

but of his admirers as well. For since it is in his more substantial
and worthily representative poems that the difficulty is greatest,
and since, on the other hand, no great degree of penetration is
required for an understanding of his slighter pieces, it is not
unnatural that a wholly disproportionate degree of fame and admiration should for a long time have settled on the latter. This
happened the more easily because their fragile charm, their ease,
and their brilliance appeared to be so perfectly in accord with the
various picturesque presentations of Shelley the man that busy
pens had built up after his death—Matthew Arnold's 'ineffectual
angel', the Victorianized 'divine bard', Francis Thompson's
'child . . . gold-dusty with tumbling amid the stars', or the 'Ariel'
of M. André Maurois.[1] The corollary followed that this was a
poet in whom considerable ideas were hardly to be expected.
Today all serious students of Shelley are aware not only that his
representative poetry is essentially a poetry of ideas but that those
ideas were fed, as Professor Grabo affirmed some twenty years
ago,[2] 'more by the literature he read than from emotional experiences of a purely personal character'.

The aim of this book is first to discover what Shelley's ideas
were and how they were derived and then to illustrate how he
interpreted experience through them; its basis is the evidence
which his drafts and memoranda afford. I have called it 'a
critical inquiry' and my endeavour throughout its preparation
has been to inquire and deduce rather than to theorize or construct. Quite apart from my conviction that any creative artist
should be so approached in the first place—which, if a truism, is
a frequently neglected one—such a method was imposed by
Shelley's notebooks themselves for, as my first chapter will make
plain, their nature would permit of no other. Where a personal
theory has been advanced I have indicated my responsibility by
the use of the first person singular. Documentation has been as
full as possible, but since the validity of the whole book must
depend also on the validity of the research out of which it has

[1] Matthew Arnold, *Essays in Criticism* (2nd series), New Eversley edn., 1935,
pp. 143–4. Francis Thompson, *Shelley*, Burns, Oates, and Washbourne, 1906.
André Maurois, *Ariel, ou la vie de Shelley*, Grasset, 1923. These and other 'Shelley
legends' have recently received most salutary treatment in a survey of the whole
question of Shelley's after-fame. See Sylva Norman, *Flight of the Skylark*, Reinhardt, 1954.
[2] *The Magic Plant*, Chapel Hill, N.C., 1936, p. 36.

proceeded, a brief account of the preliminary mechanics of my labours has been introduced into the first chapter.

It was, once again, Professor Grabo[1] who emphasized the impossibility of doing justice to Shelley's poetry without taking into account what it transmutes from languages and literatures other than his own. This is a field for study in which his notebooks offer exceptional opportunities; almost every page of what follows will reveal some evidence of what he gained, in particular, from his reading in Greek, Italian, and Spanish. Translations have been given with my quotations from these languages except when I wished to avoid repetitiveness or where it seemed that a translation would assist one reader less than it would encumber another. Wherever possible I have given Shelley's own versions; where none existed such others have been used as were convenient and suitable; in a few cases I have had to supply a version of my own. The subject of Shelley's translating is a field for study in itself, and, though critical digression into this had to be resisted, material for it is plentifully supplied both in the text, where his versions are printed below or close to the original, and in the appendixes. Where in translation or otherwise he may be discovered to have misinterpreted Plato, Dante, Calderón, Goethe, and others my concern has been less with niceties of accuracy—though I have always endeavoured to respect the true meaning—than with the matter of how in fact he *did* interpret these writers. For it is his interpretation, right or wrong—and it is usually the former, percipiently so—which affects his composition.

In writing this book I have incurred a deep debt of gratitude to many people and to some institutions. Thanks in the first place are due to the trustees of the Leverhulme Foundation whose award of a Fellowship made possible a year of research at Oxford, to the British Academy and the Pilgrim Trust for a generous grant towards the completion of the work, and to the Education Committee of the London County Council, Mr. Philip Wayne, and Mr. Harold Llewellyn-Smith for much kindness and patience involved in allowing me three years' leave of absence from my duties at St. Marylebone Grammar School. For the initial encouragement without which my Shelley researches would never have begun I have to thank Professor Blunden who, further-

---

[1] In the passage quoted above.

more, has been ready at all times to offer valuable suggestions or to answer queries out of his unrivalled knowledge of Shelley's poetry and Shelley's period. Professor H. W. Garrod has given me the benefit, unfailingly, of his great scholarship and experience: to him and to Sir Maurice Bowra I am indebted not only for much kindness and encouragement but for the making of certain practical arrangements entailed by my stay in Oxford. My researches in the Bodleian have owed much to the facilities arranged for me by the Keeper of Western Manuscripts, Dr. R. W. Hunt, and to the patience and skilled assistance of his staff.

Next I have to express my thanks to certain owners of copyright material. Sir Edward Bridges has very kindly permitted me to quote from a letter written to W. B. Yeats by his father, the late Poet Laureate, Mr. Maurice Buxton Forman has given me leave to quote from the privately printed *Shelley Notebooks*, edited by his father, the late Harry Buxton Forman, and Miss Ruth Draper has allowed quotation from the text and from her translation of Lauro de Bosis' *Icaro*. Lord Abinger has permitted me to quote from the manuscripts in his collection of which the Bodleian possesses microfilms, and for permission to make use of microfilms taken for the purposes of this book I have to thank the authorities of the Library of Congress, the Henry Huntington Library, and the Library of Harvard University. Mr. W. C. H. Esdaile, completing the generosity of Shelley's family, has permitted me to have a microfilm made of his precious Shelley notebook. Mr. John Wain has allowed quotation from an article on George Orwell, and the Clarendon Press have permitted me to quote from the late Professor F. M. Cornford's version of Plato's *Republic*. If through inadvertence I have made use of any other copyright material my apologies are here tendered in advance.

Among those who have helped me by their replies to queries I am grateful to Professor Gilbert Murray for his prompt assistance on several occasions and particularly for tracking down one of Shelley's more erratic Greek quotations which proved to be of much significance in relation to *Epipsychidion*. For identifying three or four other Greek quotations I am indebted to Mr. Alan Longmans who has saved me a good deal of time and labour. Professor Frederick L. Jones of the University of Pennsylvania, scholarly editor of three important volumes, my debt to which will be apparent from my bibliography and footnotes, has been a helpful correspondent and has kindly lent me his photostat facsimile of the Shelley notebook in the Library of Congress. Miss Mabel A. E. Steele, of the Houghton Library, Harvard University, has been of great assistance with her prompt replies to correspondence and her clever and accurate observation of manuscripts; Miss R. Glynn Grylls (Lady Mander) and Miss Sylva Norman have given me the advantage of their specialist knowledge whenever I had need of it.

For obtaining me access to an important manuscript, inaccessible hitherto, I am exceedingly grateful to Mr. James Lees-Milne. Mrs. Louise Boas of Orleans, Mass., has made me several generous gifts of rare books and for certain other books I am indebted to Mr. Carl Pforzheimer.

For advice or help on particular sections of the book I have to thank Signor Edoardo Cacciatore, Mr. Gordon Chapman, Mr. Cecil Grayson, Dr. Ernest Stahl, and Dr. Enid Starkie. Some perceptive suggestions were made by Miss Antonia Gianetti and by my friend and former pupil, Mr. David Woolf. Mr. Christopher Harris has kindly read certain sections of the proofs and corrected errors.

Mrs. Kilgour (Miss Dorothy Hewlett) has read my manuscript and made helpful suggestions and both she and Mr. Norman Kilgour have helped me in a score of ways: not least by their warding off from me of distractions which threatened to prevent me from finishing the book within the time available for writing.

Finally, over and above what this book owes to individuals and institutions, I should, I feel, be lacking both in courtesy and in justice if I concluded the ceremony of thanks with anything less than a comprehensive acknowledgement of its debt to a very valuable heritage of contemporary American scholarship. And as it takes off on its somewhat adventurous flight into the upper ether of Shelley's intellect and imagination let me give it for *envoi* a salute, in particular, to Professor Frederick L. Jones, Professor J. A. Notopoulos, and the late Professor Newman Ivey White, those three skilful engineers to whom it owes so much of its equipment.

N. R.

Oxford and Hampstead, May 1956

ADDITIONAL ACKNOWLEDGEMFNTS

I am particularly indebted to Dr. Duane Schneider, my friend and colleague of the Department of English at Ohio University, for the time, care, and skill he has devoted to the proofs of this second edition; my grateful thanks are likewise due to Mr. John Lazzati, of the Department of Classics at Wayne University, who has kindly checked the Greek quotations. For an interesting point concerning *Hellas* (p. 298, n. 4), as well as for a number of minor corrections, I have to thank Professor J. C. Maxwell. It would be impracticable to name all the many others who, since the publication of my first edition, have taken the trouble to send me their encouragement, corrections, and suggestions. I can do no more than thank them collectively.

N. R.

CONTENTS

LIST OF ILLUSTRATIONS   xvii

MANUSCRIPTS   xix

BIBLIOGRAPHY   xxi

PART ONE

'The wanderings of careful thought'

1. Shelley's notebooks: 'method in his madness'   1

2. The mind and its paths. Philosophy and symbolism in Shelley's poetry   15

3. Thought, Feeling, and Symbols. Necessity and the New Birth   24

4. 'Ariadne'; Love and Intellectual Beauty; Virtue and Power   37

5. Daemons and other 'monsters of his thought'   64

6. Boats. Isles   91

7. The Dome. The Eye and the Star. The Philosophic Imagination   105

8. The Veil. Mutability   120

9. The Cave   147

10. The Dream of Life   169

PART TWO

The wind, the lyre, and the labour

11. Shelley at work: a closer view. 'To a Skylark'   195

12. Shelley and the West Wind   211

13. Italian Platonics and *Epipsychidion*   230

14. 'Ginevra': Emilia to Keats   249

15. *Adonais*: Keats to Intellectual Beauty and the One 255

16. From *Hellas* to 'The Triumph of Life' 273

CONCLUSION

17. Poetry and the Power of Mind 305

APPENDIXES

I. The Bipont Plato: references collated 328

II. The temptation of Justina: Calderón's episodes: Shelley as a translator 329

III. 'A Midsummer Night's Dream Poem': Sussex, Goethe, and Rousseau 334

IV. Henry Reveley: later achievements of Shelley's engineer 339

V. (*a*) Shelley's memoranda on Dante's *Convito* 340

(*b*) Shelley's Italian letters to Emilia Viviani 341

(*c*) Shelley's Italian versions of his own poetry 342

INDEX 344

LIST OF ILLUSTRATIONS

PLATE I. (a) The Boat, the Dome, the Isle, the Eye of
Creative Imagination *frontispiece*

(b) 'The mind . . . a wilderness of intricate
paths . . . a labyrinth.' 'Truth as fair as
Ariadne'

PLATE II. Daemons: 'monsters of his thought' *facing p.* 68

(a) (?) A κακοδαίμων in pursuit

(b) Daemons floating in the 'intermediate
space'. The Boat and the Isle again

(c) The Tan-yr-allt 'assailant'

PLATE III. Draft for opening of 'To a Skylark' *facing p.* 207

MANUSCRIPTS

(a) *Manuscripts used*

THE basis of this book is the Bodleian Collection of Shelley manuscripts, more particularly the notebooks. These latter have been collated by means of microfilms or facsimiles[1] with six Shelley notebooks in America: three in the Henry Huntington Library, California,[2] two in the Library of Harvard University, and one in the Library of Congress, Washington. Other Bodleian material consulted includes the microfilms of the manuscripts owned by Lord Abinger and the papers bequeathed by 'The Reverend Colonel Finch'. In the British Museum Library I have made use of the unpublished journals of Claire Clairmont. Through a microfilm I have had access also to the early, hitherto unpublished poems of Shelley which are contained in the famous 'Esdaile Notebook'.

Where manuscripts have been foliated or paginated, as has been done with the Bodleian notebooks, exact sources are given in the footnotes; where manuscripts are unfoliated and unpaginated such exactness is not possible.

(b) *Note on the text of passages quoted*

In quoting previously unpublished passages from Shelley's memoranda or drafts I have endeavoured, in principle, to give a text that shall reproduce as closely as possible what he wrote in the manuscript. Since, however, textual matters are not the primary concern of this book, I have noticed only such variants and other points as have significance and have reduced both discussion and apparatus to a minimum.

Where Shelley is himself quoting some printed passage and his errors and variations are of no interest, I have given the text as it appears in print.

[1] Among these *The Shelley Notebook in the Harvard College Library*. Reproduced with Notes and a Postscript by George Edward Woodberry, Cambridge, Mass., 1929.

[2] These three notebooks, given by Lady Shelley to Richard Garnett and acquired after his death by W. K. Bixby, were for a while known as the 'Bixby Notebooks'. For the avoidance of confusion I refer to them throughout as the 'Bixby-Huntington Notebooks'. (B-H I, B-H II, and B-H III.)

Passages first printed in this book will be found marked with a double asterisk ** on the pages where they are first quoted, namely:

16–17, 18, 20, 21, 28–29, 38, 44, 45, 63, 64, 66, 91, 94, 95, 102, 107, 169, 171, 176–7, 192(2), 203, 236, 238, 239(2), 240(2), 252(2), 257, 260, 261, 263, 264, 265, 288, 340–1, 341–2(5), [cf. 238–40], 342–3(2).

Besides these passages I have quoted from the manuscripts a number of others which, though not now printed for the first time, have hitherto been accessible only in limited or privately issued editions. These are marked with a single asterisk * on the pages where they first appear, which are the following:

15, 45, 199, 200, 204, 213(2), 215, 217, 218, 219(2), 220, 221, 222(4), 223(2), 224, 240, 242, 301, 318, 334.

The following signs and conventions have been used in my quotations:

blank space	a blank space in the manuscript
]	preceding word or words are lost
[	abrupt ending of passage
[]	cancellation by Shelley
⟨ ⟩	gap or tear in the manuscript
⟨?⟩	illegible word, words, or part of a word
de⟨wy air⟩	(e.g.) conjectural word, words, or part of a word.

Here and there a ⟨*sic*⟩ denotes some characteristic slip on Shelley's part, e.g. in his Greek, Italian, or Spanish grammar, though neither here nor elsewhere has it been my purpose to notice his many slips at all systematically.

BIBLIOGRAPHY

MANY books have been read during the preparation of this present volume, but those only are listed of which direct use has been made. Such abbreviations as have been used in the footnotes will be self-explanatory.

1. *Printed texts of Shelley's writings*

The Complete Poetical Works of Shelley. Edited with textual notes by Thomas Hutchinson, Clarendon Press, 1904.

The Complete Works of Percy Bysshe Shelley. Newly edited by Roger Ingpen and Walter E. Peck. In ten volumes. Published for the Julian Editions in London by Ernest Benn, Ltd., and in New York by Charles Scribner's Sons, 1926–7.

New Shelley Letters. Edited by W. S. Scott. The Bodley Head, 1948.

The Shelley Notebooks.[1] Deciphered, transcribed, and edited with a full commentary by H. Buxton Forman. Privately printed for the Boston Bibliophile Society, St. Louis, Mo., 1911.

Plato's Banquet. Translated from the Greek, 'A Discourse on the Manners of the Ancients Relative to the Subject of Love', also 'A Preface to the Banquet', by Percy Bysshe Shelley. Revised and enlarged by Roger Ingpen from manuscripts in the possession of Sir John Shelley-Rolls, Bart. Privately printed, 1931.

Verse and Prose. From the Manuscripts of Percy Bysshe Shelley. Edited by Sir John Shelley-Rolls, Bart., and Roger Ingpen. Privately printed, 1934.

The Esdaile Poems. Early Minor Poems from the Esdaile Notebook. Edited from the manuscripts with introduction, commentary, and notes by Neville Rogers, Clarendon Press, 1966.

The Letters of Percy Bysshe Shelley. Edited by Frederick L. Jones, Clarendon Press, 2 vols., 1964.

Kenneth Neill Cameron, *Shelley and His Circle*, vols. i–ii, Oxford and Harvard, 1961.

[*Note.* In quoting printed passages of Shelley's writing I have followed, as a rule, the texts indicated in my footnotes, correcting only one or two undoubted errors of punctuation. An exception, however, is the text of the *Symposium* translation where I found it necessary not merely to depart from some of the accepted punctuation where it impeded the sense but also to interpolate an occasional word where the accepted text was nonsensical.]

---

[1] i.e. the 'Bixby-Huntington' Notebooks. See above, p. xix, n. 2.

2. *Contemporary sources of facts and chronology*

The Letters of Mary W. Shelley. Edited by Frederick L. Jones, Univ. of Oklahoma Press, 1944.

Mary Shelley's Journal. Edited by Frederick L. Jones, Univ. of Oklahoma Press, 1947.

Maria Gisborne and Edward E. Williams, Their Journals and Letters. Edited by Frederick L. Jones, Univ. of Oklahoma Press, 1951.

3. *Recollections of Shelley's contemporaries*

THOMAS MEDWIN: *Revised Life of Shelley*. Edited by H. Buxton Forman, O.U.P., 1913.

T. J. HOGG: *The Life of Shelley*.
E. J. TRELAWNY: *Recollections of Shelley, Byron and the Author*
T. L. PEACOCK: *Memoirs of Shelley*.

} Combined edition entitled *The Life of Shelley*, ed. Humbert Wolfe, Dent, 1933.

4. *Later biographies*

Among later biographies the one chiefly used has been:

NEWMAN IVEY WHITE: *Shelley*, 2 vols., Secker and Warburg, 1947.

The following have also been consulted:

EDWARD DOWDEN: *The Life of Percy Bysshe Shelley*, 2 vols., Kegan Paul, 1886.
W. E. PECK, *Shelley, His Life and Work*, 2 vols., Boston and New York, 1927.
EDMUND BLUNDEN: *Shelley*, Collins, 1946.
A. H. KOSZUL: *La Jeunesse de Shelley*, Paris, 1910.
ANDRÉ MAUROIS, *Ariel, ou la vie de Shelley*, Grasset, 1923.
R. GLYNN GRYLLS: *Mary Shelley*, O.U.P., 1933.
R. GLYNN GRYLLS: *Claire Clairmont*, John Murray, 1939.
ELIZABETH NITCHIE: *The Reverend Colonel Finch*, New York, Columbia University Press, 1940.
ENRICA VIVIANI DELLA ROBBIA: *Vita di una donna*, Florence, Sansoni, 1936.

5. *Special Studies*

In the all-important field of Shelley's Platonism I have made much use of the careful survey made in

The Platonism of Shelley, A Study of Platonism and the Platonic Mind, by James A. Notopoulos, Duke University Press, 1949.

My debt to Professor Notopoulos is far greater than can be acknowledged in footnotes.

It has been no part of my purpose to make a systematic reading of the many special studies of Shelley and of particular aspects of his work, though I have read many of them. Of these the following books and periodicals have been quoted or referred to:

CARL GRABO: *A Newton among Poets*, Chapel Hill, N.C., 1930.
CARL GRABO: *Prometheus Unbound, An Interpretation*, Chapel Hill, N.C., 1935.
CARL GRABO: *The Magic Plant*, Chapel Hill, N.C., 1936.
A. M. D. HUGHES: *The Nascent Mind of Shelley*, Clarendon Press, 1947.
SYLVA NORMAN: *Flight of the Skylark, The Development of Shelley's Reputation*, Reinhardt, 1954.
MATTHEW ARNOLD: *Essays in Criticism* (2nd series), New Eversley edn., Macmillan, 1935.
FRANCIS THOMPSON: *Shelley*, Burns, Oates, and Washbourne, 1906.
DESMOND KING-HELE: *Shelley; His Thought and Work*, Macmillan 1960.
DONALD H. REIMAN: *Shelley's 'The Triumph of Life'*, Univ. of Illinois Press, 1965.
The Keats–Shelley Memorial Bulletin, ed. Sir Rennell Rodd and H. Nelson Gay, no. 2, Macmillan, 1913.
The Keats–Shelley Memorial Bulletin, ed. Dorothy Hewlett, nos. 3–5 (1950, 1951, 1952), pub. for the Keats–Shelley Memorial from 11, Lion Gate Gardens, Richmond, Surrey.
The Keats–Shelley Journal, ed. Mabel A. E. Steele, nos. I–III (1952, 1953, 1954), pub. by the Keats–Shelley Association of America, Inc., New York.

To these books and periodicals must be added the following special articles:

G. M. MATTHEWS: 'The Triumph of Life', A New Text, in *Studia Neophilologica*, vol. xxii, no. 21, 1960.
G. M. MATTHEWS: 'Shelley and Jane Williams', in *Review of English Studies*, Feb. 1961.
PAUL BUTTERS: 'Sun and Shape in Shelley's "The Triumph of Life"', *Review of English Studies*, Feb. 1962.
DONALD H. REIMAN, 'Shelley's "The Triumph of Life"': the Biographical Problem' in *Publications of the Modern Language Association*, Dec. 1963.
A. M. D. HUGHES: 'The Triumph of Life', in *Keats–Shelley Memorial Bulletin*, no. xvi, 1965.

6. *Latin, Greek, Spanish, Italian, and German texts*

For Latin and Greek authors I have used:

Scriptorum Classicorum Bibliotheca Oxoniensis, Oxonii, e Typographeo Clarendoniano (the 'Oxford Classical Text').

For the plays of Calderón:

Don Pedro Calderón de la Barca, Obras Completas. Textos íntegros según las primeras ediciones y los manuscritos autógrafos que saca a luz Luis Astrana Marín, Tomo I, Dramas, Aguilar, S.A. de Ediciones, Madrid, 1951.

For Dante:

Biscioni's edition, 1793 (see App. V, p. 340), *Opere di Dante Alighieri*, a cura del Dr. E. Moore, nuovamente rivedute nel testo dal Dr. Paget Toynbee, quarta edizione, Oxford, 1908.
The Convivio of Dante Alighieri, ed. P. H. Wicksteed, Dent, 1908.

For Petrarch:

Francesco Petrarca, *Le Rime*. Collezione Salani, Firenze, 1924.

And for Goethe:

Faust, Der Tragödie erster Teil, Reclam Verlag, Stuttgart.

7. *Miscellaneous*

C. M. WIELAND: *The History of Agathon*, translated from the German, London, 1773.
M. LASTRI: *L'Osservatore Fiorentino sugli edifizi della patria, per servire alla storia della medesima*, terza edizione, Firenze, 1821.
WILLIAM DRUMMOND, *Academical Questions*, London, 1805.
SIR HUMPHRY DAVY, *Elements of Agricultural Chemistry*, London, 1813.
C. D. LOCOCK: *An Examination of the Shelley Manuscripts in the Bodleian*, Clarendon Press, 1903.
A. H. KOSZUL, *Shelley's Prose in the Bodleian Manuscripts*, Henry Frowde, 1910.
Shelley Memorials, ed. Lady Shelley, Smith Elder, 1859.
Relics of Shelley, ed. Richard Garnett, Moxon, 1862.
A Lexical Concordance to the Works of Percy Bysshe Shelley, compiled and arranged by F. S. Ellis, Quaritch, 1892.
Letters of John Keats, ed. M. Buxton Forman, O.U.P., 1935.
Biographia Literaria, by S. T. Coleridge, ed. J. Shawcross, 2 vols., O.U.P., 1907, repr. 1949.
The Republic of Plato, translated with Introduction and Notes by Francis Macdonald Cornford, O.U.P., 1951.
THOMAS TAYLOR: *The Cratylus, Phaedo, Parmenides and Timaeus of Plato* (translated), London, 1793.
Icaro, by Lauro de Bosis, with a translation from the Italian by Ruth Draper and a Preface by Gilbert Murray, O.U.P., New York, 1933.
La storia della mia morte, di Lauro de Bosis, Prefazione di G. Salvemini, Torino, Francesco de Silva, 1948.
Selected Poems of Friedrich Hölderlin, the German text translated with an Introduction and Notes by J. B. Leishman, Hogarth Press, 2nd edn., 1952.
C. M. BOWRA: *The Romantic Imagination*, O.U.P., 1950.
ENID STARKIE: *Arthur Rimbaud*, Hamish Hamilton, new and revised edn., 1947.
The Novels of Thomas Love Peacock, edited with Introduction and Notes by David Garnett, Hart Davis, 1948.
UMBERTO CALOSSO, *L'anarchia di Vittorio Alfieri*, Seconda edizione, riveduta, Bari, Laterza, 1948.

PART ONE
'The wanderings of careful thought'

1. Shelley's notebooks: 'method in his madness'

'THE source of poetry', Shelley once remarked, 'is native and involuntary but requires severe labour in its development.' He was replying to Medwin[1] who, seeing him in the throes of composition, had commented on his constant *'pentimenti* and self-hypercriticism'. If we cannot, like Medwin, look over Shelley's shoulder as he wrote, we can still see from a first glance at almost any of his drafts the force of both the comment and the reply.

Far and away the most valuable primary source for study of his poetry is to be found in his working notebooks, those 'manuscript books' of which Mary Shelley speaks. Twenty-eight of them survive in England and America. Two are different from the rest, being fair copy books. One of these, now at Harvard, has long been known as a vital textual source for the poems mainly of 1819–20 copied into it by Shelley and Mary; the other, the famous 'Esdaile Notebook',[2] was used by Shelley about 1812 for collecting together some of his poems of the previous years: certain quotations will be made in the ensuing chapters from the unpublished material which it contains. But it is the remaining twenty-six notebooks that will command most of our attention, for it is in them that we really meet the poet in his workshop. The figure lurking there is, we notice straight away, something very much more substantial than the inspired writer of well-anthologized and apparently effortless lyrics who is most commonly taken to constitute the true, the total Shelley.

It is, above all, a worker and a thinker that we meet. Inspira-

---

[1] Thomas Medwin, *Revised Life of Shelley*, ed. H. Buxton Forman, O.U.P., 1913, p. 347.   [2] Now in the Carl H. Pforzheimer Library.

tion indeed, unlike the generality of verse writers, he hardly ever lacked and it was for this reason that, as Mary Shelley tells us,[1] 'he never wandered without a book and without implements of writing'. Thus, when the inspiration came to him—which was as likely to occur in the Baths of Caracalla or in a boat on the Thames, the Serchio or the Bay of Lerici as in his study at home—he was equipped and ready for the drafting of poetry. Unfortunately— and here was his especial problem—when the inspiration did come it was liable to visit him with a strength that was frequently beyond his management, and hence came his difficulty in attaining, as Keats so shrewdly pointed out, that 'self-concentration'[2] necessary to him as an artist. Hence came the struggle involved in his '*pentimenti* and self-hypercriticism'. To glance at these today is to be astonished as Medwin was by the 'severe labour' which went towards the 'development' even of some of his slighter lyrics from their 'native and involuntary source' and which, quite frequently, gave to the final form in which they have become familiar to us the appearance of a string of easily-captured *vers donnés*. To study the record which his notebooks have preserved for us of the successive stages of that labour is to have a new notion of Shelley's art.

Here too, intermingled with poetry in all the stages of its composition, lies a mass of other matter still more instructive for a student: drafts of many of his prose works, notes for these or for other projected writings in prose or verse, abstracts from his philosophical, historical, or scientific reading, extensive quotations in Greek and Italian together with an occasional one in Spanish, Latin, or French, translations from these languages or from German, personal and domestic memoranda, pen and pencil sketches, and a good deal else besides. All this material, when identified and subjected to the light of a critical analysis, has a great deal to reveal about the many ways in which Shelley was busied, and can enable us to see behind the 'severe labour' expended upon individual poems into the evolution of his mind as a 'native and involuntary source' from which poetry was ready to spring. This latter subject, the evolution of Shelley's mind, will occupy us in Part I of this book and later, in Part II, we shall

---

[1] 'Note on Poems of 1817': Thomas Hutchinson, *The Complete Poetical Works of Shelley*, Clarendon Press, 1904, p. 551.

[2] M. Buxton Forman, *Letters of John Keats*, 2nd edn., 1935, p. 507.

apply the same analytical procedure in examining the genesis of certain of the major or more significant poems. Since the validity of such an analysis must depend on the researches on which it is founded, an account of these will be a necessary preliminary. But first of all some description must be attempted of Shelley's idiosyncratic habits of work and the resultant problems with which research had to deal.

Recurrent at every turn were the problems arising from Shelley's handwriting. Though examples are not lacking in his notebooks of the beautiful, triumphant calligraphy he could display in his fair copies these, comparatively, are rare and the drafts and memoranda which fill them for the most part are little more than a welter of near-illegibility and conflicting corrections built up in tiers. Trelawny's description[1] of a single page, now lost, is by no means untypical: 'It was a frightful scrawl . . . it might have been taken for a sketch of a marsh overgrown with bulrushes and the blots for wild ducks.' Sometimes he has either been too busy to sharpen his quill or has forgotten his penknife, so that the words are formed with the utmost difficulty and can only be guessed from their general shape or from their context. Sometimes too—perhaps when he is out of doors—his ink runs out and a draft will degenerate into a series of pen-sketches eked out with a pencil; quite a number of pages are written wholly in pencil and some of them in consequence have become so severely rubbed in the course of the years as to be quite indecipherable. Not uncommonly ink and pencil conflict upon a page: satirical lines on the Lake Poets, for example, emerge in pencil from under lines written in ink for 'A Vision of the Sea',[2] and over the pencil draft of three stanzas for the 'Ode to the West Wind' we find drafted in ink the Italian prose story 'Una Favola'.[3] Then again, peeping out from under the fragment 'To Constantia'—'The rose that drinks the fountain dew . . .'[4]—we come upon some Greek script and

[1] *Recollections of the Last Days of Shelley and Byron*, in Humbert Wolfe's combined edition of Hogg, Peacock, and Trelawny, *The Life of Percy Bysshe Shelley*, Dent, 1933, ii. 197.

[2] Bixby-Huntington Notebook, II, *27ᵛ. The three Shelley notebooks in the Henry Huntington Library will hereafter be referred to as 'B-H I', 'B-H II', and 'B-H III'. For a list of principal manuscripts referred to see Bibliography above.

[3] B-H I, *4ʳ, *4ᵛ, *5ʳ, *5ᵛ, *6ʳ. Cf. below, pp. 241, 226, n. 1.

[4] Bod. MS. Shelley adds., e. 10, p. 219 rev.

recognize a quotation from Plato's *Apology*; Shelley's Greek script, incidentally, is untrammelled as a rule by breathings, accents, or iota subscripts, and his running together of the words gives them the appearance at first of a series of Aristophanic coinages. Should a notebook have a plain cover, of parchment, leather or cardboard, it is as likely as not to receive an overflow of English or Greek writing upon the outside of it. 'When my brain gets heated with thought', said Shelley to Trelawny on the occasion just referred to, 'it soon boils and throws off images and words faster than I can skim them off. In the morning, when cooled down, out of the rough sketch (as you so justly call it) I shall attempt a drawing.' In the morning, as it often turned out, he would be busied and heated with something quite different, and so it was Mary Shelley who, after his death, had to 'attempt a drawing' of so many of the rough sketches he left behind him.

But the complications arising from illegibility and the other vagaries that have been mentioned are more than doubled by the way he frequently has of turning the book upside down and sideways as he works on it. We will take, for example, a notebook which by reason of its size and shape lends itself very readily to the habit.[1] Its leaves number 88 and they measure 236 × 186 mm. Let us imagine it placed before us in Fig. (i), ready to open at page 1, *AB* representing the top edge, *DC* the bottom edge, and *AD* the spine:

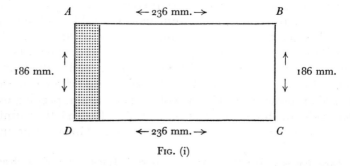

FIG. (i)

In addition to working forward in the normal manner from f. 1 towards f. 88, what he does is to invert the book, open it as if the back cover were the front one, and proceed to work backwards. The consequence is that on any given page we find that the

[1] Bod. MS. Shelley E. 4.

positions of the top and bottom are reversed, as in Fig. (ii), and that the writing is running from f. 88ᵛ towards f. 1ʳ, 'reversed'.

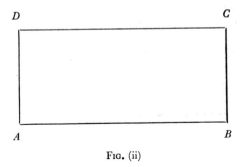

FIG. (ii)

But a page may be turned, and so Shelley turned it, two other ways: to the right, as in Fig. (iii), and to the left, as in Fig. (iv).

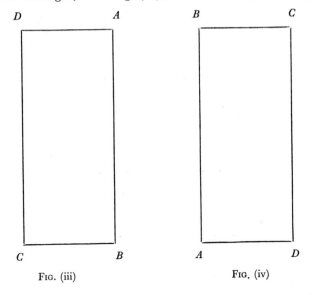

FIG. (iii)   FIG. (iv)

It will thus be seen that there are *four* ways in which the handwriting may be found running on any given page of a notebook.

The first complication arises when the forward-running writing proceeding from the use of the book in the first position—Fig. (i) —coincides with writing in reverse—Fig. (ii). If we represent the directions of both sets of writing by arrows the appearance of a page when the book is held in the first position will be something like what is shown in Fig. (v).

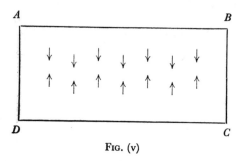

FIG. (v)

When, in addition to writing running forwards or in reverse, Shelley elects to write a few notes or lines of verse with the book turned to the right or to the left confusion reaches a climax: the effect as seen, once again, when the book is held in the first position—Figs. (vi) and (vii)—is almost beyond diagrammatic representation:[1]

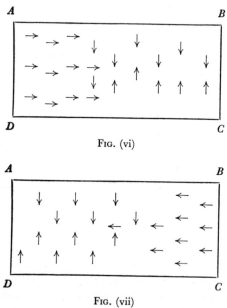

FIG. (vi)

FIG. (vii)

[1] I have not noticed a page with the writing running *four* ways, but such may quite possibly exist.

The problems created for the student by such habits need hardly be emphasized. It will be enough to mention, for instance, the hazards of following a note or a poem when it is not only nearly illegible to start with but inconsecutively drafted, its course being constantly broken up by other writings running in other directions so that, as Shelley did, we have to skip pages and be ready, if necessary, to jump out of one notebook into another— when, moreover, it may itself be partially written 'in reverse' so that we have to be constantly turning the book around as Shelley turned it. Even in the case of a familiar, long-printed poem, and with the aid of the invaluable *Shelley Concordance*,[1] it is at times by no means easy to identify scattered lines or portions of them. 'I think Cyprian',[2] wrote Mary Shelley at the head of one page, tentatively identifying a piece of the draft of Shelley's translation from *El mágico prodigioso*.[3] She was right, as it happens, but with all her first-hand knowledge and pioneering skill even she could not be sure for the moment.

From the twenty-six notebooks we have been thus describing in general terms let us now select a typical example for closer examination. The volume we will choose[4] is of Italian manufacture, is bound in coloured parchment and measures 185×130 mm.: there are 172 pages and the writing which runs, as usual, from both ends continues on to the endpapers and on to the front cover where we find drafted the fragment: 'Is it that in some brighter sphere . . .?' Working forwards—see Fig. (i)—in accordance with the Bodleian pagination we find the following among its contents:

p. 1	Drawing of trees.
pp. 2–7	Calculation of statistics for milk and potato production.
p. 10	Draft of part of 'Lines written during the Castlereagh Administration'.
pp. 14–16	Draft for 'Liberty' ('The fiery mountains answer each other . . .').

[1] *A Lexical Concordance to the Works of Percy Bysshe Shelley*, compiled and arranged by F. S. Ellis, Bernard Quaritch, 1892.

[2] Bod. MS. Shelley adds. e. 18, p. 65.

[3] Shelley and his circle seem usually to have referred to the play as 'Cyprian' from the name of its protagonist, Cipriano: see below, p. 81, and also Frederick L. Jones, *Maria Gisborne and Edward E. Williams, their Journals and Letters*, Oklahoma Press, 1951, p. 135.

[4] Bod. MS. Shelley adds. e. 6.

p. 17   Some lines for 'Song to the Men of England'.
p. 18   Draft of a stanza, later redrafted for *Adonais*, xxxii, beginning 'Panther-like Spirit, beautiful and swift...'.
p. 21   A line for 'The Cloud'.
pp. 22–25   Draft for 'Hymn of Apollo'.
pp. 27–29   Draft for 'Hymn to Pan'.
p. 31   Continuation of draft for 'The Cloud'.
pp. 35–37   Fair copy of 'The Cloud', line 35–end.
pp. 39–42   Draft of 'Matilda Gathering Flowers' (translation from Dante, *Purgatorio*, xxviii, 1–51).
p. 44   Drawing of the butt of a pistol.
pp. 45–59   A discussion of sexual ethics, arising out of Plato's *Symposium*—part of Shelley's 'Discourse on the Manners of the Ancients Relative to the Subject of Love'.
pp. 60–65   A more general discussion of the *Symposium* (the draft of Shelley's intended Preface to his translation).
pp. 67–69   Two lines of Greek [Euripides, *Hippolytus*, 1004–5] connected with the preceding discussion: also notes on a passage in Athenaeus [*Deipnosophistae*, 217a].

As, however, we thus work forwards, the greater part of the writing appears in reverse and in order to follow it we must turn the book upside down—see Fig. (ii)—and work backwards from p. 172:

pp. 172 rev.– ⎱Abstracts from Sir Humphry Davy's *Elements of*
    155 rev.   ⎰*Agricultural Chemistry*, 1813.
pp. 154 rev.– ⎱Draft for 'Arethusa'.
    149 rev.   ⎰
p. 144 rev.   Two passages of Greek prose [Plato, *Phaedo*, 108c. 5, 115c. 6].
p. 146 rev.   Part of draft for 'Ode to Liberty'.
p. 141 rev.   A fine drawing of trees, crags, and water.
pp. 138 rev.– ⎱Draft of last two stanzas of the 'Ode to the West
    137 rev.   ⎰Wind'.
p. 136 rev.   Beginnings of a draft for a ballad on a woman driven by her betrayer to starvation and prostitution.[1]
pp. 135 rev.– ⎱Continuation of draft for the 'Ode to Liberty'. On
    131 rev.   ⎰p. 131 is a drawing suggestive of Capri.
p. 130 rev.   A few more lines for the ballad.
pp. 129 rev.– ⎱'Ode to Liberty' continues. On p. 118 rev. also is a
    118 rev.   ⎰draft of 'Good-night'.

[1] See *The Complete Works of Percy Bysshe Shelley*, edited by Roger Ingpen and Walter E. Peck. In ten volumes. Benn and Charles Scribner's Sons, 1927 (the 'Julian Edition'), iii. 152. Mr. W. J. McTaggart has noticed that 'Young Parson Richards' is a misread title: the Harvard Fair Copy Book has 'A Ballad'.

pp. 117 rev.–
110 rev. } The ballad continues, partly in pencil.

pp. 108 rev.–
107 rev. } More of 'Ode to Liberty'.

p. 97 rev.   Very rough draft for beginning of 'To a Skylark'.

p. 96 rev.   More of the ballad.

pp. 94 rev.–
70 rev. } Very rough draft for 'The Witch of Atlas'.

I have chosen for illustration not the richest of Shelley's note-books but one rather which may be fairly taken as characteristic. Even though its contents have been somewhat abbreviated from my full list, the versatility and energy of which these pages give evidence are quite startling: it might be hard to find many minds which, amid the composition of 'The Cloud' and the 'Ode to Liberty', the 'Ode to the West Wind', and 'To a Skylark' could freely range through Dante, Euripides, and thoughts of pistol practice (a favourite recreation with Shelley) to contemporary science or the immortality of the soul, agriculture, or Greek homosexuality—pausing, meanwhile, to dash down an efficient and indeed moving political ballad or to make a drawing of some observed or imagined scene of Nature. Here is the heat of thought and the boiling of the brain of which Shelley spoke, and out of it we can see the poetry emerging, as he said, in words and images 'thrown off faster than I can skim them off'.

But to trace this exciting emergence of thought and poetry was impossible until some practical mechanism was available for surmounting the obstacles presented by the notebooks them-selves. It becomes necessary at this point to describe the making of such a mechanism. Two things were necessary for a start: an analysis of the contents of each individual notebook and a system of reference to cover *all* the notebooks by means of which the scattered portions of individual drafts and memoranda might be at once traced, assembled, and collated when required.

First, as each notebook was examined, its contents, in order of pagination or foliation, were listed on loose quarto pages which were then clipped together into a sheaf. In some cases—e.g. where a single notebook had been devoted to a single draft—this was the matter of a few minutes' work only: in the case of others, though detailed deciphering could be postponed, a considerable amount of time had to be spent upon the mere identification of many of the drafts and fragments, published and unpublished: still more time was needed to trace quotations from Greek, Italian, Spanish, Latin, and French authors and from Shelley's vast reading in his own language. Finally, however, all his notebooks in the Bodleian had been worked through in this manner, as well as microfilms of all those in America with the exception of one, the contents of which had already been listed in a manner adequate to my needs. Other material too had to be inventoried which bore upon or might bear upon his notebooks, e.g. a large box of his loose manuscript sheets[1] and various notebooks of Mary Shelley's.

Dating was the next step. From the known dates of certain compositions, from biographical facts and dates available from such sources, notably, as Mary Shelley's *Journal*[2] and the letters of both Shelley[3] and Mary,[4] as well as, sometimes, certain dates obligingly jotted down by Shelley himself amid his drafts and memoranda, my quarto pages were first marked with a series of chronological glosses and then, by using these with caution proportionate to the degree of certainty which could be credited to each, it became possible to assign a general date to the sheaves, each representing a notebook, into which they had been fastened. Here more caution was required, since it was apparent that Shelley did not always use a notebook consecutively or continuously so that two or three of them at times might combine to cover a period. Allowance had also to be made for the likelihood, of which evidence was to be found, that he was liable to copy or revise in a notebook he happened to be using something he had actually composed at an earlier date: at times too he would seem to have composed in an old rather than a current notebook if it came handy when the impulse was upon him. But although, in consequence, no dating of the notebooks as a whole could pretend to a total accuracy yet most of them do supply quite strong internal evidence of the period in which they were in general use. A con-

---

[1] Bod. MS. Shelley adds. c. 4. A few of these loose sheets proved to be identifiable as pages torn from Shelley notebooks in England or America. See 'Four Missing pages from the Shelley Notebook in the Harvard College Library' by Neville Rogers, *Keats–Shelley Journal of America*, iii. 47–53, 1954.

[2] Frederick L. Jones, *Mary Shelley's Journal*, Oklahoma Press, 1947.

[3] Frederick L. Jones, *Letters of Percy Bysshe Shelley*, Clarendon Press, 1964.

[4] Frederick L. Jones, *Letters of Mary W. Shelley*, Oklahoma Press, 1944.

venient example is afforded by the one we have examined above. One general clue appears in the persistence throughout its pages of draftings for the 'Ode to Liberty'. This Ode, we know, was inspired by news of the success of the Spanish insurgents in 1820: we know also from a reference in Claire Clairmont's journal[1] for 16 March that the news had reached the Shelley household by then and Mary's letters to Mrs. Gisborne of 26 March and 31 March[2] contain further enthusiastic references to the events in Spain. It was on 12 July that Shelley wrote to Peacock[3] enclosing the Ode and it would seem likely that the period in which the volume was in general use lay between mid-March and that date: into this period, consistently, would fall the drafting of 'To a Skylark' which has been fairly conclusively dated by Professor White to 22 June:[4] likewise perhaps the quotations from the *Phaedo* which Shelley read on 9 May.[5] That the earlier pages were in use somewhat previously is suggested by the drafts of the 'Ode to the West Wind' and of the two political poems, usually believed to have been written in the autumn of 1819:[6] that its use continued into August is shown by the draft of 'The Witch of Atlas', composed on 12–14 of the month.[7] This notebook, incidentally, must have been the one lent to Medwin[8] by Shelley during the former's illness at Pisa, 20–23 November 1820 which, he mentions, contains 'Arethusa' and the 'Ode to Liberty': he mentions also the 'Sensitive Plant' which may well have appeared on pages now missing: that poem is dated in the Harvard Fair Copy Book 'March 1820', which is consistent with our general date for the volume.

One particularly interesting question of dating arises from the 44-leaved volume[9] which has been described as 'Shelley's Last Notebook since it has been believed to have accompanied the poet when he was drowned on 8 July 1822. In view of the

---

[1] British Museum MS., quoted by Newman Ivey White, *Shelley*, Secker & Warburg, 1947, ii. 191. The poem 'Liberty' drafted on pp. 14–16 of this notebook may be regarded as a preliminary product of the same excitement.

[2] Jones, *Letters of Mary W. Shelley*, i. 103, 104.

[3] Jones, *Letters of Shelley*, ii. 212.   [4] White, *Shelley*, ii. 594.

[5] Jones, *Mary Shelley's Journal*, p. 132.

[6] White, *Shelley*, ii. 107, 576.

[7] Mary Shelley's Note on *The Witch of Atlas*, Hutchinson, p. 388, and Jones, *Mary Shelley's Journal*, p. 137.

[8] Forman, *Revised Life*, p. 236: see also Jones, *Mary Shelley's Journal*, p. 141.

[9] Bod. MS. Shelley adds. e. 20.

tradition one is immediately struck by the fact that its contents belong not to 1822 but to the previous year. Exactly half of its pages are taken up with a draft for *A Defence of Poetry* and much of the remainder relates to Keats and *Adonais*. Together with these indications may be mentioned the presence of a draft for the poem 'To Emilia Viviani'—'Madonna, wherefore hast thou sent to me . . .?'[1]—besides Shelley's attempts to compose verses in Italian which Ingpen and Peck rightly printed under the same title. Then, not least, there is a curious drawing[2] of a naked male figure bearing a lance, the appearance of which amid the draft of *A Defence of Poetry* recalls Shelley's remark in a letter to Peacock written on 15 February 1821,[3] when he was promising a reply to his friend's 'The Four Ages of Poetry'—'I had the greatest possible desire to break a lance with you'; in stealthy retreat from the lance-bearer we may notice the still more curious figure of an anthropomorphous peacock. The little volume, undoubtedly once soaked in water, has been scientifically treated and is mostly legible. Whether it is supposed to have been found in Shelley's pocket, or subsequently recovered from the lockers of the 'Don Juan', has never been made clear and inquiries have failed to elucidate the family tradition. The first possibility is not supported by any contemporary references among those who conducted Shelley's burial: for the second some support might be discoverable in Captain Roberts's letter to Trelawny of September (?) 1822:[4] this mentions three 'memorandum books' as having been salvaged and the possibility that a notebook of the previous year *might* have been taken aboard is by no means negligible.[5] But Shelley's boating habits rendered his books liable on more occasions than one to damage by water, and in view of the strong *Adonais* element in this notebook, there seems a very likely chance indeed that it became immersed not on 8 July 1822, when he was

[1] Jul. iv. 87–88.

[2] Bod. MS. Shelley adds. e. 20, f. 34.   [3] Jones, *Letters of Shelley*, ii. 261.

[4] Trelawny, *Recollections*, in H. Wolfe's combined *Life*, ii. 229.

[5] Since I first raised this query about the 'Last Notebook' (*T.L.S.*, 30 July 1951), the whole story of Shelley's shipwreck has been freshly surveyed from manuscript evidence: see Leslie Marchand, 'Trelawny on the Death of Shelley', *Keats–Shelley Memorial Bulletin*, ed. Dorothy Hewlett, vol. iv, 1954. Amongst other matters Professor Marchand was able to show that earlier than 1858 there is no evidence to authenticate the Sophocles volume so long believed to have been taken from Shelley's dead hand and this in consequence has been removed from permanent exhibition at the Bodleian.

drowned, but on 16 April 1821 when, in company with Henry Reveley, who then saved his life, he met with his 'ducking' in the Pisa canal—the very day, incidentally, when he wrote the letter to Byron which gives us one of the earliest known indications of his knowledge of the death of Keats.[1]

The notebooks being thus dated one by one from internal and other evidence, the sheaves representing them were now marked in their turn with indications of the periods covered by each. To complete the process of dating they were next arranged in chronological order and fastened into loose-leaf binders: where the chronological arrangement was obscured by the overlapping of two notebooks in point of date precautionary cross-references were added. Three such binders, containing between them over four hundred closely written pages of analysis, and each prefaced with a list of the notebooks by which it was divided into sections, now formed a chronological guide to the greater part of Shelley's working life from 1814 to 1822—not complete since, missing pages apart, one or two whole notebooks seem to have been lost, and not final, since the analysis itself must contain errors corrigible from subsequent research, but adequate, none the less, for practical up-to-date use.

But this piece of equipment was not in itself sufficient: in order to reach the secrets of Shelley's notebooks it was necessary to follow him at work in order not merely of time but also of direction. Of the difficulty of following through the pages of a notebook the scattered and inconsecutive portions of a draft one example has already been seen in the 'Ode to Liberty': worse than this was the difficulty of following the many drafts, such as that of the 'Ode to the West Wind',[2] which were scattered through not one but several notebooks. For the following of these what was needed, and had to be made next, was a card-index by means of which their scattered portions could be instantly traced and brought together when necessary. As this index developed it had necessarily to be extended to cover not only Shelley's notebooks but all other sources of his poetical text and so elaborated as to distinguish printed from unprinted material. The addition

[1] See Ch. 16 below for the circumstances of the composition of *Adonais* with which this theory seems to fit.
[2] See below, Ch. 12 *passim.*

subsequently proved necessary as well of a companion index to show the whereabouts of accompanying prose drafts.

With this second set of equipment added to the first it became possible at last to begin the charting of the 'wilderness of intricate paths' running through the notebooks—this phrase of Shelley's which I am here applying to them, a phrase used by him in describing the human mind, is an apt description both of them and of his own mind.[1] What sifting, grouping, and regrouping of material was involved in the survey that followed, and what further apparatus had to be improvised before the paths began to stand out, need not be related here. Some of them proved disappointing enough: though promising at first they would merely lead into dense undergrowth or to the brink of a chasm; others, tangled to start with, would become clearer as they were followed; most of them as they proceeded would twist and ramify and interlace. Yet at every turn and every intersection there were points from which new bearings could be taken, and all the while new perspectives were appearing through which things not previously known to be related could be seen in their relationship to each other: the relationship in Shelley's writings between one poem and another, of verse pieces to prose pieces, of fragments to finished poems, the relationship of his Greek studies to his studies in other languages or in science and of his translating to his composition, the relationship in his thinking of the political to the philosophical and of his thinking generally to his creative processes, the relationship of both to the experiences of his life. Many of his drawings too had unexpected meanings to reveal. Here, awaiting exploration could the way be found, lay the mind of Shelley.

For the pathfinder it turned out in the end that Shelley himself had blazed the main trails, since the most valuable clues proved to lie in those memoranda of his, so enigmatical at first.

[1] See Ch. 2 below.

2. The mind and its paths. Philosophy and symbolism in Shelley's poetry

THE memorandum from which we will make our start is one from which a phrase was quoted in the last chapter, and it is one that has often been quoted and discussed since it was first printed by Mary Shelley in 1839. Though she brought it into her 'Note on *Prometheus Unbound*'[1] it appears in Shelley's notebook[2] as a footnote to the draft Preface for *The Cenci*:

... in the Greek Shakespeare, Sophocles, we find this image,

Πολλὰς δ' ὁδοὺς ἐλθόντα φροντίδος πλάνοις

a line of almost unfathomable depth of poetry; yet how simple are the images in which it is arrayed!

'Coming to many ways in the wanderings of careful thought.'[3]

... What a picture does this line suggest of the mind as a wilderness of intricate paths, wide as the universe, which is here made its symbol; a world within a world which he who seeks some knowledge with respect to what he ought to do searches throughout, as he would search the external universe for some valued thing which was hidden from him upon its surface.[4] *Such is the dim ghost of an imagination which is now dead for want of breathing the native air in which it was conceived and born.*

What Shelley says about Sophocles is very close to what he reveals obliquely of himself when commenting in the Preface to *Prometheus Unbound* upon its imagery drawn, he tells us, 'in many instances . . . from the operations of the human mind'; this means, without a doubt, their reflection in Shelley's—so much so that, as Mary says, 'it requires a mind as subtle and penetrating as his own to understand the mystic meanings scattered throughout the

---

[1] Hutch., p. 273.
[2] B-H (see above, p. xix, n. 2) II, *18ʳ.
[3] *O.T.* 67. Shelley's translation is inexact: it should read 'Having come by many ways . . .'.
[4] In quotation from Shelley's manuscripts, passages previously unprinted, both prose and verse, will be enclosed thus **. . .**, while passages hitherto accessible only in privately printed or limited editions will be enclosed, as here, thus *. . .*. The contents of the three Bixby-Huntington Notebooks were transcribed by H. Buxton Forman and privately printed by him in *The Shelley Notebooks*, St. Louis, Boston, 1911. For signs and conventions used in quotations from manuscripts see above, p. xx.

poem'. Now in *Prometheus* lies the quintessence of all Shelley's
subtlety: he himself recognized this[1] and we shall find in the
ensuing chapters that the deeper we get into his thought the more
frequently we come round to it. What is true of the mind we see
at work there will serve at the same time as an apt description of
the mind we have seen well illustrated in a single Bodleian notebook: 'wide as the universe which is here made its symbol'. It
might be said that in those two words 'universe' and 'symbol' lie
Shelley's whole conception of the stuff of poetry and of the
manner of its expression, and it is the universality of his thought
combined with the symbolism of his language which so often
obscure the clarity of his 'mystic meaning'. To follow him across
the universal spaces in which he so often seems to have ranged
too far and got lost is a hazardous journey whereon many perish:
his symbols, however, are the paths and fortunately they are not
undiscoverable though they are often remote and liable, as Mary
says, 'to elude the ordinary reader'. Even here he is hinting where
they chiefly lie, namely in the thought of ancient Greece, the 'dim
ghost of an imagination . . . now . . . dead'. Into this, with all its
kindred imagery, he sought to breathe new life 'not imitating the
Greek . . . [but gifting] it with that originality of form and colouring which sprang from his own genius'.

About the difficulties he presented to his readers Shelley had no
illusions. Elsewhere we find him beginning to draft what seems to
be a dialogue between himself, or some supporter of his, and a
baffled critic. (The bantering tone of this, the more noticeable
perhaps when contrasted by quotation here with the tone of
Mary's pardonable hagiography, is an incidental reminder of the
humour that is too commonly denied him. He could at times
display, like many young Englishmen of his order, a most per-
plexing capacity for laughing in the same breath at both himself
and his enemies.) The reviewer speaks first:[2]

**'A strange fellow', he says 'that Lionel—but there is a kind of
method in his madness which I should be glad to [find] see un-
ravelled.—'**

[1] See (Hutchinson, p. 274) Shelley's own comment when he finished the poem,
another example of Mary's skilful annotation: 'It is a drama, with characters and
mechanism of a kind yet unattempted; and I think the execution is better than any
of my former attempts.'

[2] Bod. MS. Shelley adds. e. 8, pp. 70–71. Only with great difficulty is the

The next two lines are cancelled in the manuscript:[1]

    **[It is a labyrinth without a thread
    I think that I possess]**

Then the reviewer goes on[1]

If we could for the sake of some truth as fair as Ariadne vanquish the monster of his thought [and ⟨? its⟩] I fear lest we should find no thread [unwinds, as] to guide us back thro the labyrinths [of his winding sophistries] which led us to its den. We should have arrived at a conclusion & have forgotten the premises which led to them. We should have scaled the [inaccessible] with a ladder which is immediately withdrawn.

To this indictment—one may catch, I think, an echo of Peacockian raillery rather more than the voice of the *Quarterly*—the defence begins[1]

Such is your conception of the intellectual & universal system of which Lionel is a disciple. The mechanical philosophy of the day which is popular because it is superficial and intelligible because it is conversant alone with the grosser objects of our thoughts[

With the full context of this memorandum—it can be traced and it is a most interesting one as we shall see later[2]—we shall not be concerned here. What is of importance for the moment is to discover its intrinsic meaning and significance. 'Lionel', as we know from the use of this name in 'Rosalind and Helen' and 'The Boat on the Serchio', is Shelley himself, and it is of himself therefore that he is talking, or, rather imagines one of his puzzled readers to be talking. We note immediately that both the thought and the language are almost identical with the thought and language of his other memorandum: the notion of thought as a 'labyrinth', having a monster within it, is but an extension of his phrase about the implication of Sophocles' line. And just as Man's mind, in Sophocles' implication, is a symbol of the universe, so Shelley's mind here may be taken as a symbol of Man's: he is in fact telling us directly what we gather indirectly from the *Prometheus* Preface. Now though we do not know exactly how the defence would have proceeded, it is not difficult to deduce something from those

passage to be deciphered. Here, as elsewhere, I have done my best to minimize reproduction or discussion of non-significant anomalies in the manuscript.

    It was in a contemporary notebook, Bod. MS. Shelley adds. e. 9, p. 366, that Shelley made the sketch of a woman, a landscape, and a maze (see Plate I *b*) which seems to illustrate his phrase 'truth—an Ariadne'.   [1] Ibid.

    [2] See below, p. 256.

words 'truth as fair as Ariadne', which are put into the mouth of the critic, and from the few words of it which do remain. Twitted for his labyrinthine subtlety, the inaccessibility of his central thought, Shelley's reply would have been, broadly speaking, that he at any rate, unlike others, did aim at 'truth' and a 'universal system' unlike 'the mechanical philosophy of the day', i.e. the system derived from Locke which regards poetry as a matter of 'wit' and is not concerned with truth or reality. Like other Romantics Shelley deplored its lack of respect for the human self. 'I am prepared', he says, 'to be unpopular rather than popular... because superficial and intelligible'; 'for truth', he might have added, 'is not to be expressed in ordinary mortal language, in fact'—and here he might have plunged straight into a crucial point of *Prometheus Unbound*[1]—

'the deep truth is imageless'.

For Shelley's way was not to explain truth but to express it in his own peculiar symbolical language, to be understood by those only whose perceptions were equal to it: in line with this is his abhorrence of didactic poetry expressed in the Preface to *Prometheus*. Here he breaks off the dialogue, or rather diverts it elsewhere as we shall see in a later chapter.[2] Symbolically, however, he has given us one very valuable hint. By 'truth', like Keats and others, he meant 'reality', *'real* truth'. If we would unravel the 'method in his madness' the way into the labyrinth must be sought, as we have said, by following the correspondingly 'intricate paths' of his notebooks. Broken and winding as these are, most of them can be mapped out in time: quite often several of them come together to form a single path proceeding in a single direction—a path of Grecian thought, signposted by Shelley's memoranda.

There are practically none that do not have something to tell us if their connexions can be traced. On a page, for instance, which bears a draft for the last two stanzas of the 'Ode to the West Wind'[3] we find inscribed the line

ἀρετῇ σε νικῶ θνητὸς ὢν θεὸν μέγαν

By virtue I, a mortal, vanquish thee, a mighty god.

[1] II. iv. 116, Hutch., p. 238. Cf. below, p. 159.   [2] See below, pp. 256–8.
[3] Bod. MS. Shelley adds. e. 6, p. 137 rev.

Less striking at first than any connexion with the West Wind is an Aeschylean ring about the line recalling the fact that in October 1819, when the Ode was conceived, Shelley was close to the writing of the fourth act of *Prometheus Unbound*. Then, as we examine the untidy draft, we see that there *is* such a connexion, for in place of line 56 as we know it Shelley originally wrote (my italics)

> One too like thee, *yet mortal*, swift and proud.

And though, we reflect, by the time Shelley had reached Act IV the original Aeschylean feeling of the drama had been superseded by a Platonic feeling, the Greek line does have as well a discernible relation to Prometheus. Altogether a triple link may be perceived: Shelley, defying the forces of despotism and institutional religion, is identified with the tortured Titan, like him suffering liberator and pioneer of scientific enlightenment: at the same time, speaking as the voice of truth and ἀρετή, he is identified with the power of the West Wind:

> Scatter, as from an unextinguished hearth
> Ashes and sparks, my words among mankind!

When we pursue the ἀρετή quotation to its source still further correlations can be made. It does not, in fact, derive from Aeschylus at all but from Euripides, *Hercules Furens*, 342. According to the strange mythological background of this play Alcmena was the mother of Heracles and a twin brother, the result of intercourse both with her husband Amphitryon and with Zeus who has visited her in his likeness. In the speech where the line occurs Amphitryon is upbraiding Zeus, his ὁμόγαμος, for permitting the state of affairs whereby he and the whole family of the hero are faced with extermination at the hands of the tyrant Lycus, i.e. for lacking just that sense of ἀρετή seen in a concern for his responsibilities towards humanity which is displayed by the mortal who is speaking. The reproach is suggestive enough both of Prometheus and of Shelley, still more so the sentiment of the last line of the speech, ἀμαθής τις εἶ θεός, ἢ δίκαιος οὐκ ἔφυς, 'a rather stupid god, or else unjust'. Later in the play Heracles becomes mad and kills his children; overcome by remorse he threatens suicide but is restrained by the exhortations of Theseus to endure woes that have arisen from the misdeeds of the gods. The situation of Heracles, like that of Amphitryon, offers a notable parallel with that of the Shelley of 1819, crushed under the world's sorrows which he has attempted to shoulder and bowed by the loss of his children, faltering for a moment and then recovering his courage. Nor, if we observe the addition by Shelley of a note of hope hardly found in the Euripides context, is this recovery of courage very far from the feeling of the close of the Ode:

> O Wind,[1]
> If Winter comes, can Spring be far behind?

And this brings us to another frequent Shelleyan motif: the idea of the regenerating processes of Nature, symbolizing the working in humanity of a hidden ἀρετή which produces a moral palingenesis or 'New Birth', not by revolutionary but by gradual means. Another memorandum, scribbled in 1822 inside the front cover of another notebook,[2] sets down the same idea:

> **The spring rebels not against winter but it succeeds it—the dawn rebels not against night but it disperses it.**

One memorandum, a single Greek line pointing the way through a Prometheus–Shelley allegory to the symbol of the Seasons has taken us far. Our next path may be picked up from a single word, several times jotted—'Diotima'.[3] This, of course, brings us at once to that point in Plato's *Symposium*[4] where Socrates begins his account of the discourse of the Mantinean woman on the subject of Love. It is not long before we come to the latter's definition of Love ("Ερως) as a being 'between a mortal and an immortal'. 'What is that, O Diotima?' asks Socrates, and she replies[5]

> Δαίμων μέγας, ὦ Σώκρατες· καὶ γὰρ πᾶν τὸ δαιμόνιον μεταξὺ ἔστι θεοῦ τε καὶ θνητοῦ.

A great Daemon, Socrates; and every thing dæmoniacal holds an intermediate place between what is divine and what is mortal.[5]

The terms here, θεοῦ τε καὶ θνητοῦ, are precisely those of our former antithesis, θνητὸς ὢν θεὸν μέγαν, which represent the conflict of *Prometheus Unbound* and the 'Ode to the West Wind'. "Ερως,

---

[1] See below, p. 228, for the original drafting of the last line. And for the significance of the Euripides quotation cf. below, pp. 53–55, 60, 226–7, 293–9.

[2] Bod. MS. Shelley adds. e. 18.

[3] In more than one notebook. [4] 201d.

[5] *Symp.* 202e. Jul. vii, 197. This and other translations from the *Symposium* are taken from Shelley's version unless otherwise stated.

this latest path to which we have been directed by the jotting 'Diotima', has joined with the ἀρετή path and the two together have led us well into the centre of Shelley's labyrinth. 'These daemons', continues Diotima in Shelley's translation, 'are indeed many and various, and one of them is Love.' Many and various were the notions of ἀρετή pursued by Shelley, but the greatest of these, an all-mastering concept into which other concepts were usually merged, was a too-frequently elusive, most Shelleyan notion of Love. For him Love became the guiding thread—'truth as fair as Ariadne'.

Scribbled in the same 1822 notebook[1] to which we have just made reference—inside the back cover this time—are two more Platonic pointers down the path of Love and Ariadne; they are from the *Republic*.[2]

** Οἴει ἂν οὖν ἧττόν τι ἀγαθὸν ζωγράφον εἶναι ὃς ἂν γράψας παράδειγμα οἷον ἂν εἴη ὁ κάλλιστος ἄνθρωπος καὶ πάντα εἰς τὸ γράμμα ἱκανῶς ἀποδοὺς μὴ ἔχῃ ἀποδεῖξαι ὡς καὶ δυνατὸν γενέσθαι τοιοῦτον ἄνδρα;**

Ὁ οὖν καλὰ μὲν πράγματα νομίζων, αὐτὸ δὲ κάλλος μήτε νομίζων μήτε, ἄν τις ἡγῆται ἐπὶ τὴν γνῶσιν αὐτοῦ, δυνάμενος ἕπεσθαι, ὄναρ ἢ ὕπαρ δοκεῖ σοι ζῆν; σκόπει δέ. τὸ ὀνειρώττειν ἆρα οὐ τόδε ἐστίν, ἐάντε ἐν ὕπνῳ τις ἐάντ' ἐγρηγορὼς τὸ ὅμοιόν τῳ μὴ ὅμοιον ἀλλ' αὐτὸ ἡγῆται εἶναι ᾧ ἔοικεν;

Then suppose a painter had drawn an ideally beautiful figure complete to the last touch, would you think any the worse of him if he could not show that a person as beautiful as that could exist?

Now if a man believes in the existence of beautiful things, but not of Beauty itself, and cannot follow a guide who would lead him to a knowledge of it, is he not living in a dream? Consider: does not dreaming, whether one is awake or asleep, consist in mistaking a semblance for the reality it resembles?[3]

The full implications of this memorandum appear when it is considered in conjunction with the Lionel–Ariadne dialogue and when both are placed in their biographical context. Of this it will be sufficient here to note that the two notebooks involved are among those which may be fairly accurately dated, and that there is evidence to show beyond a doubt both that the Lionel dialogue

---

[1] Bod. MS. Shelley adds. e. 18, 154–64 rev.   [2] 472d, 476c.

[3] Francis Macdonald Cornford, *The Republic of Plato*, translated with Introduction and Notes, Clarendon Press, 1941, pp. 173, 179. All subsequent translation from the *Republic* is from Professor Cornford's version.

belongs to the Emilia Viviani-*Epipsychidion* period of early 1821
and that the *Republic* quotation was noted down during those
months of 1822 when Shelley was none too happy with Mary
and Jane Williams was ascendant in his imagination. For Shelley
love, which gave the guiding thread to 'truth', i.e. 'reality' and
also beauty: something which he pursued philosophically in his
poetry and of which, at the same time, he sought a living likeness
in his own life. In *Epipsychidion* and elsewhere he had 'drawn an
ideally beautiful figure': throughout a series of baffling relationships, ranging from poor Harriet Shelley, through Miss Hitchener
(subsequently a 'brown demon'), to Emilia (in turn a disappoint-
ment), he had tragically endeavoured to 'show that such a beautiful
person could exist': now, between Mary, the most faithful of his
Ariadnes, and Jane, his 'anticipated cognition', as he called her,
he asked in the language of Greece the question—to which not all
his critics have supplied the negative answer that follows in
Plato's context—'Would you think the worse of him?' But Shelley
was not concerned to judge or be judged: what mattered was
that the quest for Truth and Beauty must go on: 'I always go on
till I am stopped', he once said,[1] and nine days before his death
he was writing to Horace Smith[2]—'Let us see the truth whatever that may be.' Till his last moment he continued in his
'wanderings of careful thought', and the problems of semblance
and reality, life and dreaming, were the subject of his last, unfinished poem. Their answer—the answer to the question formu-
lated in its last lines 'Then, what is life?' I cried—is one at which
we were left guessing by his death.

The universal system of which Lionel is a disciple

is, in fact, Platonic philosophy: it was out of this that he, Shelley-
Lionel, sought to gain an apprehension of Reality. Yet Shelley,
though gifted for philosophy, was not a philosopher but a poet
and what he took from philosophy he took for his own poetical
purposes, gifting it with his own 'originality of form and colouring'. To attempt to formulate a reasoned exposition of his derived
notions, which, even at the end, had hardly achieved the status
of a system of his own, would indeed be to 'scale the inaccessible
with a ladder which is immediately withdrawn'. What is of import

---

[1] Trelawny, *Recollections*, in H. Wolfe's combined *Life*, ii. 194.
[2] Letter of 29 June 1822. Jones, *Letters of Shelley*, ii. 442.

to Shelley studies is not so much Plato's philosophy as such, nor Shelley considered in a philosopher's role; it is what Shelley took from Plato and how he absorbed and transmuted it; the same, *mutatis mutandis*, applies to Goethe, Calderón, Dante, and the other great minds on which he drew, by no means all of whom are mentioned in his notebooks or can have their proper places in this book. The relation of transmutation to originality will appear in Part II, when we shall see Shelley at work on individual poems: in the next few chapters, although much poetry will come up for incidental examination, we shall be concerned chiefly with the process of absorption, for hereby we may hope to discover something about the mind from which the poems derived their life, their form, and their colour.

What we must be prepared to find might be best expressed perhaps in general terms by an adaptation of Shelley's own image: it will neither prove to be, as might first have been expected, an entangled pathless jungle, nor, as might next have seemed possible, the formally-designed garden-home of a systematically planted philosophy: we may expect instead a vast, fertile tract, wild and half-unexplored, interlaced by winding, well-worn paths of symbolical thinking, down which in endless directions move its operations, the operations of poetry. Some of the paths have already been indicated and these and the concepts which grow along them we shall follow, since their windings and interlacings forbid anything like an arbitrary sequence or method, in an order that is more convenient than methodical—the New Birth of Nature and Thought, ἀρετή and Ἔρως and their meanings and relationships in the Ariadne quest, Daemons and the 'intermediate place' they hold between divine and mortal, the idea of 'living in a dream'. These, our first paths, will lead us into other paths and concepts into which they merge at various points—Necessity, Boats and Isles, the Dome and the Eye, the Veil and Mutability, the Cave of Thought. We shall pause at times to take our bearings from Shelley's varied memoranda and sometimes from the curious drawings that decorate the pages of his manuscripts: then we shall travel onwards on our Platonic way, a way which, we shall find, leads us not only in and out of Plato but also through poets and prose writers in the several languages read by Shelley. Here and there too we shall come upon his explorations into contemporary science.

3. Thought, Feeling, and Symbols. Necessity and the New Birth

BEFORE we look at the first among Shelley's symbols and concepts which we are to examine, it may be well to take a glance at something he wrote about himself which casts a little more light upon the relation to him and his poetry of his concepts and symbols generally. It is something written to Godwin on 11 December 1817, and it is one of those little things like the note on Sophocles' mind-image which Mary Shelley, with her ready eye, once again, for any passage that illuminated her poet as she knew him, chose for inclusion among her notes in 1839.[1]

I am formed, if for anything not in common with the herd of mankind, to apprehend minute and remote distinctions of feeling, whether relative to external nature or the living beings which surround us, and to communicate the conceptions which result from considering either the moral or the material universe as a whole.

His possession of the faculty here claimed is well illustrated in the note on Sophocles, and had he continued with the Lionel dialogue he must have had a word or two to say about it in reference to his critic-baffling subtlety: it is a faculty illustrated throughout his poetry, and one which even today has not lost its power to baffle— one might comment, perhaps not unfairly, that though Shelley does seem to have been *formed* to communicate the conceptions in question, he does not always succeed or appear to succeed in so doing. The passage takes us to the heart both of Shelley's poetry and of 'Romantic' aspiration. Three days before writing to Godwin Shelley had 'read and finished Coleridge's Literary Life'.[2] Later editions were to print these words.[3]

To make the external internal, to make nature thought and thought nature, this is the mystery of genius in the Fine Arts.

Shelley, such was his kinship with the *Zeitgeist*, had anticipated

---

[1] 'Note on *The Revolt of Islam*', Hutch., p. 158. In subsequent references Shelley's original title *Laon and Cythna* will be preferred for the poem.

[2] Jones, *Mary Shelley's Journal*, p. 87.

[3] *Biographia Literaria*, ed. J. Shawcross, Oxford, 1907, ii. 258.

them: 'the cloud of mind' was 'discharging its collected lightning'.[1]

And if, instead of writing with a general implication, Coleridge had been referring specifically to Shelley, he could hardly have given a more succinct and apposite expression for Shelley's particular way of conceiving the material universe in terms of the moral, Nature in terms of thought and vice versa: he might seem, almost, to speak for Shelley more plainly than Shelley speaks for himself. But one phrase of Shelley's is to be noted: he does not say 'distinctions of *thought*' but 'distinctions of *feeling*'. His symbolism does of course consist, essentially, of minute and remote distinctions of thought: nevertheless the distinctions of thought *are* at the same time 'distinctions of feeling'. To those who do not realize this such a poem as *Adonais* might seem cold and unemotional, hardly more perhaps than a formal exercise in the manner of the Greek Bucolic poets. It is vital for an understanding of Shelley's symbolism to realize at the outset that in him thought and feeling were blended through the language and that the subtlety of the one is the subtlety of the other. Only if we qualify what Coleridge says about the whole 'mystery of genius in the fine arts' by the implications of Shelley's phrase about himself can we begin to understand the mystery of genius in Shelley. All this, of course, is true of other poets: of Shelley it needs to be particularly emphasized, not only because it happens to be peculiarly true in his case but because there is more than a chance that the truth may be obscured by the many source-hunters and writers of theses who, by concentrating on the mere tabulation of his thought as it may be chased from book to book, are in danger of building up an academic picture of his poetry as little more than a patchwork of borrowings, literary, philosophical, or political according to taste. Throughout Shelley's work in both prose and verse instinctive feeling and derivative thought—the first coloured by the emotions arising out of experience and the second elaborated by a great deal of original invention—are so closely interwoven that, beyond a certain point, they defy disentanglement: all we can do —and this precaution is always necessary in our studies—is to allow for thought when we are considering feeling and for feeling when we are considering his thought. The great point, however,

[1] *Prom.*, Preface, Hutch., p. 206.

is that while the nice distinction between the two elements is unimportant the effect of the amalgam is vital. 'It is', says Professor Carl Grabo,[1] in truthful summary, 'when he gives lyrical expression to ideas that he reaches his poetic heights.'

An admirable illustration is afforded by the symbol I have called 'the New Birth', a symbol frequent in Shelley's poetry: its significance evaporates unless we remember its dual origin, and realize that, although a thought may be derivative in part, it becomes so blended into his sentient nature that, when feeling begets the poem, idea and expression are lyrically born together. Thus upon him, even more than upon most people, the seasons cast not only a physical but an intellectual and moral influence which poetically *became* a feeling. Hence, for instance, in 1818–19, the 'dejection' at Naples and elsewhere, the abandonment of *Prometheus Unbound* after the completion of Act I, and later on the inspiration of Acts II and III, as the Preface tells us, by[2]

The bright blue sky of Rome, and the effect of the vigorous awakening spring in that divinest climate, and the new life with which it drenches the spirits even to intoxication. . . .

Here indeed is Nature in terms of thought, for Spring it is, as Professor White remarked,[3] that dominates these two acts. Among examples of Shelley's correlated faculty for seeing, or feeling, thought in terms of Nature a particularly touching one is to be found on the loose manuscript sheet bearing the lines 'On Fanny Godwin',[4] ('Her voice did quiver as we parted . . .'): by their side is one of his frequent sketches of a flowering plant and on the verso side is another of a grave and a plant in an urn: when the seasons came round again he added beside the latter 'I drew this in 1816 and now it is 1817'. Later, when 'the bright blue sky of Rome' had suddenly become dimmed for him by the death of William Shelley, he wrote out on the recto side that other memorial poem beginning 'Thy little footsteps on the sands . . .'. The revival of his spirits came towards the end of that October when he was expecting another child—'the new birth' was his

---

[1] *The Magic Plant*, p. 33. For a particularly interesting remark of Shelley's about the relative sensitiveness of 'head and heart', see below, p. 77.

[2] Hutch., p. 205.   [3] *Shelley*, ii. 115.

[4] Bod. MS. Shelley adds. c. 4, f. 68, Hutch., p. 546.

own phrase in a letter and coincided with the 'Ode to the West Wind', inspired by reflections on the regeneration of Nature out of its own decay.

In its early manifestations the New Birth concept is hardly distinguishable from the doctrine of Necessity enunciated in *Queen Mab*:[1]

> Spirit of Nature! all-sufficing Power,
> Necessity! thou mother of the world!

It seems probable that this doctrine reached Shelley through the eighteenth-century philosophers many among whom, though opposed to Plato, may have had it from indirectly Platonic sources. In its Shelleyan form it was a fusion of two Platonic ingredients, Necessity and the World Soul, and, though the emphasis later shifted towards the second of these, it was identifiable originally chiefly with the first, that Necessity which in the *Republic*[2] is the Mother of the Fates, on whose spindle turn the orbits of the world. It is, for Shelley, the spirit of Nature and of life, an impersonal, impartial power, unlimited and outlasting decay; all actions and thoughts in the universe are subject to it; actions are predestined and were always so.[3] In the year before he wrote *Queen Mab* he thus affirmed his belief to Miss Hitchener.[4]

Certainly everything is connected, both in the moral & physical world there is a train of events, & tho' not likely, it is impossible to deny but that the turn which my mind has taken, originated from the conquest of England by William of Normandy.

Men, he believed with Rousseau, Montesquieu, and others, are naturally virtuous and happy but have been corrupted by the evils resulting from false sophistication and false civilization; in *Queen Mab* he added, and made much of, his own peculiar belief in the evils engendered by an animal diet. God he regarded, with Voltaire, as a creation of the human mind based on the example of earthly tyrants and no less depraved than they: tyranny and warfare were produced by men's ignorance and selfishness as manifested in kingcraft, priestcraft, and commerce; marriage was a selfish institution, a violation of liberty. All these evils would perish in time, destroyed by their own corruption; meanwhile

---

[1] vi. 197–8, Hutch., p. 786.   [2] 616c–617c.
[3] See J. A. Notopoulos, *The Platonism of Shelley*, Duke Univ. Press, 1949, p. 176.
[4] Letter of 15 or 16 Oct. 1811. Jones, *Letters of Shelley*, i. 150.

what held back the restoration of mankind to virtue and happiness—and here he is hardly consistent with the tenet of predestination—was that 'man's all-subduing will', corrupted itself
by the selfishness, superstition, and lust which produced them,
was weak enough to tolerate their existence. So much the past
had taught; in a poem probably written in 1812 and entitled
'A Retrospect of Times of Old'[1] he points the lesson for the future:

> **The mansions of the Kings are tenantless,—
> Low lie in dust their glory and their shame!
> No tongue survives their virtuous deeds to bless,—
> No tongue with execration blasts their fame!**

The poem is not a cheerful one. After much about the pomp,
vileness, and decay of tyrants and priests it ends in an apostrophe
to the past possessors of earthly glory:[2]

> **Sesostris, Caesar, and Pizarro,—come!
> Thou, Moses, and Mahommed,—leave that gloom!
> Destroyers, never shall your memory die!
> Approach, pale Phantom, to yon mouldering tomb
> Where all thy bones, hopes, crimes, and passions lie!
> And thou, poor peasant, when thou pass'st the grave
> Where, deep enthroned in monumental pride,
> Sleep low in dust the mighty and the brave,
> Where the mad conqueror, whose gigantic stride
> The earth was too confined for, doth abide,
> Housing his bones amid a little clay,—
> In gratitude to Nature's Spirit bend,
> And wait in still hope for thy better end.**

And to bring the lesson a little closer to contemporary experience
he adds a footnote in the manuscript:[2]

**To this innumerable list of legal murderers our own age affords
numerous addenda, Frederic of Prussia, Buonaparte, Suvoroff, Wellington and Nelson are the most skilful and notorious scourges of their
species of the present day.**

In a long poem 'The Voyage'[3] he describes the uncontaminated

---

[1] Neville Rogers, *The Esdaile Poems*, Clarendon Press, 1966, p. 50, 1–4. Edward
Dowden's ascription to 'Lynmouth, August 1812' is probably correct: see *The
Life of Percy Bysshe Shelley*, 2 vols., Kegan Paul, 1886, i. 285.

[2] Ibid., pp. 52–53, 70–83.

[3] Ibid., pp. 53, 102–11. Other lines from this poem are quoted on pp. 91–92. The
manuscript is dated by Shelley 'Devonshire, 1812'.

life of merchant seamen and is rhetorical on the subject of the
true friendship that their life involves:

> **Who that had shared his last and nauseous crust
> With Famine and a friend would not divide
> A landsman's meal with one who needed it?
> Who that could rule the elements and spurn
> Their fiercest rage would bow before a slave
> Decked in the fleetingness of earthly power?
> Who that had seen the soul of Nature work,
> Blind, changeless, and eternal in her paths,
> Would shut his eyes and ears, quaking before
> The bubble of a Bigot's blasphemy?**

At this point, further to drive home the lesson, another footnote
is supplied in the manuscript:[1]

> **It is remarkable that few are more experimentally convinced of
> the doctrine of Necessity than old sailors, who have seen much and
> various service. The peculiarly engaging and frank generosity of sea-
> faring men probably is an effect of this cause. Those employed in
> small and ill-equipped trading-vessels seem to possess this generosity in
> a purer degree than those of a King's ship. The habits of subjection
> and coercion imbued into the latter may suffice to explain the cause
> of the difference.**

The seafaring men at Lynmouth and elsewhere who enjoyed
their easy chats with the talkative young Shelley can hardly
have realized that for him they were showing themselves in
their reminiscences 'experimentally convinced of the doctrine
of Necessity'. With them is contrasted the landsman,

> **Rapacious, mean, cruel and cowardly,
> Casting upon the loveliness of day
> The murkiness of villainy.
> By other nurses than the battling storm,
> Friendship, Equality and Sufferance,
> His manhood had been cradled,—
> Inheritor to all the vice and fear
> Which kings and laws and priests and conquerors spread
> On the woe-fertilized world.**

The development of the doctrine of Necessity in Shelley's mind
might be regarded, to some extent, as a conflict between his
intellect, which long stood firm upon it, and his instincts which

---

[1] Ibid., p. 56, whzrz 'habit' is a misreading.

rebelled against its cold, unrelieved gloom. The point at which the New Birth idea was to break away from it was the idea, involved in the doctrine, that evil must perish of its own corruption, and, at the risk of reading too much, perhaps, into a single phrase, we might already detect in 'the woe-fertilized world' of 'The Voyage' the germs of a corollary that out of decay comes regeneration, both in 'the moral and the material universe'. And *c.* 17 November 1811 we find Shelley writing to Miss Hitchener.[1]

> You must not *quite* despair of human nature—Our conceptions are scarcely vivid enough to picture the degree of crime of degradation which sullies human society—but what words are equal to express their inadequacy to picture its hidden virtue—

A weakness and inconsistency in the doctrine was, as we have remarked, the combination within it of a belief in predestination and a limited allowance for the power of human will. About freedom of will Shelley does not seem to have been able to make up his mind when writing *Queen Mab* in 1812 : though it is asserted in the text it is practically denied in the note on vi. 197–8.[2] So when we find him thus detecting in the previous year a hidden ἀρετή in human nature, his thoughts seem to be overleaping *Queen Mab* and moving towards a conception of the ideas of good and evil to be voiced seven or eight years later in *Prometheus Unbound* and the 'Ode to the West Wind'. Much has been and will be written about the progress of Shelley's thinking as it can be traced from his reading :[3] it seems likely, however, that at this period, as often, he was reaching new conceptions of the human mind as a result more particularly of his explorations into his own. A month or so before writing to Miss Hitchener[4] of the 'hidden virtue' in human society he had written thus of himself as a particular instance :

> I have long been convinced of the eventual omnipotence of mind over matter; adequacy of motive is sufficient to anything, & *my* golden age is when the present potence will become omnipotence. . . . Will it not be the task of human reason, human powers . . . ?

Herein we have one of the central ideas of *Prometheus Unbound* : that in the omnipotence of Man's mind was to be found his all-powerful weapon against tyranny. 'Human reason, human

---

[1] Jones, *Letters of Shelley*, i. 185.   [2] Hutch., p. 809.

[3] See, for instance, Not., pp. 176–8 for Platonic and Neoplatonic derivatives among his ideas at the *Queen Mab* period.

[4] 19 Oct. 1811. Jones, *Letters of Shelley*, i. 152.

powers', Shelley's words here, are an anticipation of his belief allegorized throughout the poem, that[1] 'evil is not inherent in the system of the creation, but an accident that might be expelled ... that mankind had only to will that there should be no evil, and there would be none': already this belief is gaining the strength which will finally oust the belief in predestination so incongruously existent with it inside the doctrine of Necessity. And already he is anticipating that mood of 1819, ἀρετῇ σε νικῶ θνητὸς ὢν θεὸν μέγαν, when the virtue and power[2] of his own will would reach their climax and be projected poetically both into Prometheus and the West Wind: such would be his 'golden age' when his 'omnipotence' would be one with theirs. What we have said about the unity of thought and feeling reflected together in the symbolical expression of the 1819 mood may be more readily understandable for the evidence that as far back as 1811 thought and feeling had so far anticipated the mood.

If *Queen Mab*, begun in about August 1812, marks the climax of the doctrine of Necessity in Shelley's poetry enough has been said to show that in his mind it had passed its climax and begun to move in other directions. Its movement, as briefly illustrated here from the Hitchener correspondence, might be said to represent a shift of the original emphasis upon Necessity in its more materialistic form towards a 'spirit of Nature' or World Soul conceived as Mind: an approximation to the Platonic idea from the *Timaeus*[3] of Mind as 'the ruling power that persuaded Necessity to bring the greater part of created things to perfection'. This in *Queen Mab* is the 'pervading spirit co-eternal with the universe'— Shelley's substitute for God. The conception of the universe as a sentient organism, making possible the feeling of a union between the poet's soul and the soul of nature, is one that appealed to Shelley's instincts and became both a theme and a principle in his poetry: it involved the immortality of the soul, found in *Queen Mab*, and drew him to manifestations of immortality in Nature. Here is Shelley, the politician, some months

---

[1] Mary Shelley, 'Note on *Prometheus Unbound*', Hutch., p. 271. But see below, pp. 71–73, 125–7.
[2] Exactly what ἀρετή meant to Shelley may be deduced from the fact (see p. 52) that in translating the *Symposium* he actually used this phrase 'virtue *and power*' to render the word. On these grounds it seems safe to equate the meaning it had for him in 1819 with what he meant by 'omnipotence' in 1811.   [3] 48a.

before he began *Queen Mab*; he is attacking Malthus and those
who used the Malthusian argument of pressure of population to
justify complacency in face of 'war, vice and misery'—it is, we
may note, at the same time, the later poet fighting for the 'intellectual and universal system of which he is a disciple' against 'the
mechanical philosophy of the day . . . popular because conversant
alone with grosser objects':[1]

To how contemptible a degradation of grossest credulity will
not prejudice lower the human mind!—We see in Winter that the
foliage of the trees is gone, that they present to the view nothing
but leafless branches—we see that the loveliness of the flower decays,
though the root continues in the earth. What opinion should we
form of that man who, when he walked in the freshness of the spring,
beheld the fields enamelled with flowers, and the foliage bursting
from the buds, should find fault with this beautiful order, and murmur
his contemptible discontents because winter must come, and the landscape be robbed of its beauty for a while again? Yet this man is
Mr. Malthus.

Once again in 1812 we are looking forward to 1819: in that
'winter must come' we have the very words of the 'Ode to the
West Wind', and implicit throughout is the question which points
the Ode, 'can Spring be far behind?' The seasons in the material
universe have become the symbol of immortality in the spiritual
and moral universes: with the latter, since for Shelley the intellectual is a portion of the moral, they are a symbol for the immortality of thought and poetry: more than this they symbolize
the cycles of good and evil which can be moved around by the
power of thought and Mind.

As we have said, the paths of Shelley's symbols are seldom
straight ones: rather do they wind and interlace most of the time.
Lest we lose our way thus early in our journey along the first of
them let us look back for a moment upon the way we have so far
come. Starting, probably, from the eighteenth-century philosophers to whom he was early attracted by his humanitarian
instincts, came the doctrine of Necessity, a fusion in his mind of
two originally Platonic doctrines, Necessity and the World Soul,
the emphasis initially being principally upon the first. But a
weakness always inherent in this was the inconsistency about
predestination and free will. Shelley, therefore seeking intel-

---

[1] *A Proposal for Reform*, pub. in Dublin, 2 Mar. 1812. Jul. v. 266.

lectually a firmer path, branched out from the pure doctrine of Necessity—a convenient juncture being the conception of evil as something that must perish through its own decay—into the belief that out of decay comes regeneration: a New Birth in the moral (involving the intellectual) universe symbolized in the material universe by the New Birth of Nature with the Spring,[1] this symbolizing at the same time the cyclic succession of evil by good. In its turn this more poetical and more humane concept of the universe as a sentient organism had caused a revulsion against the materialistic aspect of Necessity and drawn him more and more into the doctrine of the World Soul which from the first he had always partially attached to it: herein lay a firmer path of thought. For as the World Soul, by ruling Necessity according to Platonic belief, could rule the universe, so Man's mind, its microcosm, had freedom of will, always supposing it could develop a sufficient power of ἀρετή, its 'hidden virtue', to control the course of good and evil in human events.[2]

But *how* does the World Soul control Necessity and the Universe? Shelley looked to the material universe for the analogy which would supply his answer and he saw that in Nature it is love that causes procreation: the poetical aspects of this were bright in his mind from his reading of Lucretius. And so in the moral universe the 'Spirit of Nature', identified in *Queen Mab* originally with Necessity, became identified more and more with love, and love was viewed as a cosmic force:[3]

> All things are recreated, and the flame
> Of consentaneous love inspires all life. . . .

Wielding this cosmic force the World Soul becomes the Absolute, the cause of causes (the 'Life of Life' in *Prometheus Unbound*), the One that is eternal (in Adonais 'The one remains, the many change and pass'), again the Cloud: 'I change but I cannot die.' It was Shelley's weighty mission, as man and as poet, to seek truth and to lead others towards it: with truth went liberty and the banishment of evil since tyranny and evil of every kind were

---

[1] The Ode is strongly anticipated too in *Queen Mab* by the notes on v. 1, 2 and v. 4–6 (Hutch., p. 803), especially by Shelley's quotation from Hom. *Il.* vi. 146: οἵη περ.φύλλων γενεή τοιήδε καὶ ἀνδρῶν.

[2] Though Shelley never conceived the victory of the human will as permanent. If it weakened, evil would return with the same cyclic certainty. Cf. below, pp. 125–7.

[3] viii. 107–8, Hutch., p. 794.

existent only when bound up with false beliefs—the whole knot
of false beliefs which he comprehended in the Lucretian 'religio'
when he set out his manifesto in the lines attached to *Queen Mab*

> . . . magnis doceo de rebus; et arctis
> religionum animos nodis exsolvere pergo.

I am telling of great matters; and I shall proceed to loose the bonds
of superstition and to free men's minds.

From this determination he never swerved. He was not a trained
philosopher nor did he aspire to be one, and his 'universal system',
as we said in the last chapter of this section, was not really a
system of philosophy but a poetical vision of reality shining ahead
of him as, in his 'wanderings of careful thought', he moved towards it down a criss-cross of symbolical paths. Tangled as the
symbols become they all point in the same direction, and with a
knowledge of their affinities and their respective meanings it is
possible to feel that they make each other clearer while, at the
same time, the 'system' yields a meaning too.

Queen Mab, then, marks not only the climax in Shelley's mind
of the particular doctrine, Necessity, of which it was the poetical
manifesto in 1812, but also a very notable stage in the evolution of
his whole poetical philosophy and the system of symbols by which
it was to be expressed throughout his poems. About Necessity,
however, there is a point which needs to be made here because it is applicable, equally, to other concepts and symbols
of Shelley's and consequently important for the comprehension
of his 'system' as a whole: this is that it does not disappear
merely because it has been superseded but instead, having
reached the moment when its path is broadest and most direct,
narrows down to a thinner path and continues to wind its way
in and out of the rest of the symbolical network. Such is Shelley's
way, and how effective it can be when understood is well illustrated, five years after *Queen Mab*, in the ninth Canto of *The
Revolt of Islam* where within the space of a few stanzas he uses
in conjunction most of the several notions we have just been
discussing. First, in language strikingly anticipative of the 'Ode
to the West Wind', comes the notion of the evocative, regenerative power of Spring:[1]

[1] Stanza xxi, Hutch., p. 127.

The blasts of Autumn drive the wingèd seeds
    Over the earth,—next come the snows, and rain,
And frosts, and storms, which dreary Winter leads
    Out of his Scythian cave, a savage train;
    Behold! Spring sweeps over the world again,
Shedding soft dews from her ethereal wings;
    Flowers on the mountains, fruits over the plain,
And music on the waves and woods she flings,
And love on all that lives, and calm on lifeless things. . . .

Spring, it will be noticed, has its effect both in the material
universe where it brings about the New Birth of the things of
Nature and in the moral universe where it sheds 'consentaneous
love'. Then in three more stanzas[1] the passing of tyranny is proclaimed as part of the general cyclic course of good and evil of
which the seasons are the symbol:[2]

The seeds are sleeping in the soil: meanwhile
    The Tyrant peoples dungeons with his prey,
Pale victims on the guarded scaffold smile
    Because they cannot speak; and, day by day,
    The moon of wasting Science wanes away
Among her stars, and in that darkness vast
    The sons of earth to their foul idols pray,
And gray Priests triumph, and like blight or blast
A shade of selfish care o'er human looks is cast.

This is the winter of the world;—and here
    We die, even as the winds of Autumn fade,
Expiring in the frore and foggy air.—
    Behold! Spring comes, though we must pass, who made
    The promise of its birth. . . .

A comparison with the lines quoted in this chapter from the early
poem 'A Retrospect of Times of Old' will show how Necessity is
still a strong motif but has been absorbed into the New Birth, the
emphasis no longer being on the idea of *decay* implied in the first
doctrine but on the moral regeneration inherent in the second:
'Spring . . . we . . . the promise of its birth.' Next, in the Spring,
we have a symbol of the renewal of human love, no less than of
the all-pervading love of the World Soul—a typical Shelleyan
transition from thought to feeling, blending both:

[1] xxiii, xxiv, xxv, Hutch., pp. 127–8.
[2] Stanza xxiv, 3676–84, Hutch., pp. 127–8.

> Alas! gaze not on me, but turn thine eyes
>   On thine own heart—it is a paradise
> Which everlasting Spring has made its own. . . .

Finally, in this Canto, we find Necessity again,[1] still the histori-
cally ineluctable spectre of early poems but tempered now by
Free Will and the conception of the One:

> In their own hearts the earnest of the hope
>   Which made them great, the good will ever find;
> And though some envious shades may interlope
>   Between the effect and it, One comes behind,
>   Who aye the future to the past will bind—
> Necessity, whose sightless strength for ever
>   Evil with evil, good with good must wind
> In bands of union, which no power may sever:
> They must bring forth their kind, and be divided never!

There appears too, in cyclic succession to the time of Tyranny
when 'The moon of wasting Science wanes away', the triumph of
Mind through poetry and thought, an anticipation of the Platonic
keynote of *Prometheus Unbound*, of the 'Ode to the West Wind',
once again, and of the general idea of *A Defence of Poetry*:

> The good and mighty of departed ages
>   Are in their graves, the innocent and free,
> Heroes, and Poets, and prevailing Sages,
>   Who leave the vesture of their majesty
>   To adorn and clothe this naked world. . . .

No better example than this canto could be found in illustration
of Shelley's power to 'make the external internal, the internal
external', etc. It was in reply to Godwin's strictures on this poem
that he made the claims we have quoted at the beginning of this
chapter.

---

[1] Stanzas xxvii, xxviii. 3712–16, Hutch., p. 128.

4. 'Ariadne'. Love and Intellectual Beauty; Virtue and Power

WE have seen how at the time of *Queen Mab* the doctrine of Necessity had begun to be superseded in Shelley's mind by the doctrine of Love. For Shelley Love, which was also Beauty, was something to be pursued on two planes, the one abstract and universal and the other concrete and earthly. Love in the abstract was philosophical reality, 'truth . . . an Ariadne' to gain which was the object of his wrestling with 'the monster of his thought'; in his life, at the same time, he sought an Ariadne who should embody the qualities of the universal love in her earthly Woman-love and by it be his guide to the universal. This is the point, precisely, of the two Platonic memoranda which were quoted in Chapter 2, for the universal kind of Shelleyan love corresponds on the one hand to 'Beauty itself . . . a knowledge of it' and, on the other hand, is the 'ideally beautiful figure complete to the last touch' created by the painter—in the context the meaning of ζωγράφος amounts practically to 'symbolist'. These memoranda come ten years later than *Queen Mab* and love in the meantime had become more and more the basic concept in Shelley's poetry, poetry being a quest for Beauty wherein, in accordance with the regular identification of thought with feeling, Love and its human symbol frequently became blended into one.

Shelley's quest for an idealized object of love is early perceptible in his affection first for his sisters and then for his cousin Harriet Grove: childish and instinctive at first this seems to have been very soon tinged with the colours of contemporary romantic fiction. How readily the feeling found its way into verse may be seen in a poem written when he was thirteen years old,[1] in which Harriet appears amid the usual Gothic trappings of gloomy turrets and howling winds. One stanza deserves quotation for its possible anticipation of things to come:

[1] Rogers, *The Esdaile Poems*, p. 113. The manuscript, in Harriet Shelley's handwriting, is headed 'Feb. 28th 1805, To St. Irvyne': underneath she has written 'To H. Grove'.

**My Harriet is fled, like a fast-fading dream,
 Which fades ere the vision is fixed on the mind,
But has left a firm love and a lasting esteem
 That my soul to her soul must eternally bind.**

From this to *Epipsychidion*[1] is a far cry, yet already we have something like the germ of the 'soul of my soul' idea; the turrets too might seem to have been transferred, gloom and all, into the imagery:

I questioned every tongueless wind that flew
Over my tower of mourning, if it knew
Whither 'twas fled, this soul out of my soul.

Three more early poems, written in 1810 at the age of eighteen[2] and entitled 'To Mary', lament the suicide by poison of a maiden whose story, an unhappy love affair, purports to be the experience of a friend of the poet—an anticipation, it might seem, of the device that was to be used with *Alastor* and again with *Epipsychidion*. Shelley tells in a footnote that had he had his friend's opportunity to share the poison, he would not have failed to avail himself of it. It is interesting to notice that he attaches to these three poems the same sentence from St. Augustine which in 1815 he was to attach to *Alastor*. Nothing could better express his gropings:

Nondum amabam et amare amabam, quaerebam quid amarem, amans amare.

Perhaps that feeling of 'not yet loving and wanting something to love' may go some way towards explaining the beginnings of the attraction to Harriet Westbrook. That he had certainly learned to love her during the course of their tragic married life is attested by a number of poems both published and unpublished, not least the Dedication to *Queen Mab*:[3]

Whose eyes have I gazed fondly on,
And loved mankind the more?

Harriet! on thine:—thou wert my purer mind;
Thou wert the inspiration of my song. . . .

It is significant here that Shelley's love is finding a broader basis:

[1] 236–8, Hutch., p. 417.
[2] Rogers, *The Esdaile Poems*, p. 69. Dated by Shelley. [3] Hutch., pp. 762–3.

it is passing beyond the dedicated love for a single individual to reflect a general love for humanity:[1] such indeed is the 'consentaneous love' which pervades the poem that is to follow. Again both here in the Dedication and in *Queen Mab* itself we already meet another important idea pervasive, for instance, in *Epipsychidion*: the idea of Love as a fount of poetry.

Feelings derived in the first place from instinct and later strengthened from experience were now broadened further by a strain of thought proceeding out of study. It was, as yet, a year or two before he was to come under the direct influence of direct Platonic philosophy but his mind had a natural affinity with it and he was quick to absorb its ideas from indirect sources. One such source, notably, was C. M. Wieland's romance *Agathon*, well described by Professor Notopoulos[2] as 'a kaleidoscope of Platonism', which he read in 1813 and again in 1814. Among the motifs in his life which might at this period be traceable to his thought and study there are several for which a counterpart is to be found in *Agathon*: the young and persecuted idealist hero, who 'loves mankind the more' for his attachment to his lady Psyche, the 'guide' to his Platonic instincts, might be a blue-print for Shelley himself, and Shelley's pathetic suggestion to Harriet that she should come as his 'sister' to live with him and Mary finds a corresponding situation where Agathon does actually contrive to live with two loves in such circumstances. In *Agathon* too appears the brother-and-sister-love motif, so popular in Romantic writers, which comes out not only in poems like *The Revolt of Islam* but also in his relationships with Miss Hitchener and others. Another novel of Wieland's, *Peregrinus Proteus*, was also read by Shelley in 1814, and its hero's attraction to Agathon's song of Love in the *Symposium* and to the speeches of Socrates and Diotima might well be a contributory cause of Shelley's. Next year, 1815, we come to *Alastor*. Here the unhappy poet, whose mind 'thirsts for intercourse with an intelligence similar to itself' and who 'seeks in vain for a prototype of his conception', is again Shelley, thinly disguised, and carefully patterned on Wieland; the veiled maid, whose 'voice was like the voice of his own soul', is a prototype of most of Shelley's earthly 'loves', and the Poet's tragedy is the

[1] Cf. below, pp. 56–57. See below, p. 63.
[2] p. 142; also pp. 196 ff. and for Indirect Platonism generally, pp. 78–171.

tragedy of Shelley, caught always between the ideal Love and the terrestrial.

Much has been written and much disputed about the manner in which Mary Godwin first fitted into the pattern of his life. What is relevant here is the fact that at the time of their encounter she fell naturally into the pattern of his symbolical thought and feeling. Part of the Platonic love-procedure adapted by Wieland into Agathon was the training of the mind of the beloved; Shelley had undertaken this with Harriet, but her enthusiasm had waned with motherhood. Mary Godwin, as the daughter of Mary Wollstonecraft, was not only a promising pupil but almost a symbolical figure from the very first. She too was a keen student, ready to follow him in books; her early labours in Latin may be seen today in the notebook[1] which he is believed to have given her at the time of their betrothal. This notebook contains her translation of the Cupid and Psyche episode from Apuleius and it is difficult not to wonder, as one reads through it, whether she may not have seen herself as Psyche being rescued from a family of tiresome sisters by the unusual and attractive stranger; rescue of young ladies from their 'prisons', whether in Clapham, Skinner Street, or Pisa, was, as we know, a speciality of Shelley's. One way and another we can be sure that he found Mary apt in apprehension of his Platonic love-feelings. Other affinities apart, the love-idyll in which they were sharers was a practical expression of contemporary Romantic dreamings, much tinged with Rousseau and none the less Platonic for the strong undercurrent of Platonism in Rousseau's philosophy and romances. During their 1816 visit to Switzerland they seem to have been reliving, as far as they could, *La Nouvelle Héloïse*.

A thousand times [wrote Shelley][2] have Julie and St. Prieux walked on this terraced road looking towards those mountains which I now behold—nay treading on the ground where now I tread. From the window of our lodging our landlady pointed out the 'bosquet de Julie'. At least these inhabitants . . . impressed me with an idea that the persons of that romance had actual existence.

Together with Mary and the shades of Julie and St. Prieux Shelley

---

[1] Now in the Library of Congress, Washington.

[2] Bod. MS. Shelley adds. e. 16. See below for manuscript of Shelley's journal. Printed in *Verse and Prose from the Manuscripts of Percy Bysshe Shelley*, ed. Sir John Shelley-Rolls and Roger Ingpen, London, privately printed, 1934, p. 84.

had 'the magnificence and beauty of the external world' everywhere about him and ready, as with the poet in *Alastor*, to 'sink
into the frame of his conceptions': for the self-regenerative
mightiness of thought and love the River Arve was a symbol of
symbols, while the shadow of Mont Blanc, seeming itself

> The awful shadow of some unseen Power,

was the symbol for everything he meant by Intellectual Beauty,
a phrase which he used for the first time just then enshrining his
meaning in a hymn,[1] the testament of his natural Platonism.

> Spirit of BEAUTY, that dost consecrate
> With thine own hues all thou dost shine upon
> Of human thought or form. . . .

Professor Notopoulos[2] makes an illuminating comparison of
Shelley's idea of Intellectual Beauty as it appears in the poem
with Plato's as it is revealed first in the *Phaedrus*[3] and then in the
Symposium.[4] In the Hymn and the *Phaedrus* the conceptions are
very similar, for both of them are expressions of the natural
philosophy of a mind which sees immanent and transcendental
relationship between the intellectual and the relative world and
both express this relationship in terms of the imagery of light and
shadow: again the lovers have much in common, for in both they
are moved, to start with, by the intensest possible degree of
excitement—magnificently described in poetical language—and
subsequently refreshed, consoled, and calmed. But a comparison
of Shelley's poem with the *Symposium* shows the great fundamental difference between the Shelleyan lover and the Platonic
one. It is that whereas the former is constantly seeking on this
earth for the shadow of an abstract, eternal Beauty, the latter
starts with the shadow of earthly Beauty and immediately trans-
cends it in a dialectical pursuit of its shadows in morals and
sciences. In the *Symposium*[4] Plato describes the progressive ascent

---

[1] Hutch., pp. 529–30. The phrase 'Intellectual Beauty' does not occur in Plato:
it seems to have been coined by Plotinus and to have first appeared in *Enneads*,
v. viii, which is entitled περὶ τοῦ νοητοῦ κάλλους. Shelley may have picked it up
from some Neoplatonic or indirectly Platonic source: possibly he had noticed the
phrase *Beauté intellectuelle* which occurs several times in Pernay's French version of
Wieland's *Agathon*, which he used. Possibly again, it was a coincident invention of
his own. Cf. his deliberate interpolation in translating τὸ πολὺ πέλαγος τοῦ καλοῦ,
'the wide sea of *intellectual* beauty'. [*Symp.* 210d.]

[2] pp. 201–2.   [3] 249–52a.   [4] 210a–211d: see below, pp. 138–43.

of the lover from particular beauties to Beauty itself, each step being attained by the use of reason alone, there being only in the preliminary stage a suggestion of the senses: his conception, essentially, is an intellectual and objective one. In Shelley's poem, on the other hand, despite the 'Intellectual Beauty' to which it is dedicated, the conception is mystical and emotional, being biographical in origin: in Shelley, says Professor Notopoulos, pointing the contrast to Plato, 'we have an imaginative leap with little distinction between emotion and idea'. This is very pertinent and well said. It is that 'little distinction between emotion and idea' which renders Shelley incapable of a coherent 'intellectual and universal system' fit for dissection by the standards of a professional philosopher alone: it is that 'imaginative leap' which gives him power as a poet, an interpreter, symbolically, of the universal. It was to such a power that he was laying claim when, defending himself to Godwin, he wrote of his capacity 'to apprehend minute and remote distinctions of feeling': implicit here is a confession that feeling outweighed thought in his poetry, and if we can understand this in approaching his symbolism we shall come nearer to judging what Shelley's standards were. And these are the standards—though this is too frequently forgotten—by which he ought, in the first place, to be judged, as he wished to be. Thus in the Hymn it is from feeling that he makes his approach to 'Intellectual Beauty', a feeling of which the roots—we have traced some of the earlier ones—are biographical: 'While yet a boy . . .' he says

> When musing deeply on the lot
> Of life, at that sweet time when winds are wooing
> All vital things that wake to bring
> News of birds and blossoming,—
> Sudden, thy shadow fell on me;
> I shrieked, and clasped my hands in ecstasy!

Out of this extreme of early sensibility came the pledge

> I vowed that I would dedicate my powers
> To thee and thine—have I not kept the vow?

So far, then, the approach to Intellectual Beauty is chiefly emotional in origin and the Hymn might well be regarded as the climax of years of feeling. But here, as always, we do not have to look far before we see the other element. He goes on

With beating heart and streaming eyes, even now
I call the phantoms of a thousand hours
Each from his voiceless grave: they have in visioned bowers
Of studious zeal or love's delight
Outwatched with me the envious night—
They know that never joy illumed my brow
Unlinked with hope that thou wouldst free
This world from its dark slavery,
That thou—O awful LOVELINESS,
Wouldst give whate'er these words cannot express.

In thought as well as feeling, in 'studious zeal' as well as 'love's delight', he had found the vision of Beauty. Very soon this was to be even more so for, in addition to his instinctive Platonism and the Platonism which had worked its way into his thought indirectly from much reading of many writers, the vision was to be coloured by what his 'studious zeal' derived from direct application to Plato's "Ερως.

Time and Shelley's own influence through subsequent generations have tended to obscure the contemporary originality not only of some of his work but also of certain of his interests. It is not always recognized, for instance, how neglected an author Plato was in the England of Shelley's day; 'he wants patronage', wrote Peacock in 1818, and it is significant that not till 1847 does he appear in the papers set at Oxford in the school of Literae Humaniores.[1] And though, as Hogg tells us, Shelley had read Plato in translation at Oxford, and though he had learned something of the *Symposium* at Eton with Dr. Lind, his Greek was in those days still very inadequate and his interests lay more in materialistic philosophy, science, and social reform. What really seems to have kindled his enthusiasm for things Greek was his friendship with Peacock which became progressively an intimate one from the early part of 1813. The Grecian aspect of his 'studious zeal' is traceable through his work of 1815 and 1816 and by 1817 Plato had become an influence to counterbalance Godwinism. From then on it was steadily to gain supremacy over all other systems in his mind.

It happens by great good fortune that at this turning-point in the wanderings of Shelley's thought we come upon one of the clearest and most valuable signposts to its direction that is to be

[1] See Geoffrey Mure, 'Oxford and Philosophy', *Philosophy*, xii (1938), 296–7.

found in the whole wilderness of his manuscripts: the luck seems
almost too good to be true. It consists, as may be expected by now,
of a memorandum from one of his notebooks. It is a memorandum
so interesting in all its aspects that it shall be reproduced, in so
far as print permits, exactly as it appears in the manuscript:[1]

The wonderful description of Love in Plato Sympos., p. 214 et
passim 218
    Agathon a poem

                               particularly 214, l. 8–l. ultima
**

Symposium
215 l. 7
    l. 10
218 XX
Diotima's Atheism
228–15 l. ⟨sic⟩
231 l. 5
233 l. 7
236
239
240**

       I should say in answer that "Ερως neither
       loved nor was loved but is the *cause of*
       love in others—a subtlety to beat Plato.

Before looking into the meaning of a Shelley memorandum we
should always try to see first of all what can be gleaned from its
manuscript surroundings. What they can tell us here will prove,
it happens, to be of very considerable value for the purposes of
our Platonic direction-finding, besides affording, on the way, a
close and useful illustration of what was said more generally in
Chapter 1 about the notebooks. The notebook in question, one
from the Shelley-Rolls Collection, is a slim, much-worn little
volume which had to be re-covered in the Bodleian in 1946; it
now contains 33 leaves—i.e. 66 pages—many of them mere stubs
as there has been considerable tearing; it measures 250 × 128 mm.
and opens from top to bottom like a sketch-book; such indeed
may have been the original purpose for which it was intended.
Its presence on the Swiss tour of 1816 is attested first of all by

[1] Bod. MS. Shelley adds. e. 16, p. 37. The beautiful MS page is magnificently
reproduced in *Keats Shelley Journal*, xv, Winter 1966, with Prof. Notopoulos'
important article 'New Texts of Shelley's Plato.'

several pencil-drawings of Geneva; they are not in Shelley's style and were perhaps the work of Mary. Much of the writing is in pencil. Closer dates for its use on the tour are provided by the torn remnants of Shelley's journal covering the days of the lake excursion on which he went with Byron,[1] 23 June to 29 June; it contains also his drafts for the 'Hymn to Intellectual Beauty' and 'Mont Blanc',[2] written the one before the end of the excursion and the other on 23 July. Shelley's excitement during that holiday of poets seems reflected as much in the furious sweep of his pencil-draft as in the 'ecstasy' of the Hymn itself. Personal peril, however, excited him less than Intellectual Beauty, as may be read in the calm, laconic reference to it in his entry for 25 June[3]

The waves also are exceedingly high and our boat so heavily laden that there appeared ⟨*sic*⟩ to be some danger.

It was the same indifference which he was to show at Lerici: to lose one's life might be something perhaps that merely appeared to be dangerous. The entry continues[3]

We arrived, however, safe at Mellerie after passing with great speed mighty rocks which overhang the lake and massy mountains with bare and icy points which rose immediately from the base.

The mountains, philosophically, symbolized something *real*: 'O awful LOVELINESS . . .'. He could be excited again next day too when returning from Nature back to 'studious zeal'

I read Julie all day, an overflowing as it now seems, surrounded by its own scenes which it has so wonderfully peopled, of sublimest genius and more than mortal sensibility[4]

It was on 18 August 1816 that the Shelley who 'sought for ghosts' as a boy and daemons as a man took part in a long conversation about supernatural matters with Mary, 'Monk' Lewis, Byron, and Polidori: he recorded some of their tales.[5] One result of this

---

[1] Mary Shelley, 'Note on the Poems of 1816', Hutch., p. 536.

[2] Shelley's date, Hutch., p. 535.

[3] Shelley's record of the excursion was incorporated in his letter to Peacock of 12 July 1816 [Jones, *Letters of Shelley*, i. 480], which was printed by Mary in her *History of A Six Weeks' Tour*, 1817. Shelley-Rolls and Ingpen, in *Verse and Prose*, pp. 83–87, collated the manuscript in the notebook with the letter from which they filled up certain lacunae.

The entry for 25 June is missing from the notebook and was not reproduced in *Verse and Prose*. It is reproduced here from the missing page which I discovered in the box of loose sheets catalogued as Bod. MS. Shelley adds. c. 4 (f. 65).

[4] Bod. MS. Shelley adds. e. 16, p. 56.

[5] Jones, *Mary Shelley's Journal*, p. 57 (Shelley's entry).

conversation was the birth of Mary's novel *Frankenstein*: another
may well have been the fragment 'A Ghost Story'—'A shovel of
his ashes took . . .' which also comes in the notebook: if so it would
imply that, to relieve such a tension, Shelley could, and did at
this time, make use of his much-denied sense of fun. The probability may be sufficient to justify us in taking mid-August as the
terminus ad quem for the use of the notebook in 1816.

Thus far both dating and contents are fairly continuous and
consistent. But what happened with this notebook, as with certain
others was that Shelley took it up again at a later period, and,
working as usual for our confusion from both ends, made use
of such pages as were blank or partially so. Yet we need not be
confounded. To come to what concerns us, the note on the
Symposium: we know from Mary that he read this dialogue on
13 August 1817.[1] Next we look at what precedes and what follows.
Preceding it immediately is a draft for part of 'Rosalind and
Helen', a poem which, so Mary tells us,[2] was begun at Marlow
(i.e. in 1817) and finished, at her request, at Bagni di Lucca in
1818. To which year does the part in our notebook belong? By
chance the answer is a clear one. What we have does not include
the Italian setting (lines 1–218 and 1240–1318), it is from the
central portion; furthermore a close relationship with the initial
biographical background, the unhappy marriage of Mary's friend
Isobel Baxter to one David Booth, is seen in the fact that the
name 'Isobel' actually appears in place of 'Rosalind'. Though
this, the English portion of the poem, cannot be dated with precision, 'my pretty eclogue', as Mary called it, was evidently being
written at the time of her letter to Shelley of 26 September 1817.[3]
Following the *Symposium* note comes a draft of the poem 'To
William Shelley'—'The billows on the beach . . .'[4] inspired, as we
know, by the fear that William would be taken from his father,
like Harriet's children, by the English law:

> They have taken thy brother and sister dear,
>   They have made them unfit for thee;
> They have withered the smile and dried the tear
>   Which should have been sacred to me.
> To a blighting faith and a cause of crime
> They have bound them slaves in youthly prime,

[1] Jones, *Mary Shelley's Journal*, p. 83.
[2] 'Note on *Rosalind and Helen*', Hutch., p. 188.
[3] Jones, *Letters of Mary W. Shelley*, i. 31.   [4] Hutch., p. 544.

And they will curse my name and thee
Because we fearless are and free.

It was on 1 August 1817 that William Alexander gave the legal decision that Shelley was unfit to have the guardianship of Charles and Ianthe, so this gives a *terminus a quo* for the draft. Taken all together then the pages of the notebook in which our memorandum is found can be given with some probability a general date of 'August–September 1817', and it may not be a far guess to connect it, perhaps, with Shelley's reading of the *Symposium* in mid-August, more especially as there would be some consistency between his Platonic enthusiasm and his desire, expressed in the poem, to take little William to Italy where 'I . . . will mould / Thy growing spirit in the flame / Of Grecian lore'.

It is time to return to our Platonic trail. Our digression, made in order to show a memorandum in its manuscript setting and to afford, *en route*, a close view of another typical Shelley notebook, will have served furthermore to show the seeds of Platonism taking root at a particular point in Shelley's life and its roots pushing their way upward through his work as his mind everywhere continues to make 'nature thought and thought Nature'. It may not be without significance that the peculiar arrangement of the *Symposium* note on Shelley's page is due to the fact that he fitted it in, in 1817, framewise around a drawing of trees and rocks, a relic, without doubt, of the Swiss holiday of the year before—a reminder of natural Beauty framed, through his untidiness, within a reminder for thought and Intellectual Beauty.

Our memorandum, with the exception of the left-hand column, was printed by Richard Garnett in 1862[1] and has been more than once copied, but as far as I know no attempt has been made to relate Shelley's comments to the Greek; nor indeed could this very well have been done without the clues omitted by Garnett. Even when we have these the difficulty arises that the references he gives are *page*-references and therefore only comprehensible when applied to the text of Plato which he used. Fortunately we now know what text it was,[2] namely the tenth volume of the twelve-volume Bipont edition of 1781–7; it therefore becomes possible to collate them with the Oxford Classical

[1] *Relics of Shelley*, ed. R. Garnett, Moxon, 1862, p. 77.   [2] See Not., p. 41, n. 52.

Text edition of the *Symposium*.[1] What we then have, thanks to this most valuable memorandum, is nothing less than Shelley's own anthology of the passages on which he fed his thought: we are in the position not only to find the meaning of his comments but, by further collation with his own English renderings of the passages identified, to discover a good deal about such nuances of feeling as he drew from them. With the aid of such a triple collation, taking his translation of the *Symposium* as our basis for quotation and at the same time making constant reference to the Greek, we will now proceed to examine what is contained in the Bipont[2] pages to which our memorandum refers. Since, when marking these in 1817 and still more in the following year when he translated the whole dialogue, Shelley cannot have failed to take note of some of the adjacent or intervening passages it will be desirable not to confine our attention too strictly to what he marked: through the whole of this part of the *Symposium* much is to be found that has the closest bearings on his thought and that penetrates deeply into his poetry and his life. The path of "Ἔρως is one of the chief of our paths, and as we follow it we shall come upon many turnings which in later chapters we must follow too.

Referred in their order to the Bipont edition Shelley's first three pages, 214, 215, and 218, all prove to come from the speech of Agathon. Here is page 214: 'The wonderful description of Love.'[3]

He is young, therefore, and being young is tender and soft. There were need of some poet like Homer to celebrate the delicacy and tenderness of Love. For Homer says, that the goddess Calamity is delicate, and that her feet are tender. 'Her feet are soft,' he says,[4] 'for she treads not upon the ground, but makes her path upon the heads of men.' He gives as an evidence of her tenderness, that she walks not upon that which is hard, but that which is soft.

Agathon continues[5]—and this is the part of the page more particularly admired by Shelley—'line 8–line ultima':

The same evidence is sufficient to make manifest the tenderness of Love. For Love walks not upon the earth, nor over the heads of men,

[1] For this collation and for bibliographical details of the Bipont Plato see App. I, p. 328.

[2] References made will be to the Julian edition and to the Oxford Classical Text.

[3] *Symp.* 195d, Jul. vii. 189.

[4] *Il.* xix. 92.   [5] *Symp.* 195e–196a, Jul. vii. 189–190.

which are not indeed very soft; but he dwells within, and treads on the softest of existing things, having established his habitation within the souls and inmost natures of Gods and men; not indeed in all souls— for wherever he chances to find a hard and rugged disposition, there will he not inhabit, but only where it is most soft and tender. Of needs must he be the most delicate of all things, who touches lightly with his feet, only the softest parts of those things which are the softest of all.

He is then the youngest and the most delicate of all divinities; and in addition to this, he is, as it were, the most moist and liquid.

Here now is the passage marked from page 215 of the Bipont edition lines 7–10:[1]

... for the winged Love rests not in his flight on any form, or within any soul the flower of whose loveliness is faded, but there remains most willingly where is the odour and radiance of blossoms, yet un- withered.

We must here make a slight détour to follow Shelley's mind through some of the poetry which begins to spring up at this point in the Platonic path from 'The wonderful description of Love'.

Out of the passage on page 215, to start with, the passage beginning on the Bipont page ″Ὅμηρος γὰρ Ἄτην . . .[2], may be traced the passage about Desolation in *Prometheus Unbound*.[3] 'Desolation' is only a retranslation of Ἄτη, 'the Goddess Calamity', and the lines are a characteristic Shelleyan trans- mutation of Greek language-colour.

Ah, sister! Desolation is a delicate thing:
    It walks not on the earth, it floats not on the air,
But treads with lulling footstep, and fans with silent wing
    The tender hopes which in their hearts the best and gentlest bear. . . .

Again out of the passage on the Bipont page 214 which begins ″Ἔρωτα ὅτι ἁπαλός Urania in *Adonais*[4] derives the tenderness of Plato's Love:

Out of her secret Paradise she sped,
    Through camps and cities rough with stone, and steel,
    And human hearts, which to her aery tread
Yielding not, wounded the invisible
Palms of her tender feet where'er they fell. . . .

---

[1] *Symp.* 196b, Jul. vii. 190. [2] *Symp.* 195d, Jul. vii. 189.
[3] i. 772–5, Hutch., p. 225. [4] 208–12, Hutch., p. 437.

It is not uninteresting to notice the evolution of the '. . . stone, and steel / And human hearts' out of ἀλλ᾿ ἧτινι ἂν σκληρὸν ἦθος ἐχούσῃ ἐντύχῃ by way of Shelley's rendering—admirable in the context —of σκληρὸν ἦθος : 'a hard and rugged disposition'. The image persists and on an occasion in 1822 when Shelley feels the cruelty of Love it comes out in 'Lines: "When the Lamp is Shattered"' :[1]

> O Love! who bewailest
> The frailty of all things here,
>   Why choose you the frailest
> For your cradle, your home, and your bier?

The last line, it may be mentioned in passing, comes straight from a line of Calderón about the withering of roses, 'cuna y sepulcro en un botón hallaron', 'they found a cradle and a sepulchre in a bud':[2] there will be more about this line later: what we need to notice here is the way Calderón's image was so readily fused in Shelley's lyric with Plato's. No doubt, when having in the meantime learned the Spanish language he came upon it, it at once took its place in his mind beside the passage he had admired on page 215 of his Bipont Plato about the withering of flowers: thence it had not far to go in order to join the other passage about the frailty of Love. From page 215—out of those very phrases perhaps of Shelley's translation '. . . any soul the flower of whose loveliness is faded . . . the odour and radiance of blossoms yet unwithered'—proceeded another famous lyric, an expression of a miserable mood in 1818:[3]

> The colour from the flower is gone
>   Which like thy sweet eyes smiled on me;
> The odour from the flower is flown
>   Which breathed of thee and only thee!
>
> A withered, lifeless, vacant form,
>   It lies on my abandoned breast,
> And mocks the heart which yet is warm
>   With cold and silent rest. . . .

No italicization is necessary to emphasize the verbal heritage. A glance at the original will show the easy transference of Platonic colour and feeling:[4]

---

[1] 21–24, Hutch., p. 668.   [2] See below, p. 203.
[3] 'On a Faded Violet.' Text from Bod. MS. Shelley e. 5, which differs from that in Hutch., p. 553.   [4] Symp. 196a–b.

ἀνανθεῖ γὰρ καὶ ἀπηνθηκότι καὶ σώματι καὶ ψυχῇ καὶ ἄλλῳ ὁτῳοῦν οὐκ
ἐνίζει "Ἔρως, οὗ δ' ἂν εὐανθής τε καὶ εὐώδης τόπος ᾖ, ἐνταῦθα δὲ καὶ
ἵζει καὶ μένει.

Here he is not merely 'imitating the Greek in this species of
imagery'. 'For, though he adopted the style, he gifted it with that
originality of form and colouring which sprung from his own
genius.' Mary Shelley[1] knew her Poet.

But to return from our détour: if pages 214 and 215 of the
Bipont Plato—'particularly line 8–line ultima' of the latter page
—are more immediately and noticeably interesting as showing
the influence of Platonic imagery upon Shelley and the general
harmony of Platonic feeling with his instinctive feelings about
love and Beauty, what is still more interesting about them is the
way in which they point ahead along the trail of his thought. We
have seen how in Switzerland in 1816 love had risen from origins
largely instinctive, emotional, and biographical to the heights of
'Beauty itself', pure Intellectual Beauty: now, in continuance of
the process begun at the time of *Queen Mab* its basis becomes
further broadened. With Shelley love and beauty are almost
inseparably overlapping conceptions but in the Hymn the chief
emphasis was on Beauty: out of Platonism he now begins to
develop an altogether broader conception of the nature of the
world-pervading 'consentaneous love'. A later illustration of the
direction in which this development was proceeding may be seen
in the Urania passage from *Adonais*, which has just been quoted.
Urania in that poem[2] is something more than the personification
of Intellectual Beauty in the abstract, she is, in part at least, a
spirit of universal love come to mourn at Keats's bier, the spirit of
a Shelleyan love which runs through *Prometheus Unbound*. The love
conceived in *Queen Mab* is at first somewhat a cold, inhuman conception, hardly weaned as yet from Necessity. A broader, more
human conception emerges in Shelley's mind from the intense
Platonic study which began in 1817: it may be traced already,
perhaps to 'the wonderful description of Love' where the emphasis
is all on tenderness. The point becomes clearer when we refer
Agathon's description to the context since its purpose is to point
the contrast between the 'affection and peace, in which the Gods
now live, under the influence of Love'[3] and their crimes under the

[1] Note on *Prometheus Unbound*, Hutch., p. 273.
[2] Cf. for Urania here, pp. 125-7, below.   [3] *Symp.* 195c, Jul. vii. 189.

old rule of Necessity, such as have been described just previously.

Though Shelley's reference to page 215 seems to be specifically
concerned with the lines just quoted from the Greek, we must not
miss what immediately comes after them, for this is where we find
our old friend ἀρετή in a Platonic setting:[1]

Περὶ μὲν οὖν κάλλους τοῦ θεοῦ καὶ ταῦτα ἱκανὰ καὶ ἔτι πολλὰ
λείπεται, περὶ δὲ ἀρετῆς Ἔρωτος μετὰ ταῦτα λεκτέον. . . .

And here is Shelley's translation:[2]

Concerning the beauty of the God, let this be sufficient, though
many things must remain unsaid. Let us now consider the virtue and
power of Love. . . .

We have come to a meeting of paths. Ἀρετή was one of our first
signposts in Chapter 2, picked up from a line of Euripides, a
memorandum of 1819; we saw there how its manuscript context
involved a close relation between Prometheus and the West Wind.
We met it again in Chapter 3, in that phrase about the 'hidden
virtue' in Nature used by Shelley in a letter written to Miss
Hitchener in 1811; this was one of the points at which Shelley's
mind was making an instinctive reaction against the doctrine of
Necessity. Now, following the trail of Ἔρως, we come upon it
amongst passages of the *Symposium* picked out and marked by
Shelley himself and occurring at a point, exactly, in our trail
where Shelleyan love is about to take a new turning. The context,
as always, is important. Agathon is turning aside from the Beauty
of Love to his crucial *quality* or nature: for this ἀρετή is the word.
Of what Shelley considered the crucial quality of Love his translation leaves us in no doubt: not merely 'virtue' but

virtue *and power*[3]

was what ἀρετή meant to him and what he meant by it. What has
happened is that the 'virtue and power' of the daemon have
made him the incarnation of something much more than the

---

[1] *Symp.* 196b.

[2] Jul. vii. 190.

[3] The 'virtue and power' of love ('sua vertute e sua potenza') is among the
subjects of Cavalcanti's *Canzone d'Amore*, where the theories of love are very
Shelleyan. See below, p. 237. Shelley may have known this poem. If H. B. Forman's
date is correct, as I believe, he had translated in 1815 his sonnet to Dante. [Hutch.,
p. 731.]

ordinary human love: he now stands for a wide-embracing humanitarian feeling, approximating to something like the Christian ἀγάπη. And since, according to Shelley's 'subtlety to beat Plato', Ἔρως is 'the cause of love in others' Shelleyan love, both in Shelley himself and in Prometheus, takes on his ἀγάπη quality from the daemon. This conjunction of the Ἔρως and ἀρετή concepts is essential in Shelley: herein we have not only the central idea of *Prometheus Unbound* and of the 'Ode to the West Wind' but the centre too of much closely related ethical and political thinking: herein is perhaps the chief of all the conceptions he made it his major purpose in life to communicate, 'conceptions which result from considering the moral or the material universe as a whole'. It was his *Prometheus*, which among all his poems contained perhaps the greatest measure of 'the virtue and power of love' that he called 'my best poem'. That Shelley is less often judged according to the great conceptions which were his own standards than misunderstood or belaboured by reason of their deterrent subtlety, while being admired at the same time for the more easily penetrable excellence of his lyrics—'mere *deliciae* from his point of view', as Professor Blunden has said[1]— this is a matter which may be deplored but needs no explaining.

What Agathon has to say about the ἀρετή of Love takes us into page 216 of the Bipont text, still for the moment just outside the strict boundaries of Shelley's markings. In his translation it appears thus:[2]

What is most admirable in Love is, that he neither inflicts nor endures injury in his relations either with Gods or men. Nor if he suffers any thing does he suffer it through violence, nor doing anything does he act it with violence, for Love is never even touched with violence. Every one willingly administers everything to Love; and that which every one voluntarily concedes to another, the laws, which are the kings of the republic, decree that it is just for him to possess. In addition to justice, Love participates in the highest temperance; for if temperance is defined to be the being superior to and holding under dominion pleasures and desires; then Love, than whom no pleasure is more powerful, and who is thus more powerful than all persuasions and delights, must be excellently temperate. In power and valour Mars cannot contend with Love: the love of Venus possesses Mars; the possessor is always superior to the possessed, and he who subdues the most powerful must of necessity be the most powerful of all.

[1] *Shelley*, Collins, 1946, p. 290.   [2] *Symp.* 196b–d, Jul. vii. 190.

Here is the point of divergence between Shelley's Prometheus and the hero of Aeschylus' lost play. 'I was averse', he says,[1] 'to a catastrophe so feeble as that of reconciling the Champion with the Oppressor of mankind'; instead therefore he gives us a Prometheus not reconciled but victorious over his 'successful and perfidious adversary'; victorious because of his personal qualities: it is these that make him 'the type of the highest perfection of moral and intellectual nature' and they are summed up in the Shelleyan ἀρετή, the 'virtue and power of Love': ἀρετῇ σε νικῶ θνητὸς ὢν θεὸν μέγαν. Now the essence of the Shelleyan-Promethean love is that it 'neither inflicts nor endures injury in its relations either with Gods or men': it is out of this that Shelley makes the catastrophe of his own drama proceed. For not till Prometheus has forsworn vengeance can he prevail over tyranny: it is his possession and exercise of 'the highest temperance' in addition to his sense of justice—πρὸς δὲ τῇ δικαιοσύνῃ σωφροσύνης πλείστης μετέχει—which brings round the hour of his triumph:

> Resist not the weakness,[2]
> Such strength is in meekness . . .

is Shelley's choric version of what Agathon says[3] of the weakness of violence: 'In power and valour Mars cannot contend with Love.' The sentence is significant for one point and possibly two. The first is his translation of the single word ἀνδρείαν as 'power and valour', whereby, having translated ἀρετή as 'virtue and power', he half equates, by implication, the meanings of the two words; a typical fusion of conceptions, important when we come to interpret his notions of ἀρετή and Love. The second is that Plato himself in this sentence is adapting to his doctrine of Love a line of Sophocles about the power of Necessity: 'Necessity whom not the God of War withstands', a point of real significance only if we may assume that Shelley knew the reference, but interesting none the less.[4] Shelley believed, however, that the weakness of Tyranny lay in its inability, ultimately, to withstand the power of Man's mind, which he might exercise if he would, his will being free; to make use of his will, however, he must have a sufficiency of ἀρετή. This ἀρετή of his implied a cultivation of all

---

[1] Preface to *Prometheus Unbound*, Hutch., p. 205.
[2] II. iii. 93–94, Hutch., p. 236.   [3] *Symp.* 196c.
[4] Soph. *Thyest*, fr. 235.

the meekness, patience, &c., that are implied in Agathon's word σωφροσύνη. Such was the doctrine preached philosophically and poetically in *Prometheus Unbound*. Politically at the time when he was writing the fourth act in 1819 he had just urged the same doctrine upon the working-class men of Manchester: it was what would today be called a 'policy of passive resistance'; they are urged, in *A Mask of Anarchy*[1] to right their wrongs not by violence but by

Spirit, Patience, Gentleness. . . .

'This', says Mary Shelley of the doctrine,[2] 'also forms a portion of Christianity.'

Hastily turning over page 217 of the Bipont text—noting only that it treats of the relation to Love of poetry and the arts generally so that Intellectual Beauty is only just round the corner if we cared to turn aside from the immediate path of ἀρετή—we come to page 218, the third of the pages marked by Shelley. That he thought it a very notable page may be seen from the 'passim' which he wrote against it and from the two crosses with which, Baedeker-wise, it is recommended in his notebook. Like 'The wonderful description of Love' it follows a mention of the crimes committed by the gods under the previous rule of Necessity. 'But', continued Agathon,[3] bringing his speech to a close with a prose-hymn on the 'virtue and power' of Love,

so soon as this deity sprang forth from the desire which forever tends in the Universe towards that which is lovely, then all blessings descended upon all living things, human and divine. Love seems to me, O Phaedrus, a divinity the most beautiful and the best of all, and the author to all others of the excellences with which his own nature is endowed.[4] Nor can I restrain the poetic enthusiasm which takes possession of my discourse, and bids me declare that Love is the divinity who creates peace among men, and calm upon the sea, the windless silence of storms, repose and sleep in sadness. Love divests us of all alienation

[1] 258, Hutch., p. 343.
[2] 'Note on *Prometheus Unbound*', Hutch., p. 271. Though, as Sir Maurice Bowra has noticed (*The Romantic Imagination*, O.U.P., 1950, p. 121), Shelley forgets that Jupiter is not a person but a symbol of the very principle of Evil which, as he well knew, should not and will not be defeated by forgiveness. The result is a confusion of the philosophical scheme of the poem.
[3] *Symp.* 197c, Jul. vii. 191–2.
[4] At the turn-over [196d] comes the idea, which had been Shelley's feeling in the Dedication of *Queen Mab*, 'for everyone, even if before he were ever so undisciplined becomes a poet as soon as he is touched by Love' [Jul. vii. 191]. The word ποίησις, as below in 205b, c, means both 'poetry' and 'creation, generation'.

from each other, and fills our vacant hearts with overflowing sympathy; he gathers us together in such social meetings as we now delight to celebrate, our guardian and our guide in dances, and sacrifices, and feasts. Yes, Love who showers benignity upon the world, and before whose presence all harsh passions flee and perish; the author of all soft affections; the destroyer of all ungentle thoughts; merciful, mild; the object of the admiration of the wise, and the delight of gods; possessed by the fortunate, and desired by the unhappy, therefore unhappy because they possess him not; the father of grace, and delicacy, and gentleness, and delight, and persuasion, and desire; the cherisher of all that is good, the abolisher of all evil; our most excellent pilot, defence, saviour and guardian in labour and in fear, in desire and in reason; the ornament and governor of all things human and divine; the best, the loveliest; in whose footsteps everyone ought to follow, celebrating him excellently in song, and bearing each his part in that divinest harmony which Love sings to all things which live and are, soothing the troubled minds of Gods and men. . . .

So much can come into the world with Love. Necessity, Ἀνάγκη, like Zeus in the *Hercules Furens*,[1] was 'a rather stupid god or else unjust' because lacking, like him, in a sense of responsibility towards humanity such as the possession of ἀρετή involves: Love, on the contrary, by reason of his inherent 'virtue and power'

showers benignity upon the world.

The extremely Shelleyan word 'benignity' is to be noticed; we may notice too, for a third time, Shelley's tendency to expand a phrase in translation when he wishes to emphasize a nuance he has found in the Greek or is reading into it. He makes a good deal of πρᾳότητα μὲν πορίζων, ἀγριότητα δ' ἐξορίζων. If we understand the humanitarian turn that love was taking at this point of the main Platonic path, a good deal in *Prometheus Unbound* will become clearer, more particularly the mysterious character of Demogorgon, whom we may agree with Professor Grabo[2] in interpreting as representing Fate or Necessity, the mother of the Fates: 'By casting out hate Prometheus has identified himself with the ruling power of the universe which is Love, and Love commands Destiny, or Fate, which is Demogorgon.' What has happened at this point of the path is that, as we saw, there has been a juncture of Ἔρως and ἀρετή which then branch out together into a love of a humanitarian character approximating in its essential aspects

---

[1] See above, pp. 19-20.   [2] *The Magic Plant*, p. 280.

to the Christian ἀγάπη. It bears some relation too to the final, universal love which Dante conceives as animating the universe: in Dante, in the course of time, Shelley would re-encounter this Platonically derived notion of his.

We have not yet quite finished with Shelley's two-starred page. In his translation of the latter part of Agathon's speech may be felt the stirrings[1] of a choric movement, and much of the general feeling of the language was to underlie the choruses of *Prometheus Unbound*. We will find room for two examples: in both the image of the ship is prominent, together with Love 'our most excellent pilot' (κυβερνήτης ... ἄριστος). The first is from Asia's song:[2]

> Meanwhile thy spirit lifts its pinions
> In music's most serene dominions;
> Catching the winds that fan that happy heaven.
> And we sail on, away, afar,
> Without a course, without a star,
> But, by the instinct of sweet music driven;
> Till through Elysian garden islets
> By thee, most beautiful of pilots,
> Where never mortal pinnace glided,
> The boat of my desire is guided:
> Realms where the air we breathe is love,
> Which in the winds and on the waves doth move,
> Harmonizing this earth with what we feel above.

Here is 'the divinity who creates peace among men and calm upon the sea', and the movement is tranquil, *andante*. But in the speech of the Earth comes a stanza[3] about the will of Man: the whole speech is about Man and the movement is *maestoso*; Love here is 'defence, saviour and guardian in labour and fear':

> His will, with all mean passions, bad delights,
> And selfish cares, its trembling satellites,
> A spirit ill to guide, but mighty to obey,
> Is as a tempest-wingèd ship, whose helm
> Love rules, through waves which dare not overwhelm,
> Forcing life's wildest shores to own its sovereign sway.

[1] What Shelley meant to signify in his memorandum by 'Agathon a poem' can only be guessed; my guess is that he meant 'Agathon's speech—as good as a poem'. Another possibility is that he meant to write a poem on the subject of Agathon: perhaps 'Prince Athenase' was to have been that poem: it makes reference to 'Plato's words of light' and 'Agathon and Diotima' [224, 228, Hutch., p. 164].

[2] *Prom.* II. v. 85–97, Hutch., p. 242. *Symp.* 197e.

[3] *Prom.* IV. 406–11, Hutch., pp. 263–4.

It is difficult not to think back to the day, three years before this
was written, when Shelley was on Lake Leman with Byron and
'there appeared to be some danger'; there are so many times when
his symbolism seems to grow into or out of his life as much as his
thought. One thinks forward too to the day three years later when
Williams, who at such times had practical rather than philosophical notions of reality, was vainly trying, off Lerici, to teach
seamanship to a by no means excellent pilot—indeed a κυβερνήτης
κάκιστος:[1]

As usual Shelley had a book in hand, saying he could read and
steer at the same time, as one was mental, the other mechanical.

The remaining pages marked by Shelley bring us round to
what was one of our starting-points in Chapter 2, Socrates'
account of his talk with the Mantinean woman. If he has not
actually starred any of them as he has starred page 218 we have a
strong enough indication, from the heading 'Diotima's Atheism'
which he gives them, and from the fact that here and there in his
notebooks he jots down the word 'Diotima' again as self-reminder,
of the importance which he attached to them *passim*.

To start with page 228, which needs to be studied well beyond
line 15, the limit of Shelley's reference: throughout Agathon's
speech Love has been referred to without doubt or hesitation as
a god. Socrates now questions Diotima on the point:[2]

'But,' I said, 'love is confessed by all to be a great God.'—'Do
you mean, when you say all, all those who know, or those who
know not, what they say?'—'All collectively.'—'And how can that
be, Socrates?' said she laughing; 'how can he be acknowledged to
be a great God, by those who assert that he is not even a God at
all?'—'And who are they?' I said.—'You for one, and I for another.'

Such is 'Diotima's Atheism': in the context, though it is concerned with pagan and not Christian theology, there is everything to appeal to the Shelley who, at Oxford, had signed himself,
in the 'advertisement' prefacing his temerarious pamphlet,
'Through deficiency of proof, an Atheist'. Diotima goes on to
remind Socrates of a concession he has made just previously that
Love, who is ever seeking the good and the beautiful, cannot, in
consequence, be said to possess them; therefore, she says, he can-

[1] Trelawny, *Recollections*, in H. Wolfe's combined *Life*, ii. 209-10.
[2] *Symp*. 202b, Jul. vii. 197.

not be a god for 'How can we conceive a God to be without the possession of what is beautiful and good?':[1]

'What, then,' I said, 'is Love a mortal?'—'By no means.'—'But what, then?'—'Like those things which I have before instanced, he is neither mortal nor immortal, but something intermediate.'—'What is that, O Diotima?'

And here, in its context, is Diotima's reply which we have already quoted in Chapter 2:[2]

'A great Dæmon, Socrates; and every thing dæmoniacal holds an intermediate place between what is divine and what is mortal.'

Asked about his power and nature she goes on to explain that he 'interprets and makes a communication between divine and human things' and that he[2]

'fills up that intermediate space between these two classes of beings, so as to bind together, by his power, the whole universe of things'.

If we have been correct in assuming, as it would seem we may, that Shelley sees in 'Diotima's Atheism' a reflection of his own views, it might well be held that we have found the clue here first to his own attitude regarding 'the universe of things'—τὸ πᾶν— and secondly to his own peculiar spiritual existence. Diotima refers, in the speech just quoted, to 'those things I have instanced before'; she means 'previous examples of "intermediate" things'. Let us look back to a point in the argument which, for the moment, we have passed over; we find it, in Shelley's Bipont text, at the top of page 228 which shows her asking[3]

'Do you not perceive that there is something between ignorance and wisdom?'

and, in reply to Socrates' query 'What is that?' she replies;

'To have a right opinion or conjecture'

then, immediately, she explains that

'A right opinion is something between understanding and ignorance'

which is to say that Love stands in the same relationship to the divine and the mortal as 'a right opinion' does to understanding

---

[1] *Symp.* 202d, Jul. vii. 197.   [2] *Symp.* 202e, Jul. vii. 197.
[3] *Symp.* 202a, Jul. vii. 196. The passage may perhaps have contributed to that phrase in the Preface to *Prom.* '. . . the equilibrium between institutions and opinions'.

and ignorance: both are 'something intermediate', both fill an intermediate space. Herein, I believe, is the point of what Shelley designated as 'Diotima's Atheism' and such, I believe, was the central, operative point in his own beliefs or disbeliefs regarding 'the whole universe of things'. God, or whatever the supreme Power might be, could not 'through lack of proof' be logically apprehended, and it was illogical, ridiculous to cleave to mere faith, a dogma rooted in ignorance: however, somewhere between the extremes of understanding and ignorance on the one hand and of divine and mortal on the other lay Love and the possibility of a right opinion—τὸ ὀρθὰ δοξάζειν—a conjunction amounting to Intellectual Beauty: here was the whole of the spiritual— πᾶν τὸ δαιμόνιον—'everything daemoniacal' as Shelley translates it, and here was Love to bind together by his power 'the whole universe of things'. Here it was that Shelley had his own spiritual existence, 'between divine and mortal'—μεταξὺ θεοῦ τε καὶ θνητοῦ—following the daemon Love by aspiring to whose 'virtue and power' he might prevail over such powers as lacked it— ἀρετῇ σε νικῶ θνητὸς ὢν θεὸν μέγαν. Such was the task of 'human reason, human powers' which he set himself in *Prometheus Unbound* in his 'golden age',[1] his annus mirabilis of 1819: the West Wind was its symbol. Seeing that 'between divine and mortal' would seem to imply the existence of something divine what Shelley called 'Diotima's Atheism' appears a somewhat anomalous concept: the anomaly would correspond with the fact that he was never either clear or happy about his own atheism.[2] He contented himself, however, with the pursuit of universal Love—not a god but a daemon, 'The Daemon of the World' as he had called it in his revised version of *Queen Mab*; direct Platonic study had enlarged the concept. But Diotima goes on, taking us once more a little beyond Shelley's markings:[3]

The divine nature cannot immediately communicate with what is human, but all that intercourse and converse which is conceded by the Gods to men, both whilst they sleep and when they wake, subsists through the intervention of Love; and he who is wise in the science of this intercourse is supremely happy, and participates in the daemoniacal nature; [ὁ μὲν περὶ τὰ τοιαῦτα σοφὸς δαιμόνιος ἀνήρ] whilst he who is wise in any other science or art, remains a mere ordinary slave.

[1] Letter to Miss Hitchener, 1811, quoted on p. 30.
[2] Cf. below, pp. 276-9.   [3] *Symp.* 203a, Jul. vii. 198.

These daemons are, indeed, many and various, and one of them is Love.

To 'participate in the daemoniacal nature' was what Shelley sought to do: unfortunately he was not always wise and not always happy; at times it seemed that the Daemon was not Love but one of the 'many and various' other spirits: these were the 'monsters of his thought' with which he had to wrestle.

The next passages are concerned with 'the daemoniacal nature', i.e. the nature of this particular daemon, Love. The passage on the Bipont page '231 line 5' is thus translated by Shelley—Diotima is briefly relating[1] how, at the feast given by the gods to celebrate the birth of Venus, Poverty wishing to have a child by Plenty, on account of her low estate, lay down by him and from his embraces conceived Love:

Love is, therefore, the follower and servant of Venus, because he was conceived at her birth, and because by nature he is a lover of all that is beautiful and Venus was beautiful.

As a corollary (page 233), since Wisdom is one of the most beautiful of all things, Love is a philosopher, a follower of Wisdom. Then comes the passage beginning at line 7 to which Shelley specifically refers on this page, and which seems to have struck him very forcibly:[2]

Such is the dæmoniacal nature, my dear Socrates; nor do I wonder at your error concerning Love, for you thought, as I conjecture from what you say, that Love was not the lover but the beloved, and thence, well concluded that he must be supremely beautiful; for that which is the object of Love must indeed be fair, and delicate, and perfect, and most happy; but Love inherits, as I have declared, a totally opposite nature.—

It is, I believe, to this that Shelley refers when he notes

I should say in answer that Ἔρως neither loved nor was loved but is the cause of love in others, a subtlety to beat Plato.

Here we have the essence of the Shelleyan conception as regards love on the concrete, human plane. Love, in Diotima's myth, is not compact of perfections since Love inherits—she has explained this—certain sordid qualities from his mother Poverty and is not therefore to be identified with physical perfection in the beloved:

[1] *Symp.* 203b–c, Jul. vii. 198.
[2] *Symp.* 204b (ἡ μὲν οὖν φύσις . . .), Jul. vii. 199.

it was something—found formerly even in Miss Hitchener—
which evoked response, inspiring and ennobling, bridging the
gulf between divine and mortal, a *cause* of all the good and the
beautiful; it corresponded to the love which, on the abstract
plane, had 'virtue and power' to 'bind together the whole universe
of things'. On page 236 love is further defined as 'collectively the
desire in men that the good should be ever present to them'; this,
if we are to reconcile it with Shelley's comment that Ἔρως is 'the
cause of love in others', must be taken as implying that Ἔρως
while the 'cause' of love must also be something reciprocal to the
'cause'. Diotima continues about the cause of love in the next
few pages: Love, she says, is not so much the love of the beautiful
as a desire to procreate from the beautiful,[1]

> For the mortal nature seeks, so far as it is able, to become deathless
> and eternal. But it can only accomplish this desire by generation. . . .

The argument has much in it of the feeling of *Queen Mab*: 'All
things are recreated', and Shelley's perception at the time when
he wrote it of a spiritual and moral palingenesis corresponding
to the reproductive processes of Nature. The first phrase needs to
be noticed as it is in the Greek: ἡ θνητὴ φύσις ζητεῖ κατὰ τὸ
δυνατὸν ἀεί τε εἶναι καὶ ἀθάνατος—here, once more, is our old
antithesis of mortal/immortal: Shelley might well have attached
the words to the West Wind manuscript in place of his Euripides
quotation. Diotima goes on[2]

> Manners, morals, opinions, desires, pleasures, sorrows, fears; none
> of these ever remain unchanged in the same persons; but some die
> away, and others are produced. And, what is yet more strange is, that
> not only does some knowledge spring up, and another decay, and
> that we are never the same with respect to our knowledge, but that
> each several object of our thoughts suffers the same revolution.

Again we have come to a meeting or recrossing of paths: here is
the New Birth Symbol, out of which we formerly saw Shelley's
mind branching into the doctrine of Love, now appearing as a
path, in its turn, branching out of the Love-doctrine rather than
as an offshoot, as it formerly was, of the old doctrine of Necessity.
We might here take it further into the *Symposium* where the idea
is developed, which has already been touched on in this chapter,

---

[1] *Symp.* 207d, Jul. vii. 202.   [2] *Symp.* 207d, Jul. vii. 203.

of love as a source of poetry and the arts: this, however, must await Chapter 8, where we shall turn into it from the Veil, one of the subsidiary symbolical paths. We have had far to go in following Shelley's Ariadne quest: we have seen love rising to Intellectual Beauty, being incarnated in various 'ideal figures' in Shelley's youth and, broadened by Platonic study, merging into a humanitarian ideal of a Christian character: after necessary détours to look closely at a memorandum, at the dating and contents of a notebook and at various passages of poetry by the wayside, we came to Shelley's atheism, to the nature of Love-the-daemon and the kind of Shelleyan-Promethean love that is modelled on it, and back to the familiar path of the New Birth symbol. It has been a long road but it is a main road and careful surveying was necessary. More of the various manifestations of Shelleyan love— **πολλῶν ὀνομάτων μορφὴ μία**[1]—inescapable, and always difficult to define, will appear throughout subsequent chapters. But we must now turn aside to look more closely at what will by now have been perceived to be not least of Shelley's subsidiary symbols, the Daemon and his 'many and various' manifestations.

ADDENDUM (*See p. 39, above*)

An interesting example of what Professor Notopoulos calls Shelley's 'natural Platonism' (an instinct peculiar neither to him nor, indeed, to poets) is his frequent reference, when writing to Hogg, to the Aristotelean conception of ἀφιλαυτία and φιλαυτία—selfless and selfish love in friendship: herein, in 1811–12, he is groping his way towards the later Shelleyan-Platonic notion of ἀγάπη. See Jones, *Letters of Shelley*, i. 77, 78, 81, 96. The basis of this thinking may be found in *Nicomachean Ethics*, ix. 8, which he translated: see Kenneth Neill Cameron, *Shelley and His Circle*, ii. 659 foll., Oxford and Harvard, 1961.

[1] 'One form, under many names.' This quotation, from Aeschylus, *P.V.*, 210, is jotted at the end of a notebook Bod. MS. Shelley adds. e. 11 and a few pages away is the fragment 'Love the Universe To-day', Hutch., p. 584.

> And who feels discord now or sorrow?
> Love is the universe to-day—
> These are the slaves of dim to-morrow,
> Darkening Life's labyrinthine way.

The occurrence of the labyrinth will be noted. Shelley seems to have adapted Aeschylus' phrase in *Ep.* 267.

> In many mortal forms I rashly sought
> The shadow of that idol of my thought.

Greek quotations were sometimes liable to find their way from Shelley's notebooks into his writings without much reference to their original context: cf. the Pindar passage quoted on p. 100.

5. Daemons and other 'monsters of his thought'

Philosophers themselves have not disdained to employ under other names the useful machinery supplied by vulgar creeds. Genii, Daemons and younger gods were beings whose existence was acknowledged by the Platonists and the appellations only of these beings have been changed by other sectaries, who speak of Powers, Dominions and Thrones. But the belief in the interference of Deities and Daemons in human concerns and in the order of Nature was gradually rejected as the experience of men increased.

So wrote Sir William Drummond in his *Academical Questions*,[1] published in 1805, a book much studied by Shelley and several times praised by him, more especially in the Notes on *Queen Mab*[2] and in the Preface to *The Revolt of Islam*.[3] Like Coleridge Shelley made considerable use of some of the beliefs referred to and they are reflected in one of his jottings:[4]

I am not conscious of having deviated from the costumi ⟨sic⟩ of antique mythology. The spirits indeed belong under various names to every system of supernatural agency, it is a generic name including Genii, Lamiae, elementary powers, angels, fairies, ghosts, daemons[

A point of immediate interest is that this jotting connects with Sir William not only by its content but by its date. For it was on 22 April 1819[5] that he visited the Shelleys in Rome, and the Shelley-Rolls notebook containing it was certainly in use just about then: only a few pages away from where it is scribbled over an out-of-date draft (part of 'Julian and Maddalo') the coachman has signed a receipt for his monthly wages and the receipt is dated 'April 20, 1819'.[6] What is of greater interest is that Sir William and his views are both immediately seen in relation to

---

[1] i. 176.   [2] Hutch., p. 800 foll.   [3] Hutch, p. 32 foll.
[4] Bod. MS. Shelley adds. e. 11, p. 88.
[5] See White, *Shelley*, ii. 89, which is substantiated by Claire's Journal [Brit. Mus. MS.].
[6] Bod. MS. Shelley adds. e. 11, p. 124 rev. The donor of this valuable clue was one Vincenzo Gavita. He was able to write, if not very grammatically, and the receipt above his signature reads
** O ricevuto scudi 6 per mia mesata **
Shelley attaches a list of domestic expenses in which we read 'Coachman 6.0.'

Prometheus Unbound, which had had its New Birth that spring in the beauty of the Roman sunshine. It is true that in Shelley's letter to Peacock of April 6[1] the first three acts are described as finished, but this notebook contains one or two passages which look like afterthoughts written subsequent to the main draft[2] now, for the most part, missing: it contains also part of the draft for the Preface for which our jotting may, just possibly, have represented an intended idea or two. One way and another it certainly points deep into the drama, and does so via Sir William and his views. About the nature of the soul, for instance, he says in his book:[3]

... surely more sublime was the Platonic doctrine, which taught the pre-existence of the immaterial soul and according to which it was supposed that the spiritual and incarnate effluence of universal mind gradually awakes to reminiscence and intelligence after its first slumber has passed in its corporeal prison.

In this Neoplatonic presentation of the immortality of the soul, known to Shelley in 1812, we may trace something of the World-Soul conception pervading *Queen Mab* and much that was to come out in *Adonais*: there is much in it too which may be traced throughout the general conception of *Prometheus Unbound*. More particularly the 'Spirits' in the poem are a generic name for the means by which Shelley sought, as Mary said, 'to gift the mechanism of the universe with a soul and a voice'. Again,

Mind [says Drummond] is defined by Plato to be that which is self-moved. Plato ... appears to have believed that it is contained in a material substance which he considered as its proper organ. The later Platonists imagined that the intellectual principle, when it quits the human body, immediately attaches itself to an aerial form which becomes its vehicle.

So too did Shelley imagine the soul in 'aerial forms' such as

... Desires and Adorations,
Wingèd Persuasions and veiled Destinies.

---

[1] Jones, *Letters of Shelley*, ii. 94.
[2] Though the Bodleian has possessed, since 1893, a fine intermediate fair copy of *Prometheus Unbound* the existing MS. *drafts* are very incomplete. A good deal of Act IV is covered by Shelley-Rolls Notebooks and by the Bixby Notebooks in the Henry Huntington Library: of Acts II and III a few scraps only remain and of Act I there is, as far as I am aware, nothing. For this and other reasons I am inclined to suspect that a notebook or two of 1818–19 was lost or destroyed.
[3] i. 26–27.

But we do not have to look as far as *Adonais*:[1] the spirits are there in the notebook. We have only to turn a few pages to find, roughly scribbled in pencil,[2]

> Hark! Spirits speak. The liquid responses
> Of their aëreal tongues yet sound.
>   I hear.
>   O, follow, follow,
>   As our voice recedeth
>   Through the caverns hollow,
>   Where the forest spreadeth. . . .

And, in addition to the Echoes' song for Act II, we have in this notebook[3] a good deal of the speech of the Spirit of the Hour which ends Act III. What exactly resulted, in terms of poetry, from the Shelley-Drummond conversation we can never know, but it is tempting to infer that just as Sir William's book lent a good deal to the general conception of *Prometheus* so his presence in Rome may have conjured up a few additional spirit-voices for Acts II and III.

Immediately preceding the page where the Spirit of the Hour begins her faintly-pencilled speech we find the following curious invocation which appears over the signature, very bold and assertive, 'PERCY SHELLEY':[4]

> **To the ghost of Aeschylus
>   audisne haec Amphiarae sub terram abdite?**

The point of the Latin question, printed as a motto on the title-page of the *Prometheus* volume, becomes very much clearer if we are to imagine Shelley as saying in mock defiance to the ghost of Aeschylus 'How now, old mole? Do you hear *this*?'—'this' being his poem in which, unlike the poor ghost in its lost play, he was 'averse to a catastrophe so feeble as that of reconciling the Champion with the Oppressor of mankind'[5] and so gave his theme a Platonic twist. Such an admixture of humour and fantasy[6] would not have been untypical, more especially as the gibe,

---

[1] 109–10, Hutch., p. 434.   [2] *Prom.* II. i. 171–6, Hutch., p. 230.

[3] Bod. MS. Shelley adds. e. 11, pp. 114 rev.–113 rev.

[4] The quotation is from the 'Epigoni' of an unknown author quoted in Cicero, *Disp. Tusc.* ii. 60.

[5] Cf. the Preface to *Prometheus Unbound*, Hutch., pp. 221 and 224. And see above, pp. 55–57.

[6] Not altogether dissimilarly in the next year, 1820, by a coincidence, do we find the young Elizabeth Barrett writing her letters to Homer, Pindar, and Socrates

at once a private and a public one, would be at 'the advocates of injustice and superstition', i.e. 'if I do live to accomplish what I purpose . . . let them not flatter themselves that I should take Aeschylus rather than Plato as my model'.

But Shelley's attraction to the supernatural may be traced back to the early years of his childhood, and there too it appears in humour and fantasy; from time to time he would regale his sisters with stories of such monsters of Sussex legend as the Great Tortoise that lived in Warnham Pond, near Field Place; then there were the occasions, of which Hellen Shelley told Hogg long afterwards, when 'we dressed ourselves in strange costumes to personate spirits or fiends, and Bysshe would take a fire-shovel and fill it with some inflammable liquid and carry it flaming into the kitchen and to the back door'. Thornton Hunt too remembered,[1] after forty-six years, how, in 1817, Shelley would delight him and his brothers and sisters by his impersonations of a fiend, screwing up his long hair into the appearance of a horn, assuming a terrifying expression, and advancing 'with rampant paws and frightful gestures'. Supernatural inventions of the kind are common enough among all children but few children were ever so given to them as Shelley; in the 'Hymn to Intellectual Beauty'— 'While yet a boy I sought for ghosts . . .'—he tells how imagination turned from fantasy towards philosophy. No doubt the fashionable romances of Gothic gloom and horror helped it on its way. As he read more and more about the universe, belief in strange deities and daemons increased till they became very much more for him than merely 'useful machinery'. By about 1814, writing of Christian miracles, he could seriously explain them thus:[2]

They may have been produced by a peculiar agency of supernatural intelligences, analogous to what we read of animal magnetism and daemons good bad or indifferent who from caprice or motives inconceivable to us may have chosen to sport with the astonishment of mortals.

We see here how real these daemons, etc., could become; he tells

addressed 'Les Champs Élysées, Près du Palais de Pluton, L'Enfer'. See Dorothy Hewlett, *Elizabeth Barrett Browning*, Cassell, 1952, p. 32.

[1] Thornton Hunt, 'Shelley by One who Knew Him', in *The Atlantic Monthly*, 1863, xi. 184–204.

[2] Library of Congress Notebook, first published by Professor Fredk. L. Jones in *Studies in Philology* (45, no. 3, pp. 472–6) for July 1948.

us something too of the nature he personally attributed to the 'many and various' daemons other than Love who inhabited that mysterious 'intermediate space' of Diotima's. It is my firm conviction that the mysterious Tan-yr-allt assailant in 1812 was neither more nor less than one of these 'monsters of his thought' which had, for a moment, become real through the sheer force of creative imagination impinging upon an overwrought mood of emotion; so real indeed for Shelley that he was able to sketch the monster's appearance on a wooden screen: when the mood had subsided it would be only natural that, impelled by what would now be called 'defence mechanism', he should enlist his creative powers by inventing a practical explanation of the incident. His sketch is reproduced in Plate IIc and if anything were wanting to make the screen sketch a proof not of the reality of the figure but that what he saw was seen in his imagination rather than with the physical eye, it might be a comparison with two examples of the monsters he was sometimes wont to sketch, imaginatively, in a by no means dissimilar style: such examples may be found in Plates IIa and IIb. Both are taken from the same Shelley-Rolls notebook.[1] Plate IIb affords a particularly rich illustration of the strange and weirdly peopled world that existed in Shelley's mind: not only does it show two of the symbols we have met in the *Symposium*— the daemons floating in their space μεταξὺ θεοῦ τε καὶ θνητοῦ and the trees that stand for the regeneration of nature and thought— but it shows two more symbols, the Boat and the Isle which we shall discuss in the next chapter. Such was the world of one who sought to 'participate in the daemoniacal nature', a δαιμόνιος ἀνήρ.

Symptomatic of Shelley's Platonic progress under Peacock's influence during the years 1813–15 is his revision and abridgement of *Queen Mab* in the latter year under the title of *The Daemon of the World*.[2] Already the notion of Love as an intermediary spirit between gods and men had become a fundamental one having power even

> Where the vast snake Eternity
> In charmèd sleep doth ever lie.

The Snake is one of the most puzzling of Shelley's symbols by

---

[1] Bod. MS. Shelley adds. e. 9. Lawyers grow familiar with the fantasy-worlds which even a comparatively unimaginative witness can create. Cf. Addendum, p. 90.

[2] i. 100–1, Hutch., p. 3.

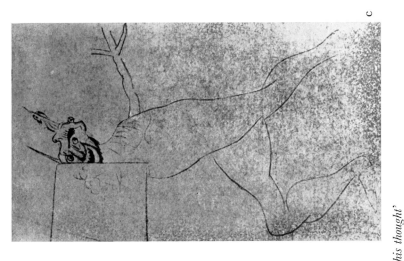

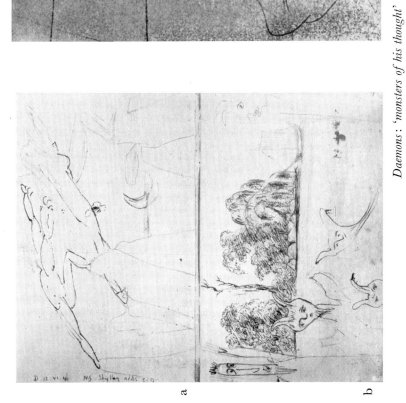

II

Daemons: 'monsters of his thought'

a. (?) *A κακοδαίμον in pursuit.* b. *Daemons floating in the 'intermediate space'. The Boat and the Isle again.*
c. *The Tan-yr-allt 'assailant'*

reason of the fact that Old Testament associations tend to tie it in our minds to the conception of evil; it is important not to misunderstand this subsidiary daemon. The symbol to which reference is made here is the δράκων οὐροβόρος, the tail-eating serpent whose figure signifies Eternity because it is without beginning or end:

Its origins are very early and it is prominent in the alchemical writings of Hermes Trismegistus, the Egyptian Thoth, from whom, it was believed, all Greek philosophy was derived: in Hermetic literature it became a symbol of the Platonic formula ἕν τὸ πᾶν which makes its appearance in *Adonais*—'The One remains, the many change and pass'; it was among the many Neoplatonic notions which were embodied in this literature.[1] Shelley is thought to have met it in such works as Volney's *Les Ruines* and Lord Monboddo's *Of the Origin and Progress of Language*. 'The subject which he loved best to dwell on', says Mary Shelley[2] apropos *Prometheus Unbound*, 'was the image of One warring with the Evil Principle', and this subject indeed is fundamental in the poem: more than once the Snake appears as the representative of the One.[3] As such it represents also the principle of the Good; this happens notably in the first canto of *The Revolt of Islam* where Evil, correspondingly, is represented by its adversary the Eagle, both daemons of the Shelleyan mid-space.

In *Alastor, or the Spirit of Solitude*, written contemporaneously with the revision of *Queen Mab*, Shelley expressed poetically the loneliness and misery of a youth of high ideals who, as he says,[4] 'seeks in vain for a prototype of his conception'. 'None of

---

[1] See Not., pp. 186–8, for a concisely detailed account of the origins of the symbol.
[2] 'Note on *Prometheus Unbound*', Hutch., p. 271.
[3] e.g. II. iii. 97 and IV. 565–7.   [4] Preface to *Alastor*, Hutch., pp. 14–15.

Shelley's poems', says Mary,[1] 'is more characteristic than this.'
Of her meaning there can be no doubt: the poem, in her know-
ledgeable opinion, related more closely to his individual mind and
his interior problems than any other. That its hero is Shelley
seeking his earthly Ariadne, his human 'guide to a knowledge of
Beauty itself', is thinly disguised in the Preface: 'The picture is
not barren of instruction to actual men. The Poet's self-seclusion
was avenged by the furies of an irresistible passion pursuing him
to speedy ruin.' What is happening is that a struggle is taking
place in the Poet's soul, a microcosm of the conflict in the universe between Good and Evil: in the course of his pursuit of the
δαίμων Love across a solitude which we may identify with Plato's
'intermediate space' he was being pursued himself by another
δαίμων—a κακοδαίμων. About the title Shelley asked the advice
of Peacock who tells us[2]

> I proposed that which he adopted: *Alastor; or, the Spirit of Solitude.*
> The Greek word Ἀλάστωρ is an evil genius, κακοδαίμων; though the
> sense of the two words is somewhat different as in the Φανεὶς Ἀλάστωρ
> ἢ κακὸς δαίμων ποθέν of Aeschylus.[3] The poem treated the spirit of
> solitude as a spirit of evil. I mention the true meaning of the word
> because many have supposed *Alastor* to be the name of the hero of the
> poem.

Idealist though Shelley was he was realist enough to know the
hazards of the Ariadne quest, and the untimely death of the Poet
in *Alastor* is an acknowledgement of them. It was not easy to
'vanquish the monster of his thought', not easy even to identify
him, to know a δαίμων from a κακοδαίμων. This was to be acknowledged again in *Prometheus Unbound*[4] where he referred to those

> Who, soothed to false repose by the fanning plumes above
>   And the music-stirring motion of its soft and busy feet,
> Dream visions of aëreal joy, and call the monster, Love,
>   And wake, and find the shadow Pain, as he whom now we greet.

Here was Love on the personal, earthly plane. The same problem
of distinction bothered Shelley about the vaster, universal Love
and had been doing so in *Queen Mab* where Christ, in a note,[5] is

---

[1] 'Note on *Alastor*', Hutch., p. 31.
[2] *Memoirs of Shelley*, in H. Wolfe's combined *Life*, ii. 341.
[3] *Persae*, 354.
[4] i. 776–9, Hutch., p. 225. Cf. the indeterminate identity of Keats's Lamia
and Coleridge's Geraldine.   [5] On vii. 135, 136, Hutch., pp. 819 foll.

divided between δαίμων and κακοδαίμων: the 'hypocritical
Daemon, who announces Himself as the God of compassion and
peace, even whilst he stretches forth his blood-red hand with the
sword of discord . . .' and 'the other who stands in the foremost
list of those true heroes who have died in the glorious martyrdom
of liberty . . .'. Shelley could never quite make up his mind about
Christ. In this, as in many things, Shelley will always defy those
who have labelled him too neatly or confidently. To set this latter
conception of Christ beside, for example, certain passages from
Prometheus Unbound and *Hellas*[1] is to realize that the Hound of
Heaven was often very close at his heels—a point curiously missed
by Francis Thompson[2] for whom the total Shelley amounted in
consequence to little more than a delightful, though heretical and
mischievous, Peter Pan.

We have come round, yet again, to *Prometheus Unbound.* Its very
first line takes Shelley with a leap into the supernatural regions:

> Monarch of Gods and Daemons and all Spirits
> But One . . .

Among the Bodleian notebooks there is a transcription by Mary[3]
of a note of Shelley's, which, being datable to October 1819, has
a bearing upon his conceptions of the supernatural as they were
when his *Prometheus* was being finished and revised; it arose
from his reading of Xenophon's *Memorabilia* and is as follows:

ON THE DAEMON OF SOCRATES
Memor. Lib I

Socrates' demon one form of augury. Socrates made a distinction
between things subject to divination and things not subject to it. He
said—a supernatural force has sway over the greatest things in all
human undertakings (p. 5), and that the uncertainty belonging to
them all is the intervention of that power, or rather that all events,
except those which the human will modifies, are modified by the
divine will.[4]

---

[1] See below, pp. 277–9 *et passim*.   [2] See above, p. x.
[3] Bod. MS. Shelley adds. d. 6, p. 1. For the date see Not., pp. 505–7. Not.
quotes from H. B. Forman with reference to the holograph which he (Forman)
appears to have seen, though I have been unable to identify the 'MS. book' containing it.
[4] The passage referred to is Xen. *Mem.* i. 2. See W. E. Peck, *Shelley, His Life and
Work*, Boston and New York, 1927, ii. 350. Professor Peck identified the passages
referred to with Shelley's markings in his own copy of Xenophon.

The 'supernatural force', of course, is the daemon: he it is who is the instrument through which 'the divine will modifies all human events except those which the human will modifies'. Had one been able to question Shelley as to *how* the human will performs its modifying there can be no doubt what his answer would have been: 'through the daemon likewise'. For the daemons in the *Symposium*[1] are conceived as the channel for a two-way, not merely a one-way, traffic: chief among them is Love, so that the δαιμόνιος ἀνήρ, he who 'participates in the daemoniacal nature', can, if he is able to command Love as Prometheus did by force of its ἀρετή, its 'virtue and power', even sway the divine will itself. It may be permissible to notice once again what Mary Shelley tells us[2] about Shelley's theories in *Prometheus Unbound* about the divine will:

> The prominent feature of Shelley's theory of the destiny of the human species was that evil is not inherent in the system of the creation, but an accident that might be expelled. This also forms a portion of Christianity . . . Shelley believed that mankind had only to will that there should be no evil, and there would be none. . . . That man could be so perfectionised as to be able to expel evil from his own nature, and from the greater part of the creation, was the cardinal point of his system.[3]

This note of Mary's and Shelley's note on the demoniacal inter-traffic might be said to be a commentary each on the other. The point of both may be seen all through the fourth act of *Prometheus* which was being composed in that autumn of 1819 when Shelley pondered the passage of Xenophon. Such was man's will. To requote what was quoted in the last chapter:[4]

> His will, with all mean passions, bad delights,
> And selfish cares, its trembling satellites,
> A spirit ill to guide, but mighty to obey,
> Is as a tempest-wingèd ship, whose helm
> Love rules. . . .

As regards Socrates' daemon what Shelley means, of course, is that this agency, of which he speaks a good deal to his judges in

---

[1] 202e–203a. Cf. above, p. 59.   [2] 'Note on *Prometheus Unbound*', Hutch., p. 271.
[3] Mary seems to imply that Shelley believed in the *permanent* victory of Good over Evil. But his belief, rather, was in *cycles* of Good over Evil: when the human will grew weak Evil again supplanted Good. See above, pp. 30–31, and below, pp. 125–7.
[4] See above, p. 57.

the *Apology*, is something that regulates his conduct in much the same way as other Greeks might allow theirs to be regulated by portents of nature, &c. This too happens to be in line with something in the *Symposium* since, immediately before the passage we have just referred to, Diotima has observed about Love:[1]

διὰ τούτου καὶ ἡ μαντικὴ πᾶσα χωρεῖ καὶ ἡ τῶν ἱερέων τέχνη τῶν τε περὶ τὰς θυσίας καὶ τελετὰς καὶ τὰς ἐπῳδὰς καὶ τὴν μαντείαν πᾶσαν καὶ γοητείαν.

Through him subsist all divination and the science of sacred things as it relates to sacrifices, and expiations, and disenchantments, and prophecy, and magic.

In *Prometheus Unbound* then, through Love (chief of the daemons, part of 'the mechanism of the universe', being at the same time a quasi-Christianized conception) Man triumphs over the divine will, synonymous in the drama with tyranny—ἀρετῇ σε νικῶ θνητὸς ὢν θεὸν μέγαν. . . .

From this universal, abstract region of philosophical love we now follow the daemon to the region of woman-love as idealized in *Epipsychidion*. Here, as in *Alastor*, we have a strong consciousness of two daemons, the good and the bad, the one striving to lead the soul from the earthly concrete plane of love to heights of Intellectual Beauty where it might become a part of the World Love if not actually identifiable with it, the other striving to drag it down to the abyss. *Epipsychidion* is, in fact, a return to the *Alastor* theme with deeper feeling, and matured thought and power of symbolical expression. Once again, in order not to make too direct a revelation of his experience with Emilia Viviani, Shelley resorted to the device of attempting to place his poem in an impersonal setting: so anxious was he about this that before writing the preface he finally published he wrote and rejected three other prefaces. The first[2] seems to reveal, when we know our Shelley, most of what it is intended to cover up:

The following Poem was found amongst other papers in the Portfolio of a young Englishman with whom the Editor had contracted an intimacy at Florence, brief indeed but sufficiently long to render the Catastrophe by which it terminated one of the most painful events of his life. . . .

[1] *Symp.* 202e, Jul. vii. 197–8.   [2] Hutch., p. 424.

He was an accomplished and amiable person but his error was, θνητὸς ὢν μὴ θνητὰ φρονεῖν,—his fate is an additional proof that 'The tree of Knowledge is not that of Life.'[1]—He had framed to himself certain opinions, founded no doubt upon the truth of things, but built up to a Babel height; they fell by their own weight, & the thoughts that were his architects, became unintelligible one to the other, as men upon whom confusion of tongues has fallen.

This, indeed, could never have concealed very much: the resemblance to *Alastor* alone is too patent: here is the same Poet who 'drinks deep of the fountains of knowledge' and 'descends to an untimely grave': the fact that this time he 'eats of a tree' and 'terminates with a Catastrophe' is the slightest of variations. Our own comment might be 'A strange fellow, that Lionel'. And, in truth here is Shelley once again, if we can only see it, quietly laughing in his English way at his most serious feelings; in the same language too, for there is next to no difference between 'opinions . . . built up to a Babel height' and 'we should have scaled the inaccessible with a ladder which is immediately withdrawn'.

Everywhere underneath *Epipsychidion* lurks a consciousness of the hazards and sorrows of Shelley's Ariadne quest; everywhere behind it lurk 'the monsters of his thought'. Their path through the notebooks at this time follows the draft of the poem. Much of this is to be found in the very volume containing the Lionel dialogue;[2] in another, overlapping with it in date,[3] we find something even more remarkable—the extraordinary creatures which he drew on its end-papers and which are reproduced in Plates II*a* and II*b*. These, there would seem very little doubt, represent the intrusion into reality, through his pen and pencil, of the daemons that peopled his imagination. That sinister, clawed figure pursuing its hermaphroditical victim[4] from crag to crag: what can it be? It is vaguely suggestive of Frankenstein's monster: perhaps this too was a kind of daemon that emerged from those conversations at Geneva. One might connect it with the 'irresistible furies' that pursued the Poet in *Alastor* (and in *Epipsychidion*, too, for that matter) or equally well with the Shelley of 1817 pursuing the Hunt children for their amusement 'with rampant paws and

---

[1] From Byron, *Manfred*, 12.

[2] Bod. MS. Shelley adds. e. 8.   [3] Bod. MS. Shelley adds. e. 9.

[4] But see Chap. 12, n. 5; cf. which chapter *passim* with these paragraphs about *Epipsychidion*.

frightful gestures', his hair screwed up into the likeness of a horn, perhaps something resembling the horns of the monsters we see in the other sketch, floating across some Shelleyan 'intermediate space' in company, we notice, with other intermediaries of his imagination, the Boat, the Isle, the expanse of water, and the trees that grow green in the spring. They, beyond a doubt, are κακοδαίμονες and I have little doubt that the Tan-yr-allt assailant (see Plate IIc) was at least a collateral relative, coexistent with Shelley upon undefinable frontiers of reality.

In *Epipsychidion* Shelley saw himself, very much in terms of the *Symposium*, as 'participating in the daemoniacal nature'. Something of a clue to what he understood by the δαιμόνιος ἀνήρ may be found in the phrase of his rejected Preface: θνητὸς ὢν μὴ θνητὰ φρονεῖν, 'being a mortal to aspire to immortal things'. As this phrase stands I am unable to trace it, but I believe it to be an adaptation from Plato's *Timaeus*. Here, in the passage in question,[1] there is a contrast between the man who by devoting himself to worldly aims has 'made great his mortal part' and the man whose aims are for higher things:

τῷ δὲ περὶ φιλομαθίαν καὶ περὶ τὰς ἀληθεῖς φρονήσεις ἐσπουδακότι καὶ ταῦτα μάλιστα τῶν αὐτοῦ γεγυμνασμένῳ φρονεῖν μὲν ἀθάνατα καὶ θεῖα, ἄνπερ ἀληθείας ἐφάπτηται, πᾶσα ἀνάγκη που, καθ' ὅσον δ' αὖ μετασχεῖν ἀνθρωπίνῃ φύσει ἀθανασίας ἐνδέχεται, τούτου μηδὲν μέρος ἀπολείπειν, ἅτε δὲ ἀεὶ θεραπεύοντα τὸ θεῖον ἔχοντά τε αὐτὸν εὖ κεκοσμημένον τὸν δαίμονα σύνοικον ἑαυτῷ, διαφερόντως εὐδαίμονα εἶναι.

In Thomas Taylor's English translation—I quote from Shelley's copy which is now in the Bodleian[2]—the passage runs as follows:

But it is necessary that he who is sedulously employed in the acquisition of knowledge, who is anxious to acquire the wisdom of truth and who employs his most vigorous assertions in this one pursuit:—it is perfectly necessary that such a one, if he touches on the truth, should

---

[1] 90b–c. For this suggestion I am indebted to Professor Gilbert Murray. Professor Notopoulos suggests *Bacchae* 396–7 as the source: τό τε μὴ θνητὰ φρονεῖν/ βραχὺς αἰών; see p. 272 Addendum. Another possibility is Aristotle, *Nicomachean Ethics*, 1177b, though here too the words are slightly different. We must not, I think, attempt exactness. Shelley was liable to fuse phrases he picked up. Cf. also *Hercules Furens* 342; see pp. 18–19 above.

For the probability that Shelley read the *Timaeus* in 1821 see Not., pp. 74–75; for Shelley and Aristotle see Not., pp. 82, 391. See also Not., p. 36. He had read the *Timaeus* in English in 1811.

[2] Thomas Taylor, *The Cratylus, Phaedo, Parmenides and Timaeus of Plato*, London, 1793. Bod. MS. Shelley adds. e. 1.

be endued with wisdom about immortal and divine concerns; and that he should participate of immortality as far has human nature permits, without leaving any part of it behind. And besides, as such a one always cultivates that which is divine and has a daemon most excellently adorned residing in his essence, he must be happy in the most eminent.

In a preceding passage of the *Timaeus*[1] Plato has explained the δαίμων συνοίκων as follows—I quote again from Taylor's version, more significant here than the Greek—

But with regard to the most principal and excellent species of the soul we should conceive as follows: that divinity assigned this to each of us as a daemon: and that it resides in the very summit of the body,[2] elevating us from earth to an alliance with the heavens.

The whole tenor of these two passages is very much in keeping with what we have seen Shelley to have picked up from the *Symposium* and with the feeling of *Epipsychidion*; yet again we have the intermediary daemon and in φρονεῖν μὲν ἀθάνατα καὶ θεῖα the mortal/immortal antithesis which we originally came across in a Euripides context in Chapter 2 and which we have so often seen to be Platonically echoed in Shelley's mind. Most striking of all, perhaps, is that phrase of Taylor's '. . . that he should participate of immortality as far as human nature permits' which, on the subject of the pursuit of true happiness, is practically identical with Shelley's phrase for the δαιμόνιος ἀνήρ in his translation of the *Symposium*:[3] 'he participates in the daemoniacal nature'. It is as if he had perceived in the *Timaeus* passage a complement to his *Symposium* ideas in the form of a definition of 'the daemoniacal nature'; the two in conjunction amount to an identification of the soul, the δαίμων συνοίκων, with the daemon Love itself: thus identified the soul in *Epipsychidion*[4] goes in search of another soul, being elevated 'from earth to an alliance with the heavens'—in fact

Into the height of Love's rare Universe.

Again that other phrase of Taylor's, 'he who is sedulous in the acquisition of knowledge', seems to lead straight to Shelley's Byron quotation[5] 'The tree of Knowledge is not that of Life'. It is here

---

[1] 90a. Cf. below, p. 234.
[2] i.e. the mind, home among men of Intellectual Beauty.   [3] 203a.
[4] 589, Hutch., p. 424.   [5] See p. 74.

that the error lies—θνητὸς ὢν μὴ θνητὰ φρονεῖν. For human nature may be too weak to enable a man to rise with his own aspirations: all depends—we are back to ἀρετή again—on the 'virtue and power' of his love.

What Shelley's capacity 'to apprehend minute and remote distinctions of feeling' owed to his Platonic studies will by now need no emphasizing. In 1822, a year after the daemon-conflicts of *Epipsychidion*, one of the climaxes of his Platonically apprehended feeling, we find that the daemon trail, together with the Ariadne trail—for both lead in the same direction—has turned aside from Plato and is passing through Goethe and Calderón, through which authors now we must duly follow his thought.

Even while Shelley was amateurishly trying in his weird sketches to give pictorial reality to his own supernatural imaginings, a German artist, Moritz Retzsch (1779–1857), was beginning to acquire a European reputation with the etchings in which he had so sensitively apprehended the feeling of Faust. When copies of these reached him he was most excited, though deploring the accompanying translations:

We have just got the etchings of 'Faust', [he wrote to John Gisborne on 12 January 1822][1] the painter is worthy of Göthe. The meeting of him and Margaret is wonderful. It makes all the pulses of my head beat—those of my heart have been quiet long ago. The translations, both these and in *Blackwood* are miserable. Ask Coleridge if their stupid misintelligence of the deep wisdom and harmony of the author does not spur him to action.

In this drawing, especially, which shows Faust and Margaret, or Gretchen, kissing in the summer-house with Mephistopheles lurking in the rear, so intensely real did the daemon-atmosphere seem to him that he wrote again:[2]

The artist makes one envy his happiness that he can sketch such things with calmness, which I dared only to look upon once, & which made my brain swim round only to touch the leaf on the opposite side of which I knew that it was figured.

It was he and not Coleridge who was spurred to action. There seems to be no evidence that he was a very profound German scholar; on the contrary, so far as we may judge from the

---

[1] Jones, *Letters of Shelley*, ii. 376. For the remarks about 'head and heart' cf. above, pp. 24–27.   [2] Jones, *Letters of Shelley*, ii. 407.

negative evidence of his notebooks, his use of this language, in comparison with others, was fairly slight. Neither German nor *Faust* however was new to him: among loose sheets in the Bodleian there is a literal translation of parts of the poem[1] which may date from 1814 or earlier, and its supernatural elements had been among the subjects of 'Monk' Lewis's conversation at Geneva in August 1816:[2] moreover, he had a fine, truthfully mimetic ear, the gift of tongues, and a rigorous self-schooling in the art of translation as such; linguistically too he had Claire Clairmont to help him. Not least of the gifts which he brought to bear upon *Faust*, as previously upon the *Symposium*, was his own subtle affinity of feeling with its subject: 'The tree of Knowledge is not that of Life.'[3]

Faust himself, like Shelley and the Poets of *Alastor* and *Epipsychidion*, has read and studied widely and *mit heissem Bemühn*: he is an idealist ever seeking for fresh knowledge and a guide who will lead him to it.[4]

> Flieh! auf! hinaus ins weite Land!
> Und dies geheimnisvolle Buch,
> Von Nostradamus' eigner Hand,
> Ist dir es nicht Geleit genug?

Though in Goethe the emphasis is on Knowledge rather than on Beauty the concept was near enough from Shelley's point of view to his own concept, Intellectual Beauty, and the *weite Land* is both the 'intermediate space' of the *Symposium* and the 'wilderness' of the Poet of *Alastor*: alike in *Alastor* and in *Epipsychidion* there is that mood of 'up, and away!'; then, in Mephistopheles, we have the daemon who has the power to go about and tempt, the κακοδαίμων who undertakes to be the guide and leads the way to destruction. Over and above the conflict of Faust is the realm where the good spirits enjoy love and Beauty, corresponding to Shelley's Platonic realm beyond the Veil[5] seen through his translation:[6]

> Doch ihr, die echten Göttersöhne,
> Erfreut euch der lebendig reichen Schöne!

---

[1] Bod. MS. Shelley adds. *c.* 4, ff. 142–76. A part of this curiosity—hardly more than a 'construe' with the English words in German order—is printed in Jul. vii. 277.

[2] White, *Shelley*, i. 460–1.   [3] See above, p. 74 n. 1.

[4] *Faust*, i. 418–21.   [5] See below, Ch. 7 and Ch. 8.

[6] *Faust*, i. 343–9. 'Scenes from Faust', i. 104–9, Hutch., p. 751.

Das Werdende, das ewig wirkt und lebt,
Umfass euch mit der Liebe holden Schranken,
Und was in schwankender Erscheinung schwebt,
Befestiget mit dauernden Gedanken!

. . . But ye, pure
Children of God, enjoy eternal beauty;—
Let that which ever operates and lives
Clasp you within the limits of its love;
And seize with sweet and melancholy thoughts
The floating phantoms of its loveliness.

There was usually a consistency of thought and purpose behind Shelley's undertakings, and in the case of his translations from Goethe and Calderón we know from a letter written to John Gisborne after they had been finished—it is dated 10 April 1822[1] —that he intended to make them the basis of a paper for *The Liberal*, the paper he was then planning to start in Italy with Byron and Leigh Hunt. Had this paper been achieved he would have shown us exactly how both *Faust* and *El mágico prodigioso* fitted into the pattern of his thought; lacking it we are reduced to mere speculation. But perhaps we have by now traced enough of that pattern in general to justify some guesses on the subject.

To start with let us consider his moods in early 1822. One clue to them is his revulsion against the *Epipsychidion* mood of the year before: he was no longer in the exalted mood of the poem but in the disillusioned one foreseen in the rejected Preface; by 18 June he could confess[2] the errors of his own quest for Beauty:

The error . . . consists in seeking in a mortal image the likeness of what is perhaps eternal.

The terms of the confession merely translate the phrase used about the 'young Englishman': 'his error was θνητὸς ὢν μὴ θνητὰ φρονεῖν'. The visionary Shelley had awakened with a start: the 'shadow of the idol of his thought' had vanished or, as he put it, Emilia had proved 'a cloud instead of a Juno': quite apart from what Shelley or Mary may have felt about her we have the opinion of that shrewd Irishwoman Lady Mountcashell: 'I believe that her chief talent was for intriguing and that the fire was more in her head than in her heart.'[3] Where the error lay was

---

[1] Jones, *Letters of Shelley*, ii. 406–7. But sometimes the translation was less purposeful: see App. II.   [2] Letter to John Gisborne, ibid. ii. 434.
[3] Letter to Mary Shelley, 31 Jan. 1824, Abinger Collection.

not in the fact that a mortal should aspire to things beyond him but in the failure to realize the inadequacy of his own ability to pursue Beauty on two planes at once. Emilia, except for a sort of final epilogue with Jane Williams, was the culmination of this double Ariadne quest: alas, 'The tree of Knowledge is not that of Life.' Here, it may well be, was the focal point of his interest in *Faust*. For Goethe Helen rather than Gretchen was the symbol of Beauty; nevertheless in Gretchen there is much to have made her seem to Shelley the 'prototype of his conception': not least the fact that in the end of Part I she triumphs in true Shelleyan fashion through the sheer 'virtue and power' of her love: it is a triumph of the human will equal, in its own sphere of Love, to the victory of Shelley's own Prometheus. What a contrast between Goethe's heroine and the heroine of *Epipsychidion*! 'Poor thing', Shelley had written of the latter,[1] 'she suffers dreadfully in her prison.' But—alas for the idealization and the teaching of Shelley-the-Liberator!—in the end she had tamely submitted to a *mariage de convenance* and had even degenerated, like other idolized friends of Shelley's, into a would-be borrower of money.[2] Gretchen, on the other hand, declining the offers of escape made by Mephistopheles the κακοδαίμων was still faithful to the 'likeness of what is eternal':

Sie ist gerichtet!

cries the evil daemon,[3] and indeed on the mortal plane she is condemned and has lost the mortal likeness of her love. But from above, in the famous, untranslatable play upon the word, comes the cry[3]

Sie ist gerettet.

For her ἀρετή, the 'virtue and power' of the integrity of Love, has saved her on the plane of the eternal and immortal—*der lebendig reichen Schöne*, where the good daemons dwell with God in eternal Beauty. In Part II of *Faust*, when it appeared after Shelley's death, Goethe's Gretchen, like Dante's Beatrice, had her place in heaven in company with the Blessed Virgin Mary herself. We may note again how, if we have not perceived it wrongly, the

---

[1] Letter to Claire Clairmont, 29 April 1821, Jones, *Letters of Shelley*, ii. 288.

[2] See White, *Shelley*, ii. 323–5, though there is disagreement from Emilia's biographer; see Marchesa Enrica Viviani della Robbia, *Vi a di una donna*, Sansoni, Firenze, 1936, pp. 130–2.

[3] *Faust*, i. 4611.

vision within Shelley's conceptions was moving unconsciously towards the visions of Christianity.

If these speculations seem in themselves a little overbold they may perhaps seem less so in the light of what has been said in previous chapters and what remains to be said in a later chapter[1] about Shelley's strange moods at Lerici when he seemed quite haunted by the shadow of *Faust*. There is consistency too in his contemporaneous attraction to *El mágico prodigioso*, the play of Calderón which offered him ideas of a similar pattern.

Writing his letter to John Gisborne on 10 April 1822 Shelley guessed that 'Cypriano' (or 'Cyprian' as he and his circle usually called the play) 'furnished the germ for *Faust*', and though its plan and structure are, in his phrase, as different from Goethe's poem 'as the acorn from the oak', the similarities are instructive. Calderón's plot originated in old martyrologies in Latin and Greek which had become current in Spanish in his day. As with *Faust* we may see a Shelleyan focal point in the heroine Justina[2]

que siendo doncella sin letras ni saber humano la escogió Dios por instrumento para convertir a un pagano, lleno de letras humanas y aun infernales.

The whole plot, likewise, hinges ultimately on this fact that she, 'being a damsel unlettered and without human knowledge was chosen by God as an instrument to convert a pagan, a man full of human learning and likewise that of hell'. Therein we have at once, though with a new and a Christian twist, the familiar motifs of Knowledge and Love, with Love working as an instrument of communication between the divine and the mortal: in conflict with Love we have the 'demonio', the κακοδαίμων who, for the perdition of Justina, enlists Cipriano, or 'Cyprian', a pagan like Shelley and a scholar and scientific speculator like both Shelley and Faust. We find him, at the opening of Act I, shunning mortal things and pondering immortal things in the form of theological problems arising out of a passage in Pliny:[3] it happens to be the very passage referred to by Shelley when commenting, among his Notes to *Queen Mab*,[4] upon that

---

[1] See below, pp. 285–90.

[2] From *La Vida de S. Cypriano y Justina Martires* as it appears in Alonso de Villegas's *Flos Sanctorum*, Madrid, 1594.

[3] *Hist. Nat.* ii. 7.

[4] vii. 13, Hutch., p. 812, where also Sir William Drummond's *Academical Questions* are referred to.

troublesome phrase 'There is no God'. The Daemon—Shelley's
word, of course, for the 'demonio'—poses as a foreign scholar;
Cyprian is amazed at his learning but he explains ironically—I
append Shelley's translation—[1]

> Sí, que de una patria soy
> donde las ciencias las más altas
> sin estudiarse se saben.

> For in the country whence I come the sciences
> Require no learning—they are known.

Cyprian's reply is full of Shelley's disillusionment :[2]

> !Oh, quién fuera de esa patria!
> que acá mientras más se estudia,
> más se ignora.

> Oh, would
> I were of that bright country! for in this
> The more we study we the more discover
> Our own ignorance.

They dispute the Pliny passage, Cyprian arguing against Pliny's
Jupiter the immorality of his behaviour among human beings as
seen in his amours. The Daemon's reply, which he does not find
satisfactory, is remarkably reminiscent of Sir William Drummond's comment on how philosophers find 'useful machinery' in
the creatures of supernatural beliefs :[3]

Cip.	Pues¿ cómo en suma bondad, cuyas acciones sagradas habían de ser divinas, caben pasiones humanas?
Dem.	Esas son falsas historias en que las letras profanas, con los nombres de los dioses, entendieron disfrazada la moral filosofía.
Cyprian.	. . . in what manner Can supreme goodness be consistent with The passions of humanity?

---

[1] *El mágico prodigioso, Obras Completas*, tomo i, Aguilar, S. A. de Ediciones,
Madrid, 1951, i. 1067. 'Scenes from the *Mágico Prodigioso*, i. 95–96, Hutch., p. 734.
[2] *M.P.*, Ag. edn., i. 1067. 'Scenes *M.P.*', i. 97–98, Hutch., p. 734.
[3] *M.P.*, Ag. edn., i. 1067. 'Scenes *M.P.*', i. 123–8, Hutch., pp. 734–5.

Daemon.   The wisdom
Of the old world masked with the names of Gods
The attributes of Nature and of Man;
A sort of popular philosophy.

The discussion[1] turns to the manner in which the Deity can or
might influence 'human undertakings'[2] and more particularly
human affections:

Dem.   Importó para esa causa
                     mover así los afectos
                     con su voz.
Cip.   Cuando importara
                     el moverlos, genios hay
                     (que buenos y malos llaman
                     todos los doctos) que son
                     unos espíritus que andan
                     entre nosotros dictando
                     las obras buenas y malas,
                     argumento que asegura
                     la inmortalidad del alma:
                     y bien pudiera ese Dios,
                     con ellos, sin que llegara
                     a mostrar que mentir sabe,
                     mover afectos.
Daemon.   To attain the end
The affections of the actors in the scene
Must have been thus influenced by his voice.
Cyprian.   But for a purpose thus subordinate
He might have employed Genii, good or evil,—
A sort of spirits called so by the learned,
Who roam about inspiring good or evil,
And from whose influence and existence we
May well infer our immortality.
Thus God might easily, without descent
To a gross falsehood in his proper person,
Have moved the affections by this mediation
To the just point.

This is similar enough to the powers of the 'supernatural forces'
in Shelley's note on the Daemon and at the same time it is not
unreminiscent of the liberty allowed to Mephistopheles in the

---

[1] *M.P.*, Ag. edn., i. 1067. 'Scenes *M.P.*', i. 163–75, Hutch., pp. 735–6.
[2] Cf. above, p. 71, Shelley's note 'On the Daemon of Socrates'.

Prologue to *Faust*. Before his exit the Daemon's Mephistophelean
function, in relation both to Cyprian and to Justina, is made still
plainer.[1]

Dem.	(*Ap.*) Pues tanto su estudio alcanza,
	yo haré que el estudio olvide,
	suspendido en una rara
	beldad. Pues tengo licencia
	de perseguir con mi rabia
	a Justina, sacaré
	de un efecto dos venganzas. (*Vase*)

Daemon.	Since thus it profits him
	To study, I will wrap his senses up
	In sweet oblivion of all thought but of
	A piece of excellent beauty; and, as I
	Have power given me to wage enmity
	Against Justina's soul, I will extract
	From one effect two vengeances. (*Exit*)

Cyprian visits Justina to settle a quarrel between two of his
friends who are enamoured of her. He falls in love with her himself, is disdained, and retired to a solitary sea-shore, not unlike
Shelley pondering his 'error' at Lerici.[2]

Cip.	Confusa memoria mía,
	no tan poderosa estés,
	que me persuadas que es
	otra alma que me guía.
	Idólatra, me cegué,
	ambicioso, me perdí;
	porque una hermosura vi,
	porque una deidad miré. . . .

Cyprian.	O memory! permit it not
	That the tyrant of my thought
	Be another soul that still
	Holds dominion o'er the will,
	That would refuse, but can no more,
	To bend, to tremble, and adore.
	Vain idolatry!—I saw,

[1] *M.P.*, Ag. edn., i. 1068. 'Scenes *M.P.*', i. 208–14, Hutch., pp. 736–7.
[2] *M.P.*, Ag. edn., i. 1077. 'Scenes *M.P.*', ii. 1–11, Hutch., p. 739.

And gazing, became blind with error;
Weak ambition, which the awe
Of her presence bound to terror!
So beautiful she was. . . .

The Platonism which had indirectly found its way into Calderón from the general European tradition and which magnetized Shelley in his work, as it always did everywhere, will have been apparent in several of the quotations we have made: in this last we find once again the familiar search for a guide to Beauty: Shelley's version, remarkable as a rule, where Calderón's lyrics are concerned, for its fidelity to the original, is here unusually free[1] and, paradoxically, the Shelleyan feeling comes out almost more clearly in the literal meaning: 'O my perturbed memory, be not strong enough to persuade me that it is another soul that is guiding me. An idolater, I blinded myself: I lost myself in my ambition because I saw a beauty, because I gazed on a form divine.' In his despair Cyprian resorts to the Faust-compact and offers his soul to the worst *genio* of Hell in return for Justina. The Daemon's voice is heard off-stage accepting the compact. There is thunder, lightning, and a shipwreck; the Daemon comes ashore in the guise of a man saved from a wreck. In an aside he explains how he is to make a new assault upon the soul of Cyprian—by 'forging the instruments of his destruction / Even from his love and from his wisdom'.[2] The next scene translated shows the temptation of Justina in her turn. The Daemon calls upon the Powers of Hell to fill all living things with love, and there follows a magnificent choric passage[3] in which the nightingale, the vine, and the sunflower are invoked as emblems and the refrain 'Love, oh Love!' is one which strikes a note very similar to the effect of one of the Moon's songs in *Prometheus Unbound*.[4] Justina becomes inflamed by passion for Cyprian—it is the 'irresistible passion' of *Alastor*

---

[1] Though that phrase 'the tyrant of my thought', so suggestive of Shelley's struggles with thought's monsters, is not so much an interpolation like his exegetical interpolation in the *Symposium* translation (see above, pp. 52 and 54) as a transference from the passage quoted below. But in the *Symposium* too he sometimes transfers as well as interpolates when he wants to show what he thinks a consistency of meaning between two passages: see p. 141.

[2] 'Scenes *M.P.*', ii. 77–78, Hutch., p. 740. *M.P.*, Ag. edn., i. 1088.

[3] 'Scenes *M.P.*', iii. 24–79; see App. II, pp. 329–33. This is a good example of the Calderón 'episodes' (see below, pp. 180–1) that Shelley imitated in the 'Ode to the West Wind' (see p. 226 below).

[4] iv. 356–69, Hutch., pp. 262–3.

pursuing, this time, a woman. Will she be able to distinguish the true δαίμων Love from the κακοδαίμων or will she be like those mentioned in *Prometheus Unbound*[1] who

> Dream visions of aëreal joy, and call the monster, Love,
> And wake, and find the shadow Pain . . .?

The Daemon enters and offers to take her to Cyprian:[2]

Just.	¿Quién eres tú, que has entrado
	hasta este retrete mío,
	estando todo cerrado?
	¿Eres monstruo, que ha formado
	mi confuso desvarío?
Dem.	No soy, sino quien movido
	dese afecto que tirano
	te ha postrado y te ha vencido,
	hoy llevarte ha prometido
	a donde está Cipriano.
Just.	Pues no lograrás tu intento. . . .

Justina.   And who art thou, who hast found entrance hither,
Into my chamber through the doors and locks?
Art thou a monstrous shadow which my madness
Has formed in the idle air?
Daemon.   No. I am one
Called by the Thought which tyrannizes thee
From his eternal dwelling; who this day
Is pledged to bear thee unto Cyprian.
Justina.   So shall thy promise fail.

The woman has recognized the κακοδαίμων and her reaction is instantaneous: she will defy him and her love shall remain on the ideal plane. It is a test for the power of the human will. The Daemon does not easily give in; he talks of forcing her will and tries to drag her away. Here comes her final triumph:[3]

Jus.	Mi defensa en Dios consiste.
Dem.	Venciste, mujer, venciste
	con no dejarte vencer.

---

[1] i. 776–7, Hutch., p. 225.
[2] *M.P.*, Ag. edn., i. 1089. 'Scenes *M.P.*', iii. 102–9, Hutch., p. 745.
[3] *M.P.*, Ag. edn., i. 1090. 'Scenes *M.P.*', iii. 133–5, Hutch., p. 746.

Justina.   My defence
                    Consists in God.
Daemon.   Woman, thou hast subdued me,
                    Only by not owning thyself subdued.

That
                    Mi defensa en Dios consiste

is exactly Gretchen's[1]

                    Dein bin ich Vater! Rette mich!

and the Daemon's

                    Venciste, mujer, venciste

is the[2]

                    Sie ist gerichtet!
                            Ist gerettet.

Such were the scenes translated by Shelley; something must now be said of the ending of the play. Cyprian tries all his learning and all his magic art in his efforts to gain the love of Justina but he discovers that they are not enough; though she is extremely poor and ignorant, 'her virtue is her dowry' and she will not debase her ideal love. In one scene he summons up a ghostly *figura fantástica* of her, rather like the Phantasm of Jupiter in *Prometheus Unbound*, but though it duly appears, obedient to the call of love, it vanishes before he can prevail upon her will; in another scene he grasps a closely veiled figure which seems to be Justina but finds it to be a skeleton which says, 'Thus, Cyprian, are all the glories of the world.' The inadequacy of mere knowledge is admitted by the Daemon who laments that in his fall from heaven he 'lost grace alone but did not lose his knowledge'. The Daemon claims his bargain: Cyprian is to be his slave. In despair, as the Daemon grapples with him, Cyprian calls upon the God of the Christians and the Daemon is baffled. Brought before the pagan governor of Antioch who is persecuting Christians, he glories in his Christianity. Justina, also a captive, is brought in with him; she strengthens his faith in the divine pardon and both are martyred, happy in the conviction that they are sacrificing the mortal for the immortal. In an epilogue the Daemon, sent by God for the purpose, proclaims that his power has been unequal to the

[1] *Faust*, i. 4607: 'I am thine Father! Save me!'
[2] *Faust*, i. 4711: 'She is condemned to die / Is redeemed on high' [Philip Wayne, *Faust*, Part One, Penguin edn., p. 197].

power of Justina's virtue and that Cyprian, in following her, has
vanquished him no less than she.

There is more than enough in *El mágico prodigioso* to make us
curious as to what Shelley might or might not have said about
it in his paper for *The Liberal*. Even for making guesses on the
subject we should require in the first place an understanding of
his 1822 thoughts and moods which would probably need to
exceed his own understanding of them. On this point, however,
there is one small hint among his notes which seems to invite
some interpretation: it is afforded by two Platonic quotations
jotted down in a notebook[1] which can be confidently ascribed to
the first three or four months of the year; they are both from the
Republic.[2] Though they have already been given in Chapter 2[3]
and many times referred to they need to be seen in their context and we will therefore repeat them in Professor Cornford's
translation.[4]

Then suppose a painter had drawn an ideally beautiful figure complete to the last touch, would you think any the worse of him if he
could not show that a person as beautiful as that could exist?

Now if a man believes in the existence of beautiful things but not of
Beauty itself, and cannot follow a guide who would lead him to a
knowledge of it is he not living in a dream? Consider: does not dreaming, whether one is awake or asleep, consist in mistaking a semblance
for the reality it resembles?

We must carefully notice too what we find, written in reverse,
above the first of these two quotations: it is a copy of the lyric
A Lament,[5] 'O world! O life! O time! . . .', and above the second
stanza Shelley has written the word 'Mary':

> Out of the day and night
> A joy has taken flight;
>   Fresh spring, and summer, and winter hoar,
> Move my faint heart with grief, but with delight
>   No more—Oh, never more!

There are, it happens, no less than four copies of this lyric among
Shelley's notebooks: the earliest seems to belong to 1819, which is
two years earlier than the date assigned to it by Mary Shelley and
followed by other editors. It seems to have been one of those little

[1] Bod. MS. Shelley adds. e. 18.
[2] 472d, 476c.   [3] See above, p. 21.
[4] pp. 173, 179.   [5] Hutch., p. 643.

poems, expressive of a recurrent mood, which Shelley, and sometimes Mary, were wont to recopy when the mood came round
again: so it was with the laments on Fanny Godwin and on
William Shelley. What does it signify here? May we assume that
Shelley is thinking of his domestic disappointments of that time?
His imagination just then was trying to fashion Jane Williams,
his last 'anticipated cognition', into the 'ideally beautiful figure'
—not many pages away are drafted the lines written to accompany his gift of the guitar—and it is difficult not to feel as we look
at that particular manuscript page that it is asking us whether we
think any the worse of Shelley for persisting, even after Emilia
had proved 'a cloud instead of a Juno' in his quest for a mortal
Ariadne: perhaps this is what his conscience and such common
sense as he could muster in these matters were asking themselves.

Meanwhile, if Ariadne in his life was an illusory ideal, here she
was in Calderón, as in Goethe, in full Shelleyan perfection:

¿Eres monstruo, que ha formado
Mi confuso desvarío?

—here she is, in Shelleyan phrase even, fighting the 'monster of
her thought' and conquering him too: a real 'guide' and an
example to Shelley, so often worsted in that fray. Again the
Daemon identifies himself with the *tyranny* of love—in this passage
Shelley does not have to interpolate anything, as we saw him
doing in a previous one, to bring out the concept from the play—
and with this identification the triumph of Justina becomes level
with that of Shelley's Prometheus, also a conqueror of tyranny by
the strength of Free Will. No doubt Shelley was struck by the fact
that the woman's ideal love had succeeded where the man's
earthly love had failed, that all Cyprian's learning was as nothing
compared to the 'virtue and power' of Justina's *afectos*—it is the
woman who can say to the κακοδαίμων 'ἀρετῇ σε νικῶ θνητὸς ὤν . . .'.
So much for Shelley's efforts at schooling Mary and Emilia in the
Platonic doctrines of Love. Through Love, the *good* daemon, the
divine will had operated in the play upon a damsel 'unlettered
and without human knowledge': her ignorance and simplicity
made no difference—'The tree of Knowledge is not that of Life'.
The 'virtue and power' of her Love being strong enough there
was no 'error' in the fact that she, 'being a mortal, aspired to
immortal things': she could live on the plane where Emilia and
Mary had failed to live and where Shelley himself could not

remain, whatever his aspirations, without a 'guide'. Here came his mistake confessed to Gisborne:

> The error consists in seeking in a mortal image the likeness of what is perhaps eternal.

Such is the trail of Shelley's ideas in so far as it can be traced through *El mágico prodigioso*. Had Shelley written his intended essay, it would have been interesting to learn from it, in particular, what he had to say about the identification by Justina of her Free Will and the power of God. That he, working from the doctrine of Necessity and making use of a Pliny passage to support an assertion that 'there is no God' should, by way of Platonic ideas, have come near a point coincident with the Jesuitical doctrine of Free Will as embodied in the poetry and drama of a Spanish genius of the seventeenth century—who, incidentally, made use of the same passage of Pliny—this is strange indeed: Shelley's mind, 'coming to many ways in the wanderings of careful thought', had here come to one of the strangest. It may well be that he was moving nearer than he knew towards Christianity. But though he had gone far we must not try to push him farther: he has yet, as far as I know, to be claimed as a Jesuit.

The daemons too had travelled far between Field Place and Lerici, but once at least in one of the latest notebooks[1] Shelley's mind takes them home to Sussex and they become once again the goblins, ghosts, and fairies of a dreamy schoolboy's imagination. We shall meet them again in many forms as we follow Shelley's symbolism.

ADDENDUM (See above, p. 58)

There has been astonishing credulity about the Tan-yr-allt 'attack'. Harriet's account, commonly treated as corroborative, has no significance: she was not a witness. The really significant point is that this is but one of three 'attacks'[2] for which there is no evidence beyond hearsay emanating from Shelley himself, the only eyewitness. Each 'attack' was followed by a sudden change of residence. Cf. too Shelley's tale[3] of his mysterious visitor at Bishopsgate, a tale hall-marked by his recourse, under pressure from Peacock, to that age-old trick of the 'cornered' witness—piling up non-significant details in the hope that by their number or their colour they may *seem* corroborative. (See also p. 323 n.)

[1] B-H III, see App. III, pp. 334–8.
[2] See Dowden, *Life*, i. 227, ii. 327, Peacock, *Memoirs*, in H. Wolfe's combined *Life*, ii. 354.   [3] Peacock, ibid. ii. 341–3.

6. Boats. Isles

THE most cursory glance through Shelley's manuscripts would reveal his intense concern with boats: of one sort or another they are abundantly sketched by his pen or pencil amid scenes of lake, river, or sea like those amid which he spent many of the happiest hours of his life; it was in a boat that he met his death and the Boat, in his poetry, is a persistent symbol. A reader not aware of this need only refer to the *Shelley Concordance*[1] to discover the number and significance of the passages grouped under the headings 'boat', 'bark', 'ship', etc. The Boat, like the Daemon, was a symbol belonging equally to Shelley's mortal life and to his visionary world. Starting as something signifying an escape it often came to represent a means of communication from the one to the other.

Biographically a symbol of Shelley's recurrent escapes and endless journeyings might perhaps be detected in the paper boats which he launched on the Serpentine in 1811. Poetically, in the next year, 1812, the symbol is the basis of 'The Voyage', a long poem,[2] the work of one still, by vocation, chiefly a political reformer:

> **The young and happy spirits now
> Along the world are voyaging;
> Love, friendship, virtue, truth,
> Simplicity of sentiment and speech,
>   And other sensibilities
> Known by no outward name—
> Some faults that Love forgives,
> Some flaws that Friendship shares;
> Hearts passionate and benevolent,
> Alive, and urgent to repair
> The errors of their brother heads—
>   All voyage with them too.
> They look to land, they look to sea,—
> Bounded one is, and palpable
> Even as a noonday scene,

[1] F. S. Ellis, *A Lexical Concordance to the Works of Percy Bysshe Shelley*, Quaritch, 1892.

[2] Rogers, *The Esdaile Poems*, pp. 54–55, ll. 40–62. Other lines from the poem are quoted on p. 28.

The other indistinct and dim,
    Spangled with dizzying sunbeams,
    Boundless, untrod by human step,
Like the vague blisses of a midnight dream,
    Or Death's immeasurable main,
Whose lovely islands gleam at intervals
Upon the spirit's visioned solitude
Through Earth's wide-woven and many-coloured veil.

The emphasis here is as much on what lies ahead of the voyagers
as on what has been left behind them: and the Boat is a means of
conveyance away from the evil landsman's world, described later
in the poem, towards an ideal world of unspoiled humanity
patterned by Rousseau. We may not be wrong to regard the sea
across which the escape takes place as constituting, implicitly,
a symbol in itself, an anticipation of what Shelley was later to
express as 'the wide ocean of intellectual beauty',[1] the in-between-
ness and vastness of which suggests at the same time the barrier
between Life and Death; 'veil', rather than barrier, is the figure
he prefers.

    In 'The Voyage' it is from social evils that the imagination of
the young Shelley is taking flight. In 1817 imagination sails with
Laon and Cythna in search of a realm where pure love may exist
unpersecuted.[2]

We know not where we go, or what strange dream
    May pilot us through caverns strange and fair
Of far and pathless passion, while the stream
    Of life, our bark doth on its whirlpools bear,
    Spreading swift wings as sails to the dim air;
Nor should we seek to know, so the devotion
    Of love and gentle thoughts be heard still there
Louder and louder from the utmost Ocean
Of universal life, attuning its commotion.

Again comes the feeling of something pure and ennobling in life
on the water, some purity in the element which both calls to and
responds to the nobility innate, though often spoiled, in Man:[3]

To the pure all things are pure! Oblivion wrapped
    Our spirits, and the fearful overthrow
Of public hope was from our being snapped. . . .

---

[1] Cf. above, p. 41, n. 1.
[2] *The Revolt of Islam*, vi. 2587–95, Hutch., p. 101.
[3] Cf. above, p. 29, Shelley's note on 'The Voyage'.

Given, in place of Spenser's measure which it has here, the movement of Southey's *Thalaba* the Boat seems metamorphosed from a galleon to a highly-powered speed-boat.[1]

> The waters are flashing,
> The white hail is dashing,
> The lightnings are glancing,
> The hoar-spray is dancing—
> Away!

This little craft in which Shelley's imagination dashed away with Emilia Viviani was but one of the thousand ships that might have been launched in his poetry by that Ariadne of early 1821.

Besides being a means of escape, etc., the Boat was also a bearer of Knowledge: possibly this too was among the imagined functions of the paper dream-boats launched on the Serpentine: certainly it was the practical function, if practical is the word, of those 'Vessels of heavenly medicine' which were launched at Lynmouth in 1812:[2] the balloons too, for, symbolically, a vessel of the air was not different from a vessel of the sea. It was these and other such efforts for the dissemination of Knowledge which brought upon Shelley the attention of Lord Sidmouth and his agents, men not interested in the poetical symbolism of such proceedings but very much concerned about their unusualness and possible political subversiveness. Shelley's love of toy boats was not left behind him in England: in 1820 he delightfully described[3] his latest one, made to float upon quicksilver in the workshop of Mrs. Gisborne's son, Henry Reveley:

> And in this bowl of quicksilver—for I
> Yield to the impulse of an infancy
> Outlasting manhood—I have made to float
> A rude idealism of a paper boat:—
> A hollow screw with cogs—Henry will know
> The thing I mean and laugh at me. . . .

It was at this period that he was planning to start a steamboat service operating between Leghorn and Marseilles,[4] Henry being

---

[1] 'The Fugitives', 1–5, Hutch., p. 639. For the relation of this poem to *Epipsychidion* see below, pp. 102, 244, and this chapter, p. 102.

[2] Sonnet: 'On Launching some Bottles filled with Knowledge into the Bristol Channel', Hutch., p. 877.

[3] 'Letter to Maria Gisborne', 72–77, Hutch., p. 365.

[4] Cf. Addendum, p. 104.

the engineer and designer of the vessels. He was not slow to see
the benefits as well as the perils of contemporary scientific inventions and was inspired by thoughts of the uses to which mankind
might put its newly discovered powers.

Your volcanic description of the birth of the Cylinder [he wrote to
Henry Reveley[1]] is very characteristic both of you & of it. One might
imagine God when he made the earth, & saw the granite mountains
& flinty promountories flow into their craggy forms, & the splendour
of their fusion filling millions of miles of the void space, like the tail of
a comet,[2] so looking, & so delighting in his work. God sees his machine
spinning round the sun & delights in its success, & has taken out patents
to supply all the suns in space with the same manufacture.—Your
boat will be to the Ocean of Water what the earth is to the Ocean of
Æther—a prosperous & swift voyager.—

Those who find difficulty in believing Shelley to be other than
a delicate and ornately plumed song-bird might do well to commit
this passage to memory. Here is poetry springing fully alive from
its 'native and involuntary sources', and those sources represent
conceptions 'wide as the universe' ranging from engineering to
astronomy and theology, the whole blended with an underlying
humour, itself wide enough to enfold the cosmic and expressed in
language not a little tinged by contemporaneous study of Calderón
—here is the poet 'formed . . . to communicate conceptions which
result from considering either the moral or the material universe
as a whole'. Shelley's Boat as a symbol is here something quite
overshadowing his life as well as his poetry:

monstruo de fuego y agua

he called it this ship of ships,[3] almost a daemon itself, destined to
do both symbolically and in practice all that such a mighty intermediate spirit could do. He sketches it with its paddles in the
margin of his manuscript[4] and tries to contain his conceptions in
a poem; adapting his Spanish phrase to make its second line:

[1] 17 Nov. 1819. Jones, *Letters of Shelley*, ii. 157–8. Shelley seems to be smiling at
the contemporary theological argument, based on Newton, that the great machine
of the world implies a mechanic. Locke argued in the same manner: this was inherent in 'the mechanical philosophy of the day': cf. Shelley's memorandum,
Ch. 2, p. 17.   [2] For Shelley and comets see below, p. 205.
[3] Letter to Henry Reveley, 28 Oct. 1819, Jones, ibid. ii. 131.
[4] B-H II, *24[r].

*Child of despair and desire
Monster of water and fire
Wingless sea-bird outspeeder[*

The poetry is too much for the poem, which breaks away. The steamboat project too was to come to grief, nearly wrecking Shelley's friendship with Reveley: it managed, however, to survive with the result that eighteen months later, just when *Adonais* was about to be written, the poet's life was saved by the engineer,[1] a fact now recorded in an inscription on the Technical College in Perth, Western Australia, incidental to the commemoration of his very considerable contribution, by means of his mechanical and scientific accomplishments, to the establishment of settlements in that new continent which the 'monsters of water and fire' began to open up, more and more, as the nineteenth century went on.

To return to 1819—when Shelley might imagine but could never know how soon either his young friend or the newly invented steam-power would catch up with his conceptions of them—it would be surprising if we did not find him chasing his steamboat and its significance into the Greek classics, and this indeed he does, for in the same notebook[2] in which he started his poem comes an extract from Pindar[3] very much on the subject:

*θεός, ὃ καὶ πτερόεντ' αἰετὸν κίχε, καὶ θαλασσαῖον παραμείβεται
δελφῖνα, καὶ ὑψιφρόνων τιν' ἔκαμψε βροτῶν
ἑτέροισι δὲ κῦδος ἀγήραον παρέδωκ'. . . .**

To understand what this meant for Shelley we must first understand that for him 'God' in such a context had no particular reference either to the Christian God or to any pagan deity: what he understood here by 'God' was the whole creative power behind art and 'science', aspects both of ποίησις, creation. So understood the God in Pindar that

not only overtakes the winged eagle but surpasses the dolphin on the sea and bends many a proud mortal beneath his sway while to others he gives glory that grows not old

is exactly the God Shelley had defined in 1814 or 1815 as[4]

the vast sum of action and of thought which disposes and animates the universe.

[1] See below, p. 261, and Note on Henry Reveley in App. IV, p. 339.
[2] B-H II, *27ʳ.   [3] *Pyth.* ii. 50–53.
[4] 'On the Punishment of Death', Jul. vi. 186.

It is the World Spirit of *Queen Mab* and, exactly, the God conceived in the letter to Reveley where, interpreting the delights
enjoyed by Universal Mind in terms of the delights enjoyed by the
Shelleyan mind, he pictures him as revelling in his own creation.
One remembers his Tasso quotation in *A Defence of Poetry*—'Only
God and the Poet deserve the name of Creator.'[1] What so moved
him at the time he wrote was the feeling of the power of creation,
both in science and in poetry, that he held in his hands: growing
out of his steamboat and what it symbolized might have come
a large-scale poetical conception of the power of scientific thought
in the universe. But as he said,[2] 'A man cannot say "I will compose poetry" . . . the mind in creation is as a fading coal', and thus
it was that the poem merely flickered and went out. The reason
for this was that the furnace was overloaded with fuel, the poetry,
as we have just observed, was too much for the poem. As we look
through his notebook we may feel that his stature is as much to
be measured by his failures as by his successes; many chapters
might be written on the evidence they afford of the numerous
occasions when he failed precisely because 'the conceptions
which result[ed] from considering the moral or material universe
as a whole' were too vast for him. It should be added that the
autumn and winter of 1819 were amongst the busiest creative
periods in Shelley's life and that a good deal of what might have
gone into the abandoned poem about the progress of physical
science found its way into the fourth act of *Prometheus Unbound*.

But what the Boat symbolized for Shelley above all—above
even its function as a bearer of Knowledge—was the aspiration of
Man's soul in its quest for Love and Beauty, the aspiration to
swim into[3]

> Realms where the air we breathe is love,
> Which in the winds and on the waves doth move,
> Harmonising this earth with what we feel above.

To the Boat used symbolically in this sense Professor Grabo
ascribes a Neoplatonic origin and quotes in support a passage by
Synesius upon Porphyry:[4]

---

[1] 'Non merita il nome di creatore se non Iddio e il Poeta', Jul. vii. 138. As it stands
this does not appear verbatim in Tasso. Shelley is thought to have come across it
given as an utterance by Tasso in John Cam Hobhouse's *Historical Illustrations of the
Fourth Canto of Childe Harold*, 1818, p. 26. Cf. the double sense of ποίησις, Ch. 4, n. 52.

[2] *A Defence of Poetry*, Jul. vii. 135.   [3] *Prom.* II. v. 95–97, Hutch., p. 242.

[4] Carl Grabo, *Prometheus Unbound: An Interpretation*, Chapel Hill, N.C., 1935, p. 89.

But the soul in its first descent derives this spirit from the planetary spheres, and entering this as a boat associates itself with the corporeal world, earnestly contending that it may either at the same time draw the spirit after it on its flight or that they may not abide in conjunction.

The Boat thus becomes a vehicle for conveyance of the disembodied spirit through the mysterious intermediate space μεταξὺ θεοῦ τε καὶ θνητοῦ, an idea very cognate to the Shelleyan daemon-pattern, whether or not it was consciously derived from Neoplatonism: my own belief is that, although Professor Grabo's quotation happens to form an admirable definition of the notion as Shelley used it, the symbol is not derivative but, like many other things in his poetry, an emotional coinage which happens to approximate through kinship of feeling to something written earlier. In the 'intermediate space' there seems to be no very clear distinction between 'the *Ocean of water*' and 'the ocean of air':[1] it is an expanse common to both, nothing less in fact than 'the wide ocean of intellectual beauty';[2] we may note how in consequence in the passage from *The Revolt of Islam* quoted above the sails quite naturally take on the form of wings. Music was particularly apt to give Shelley this feeling of release, as when he listened to the singing of Claire Clairmont at Marlow:[3]

> The cope of Heaven seems rent and cloven
>   By the enchantment of thy strain,
> And o'er my shoulders wings are woven
>   To follow its sublime career
> Beyond the mighty moons that wane
>   Upon the verge of Nature's utmost sphere
> Till the world's shadowy walls are past and disappear.

It would seem that among symbolist writers at all times there are common funds of feeling and expression; just as Shelley has notions in common with the Neoplatonists and not necessarily derived from them so, at times, he seems to anticipate the French symbolists of the later nineteenth century, writers who certainly

---

[1] Contemporary aeronautical experiments with steam-power were discussed by Byron, Shelley, and Williams on 6 Jan. 1822, Byron having been requested by 'a mechanic' at Bologna and a number of professors at the University to give financial support. [Fredk. L. Jones, *Gisborne and E. Williams, Journals and Letters*, pp. 122, 123.]   [2] Cf. p. 41, n. 1.

[3] 'To Constantia Singing', 27–33, Jul. iii. 156, text from Harv. MS. Eng. 258.2. 'The cope', again, is Plato's ὑπερουράνιος τόπος, cf. below, p. 142.

derived nothing from him. Here, for instance, there is something
to invite comparison with Rimbaud, a poet who, incidentally,
would have enjoyed his letter to Reveley. 'Rimbaud', says Dr.
Starkie, 'would not be tied down nor shackled by the *ennui* of this
world nor its limitations. Disgust he knew and understood, and
revolt, but never *ennui*. He was a *voyant* and he would sail in his
mad boat—for it was his right—into the very kingdom of the
future.'[1] Though Rimbaud's 'Bateau Ivre' was as different from
Shelley's Boat in most ways as Rimbaud from Shelley, this is
applicable as much to the latter as to the former. Like Rimbaud
Shelley felt that escape of the spirit of a living man not so much
as a flight from the things of everyday life but as a soaring towards
a reality which might exist beyond and above the limits of the
world. Enchanted by the music his vision soars upward like
Rimbaud's across the 'intermediate space' towards 'the cope of
heaven', an image in itself not at all dissimilar to the *ardent
entonnoir* which forms the summit of the universe in 'Bateau Ivre'.

The Boat symbol, the more vivid no doubt in Shelley's mind
at Marlow for the hours he was spending on or near the Thames,
seemed particularly liable to come into his thoughts of Claire
Clairmont. We find it again in *To One Singing*:[2]

> My spirit like a charmèd bark doth swim
>   Upon the liquid waves of thy sweet singing,
> Far far away into the regions dim
>
> Of rapture—as a boat, with swift sails winging
>   Its way adown some many-winding river,
> Speeds through dark forests o'er the waters swinging [. . . .

The terza rima breaks away at this point, but the notebook[3] containing it travelled with Shelley to Italy and the language re-
appeared next year in Asia's lyric:[4]

> My soul is an enchanted boat,
>   Which, like a sleeping swan, doth float
> Upon the silver waves of thy sweet singing. . . .

Whatever may or may not be the truth about Shelley's feelings
for Claire there can be no doubt that at times, if only by reason
of her singing, she satisfied some of his spiritual needs and that

---

[1] Enid Starkie, *Rimbaud*, 2nd edn., Hamish Hamilton, 1947, p. 142.
[2] Hutch., p. 541.   [3] Bod. MS. Shelley E. 4.
[4] *Prom.* II. v. 72–73. See Neville Rogers, 'Music at Marlow', in the *Keats-Shelley
Memorial Bulletin*, no. v, ed. Dorothy Hewlett, London, 1954.

something of her went into the figure of Asia. Thus the Boat, being a vehicle of Shelleyan love, becomes very often concomitant with Ariadne.

Sometimes, as we have said, the Boat becomes a kind of daemon itself: more often it appears with the daemon at its helm, as for instance in *Alastor* where the Poet's frail shallop is carried on by the waves:[1]

> As if their genii were the ministers
> Appointed to conduct him to the light
> Of those belovèd eyes . . .

or, like the boat of the Witch of Atlas[2] scooped for her by Love out of a gourd:

> woven tracery ran
> Of light firm texture, ribbed and branching, o'er
> The solid rind, like a leaf's veinèd fan—
> Of which Love scooped this boat—and with soft motion
> Piloted it round the circumfluous ocean.

Very important was its delicacy. For the Witch, delicate child of Shelley's Platonic fantasy, is a personification of Intellectual Beauty itself and she has as her driver none other than the daemon Love, a 'most excellent pilot', we remember from the *Symposium*[3] and he, we remember as well, is 'the most delicate of all things', a point not forgotten by Shelley, his naval architect. Hardly more real or less fragile can the little shallop of 'laths and pitched canvas' have seemed in which, to the horror of the Tuscan peasants, Shelley himself was wont to venture on the Arno. 'Ma va per la vita!' they might well exclaim.[4]

We have just referred to Cythna's boat in *The Revolt of Islam*; of still greater significance is the other boat in the poem, the boat of the Woman in the first canto. For this woman 'beautiful as morning' is the Guide who leads Shelley to the place where Laon and Cythna are to be found, an Ariadne of his imagination who takes him, or his detached vision-self, to the Isle of Beauty and Freedom where dwell the Shelleyan-Platonic lovers who are to unfold their tale: her boat, a visionary conveyance rushing him

[1] 330–2, Hutch., p. 22.   [2] 308–12, Hutch., p. 379.
[3] 197e, 195e.
[4] Mary Shelley, 'Note on the Poems of 1821', Hutch., p. 663.

into the vision which is the poem, is a frenetical, Rimbaudian
vessel of escape, a daemon itself, gifted with the secret of an almost
perpetual and ever faster motion together with a range surpassing
mortal limits :[1]

> And swift and swifter grew the vessel's motion,
>   So that a dizzy trance fell on my brain—
> Wild music woke me : we had passed the ocean
>   Which girds the pole, Nature's remotest reign. . . .

Of the symbolic significance which Shelley meant this Boat to
have he gives a cryptic hint in the Greek lines prefixed to the
poem—like Reveley's Boat it has set him thinking in terms of
Pindar :[2]

> Ὅσαις δὲ βροτὸν ἔθνος ἀγλαίαις ἀπτόμεσθα
> περαίνει πρὸς ἔσχατον
> πλόον· ναυσὶ δ' οὔτε πεζὸς ἰὼν ἂν εὕροις
> ἐς Ὑπερβορέων ἀγῶνα θαυματὰν ὁδόν.

But as for all the bright things that we, the mortal race, attain he
reaches the utmost limit of that voyage. Neither by ships nor by land
can you find the wondrous road to the festival place of the Hyperboreans.

Pindar, in the context, is talking of the glory of an athlete's
father and the limitations of mortal achievements : not very con-
sequentially he goes on to the subject of song and music at
banquets, the delight of Apollo. What Shelley seems to have
fastened upon in the passage is an antithesis—if it was intended
by Pindar it is by no means a clear one—between the limitations
of the material, mortal world and the unlimited power of immortal song, delight of gods; his implication would seem to be
that in the visionary, immaterial world a voyage may be made
of which the speed and range would have no like in the material :
just as the Witch's boat is driven by Love so the Woman's boat is
impelled magnetically by the attraction to Intellectual Beauty.
His is the unseen power which gives it motion, a motion strong
enough to take it across the 'intermediate space' between divine
and mortal to the point beyond where lies the wondrous 'festival
place of the Hyperboreans' : here is the wondrous trysting-place

---

[1] I. xlviii. 550–3, Hutch., p. 51.

[2] *Pyth.* x. 28 ff. Text from Hutch., p. 31. For Shelley's occasional disregard of context in quotation cf. above, p. 63, n. 1, and below, p. 252.

of Laon and Cythna. It will be observed that he has practically translated the last line of Pindar's:

> ... we had passed the ocean
> Which girds the pole, Nature's remotest reign.

There was, indeed, in Shelley's mind very little that a boat might not do. Was it not natural that for him even his Boat on the Serchio should take on a life of its own and seem something[1]

> sleeping fast,
> Like a beast, unconscious of its tether,

so that he wondered whether, in its sleep, it had reached that dream-world of its own lying, like the dream-world of his poetical boats, beyond 'Nature's remotest reign'?[1]—

> 'What think you, as she lies in her green cove,
> Our little sleeping boat is dreaming of? . . .'

It was necessary for Lionel 'according to his art / weaving his idle words'—his boat getting all mixed up with the other 'monsters of his thought'—to be brought back to earth by Melchior, the more practical and the nautically long-suffering Williams:[1]

> 'Of us and of our lazy motions',
> Impatiently said Melchior,
> 'If I can guess a boat's emotions;
> And how we ought, two hours before,
> To have been the devil knows where.'

Once again, as Shelley writes this poem, we catch him smiling at himself. We may guess that he smiled a good deal during those happy expeditions with his Eton friend, when the water stood between him and the mortal prototypes of Ariadne.

Almost as often as not, when the Boat appears in Shelley's poetry, the Isle is found to appear with it; we have seen, for instance, how in 'The Voyage' (1812) the mariners are looking across the ocean towards the place where

> lovely islands gleam at intervals
> Upon the spirit's visioned solitude.

Such islands, as a rule, are the goal of the voyage: the hope of

---

[1] 'The Boat on the Serchio', 5–6, 46–48, 61–62, Hutch., pp. 654–6.

them makes the voyage possible and their beauty is the aspiration of the Boat:[1]

> Many a green isle needs must be
> In the deep wide sea of Misery,
> Or the mariner, worn and wan,
> Never thus could voyage on. . . .

Here during Shelley's unhappiness of 1818 the optimism about the voyage itself had disappeard and the sea, so far from being 'like the vague blisses of a midnight dream', is 'the deep wide sea of Misery' which has to be crossed: even greater, however, for this seem in the poem the anticipated blisses of the Islands. More especially did the Isle come to be the abode of Love, the goal of the Ariadne-quest. Thus Asia's 'enchanted boat' is driven on, like that of the Witch, with Love at the helm:[2]

> And we sail on, away, afar,
> Without a course, without a star,
> But, by the instinct of sweet music driven;
> Till through Elysian garden islets
> By thee, most beautiful of pilots,
> Where never mortal pinnace glided,
> The boat of my desire is guided:
> Realms where the air we breathe is love,
> Which is the winds and on the waves doth move,
> Harmonizing this earth with what we feel above.

It was the refuge, too, to which the fugitive could repair in company with Beauty:[3]

> **Now steer, Master Pilot,
> Right up to that islet—
> In the halls of a friend
> All our griefs there will end
> Lady mine**

Such, identically, is the Dream-Isle of *Epipsychidion*. In this poem, the climax of so much of Shelley's quest for an Ariadne on the mortal plane, symbolic paths merge and spread out together: Emily is not only[4]

---

[1] 'Lines written among the Euganean Hills', 1–4, Hutch., p. 554.
[2] *Prom.* II. v. 88–97, Hutch., p. 242.
[3] 'The Fugitives.' From Bod. MS. Shelley adds. e. 8, p. 113. For the relation of this poem to *Epipsychidion* see above, p. 93, and below, p. 244.
[4] *Ep.* 131–2, Hutch., p. 414.

Spouse! Sister! Angel!

but also

Pilot of the Fate
Whose course has been so starless! . . .

She is, in fact, a personification of the Love of the *Symposium*,[1]
Ariadne, and *Ἔρως* in one: it is the vessel of that 'most excellent
pilot' himself which awaits her:

Emily,
A ship is floating in the harbour now. . . .

In a long and famous passage Shelley pours out the full passion
of his descriptive imagination. Off they will go, across a sea where
halcyons brood—no longer the 'deep wide sea of misery' but the
sea of 'The Voyage' for 'The merry mariners are bold and free'—
until they reach the Isle of Isles:

It is an isle under Ionian skies,
Beautiful as a wreck of Paradise. . . .

And though for a moment it is given a local habitation, if not a
name, at the same time

It is an isle 'twixt Heaven, Air, Earth, and Sea,
Cradled, and hung in clear tranquillity;
Bright as that wandering Eden Lucifer,
Washed by the soft blue Oceans of young Air.

Where it really lies, of course, is somewhere in Plato's daemonic
'intermediate space', placed there by Shelley and peopled and
painted by him. In his excitement Shelley's symbols run more and
more into each other. Ariadne, who has just become identified
with Love-the-Pilot, is now identified also with the Isle[2]

Till the isle's beauty, like a naked bride
Glowing at once with love and loveliness,
Blushes and trembles at its own excess . . .

Then, finally, the Isle becomes a 'realm of abandonment' having a
soul into which the Beloved and the Lover, Shelley and Ariadne,
are merged together:[3]

Let us become the overhanging day,
The living soul of this Elysian isle,
Conscious, inseparable, one. . . .

[1] *Ep.* 407 ff.   [2] *Ep.* 474–6.   [3] *Ep.* 538–40.

Such is the Isle, another 'festival place of the Hyperboreans', midway between divine and mortal, to which Shelley's vision arrived in *Epipsychidion*, the isle with which both he and Beauty itself become identified at the climax of his quest for a mortal prototype of Ariadne. Of his quest on the other, the abstract, universal plane *Adonais* is the climax. Here too the final port is an island-port as it had been in *Queen Mab*:[1]

> Death is a gate of dreariness and gloom,
> That leads to azure isles and beaming skies . . .

and towards this his 'spirit's bark is driven', beaconed by the soul of Adonais, that is by the soul of the dead bard, the light of pure Intellectual Beauty itself. As he goes on his way to be identified finally with that far-distant light beyond the Veil he is more and more identified with the visionary Boat itself which is carrying him across the mid-space. There are times when it becomes difficult not to experience about Shelley the feeling first of a reality beyond the Veil melting into reality such as we know it on the nearer side and of poetry descending into life; to this succeeds the feeling that, all the time, a reverse process has been in operation, symbolized in the final merging of the poet and all his symbolism into one fatal, daemonic Boat-symbol rushing madly into a poetic, philosophic reality beyond the Tyrrhenian sea-mists—almost as if, in the overtones of some of his later sayings, we could catch a note from the 'Don Juan' itself:

> O que ma quille éclate, que j'aille à la mer.

ADDENDUM (*see above, p. 93*)

Perhaps something of Shelley's interest in steam transport infected Peacock; he it was who instituted monthly steam mails for India to replace the six-monthly mails of the sailing-ship era.[2]

[1] ix. 161–162, Hutch., p. 799.
[2] See David Garnett, in his Introduction to *The Novels of Thomas Love Peacock*, Hart-Davis, 1948.

7. The Dome. The Eye and the Star. The Philosophic Imagination

SINCE it may well have seemed that in following the Boat–Isle symbolism to and fro in Shelley's imagination between his poetry and his life our own excursions have been a trifle over-imaginative, it is time to give a piece of evidence which will show that we have by no means overleaped him or exaggerated the significance they held for him. So powerful indeed was his imagination in its search for philosophical reality that these particular symbols could actually take on a reality that was physical as well. They came, in fact, to form part of a landscape which, like the daemons, he was even able to embody in a drawing.

A facsimile of this drawing, a pen-sketch found inside the front cover of a notebook of 1817,[1] may be seen in Plate Ia. It has been reproduced at least once[2] before but never, I believe, studied in relation to its connexions, which are clearly demonstrable—first with passages from *The Revolt of Islam* with which it is contemporary and secondly with the 'Fragments of an Unfinished Drama' written five years later. Over and above its interest in relation to the Boat and the Isle it leads us on to two other paths of symbolism and takes us eventually deep into Shelley's inner world of philosophical imagination.

Professor White is somewhat in error in describing the notebook containing the drawing as 'the MS of *Laon and Cythna*' since beyond one jotting, a memorandum (on the opposite page) of Shelley's revised title, 'The Revolt of Islam', it contains little or no writing connected with the poem. But the memorandum itself is a useful enough hint that, anyhow, the book was in his hands when the poem and its revision were in his thoughts—possibly somewhere around 15 December 1817, for we have Mary's record that 'alterations for Cythna' were made on that day.[3] Not that we really need any such testimony of dating: a single thoughtful glance will reveal the connexions of the pen-sketch. What Shelley has illustrated—with some minor variations and with some fairly

---

[1] Bod. MS. Shelley, E. 4.   [2] White, *Shelley*, i. 530.
[3] Jones, *Mary Shelley's Journal*, p. 87.

liberal telescoping of times of day and the sequences of events—is
his own dream-voyage in Canto I and the scene of the tale told
by the Woman, his Guide to Beauty. There in the centre is the
Isle and the Boat—the 'boat of rare device'—is approaching it in
the left of the foreground. According to the poem[1] it

> had no sail
> But its own curvèd prow of thin moonstone.

This detail would seem either to have been later than the sketch
or to have been forgotten when Shelley made it; I conceive him,
however, as drawing from the vision, in any case, rather than the
text and it is the more remarkable that even more of its details did
not become blurred or varied. Behind the Isle and in the background, everywhere[2]

> . . . the mountains hang and frown
> Over the starry deep that gleams below.

If those weird eyes are 'starry'—they certainly take the place of
stars, a Platonic substitution as we shall see—then, no doubt, so is
the deep that reflects them, and furthermore, at the top of the
drawing just to the right of the centre, one of the mountain-peaks
passes into a weird face seen in half-profile which might well be
interpreted as a frown. Then, as in the poem[3]—though we perceive it to be somewhat multiplied—

> . . . *the Morning Star*
> Shone through the woodbine-wreaths which round my casement
> were.
> *'Twas like an eye which seemed to smile on me.*

These last lines come from the Woman's account of the vision
which had appeared to her in her island home towards which, as
she speaks, Shelley is returning with her on his dream-voyage.
The voyage proceeds past 'Nature's remotest reign'[4] and its
details are now illustrated with more exactitude:

> And we glode fast o'er a pellucid plain
> Of waters, azure with the noontide day.
> Ethereal mountains shone around—*a Fane*
> *Stood in the midst, girt by green isles which lay*
> *On the blue sunny deep, resplendent far away . . .*

---

[1] *Revolt of Islam*, i. xxiii. 325–6, Hutch., p. 45.   [2] Ibid., 331–2, Hutch., p. 45.
[3] Ibid., 485–7, Hutch., p. 49.   [4] Ibid., 554–8, 577–81, Hutch., p. 51.

Winding among the *lawny islands* fair,
   Whose blosmy forests starred the shadowy deep,
The wingless boat paused where an *ivory stair*
   Its fretwork in the crystal sea did steep,
   Encircling *that vast Fane's* aërial heap. . . .

The 'green isles' or 'lawny islands' are identifiable in the drawing
and the 'fane'—also described as *this vast* dome[1]—is clearly to be
seen in the distance half-way up the right-hand side. By now the
voyagers have sailed into the background of the picture and the
'ivory stair' where they landed is invisible to us. Shelley's imagination, however, was not bounded by the two-dimensional limits of
his sketch and could perceive it as we shall see below, lying just
inside the Looking-Glass land on the far side of the island, near
the Fane: four years later this detail reappears amid kindred
scenery in 'The Fugitives':[2]

> **The storm-bound pavilion
>   Its *stairs* in vermilion
>   The *mountains*, the *stars*. . . .**

Later in *The Revolt of Islam* comes a passage which will interpret
the mysterious starry eyes of the drawing: it comes at the
moment when Laon's bliss is at its height:[3]

'Fair star of life and love', I cried, 'my soul's delight,
Why lookest thou on the crystalline skies?
O, that my spirit were yon Heaven of night,
Which gazes on thee with its thousand eyes!'
She turned to me and smiled—that smile was Paradise!

The words which Shelley puts into Laon's mouth are a translation of an epigram of Plato's[4] where the lover is conceiving his
love as a microcosm of the all-pervading spirit of World Love:
this is the Spirit which in the drawing looks upon beauty embodied in a woman on her dream-isle. Here, of course, is an
idealized projection from the Marlow days of Shelley's own love
when he wrote the poem and gave it its delightful dedication to
his wife:[5]

[1] *Rev. Isl.*, i. l. 568, Hutch., p. 51.
[2] MS. Shelley adds. e. 8, p. 114 (unpub. stanza).
[3] *Rev. Isl.*, ix. xxxvi, 3788–92, Hutch., p. 130.
[4] Ἀστέρας εἰσαθρεῖς Ἀστὴρ ἐμός. εἴθε γενοίμην
    οὐρανός, ὡς πολλοῖς ὄμμασιν εἰς σὲ βλέπω, *Anth. Pal.* vii. 669.
[5] Hutch., p. 37. But the Platonism is derived, more directly, through Spenser.
See below, pp. 120–1.

> So now my summer task is ended, Mary,
>   And I return to thee, mine own heart's home;
> As to his Queen some victor Knight of Faëry,
>   Earning bright spoils for her enchanted dome;
>   Nor thou disdain, that ere my fame become
> A star among the stars of mortal night,
>   If it indeed may cleave its natal gloom,
>   Its doubtful promise thus I would unite
> With thy belovèd name, thou Child of love and light.

The language, the symbolism, belong as much to Shelley's life as to his poem: the 'enchanted dome' was the home of Mary as much as of Cythna: it was for her that Beauty in his poetry could rise up to the stars: whatever she may have been to him in their later domestic difficulties, at this time she was his Cythna, his 'Child of love and light'.

A truly astonishing point to be noticed concerning this landscape and its details is their persistence in Shelley's mind. The proof of this is that five years later, when he is writing the piece for Trelawny which Mary entitled 'Fragments of an Unfinished Drama', he introduces from his drawing of 1817 both details which he has used in *The Revolt of Islam* and details which he has not. For instance, the Lady says[1]

> Alas! Why must I think how oft we two
> Have sate together near the river springs,
> Under the *green pavilion which the willow*
> *Spreads* on the floor of the unbroken fountain?

The *willow*, forming a *pavilion*—a favourite Shelleyan form of canopy which, as we have seen, reappears in 'The Fugitives'— is conspicuous enough. Then in the Indian's speech we find[2]

>   . . . God of Heaven!
> From *such an islet*, such a river-spring—!
> I dare not ask her if there stood upon it
> *A pleasure-dome surmounted by a crescent,*
> *With steps to the blue water. . . .*

Once again in 1822 come features of the landscape of 1817: the 'islet' of Cythna, seen also in the drawing, the 'dome' also found in both—here, we may note, duly 'surmounted by a crescent' in accordance with the drawing, a detail omitted in *Laon and Cythna*

---

[1] Unf. Dr.', 61–64, Hutch., p. 484.   [2] 'Unf. Dr.', 88–92, Hutch., p. 485.

—and, once more, as in 'The Fugitives', that occasional variant on the vision, the 'steps'.[1] The Indian, indeed, as he speaks out of his recollections, seems to speak as a reincarnation of Laon, and such, it might seem from his next lines, was what Shelley intended him to be[2]

> . . . It may be
> That Nature masks in life several copies
> Of the same lot, so that the sufferers
> May feel another's sorrow as their own,
> And find in friendship what they lost in love.
> That cannot be: yet it is strange that we,
> From the same scene, by the same path to this
> Realm of abandonment—. . . .

And, less by intention no doubt than unconsciously and inevitably, it is also Shelley himself who is speaking: the voice of the Indian—last of those self-projections running from the Poet of *Alastor* through Laon to the 'young Englishman' of *Epipsychidion*—is the voice of the moods of disillusionment and attempted reassessment which disquieted his last months of life and of which we shall have more to say when we come to discuss 'The Triumph of Life'. It was in these moods that his imagination escaped again in the Boat-symbol to a 'realm of abandonment', the happy Isle.

We have not yet exhausted the traceable connexions of this extraordinary drawing, a clue, certainly, which we must rank high in importance among all the clues in Shelley's notebooks, second only, perhaps, to his starred Baedeker-list of preferred places in the *Symposium*. Indeed in the rough Baedeker, which, as we follow the peregrinations of his mind, we are obliged laboriously to improvise for ourselves, it comes like an extending page of panoramic illustration, a relief-map where we may see the heights as well as the level plains. And this is very timely, for with the Boat and the Isle the paths of symbolism which we started to follow on the ordinary levels of thought, more or less, now stop short on these levels and we have to rise with Shelley to new symbols discoverable on the highest skyline of imagination. These paths are Platonic too, but they are the paths also of Shelley's

[1] It is perhaps worthy of mention that in his manuscript draft of 'The Fugitives' from which I have quoted above Shelley originally wrote *steps*, subsequently altered to *stairs*. [2] 'Unf. Dr.', 92–99, Hutch., p. 485.

great contemporary, Coleridge, who, as far as sheer imagination
was concerned, may well have influenced him more subtly and
powerfully than could ever be effectively demonstrated in the
cold light of critical research. It must have been sufficiently obvious from the foregoing how much Shelley's vision-scene owes
to the famous lines from 'Kubla Khan'[1]

> The shadow of the dome of pleasure
> Floated midway on the waves;
> Where was heard the mingled measure
> From the fountains and the caves,
> It was a miracle of rare device,
> A sunny pleasure-dome with caves of ice!

Not only in the general imaginative conception but in verbal
reflections of imagery the influence is a clear one. In *The Revolt
of Islam* he diminishes Coleridge's *pleasure-dome* to a mere 'dome'
or 'Fane' and borrows from it to make Cythna's boat a *boat of
rare device*; it was, however, Coleridgean enough in his imagination of 1817 as we can see from the drawing where amid 'sunny
spots of greenery' he has sketched it with a little additional
Eastern detail of his own: five years later, thus embellished as a
pleasure-dome surmounted by a crescent, it duly finds its way out of
Shelley's memory or his notebook into the recollections of the
Indian in the 'Unfinished Drama'. From another manuscript
comes one other little piece of evidence of his attraction to
'Kubla Khan'. It would have been surprising if his daemonophile
eye had passed over those three other famous lines[2]

> A savage place! as holy and enchanted
> As e'er beneath a waning moon was haunted
> By woman wailing for her demon-lover

and it is therefore with a feeling of triumphant guesswork that, in
turning to his pencil draft[3] scribbled in Bisham woods, we find
when we come to the stanza beginning[4]

> Then she arose, and smiled on me with eyes
> Serene yet sorrowing, like that planet fair . . .

[1] 35–40. There seems to be no record that Shelley read 'Kubla Khan', but he
must certainly have done so when he read 'Christabel', published with it, on 26 Aug.
1816. (Jones, *Mary Shelley's Journal*, p. 61.) The drawing might suggest that his
1817 recollections of the poem included the Swiss mountains amid which he first
read it.   [2] 14–16.   [3] Bod. MS. Shelley adds. e. 19, p. 31.
[4] *Rev. Isl.*, I. xxi, Hutch., p. 45.

that above it he has written the words 'Demon Lover'. What are we to make of this? The Serpent has just coiled itself in the Woman's bosom, a Shelleyan daemon, we know: perhaps he is the 'demon-lover', perhaps Shelley's Woman, described earlier as waiting for her boat, 'Fair as herself, like Love by Hope left desolate', is a spirit-sister of Coleridge's female wailer: anyhow whatever Shelley borrowed from Coleridge he has duly treated as he treated what he borrowed from the Greeks, 'gifting it with his own originality of form and colouring'. How he has done this we shall very shortly see; for the moment we must leave the demon-lover and complete our quotation. The Woman is

> like that planet fair
> While yet the daylight lingereth in the skies
> Which cleaves with arrowy beams the dark-red air. . . .

This may or may not be related to the weird astronomical phenomena of the drawing but the love-eyes-stars feeling is the same which appears in the lines of Shelley's Platonic translation quoted above: both passages prove to be another Shelleyan pointer into Coleridge, this time into the *Biographia Literaria*.[1] Turning to this work let us look at the passage in which Coleridge, discoursing on the philosophical imagination, says that it is

a repetition in the finite mind of the eternal act of creation in the infinite I AM.

This Plotinian definition is very much akin to Shelley's idea of ποίησις as something common to God and Man: 'Only God and the Poet deserve the name of Creator.' Again the home which Coleridge has prepared for this imagination is a philosophical mysticism in which 'substances were thinned away into shadows while everywhere shadows were deepened into substances'.[2] This brings us very close to Shelley's feeling and ideas in the 'Hymn to Intellectual Beauty': in Nature, as represented by Mont Blanc, Shelley had felt 'The awful shadow of some unseen power' and the figure of *shadow* is the very figure which we now find in the concentrated Neoplatonism of the *Biographia Literaria*. We noted

---

[1] i. 202.

[2] Professor Livingston Lowes has noted—see *The Road to Xanadu*, Boston and New York, 1927, p. 29—that one of Coleridge's notebooks shows his familiarity with the shadow-notion in Plato's Parable of the Cave. For Shelley's attraction to this see Ch. 8, below.

in Chapter 4 how Shelley's notion of Intellectual Beauty varied from Plato's in being mystical and emotional rather than objective and strictly intellectual and how it is what Professor Notopoulos has called his 'imaginative leap', in place of the Platonic dialectic or λόγος, which takes his poetry beyond and above the limits of systematic philosophy. This same 'philosophic imagination' is characteristic too of Coleridge to whom Shelley, with his usual flair for discovering his own intuitive concepts in other writers, was thus readily attracted. We have already noticed how[1] he read the *Biographia Literaria* on 8 December 1817 and three days later replied to Godwin's strictures on *Laon and Cythna* in the quasi-Coleridgean terms which we have had several occasions to requote. It becomes the more interesting now to discover in the *Biographia* something else that is very pertinent both to his imagination in 1817 and to his general notions of imagination in poetry. In Coleridge too the philosophical imagination is akin to intuitive knowledge and this, he says, quoting Plotinus,[2]

we ought not to pursue with a view to detecting its secret source, but to watch in quiet till it suddenly shines upon us; preparing ourselves for the blessed spectacle as the eye waits patiently for the rising sun.

Should we be taking too big an 'imaginative leap' ourselves if, over and above associations with Plato's epigram, we were to identify those strange astral eyes in Shelley's drawing with the creative imagination, the light of Mind awaiting the rising sun,[3] that sun, the light of Intellectual Beauty, which is to awake its regenerative power and with which it will itself be merged? But here on these heights of imagination where conceptions meet and mingle we must not cling too closely to a single interpretation. We might guess, for instance, as well that there is some sort of correspondence here with the Woman's awakening as she describes it:[4]

> Deep slumber fell on me:—my dreams were fire—
> Soft and delightful thoughts did rest and hover

[1] See above, p. 24.   [2] i. 167.

[3] We know from the matter of the steps that Shelley's pictorial imagination did not stop short at the two-dimensional, so he may quite well have conceived the sun as being somewhere on the near side of the drawing, the direction in which the eyes are looking. The dark orb appearing at the top left-hand corner of the reproduction (Plate I*a*) is caused by a piece of sealing-wax in the manuscript.

[4] *Rev. Isl.* I. xl–xli. 487, Hutch., p. 49. For the significance of this dream cf. Ch. 10 *passim*. In view of the fact that Shelley read the *Biographia Literaria* on 8 Dec. and

Like shadows o'er my brain; and strange desire,
  The tempest of a passion, raging over
  My tranquil soul, its depths with light did cover,—
Which passed; and calm, and darkness, sweeter far,
  Came—then I loved; but not a human lover!
For when I rose from sleep, the Morning Star
Shone through the woodbine-wreaths which round my casement were.

XLI

'Twas like an eye which seemed to smile on me.
I watched, till by the sun made pale, it sank . . .

Here, in the Woman's love, are Shelley's sensations in the 'Hymn to Intellectual Beauty'—excitement followed by calm and refreshment. If we are right about the correspondence, and may interpret the pen-drawing in accordance with it, we have indeed attained to the Shelleyan penetralia, for it then becomes a mystical representation pictorially of those central poetic conceptions of his, the light of abstract Universal beauty and its earthly embodiment in a woman : of the whole Shelleyan-Platonic doctrine, in fact, of Love and Beauty. For want of any clear evidence of date-sequence between the writing of these stanzas, the making of the sketch, and Shelley's study of the *Biographia* we cannot trace the triple correspondence more closely. Yet in the stanzas, as in the drawing, there is some suggestion too of that passage about 'substances . . . thinned away into shadows . . . shadows . . . deepened into substances' not to speak, again, of 'the eye . . . the rising sun'. And let us remember what Shelley scribbled above that earlier stanza: he has remembered his memorandum, for that lover—'not a human lover'—is, of course, the *demon-lover* he always intended her to have : yes, now he can be recognized for what he really is: not the grim spectre of Coleridge's Germanic gloom but Shelley's own delicate Grecian

that his letter to Godwin is dated 11 Dec. it is a tempting hypothesis that the 'alterations to Cythna' mentioned on 15 Dec. included the insertion of these two stanzas. This hypothesis, unfortunately, would not be supported by manuscript evidence. So far from the stanzas being a later addition they appear—Bod.MS. Shelley adds e. 13— in what is almost certainly a first draft. The 'alterations' referred to by Mary are undoubtedly the revisions made by Shelley when adapting *Laon and Cythna* to its second form as *The Revolt of Islam* and, in any case, these do not appear to have necessitated any changes in the first canto. It may be that Shelley had read the *Biographia* at some earlier unrecorded date; if not the correspondence is a truly remarkable example of his close intuitive anticipation of ideas from another writer.

daemon, strong-winged Love himself, flying straight out of the *Symposium*, 'the divinity who creates peace among men and calm upon the sea . . . our defence, saviour and guardian in labour and fear.'

At this point, a point where the operations of Shelley's mind have become extremely complex, let us pause for a brief moment in our path-finding to consider where we are. The long path we have just been following started in the last chapter with the Boat which quickly brought us to the Isle, the Isle of Love and Beauty. Here we were fortunate enough to come upon an important signpost in the form of Shelley's drawing and, after stopping first to examine this drawing as a singular proof of the result and permanence of symbols in his mind, we follow where it pointed, namely upwards where the Boat had all along been taking us, beyond the limits of the world of thought among the high peaks of sheer imagination. In this high realm come two new symbols, the Eye and the Dome. It is before the Fane that we are now standing, the inner sanctuary of the Isle of Beauty where Woman encounters Love, the Platonic Daemon; the Fane is looked down upon by the Eye of Creative Mind which hangs over its Dome; it is an abode of bliss, a 'pleasure-dome', owing something, as the Eye does, to Coleridge. Thanks, alas, to the Person from Porlock, Coleridge never finished designing this Dome as he might have done. Shelley, however, took a hand with its interior architecture which we will shortly proceed to examine. It will be helpful if, before we do so, we take a look at those two new symbols, the Eye and the Dome, as they appear in various places in his poetry.

The power of eyes to convey a message, a power felt intuitively by all of us, is the subject of a youthful poem of Shelley's, 'How eloquent are eyes . . .',[1] most of it unpublished. Asia's eyes in *Prometheus Unbound* have a life-giving quality profoundly symbolical in the poem: Prometheus[2] remembers how he

> wandered once
> With Asia, drinking life from her loved eyes.

Panthea's eyes, likewise, are a guide to Asia:[3]

> And then I said: 'Panthea, look on me.'
> But in the depth of those belovèd eyes
> Still I saw, FOLLOW, FOLLOW!

[1] Hutch., p. 842.   [2] I. 122–3, Hutch., p. 210.   [3] II. i. 160–2, Hutch., p. 230.

Apollo himself, the God of Song, the Creative Mind—and is he
not also at the same time the Sun-god, having the radiance which
can give life to his creation?—is, not surprisingly, an Eye:[1]

> I am the eye with which the Universe
> Beholds itself and knows itself divine;
> All harmony of instrument or verse,
> All prophecy, all medicine is mine. . . .

Shelley's Hymn reminds us again of that phrase about God and
the Poet and that Poetry, in his *Defence*,[2] is 'indeed something
divine'. So too, like the divine eye which radiates life, the eye of
Man's philosophical imagination, when it has power to leap
upwards, has its place among the stars. Shelley translated the
Greek epigram where the eagle is a symbol of the Leap:[3]

> Eagle! why soarest thou above that tomb?
> To what sublime and star-ypaven home
>   Floatest thou?—
> I am the image of swift Plato's spirit,
> Ascending heaven; Athens doth inherit
>   His corpse below.

He drafted this, be it noted, in a notebook of 1821 when his mind
was much bent upon the spirit of the dead Keats. But long before
this, even before *The Revolt of Islam*, the Poet of *Alastor*[4] had had
the vision of Thought among the Stars

>   . . . two eyes,
> Two starry eyes hung in the gloom of thought. . . .

Eyes and Stars, symbolically, merge into the general Platonic
concept of *radiance*—a radiance wherein the human spirit that
has taken the Leap is at one with the World Spirit.

    The Dome as an image of all-embracing universal Beauty is,
of course, easily suggested to any poet by the sky and is a common
image in Romantic poetry:

> ever-canopying dome

as Shelley called it in the 'Ode to Heaven'.[5] It is naturally

---

[1] 'Hymn of Apollo', Hutch., p. 613.
[2] Jul. vii. 135.
[3] Ἀιετέ, τίπτε βέβηκας. . . . *Anth. Pal.* vii. 62, Hutch., p. 721.
[4] 489–90, Hutch., p. 25.
[5] 8, Hutch., p. 576.

associated, as often as not, with the image of the Stars which give it light: so it appears in *The Revolt of Islam*:[1]

> . . . that dome of woven light.

Apollo again, in the Hymn,[2] is dwelling in the dome of heaven—here the *woven light* image is further embroidered:

> Curtained with star-inwoven tapestries.

Sometimes the dome is varied to a *cope*—we saw how music like poetry could soar there when Constantia sang:[3]

> The cope of heaven is rent and cloven
> By the enchantment of thy strain. . . .

And, since a *cope* is not only woven but coloured, we can have too[4]

> The stained cope of heaven's night.

Eyes, Stars, Domes—all are transfused in Shelley's imagery of Light: we see him playing with them in his lyrics as with a box of translucent bricks. For his more serious architectural constructions he already had, by 1817, a full stockyard of these and other translucent, polychromatic materials—moonstone, sapphire, jasper, meteors, moons, hollow half-circles, and columns that mirror radiance. Out of these he built a Temple, a 'vast dome' for Laon and Cythna. It is time to go inside. To approach it we must disembark from the Boat at the 'ivory stair' which lies in Looking-Glass Land just beyond the drawing: we reach it through the poem:[5]

> The wingless boat paused where an ivory stair
>   Its fretwork in the crystal sea did steep,
>   Encircling that vast Fane's aërial heap:
> We disembarked, and through a portal wide
>   We passed—whose roof of moonstone carved, did keep
> A glimmering o'er the forms on every side,
> Sculptures like life and thought; immovable, deep-eyed.
>
> We came to a vast hall, whose glorious roof
>   Was diamond, which had drank the lightning's sheen
> In darkness, and now poured it through the woof
>   Of spell-inwoven clouds hung there to screen
>
>   Its blinding splendour—through such veil was seen
> That work of subtlest power, divine and rare;

---

[1] I. lv. 620, Hutch., p. 52.   [2] 2, Hutch., p. 612.
[3] 'To Constantia Singing', 27, Jul. iii. 155.
[4] 'Marianne's Dream', 97, Hutch., p. 538.   [5] I. li, lii, liii, Hutch., pp. 51–52.

Orb above orb, with starry shapes between,
  And hornèd moons, and meteors strange and fair,
On night-black columns poised—one hollow hemisphere!

Ten thousand columns in that quivering light
    Distinct—between whose shafts wound far away
The long and labyrinthine aisles—more bright
    With their own radiance than the Heaven of Day;
    And on the jasper walls around, there lay
Paintings, the poesy of mightiest thought,
    Which did the Spirit's history display;
A tale of passionate change, divinely taught,
Which, in their wingèd dance, unconscious Genii wrought.

Beneath there sate on many a sapphire throne,
    The Great, who had departed from mankind,
    A mighty Senate. . . .

Such was the supreme dwelling to which the Woman Guide had led Shelley's imagination, the home of love and Intellectual Beauty: Laon and Cythna, the constant Platonic lovers, were to come there, precursors of Shelley and Emilia in *Epipsychidion*: among the 'mighty Senate' not least we may be sure was Plato: certainly Shelley must have seen him there in his 'star-ypaven home' when he later came to translate that other Platonic epigram.[1] We must abbreviate the description. Overhead is a pyramid, a throne upon it, circled with fiery steps. No sooner has the Woman come into the hall than she shrieks the Spirit's name and vanishes, as many guides and symbols were so apt to vanish in Shelley's life and poetry, changing and passing into others. Darkness fills the Fane but gradually light, patterned kaleidoscopically[2] on the floor, begins to rise aloft; it rises and grows till it has become a planet hanging over a cloud of shadow cast across the fiery steps and the glowing throne. Then[3]

The cloud which rested on that cone of flame
    Was cloven; beneath the planet sate a Form,

---

[1] 'Eagle why soarest thou. . . .' See above, p. 115.

[2] I have wondered how far the contemporary popularity of the kaleidoscope lent colour to Shelley's imagery. By 1818, at any rate, it seems to have been all the rage: see Shelley's letter to Hogg of 21 Dec. of that year. And in one of his drawings, made probably at the end of 1819 [B-H I, 11ᵛ], I believe that he is representing a pattern from this toy. Something too may have been contributed by his 'solar miscroscope', said to have had some resemblance to a *camera obscura*. See Addendum, p. 119, below.   [3] I. lvii and lviii. 640-3, Hutch., p. 53.

Fairer than tongue can speak or thought may frame,
   The radiance of whose limbs rose-like and warm
   Flowed forth, and did with softest light inform
The shadowy dome, the sculptures, and the state
   Of those assembled shapes—with clinging charm
Sinking upon their hearts and mine. He sate
Majestic, yet most mild—calm, yet compassionate.

Wonder and joy a passing faintness threw
   Over my brow—a hand supported me,
Whose touch was magic strength: an eye of blue
   Looked into mine, like moonlight, soothingly. . . .

It is another sidelight on Shelley's scenic imagination that internal details of this Temple, like details of the outer landscape, could so persist in his mind as to find counterparts in a later poem: we may trace them in *Prometheus Unbound*.[1] 'A temple, gazed upon by Phidian forms . . . / Beneath a dome fretted with graven flowers, / Poised on twelve columns of resplendent stone. . . .' This other Temple we cannot pause to examine, though we must notice that it is additionally decorated with 'an amphisbaenic snake', for the presence of the δράκων οὐροβόρος symbolically brings Eternity into Shelley's conception. And Eternity too is in the Temple of Laon and Cythna: what else is that 'eye . . . like moonlight' but[2]

   . . . the white radiance of eternity?

And having asked ourselves this let us ask ourselves *who* is that Form whose Eye has this power, who remains while the Woman and Laon and Cythna change and pass, whose Light, rising upwards, kindles the Universe so that Earth's shadows flee, so that the cone of flame is cloven, the sphered skies are riven, etc.? There will be no need to labour the answer: we need only remember the *stained* cope, the *star*, and the whole concept of the Boat and we see where we have arrived:[3]

     The One remains, the many change and pass;
     Heaven's light forever shines, Earth's shadows fly:
     Life, like a dome of many-coloured glass,
     Stains the white radiance of Eternity. . . .

[1] III. iv. 112 ff., Hutch., pp. 251–2.
[2] *Adon.*, 461, Hutch., p. 443.
[3] *Adon.* 460–3, 492–5, Hutch., pp. 443–4.

I am borne darkly, fearfully, afar:
Whilst, burning through the inmost veil of Heaven,
The soul of Adonais, like a star,
Beacons from the abode where the Eternal are.

This then is the voyage of Shelley's bardic imagination. From his 1817 drawing to *Adonais*, from Coleridge's 'pleasure-dome' to the 'dome of many-coloured glass', his spirit's bark has still far to go, but the stages seem clear even if the resultant symbolism may never be entirely so. As we look at his symbolism we find that although the occasions, thoughts, and feelings that begot his poems might change and pass, his poetry, more and more consistently, becomes a Platonic vision of Light and Shadow.

Before we proceed to the chapters in which we must pursue Platonic Light and Shadow more closely, let us make yet another pause and try, for the better understanding of a major aspect of Shelley, to assess what we have learned about his imagination from this drawing and its observable connexions. If we try to add up the conceptions which have appeared from our collation of it with his poetry—the eye of Creative Imagination awaiting the rising sun, the mountains (reminders of Switzerland and the manifesto of Intellectual Beauty), the enchanted dome which is at once the home of Cythna in the poem and Mary Shelley in the poet's life, the blending of Coleridge's demon-lover with Plato's Love-daemon—and if we allow too for the probability that behind all this there may be a whole world of Platonic, Coleridgean, and other nuance which has escaped us, we may begin to have some notion of the measure of the vastness of the imagination out of which such concepts sprang. If Shelley's poetry is often difficult to read this is frequently for the reason, not least, that it was most difficult to write. How to bound imagination in language when his language itself had powers that resisted boundaries was, as his notebooks tell us again and again, the chief problem of his work.

ADDENDUM (*see above, p. 117*)

Mr. Desmond King-Hele has been so good as to remind me that a detailed description of the 'solar microscope', an apparatus very popular in Shelley's day, is to be found in Adam Walker, *Familiar Philosophy*, London, 1779, which is a useful source-book for Shelley's scientific ideas and interests.

8. The Veil. Mutability

THE Veil, one of the most subtle and complex of all Shelley's poetical concepts, is a symbol to which other symbols have already led us several times. Though it appears most characteristically and prominently as a part of the general pattern of his Platonic system it derives, to start with, from something deeper than mere philosophical thinking. Like other symbols, it had its origin in intuitive founts of imaginative feeling.

As an image for something dividing the seen from the unseen, the known from the unknown, the Veil suggests itself quite naturally to poets. Early apparent in Shelley is the feeling of something veiled in human existence: we may detect it as growing first out of his childhood visions of an ideal object of love— visions bright to the imagination yet dimmed at the same time by their distance, being beyond the range of experience. The consciousness of such a dimmed brightness, giving the idea of a Veil, is discernible in his choice of the motto from St. Augustine which he prefixed to the adolescent Mary-poems[1] of 1810:

Nondum amabam et amare amabam, quaerebam quid amarem, amans amare.

Very soon, as he matures, the Veil becomes a natural accoutrement of the ideal object of love, and it is as a Veiled Maid that the Beloved appears in various poems, e.g. in *Alastor* where she is heralded by the same tag from St. Augustine. By this time, like other creatures of Shelley's imagination, she has found her counterpart more than once in his reading: in Wieland, for instance, and in Spenser, with him, as with Keats, a favourite poet. From these writers her figure acquires indirectly more and more of a Platonic shape and colouring. *The Faerie Queene*, in particular, is steeped in Platonism: Una, the Spenserian incarnation of Platonic Love and Heavenly Beauty, appears herself as a Veiled Maid and the Red Cross Knight, in whom, together with his Christian-chivalric virtues Spenser sets forth that Platonic ideal from the *Symposium* the quest for Beauty and the One, is as fitting a soul-mate for Shelley's Veiled Maids in general as he is

---

[1] Rogers, *The Esdaile Poems*, p. 69. Cf. above, p. 38.

for Una herself—the very prototype in fact of a long succession of Shelleyan heroes starting with the Poet in *Alastor*. Most closely of all is he related to the hero of *The Revolt of Islam*, the long poem written in Spenser's metre wherein Shelley, in his own way, sets forth Spenser's theme and clothes the Platonism, as Spenser had done before him, with his own romance of action, his own poetical language, and his own symbolical incarnations. We noticed in the last chapter how its symbolism was a part contemporaneously of Shelley's own life: it may be added here that he was the Red Cross Knight quite as much as he was Laon and it was in such guise that he laid its twelve cantos, his 'summer task', before her feet. To Mary in 1817 he was her 'Elfin Knight', still a would-be slayer of legal and ecclesiastical dragons, and she was his Una and his Cythna at once, ready to be his guide into the unknown: with her love he could face martyrdom if the occasion arose:[1]

> She smiled on me, and nothing then we said,
> But each upon the other's countenance fed
> Looks of insatiate love; the mighty veil
> Which doth divide the living and the dead
> Was almost rent, the world grew dim and pale,—
> All light in Heaven or Earth beside our love did fail.

Here, as in the passages from the first canto quoted earlier, the language gives a foretaste of the pure abstract Beauty which is attained in *Adonais*: stronger, however, than philosophical feeling is the feeling of warm, romantic emotion and it is to be noticed how effectively Shelley can use the Veil image at the climax of a concrete, sensuously passionate, and satisfactorily fulfilled quest for Beauty in his own life.

Simultaneously, none the less, the Veil had been developing its more universal, philosophical significance. We saw, for instance, how the Isle to which the Boat was heading in 'The Voyage' (1812) was one of those lovely islands which[2]

> ... gleam at intervals
> Upon the Spirit's visioned solitude
> Through Earth's wide-woven and many-coloured veil.

Here too one may detect a slight anticipation of *Adonais*, notice-able for the use of the Veil as a piece of light symbolism and the

---

[1] *Rev. Isl.* xv. 4579–84, Hutch., p. 150.
[2] Rogers, *The Esdaile Poems*, p. 55, 60–62. Cf. above, pp. 91–92.

conjunction with it not only of the word 'rend', once again, but
of the epithet 'many-coloured', which already seems to be awaiting its transference nine years later to a 'dome of . . . glass': here,
however, the language, like the context, is abstract and without
emotion. In this same year, 1812, in the speech where Queen Mab
is issuing her invitation to the Spirit, the Veil takes on a more
definitely philosophical colouring and begins to pass into the
general pattern of Shelleyan symbolism:[1]

> And yet it is permitted me, to rend
> The veil of mortal frailty, that the spirit,
> Clothed in its changeless purity, may know
> How soonest to accomplish the great end
> For which it hath its being, and may taste
> That peace, which in the end all life will share.
> This is the meed of virtue; happy Soul,
>   Ascend the car with me!

The car of the Fairy is a visionary vehicle like the Boat, an ideal
Space-ship which is to take Ianthe to realms of Beauty and love,
invisible as yet save to ideal aspirations because hidden from
sight by the Veil, which is mortal frailty.

Indirectly evolved to start with and subsequently developed
through comparatively casual reading, the Platonic implications
of the symbol now begin to be developed further by more direct
reading and study of Plato and Platonic writing. In 1812 Shelley
was still full of the doctrines of the eighteenth-century materialist
philosophers and could see nothing but word-juggling in the
immaterialist doctrines of Berkeley and others. Between that year
and 1815 he became thoroughly converted to Berkeley from
whom, it may well be, he imbibed indirectly quite as much
Platonism at the time as from his direct Platonic study then being
fostered by Peacock: in particular he was attracted by Berkeley's
attempt to brush aside words and abstractions in order to penetrate beyond the veil of language to the world of ideas. A good
deal of this Platonism comes out in the sonnet of 1818:[2]

> Lift not the painted veil which those who live
> Call Life: though unreal shapes be pictured there,
> And it but mimic all we would believe
> With colours idly spread,—behind, lurk Fear

---

[1] *Queen Mab*, i. 180–7, Hutch., p. 765.   [2] Hutch., p. 569.

And Hope, twin Destinies; who ever weave
Their shadows, o'er the chasm, sightless and drear.
I knew one who had lifted it—he sought,
For his lost heart was tender, things to love,
But found them not, alas! nor was there aught
The world contains, the which he could approve.
Through the unheeding many he did move,
A splendour among shadows, a bright blot
Upon this gloomy scene, a Spirit that strove
For truth, and like the Preacher found it not.

At this stage we must abandon unprofitable and arbitrary attempts to distinguish between the germs of thought and feeling; both pass together into the language which is Shelley's natural form of poetical expression: we may recognize the components but what is more important is that we should appreciate the resultant blending of them for what it is. What the Veil comes to signify here and throughout Shelley's mature work is the illusory world of impermanence that hides or half hides the ideal world of reality. 'Mutability' was what he called this illusory world and he had explained its relation to the ideal world, in the 'Hymn to Intellectual Beauty'[1] in 1816: Beauty alone, he says—i.e. the Beauty of ideal love—can never sever

From all we hear and all we see,
Doubt, chance, and mutability.

Either as a word or as an idea the Veil appears again and again throughout Shelley's poetry and it is a vital clue, symbolically, to his whole attitude towards Life and Death: if its significance can be apprehended, much in his poetry can be understood that would be otherwise inexplicable and it is the key too to much of his otherwise inexplicable behaviour in the course of his own lifetime. The 'chasm' of the sonnet, hidden by the Veil, is but another expression for the 'intermediate space' between divine and mortal: on its near side are the things perceived by mortal senses but these are not real things, they are 'unreal shapes', the counterpart of the shadows in Plato's Cave of Thought which we shall be discussing in our next chapter. In his Ariadne-quest, pursuing love on the idealized, abstract plane, Shelley had sometimes seen a

---

[1] 30–31, Hutch., p. 530. 'Mutabilitie' was among the symbolic personifications Shelley had encountered in *The Faerie Queene*.

vision of what lay beyond the Veil and the chasm; his sorrow was his discovery that love on the near side of the Veil, when encountered in its earthly, concrete embodiment, too often proved something that merely mimicked what he would believe. We must not misunderstand the 'splendour among shadows' which might quite easily be taken for a vain and self-flattering self-description: the phrase has no reference whatever either to Shelley's physical appearance or to his personal importance as he conceived them: it is not, in fact, descriptive at all but symbolical: it is as a symbol merely that he sees himself—a symbol of reality. What makes him thus symbolical is his poetic and philosophic consciousness of the splendid world of reality behind the Veil. This it is which places him in contrast to 'the unheeding many', who are mere 'shadows', 'unreal shapes' in the 'gloomy scene' of mortal Mutability which lies on the nearer side of the Veil: shadows and shapes which are merely pictured there, imaginary and not really existent.

Amid the quintessential Shelleyan subtleties of *Prometheus Unbound* the Veil and Mutability form a subtle Platonic trail which we must now endeavour to follow. In the third act, written in the next year, 1819, the language of the sonnet is twice exactly echoed, though the symbolism has moved from a personal to a cosmic application. Here is the first passage:[1]

> Death is the veil which those who live call life:
> They sleep, and it is lifted: and meanwhile
> In mild variety the seasons mild
> With rainbow-skirted showers, and odorous winds,
> And long blue meteors cleansing the dull night,
> And the life-kindling shafts of the keen sun's
> All-piercing bow, and the dew-mingled rain
> Of the calm moonbeams, a soft influence mild,
> Shall clothe the forests and the fields, ay, even
> The crag-built deserts of the barren deep,
> With ever-living leaves, and fruits, and flowers.

There are times when Shelley's doctrine of Mutability comes close to the New Birth idea: in this passage, for instance, there is an implication of a natural process of regeneration, something productive of new bloom, beauty and vigour, which will begin when the Veil is lifted. But Mutability does not in itself imply

---

[1] *Prometheus Unbound*, III. iii. 113–23, Hutch., p. 248.

this: it is used rather to indicate Shelley's consciousness of a Heracleitean flux in earthly and human experience in contrast to the permanence of the ideal, divine realm beyond the Veil—it is this *impermanence* that the word implies, without necessarily implying more. The second passage similarly begins with a description of what happens when the Veil is rent:[1]

> The painted veil, by those who were, called life,
> Which mimicked, as with colours idly spread,
> All men believed or hoped, is torn aside;
> The loathsome mask has fallen, the man remains
> Sceptreless, free, uncircumscribed, but man
> Equal, unclassed, tribeless, and nationless,
> Exempt from awe, worship, degree, the king
> Over himself...

The Veil, now, has become a 'loathsome mask', identifiable with Evil itself, the notion being that Evil is merely something unreal and impermanent, a mask to hide the Good, and that when it has been torn aside Good will stand revealed. Such a notion is of a piece with Shelley's doctrine of love, for in the ideal world love reigns supreme and Evil cannot exist with it: Evil is mutable but love immutable because it takes on immortality from its own aspirations after the immortal: as applied to *Prometheus* this means that, since for mankind Tyranny was the chief of evils, Tyranny would vanish so that Man would have liberty[2] and be 'king over himself'. But the relation of Evil in general and of Tyranny in particular to the process of Mutability will not be clear in this passage, unless we take careful heed of what follows. Shelley continues about Man:[3]

> ...just, gentle, wise; but man
> Passionless?——no, yet free from guilt or pain,
> Which were, for his will made or suffered them,
> Nor yet exempt, though ruling them like slaves,
> From chance, and death, and mutability...

It was, it will be remembered, at the time when *Prometheus* was

---

[1] III. iv. 190–7, Hutch., p. 253.

[2] Poetry, in Shelley's belief, could assist in the rending by stimulating Man's will to be free. Thus in the 'Ode to Liberty', 86, the Spanish insurrection of 1820 made Shelley think of the 'bards and sages' whose voices had hymned the freedom of thought as 'Rending the veil of space and time assunder'.

[3] III. iv. 197–201, Hutch., p. 253.

being written that Shelley noted in his memorandum on Xenophon the power of the human will to 'modify events'.[1] The efficacy
of this power of the will depended on 'the virtue and power of
love': where this failed Man, he would not be 'exempt . . . From
chance and death and mutability'. Thus, though the process of
change might bring around the fall of Tyranny and other forms
of Evil, Man himself might again be overthrown by the very same
process of change if, weakened by his Passions, the ἀρετή and
love, on which the efficacy of his will depended, were not strong
enough to control it. For Shelley Mutability was a perpetual
process, and Good and Evil ran in cycles throughout history and
experience—such a process, of which Eternity was made up, being
symbolized by that circular-shaped emblem the Tail-eating Serpent, the creature of which one end is warring with the other:

> And the subject he loved best to dwell on,

says Mary of Shelley in her illuminating Note on *Prometheus
Unbound*,[2]

was the image of One warring with the Evil Principle, oppressed
not only by it, but by all—even the good, who were deluded into
considering evil a necessary portion of humanity; a victim full of
fortitude and hope and the spirit of triumph emanating from a reliance
in the ultimate omnipotence of Good.

It is Intellectual Beauty, alone steadfast amid the change and decay
of Mutability, through which the One operates and this is identifiable at the same time with love, that Shelleyan, all-embracing
love of humanity of which we traced the evolution in Chapter 4
out of the Platonic Ἔρως and which closely approximates to the
Christian ἀγάπη. For Shelley this quasi-Christian love together
with a Keatsian conception[3] of Beauty went to make up philosophic Goodness or Truth; witness his self-description in the
sonnet—these words at least are a self-description—

> . . . a spirit that sought
> For truth, and like the Preacher found not.

Such is the expression in *Prometheus Unbound*, in terms of the Veil-

---

[1] See above, pp. 30–31 and 71–73.   [2] Hutch., p. 271.
[3] Such affinities with Keats are due to accident. Shelley's Biblical study on the
other hand was considerable: his notebooks abound in quotations from both the
Old and the New Testament.

symbol and the doctrine of Mutability, of this kind of love, a concept which goes deep into his convictions of 1819 on the subject of the perfectibility of Man—'the cardinal point of his system', as Mary says in her Note.

If—to digress for a moment from *Prometheus Unbound*—we may look back from Shelley's cosmic application of these principles to his attempts to apply them in his own life we come to many occasions when it came his way to feel the sorrows ensuing when 'virtue and power' was wanting either in himself or in some mortal Ariadne. One such occasion was at the time when his marriage with Harriet was breaking up. With the dimming of 'the light of one sweet smile' images of dimmed radiance crowded into his poetry:[1]

> Away! the moor is dark beneath the moon. . . .

The fleeting clouds that hid the radiance were Nature's own image of mortal Mutability:[2]

> We are as clouds that veil the midnight moon. . . .

Seldom were Shelley's faculties more sensitively able 'to make the external internal, the internal external, to make Nature thought and thought Nature'. But in applying the words of Coleridge to Shelley's Veil-symbolism we must observe here again that in Shelley thought as often as not *was* feeling and feeling thought. The way in which the two alternate and overlap, corresponding to the two planes on which he pursued Beauty, is reflected in the use of the symbol as we trace it through the years, and it is where the distinction is most insignificant that its use is most effective. *Epipsychidion*, where for the moment his Ariadne-quest seemed to him to have reached its strong and final fulfilment, is a case in point: here the two planes seem to have become one, the Veil seems rent, the Beauty itself stands revealed together with Emilia Viviani, its mortal embodiment:[3]

> Seraph of Heaven! too gentle to be human,
> Veiling beneath that radiant form of Woman
> All that is insupportable in thee
> Of light, and love, and immortality!

---

[1] *Stanzas*, 1814, Hutch., p. 521.   [2] *Mutability*, I, Hutch., p. 523.
[3] 21–28, Hutch., p. 412.

> Sweet Benediction in the eternal Curse!
> Veiled Glory of this lampless Universe!
> Thou Moon beyond the clouds! Thou living Form
> Among the Dead! Thou Star above the Storm!

The Divinity here robed in the Shelleyan habiliments of Veil, Moon, Star ('most excellent pilot') is more than Beauty itself, more than Emilia, more than the conjunction of the two. She is also the Veiled Maid of *Alastor*, she is Cythna, Asia, and the Witch of Atlas on the ideal plane and, at the same time, on the earthly plane, she has in her something of Harriet and Mary Shelley, Claire Clairmont, even perhaps, spiritually, something of the poor Brown Demon—we need name no more, for as Shelley confesses[1]

> In many mortal forms I rashly sought
> The shadow of that idol of my thought.

And always there came disillusionment: in 1821 as in 1814 ἀρετή was weak and *Mutability* again provides the subject and the title of a lament:[2]

> Virtue, how frail it is!
>   Friendship how rare!
> Love, how it sells poor bliss
>   For proud despair!
> But we, though soon they fall,
> Survive their joy, and all
>   Which ours we call.

To return to the Veil-symbolism in *Prometheus Unbound*. As we have seen the love which is the core of the central doctrine of the poem is an idealized, humanitarian kind approximating to the Christian ἀγάπη and derived from the 'consentaneous love' of Queen Mab.[3] But at the same time there is in the figure of Asia a particularly striking embodiment of the usual Shelleyan-Platonic, *Symposium*-based Woman-love. We have just numbered her among the Veiled Divinities who went to make up the conception of *Epipsychidion*: her affinity with Emilia Viviani is seen still more closely in the language of the 'Life of Life' song with which she is greeted by the Voices in the Air:[4]

---

[1] *Epips.* 267. See above, p. 63, n. 1.
[2] 8–14, Hutch., p. 640.
[3] See above, pp. 33 and 51.
[4] *Prom.* II. v. 54–59, Hutch., p. 241.

> Child of Light! thy limbs are burning
> Through the vest which seems to hide them;
> As the radiant lines of morning
> Through the clouds ere they divide them;
> And this atmosphere divinest
> Shrouds thee wheresoe'er thou shinest.

The *vest* is the slightest of verbal variations for the Veil which covers Beauty in *Epipsychidion*: again[1]

> Lamp of Earth! where'er thou movest
> Its dim shapes are clad with brightness . . .

describes Asia much as Emilia is later described:[2]

> Veiled Glory of this lampless Universe!

Woman-love in Asia is a microcosm of the 'consentaneous love' of the World Spirit: she becomes herself a microcosm of the One, her radiance is of the radiance of the One which is the Beauty of the One.

Such is Asia. For Prometheus the hour of his triumph is also the hour in which he is united to her. All-important are the symbolical implications of their union. Prometheus is Mind—the mind of Man which, if it casts out weakness and develops strength, can become a microcosm of the World-Spirit: just as the World-Spirit by ruling Necessity can rule the universe so man's mind, within its own microcosm, can 'modify events', but it depends for the necessary strength on 'the virtue and power of Love'.[3] Prometheus, when he cast out hate, was given that strength through love and so could triumph over Evil by controlling Necessity, or Fate, personified in Demogorgon. Hercules congratulates him:[4]

> Most glorious among Spirits, thus doth strength
> To wisdom, courage, and long-suffering love,
> And thee, who art the form they animate,
> Minister like a slave.

Prometheus' reply quietly emphasizes the real triumph, the

[1] *Prom.* II. v. 66–67, Hutch., p. 241.
[2] *Ep.* 26, Hutch., p. 412.
[3] See above, pp. 55, 71–73.
[4] *Prom.* III. iii. 1–4, Hutch., p. 245.

triumph of his ἀρετή which is Shelley's great point in the Catastrophe:[1]

> Thy gentle words
> Are sweeter even than freedom long desired
> And long delayed.

Far greater than mere personal liberty is the *moral* triumph: here is the point which Shelley thrusts home in his Preface.[2]

> ... until the mind can love, and admire, and trust, and hope, and endure, reasoned principles of moral conduct are seeds cast upon the highway of life which the unconscious passenger tramples into dust, although they would bear the harvest of his happiness.

The overthrowing of Evil by Good, which has resulted from the triumph of Prometheus' ἀρετή, is symbolized in the language in which he turns to address Asia:[3]

> Asia, thou light of life,
> Shadow of beauty unbeheld: and ye,
> Fair sister nymphs, who made long years of pain
> Sweet to remember, through your love and care:
> Henceforth we will not part.

Shadow has been displaced by *light*: no longer is Asia 'unbeheld' since she has been unveiled. We need to note that phrase 'light of life', a variant of 'Life of life' which is comparable in form to the 'soul within my soul' of *Epipsychidion*. The last is a characteristically Shelleyan phrase the like of which are to be found in letters as early as 1811 and 1812: Professor Notopoulos[4] has coined for it the useful name 'Platonic partitive genitive' and it involves the conception, taken from the *Symposium*, of love as the union of two parts of an original soul. Closely cognate to this conception is the whole union of Prometheus with Asia—of Prometheus, who stands for Mind and Will and has become a microcosm of the World-Spirit, with Asia, microcosm of World-love: united they are a microcosm of the One, practically identifiable with the One: 'Henceforth we will not part.'

But there is more in their union than this. Asia, as we have just said, is a microcosm not merely of the love of the One but also

---

[1] *Prom.* III. iii. 4–6, Hutch., pp. 245–6.
[2] Hutch., p. 207.   [3] *Prom.* III. iii. 6–10, Hutch., p. 246.
[4] p. 279: 'Life of life' means 'thou part of the World-life', i.e. 'thou microcosm of the World Spirit': by analogy 'light of life' means 'thou microcosm of the light of the World Spirit'.

of the Beauty of the One: in their union therefore is involved not merely the philosophical triumph of Good but also the whole aesthetic principle of Beauty: it is doubly symbolical and the double symbolism is a point of immense importance. For in Shelley the two principles are indistinguishable: indeed it is a cardinal point with him that they are the same. This we can see, to start with, if we compare what he says in the Preface to *Prometheus* about 'the reasoned principles of moral conduct' with something he says in *A Defence of Poetry*:[1]

The great secret of morals is love; or a going out of our own nature, and an identification of ourselves with the beautiful which exists in thought, action, or person, not our own.

What he tells us here in his prose manifesto on the subject of poetry, written nearly two years after the third act of *Prometheus*, is extremely pertinent to the drama: he tells us *how* the veil is lifted. What lifts the veil is 'the identification of ourselves with the beautiful'. Evil in Shelley's view was something unreal and Man had only to will that it should not exist for it to be dispelled: Prometheus was given the victory because of the strength of his Mind and Will and this depended on the 'virtue and power' of his love. Now the love animating Prometheus was a *double* love: first the humanitarian ἀγάπη, which was Goodness, and secondly the Platonic, idealized love-of-woman-which-was-Beauty out of which the humanitarian love evolved;[2] this was engendered in its turn by aspirations after 'identification with the Beautiful' such as we have noticed in his attraction to Asia his Guide when he was 'drinking love from those loved eyes'—just as Shelley had done with Harriet 'And loved mankind the more'. And so he succeeds in lifting the Veil: when the unreal world of Evil is dispelled the opposite of Evil stands revealed, a world of reality, a world in which Goodness and Beauty exist equally and indistinguishably since both are the opposites of Evil. The unity of the Good and the Beautiful, of his philosophical and his aesthetic ideas, was a central point in Shelley's personal life: in him poet and fighter against Tyranny were one: never more so than in 1819 when the greater part of *Prometheus Unbound* was being written. The same unity is a central point in the argument of the *Defence*[3] where he expounds specifically about the regenerative power of poetry

[1] Jul. vii. 118.   [2] See above, pp. 56–57.   [3] Jul. vii. 117.

what he had conveyed allegorically in *Prometheus*: here too we get
the terms 'beauty . . . vesture . . . veil':

> The beauty of the internal nature cannot be so far concealed by its
> accidental vesture. . . .

> Poetry lifts the veil from the hidden beauty of the world. . . .

We must, however, continue with Prometheus' speech. He goes
on to tell Asia of the joys that await them in the realm where the
Good and the Beautiful are one:[1]

> There is a cave,
> All overgrown with trailing odorous plants,
> Which curtain out the day with leaves and flowers,
> And paved with veinèd emerald, and a fountain
> Leaps in the midst with an awakening sound.
> From its curved roof the mountain's frozen tears
> Like snow, or silver, or long diamond spires,
> Hang downward, raining forth a doubtful light:
> And there is heard the ever-moving air,
> Whispering without from tree to tree, and birds,
> And bees; and all around are mossy seats,
> And the rough walls are clothed with long soft grass . . .

What it is highly important to understand about this cave is that,
unlike the Cave of Demogorgon in the second act, which we shall
be discussing in our next chapter, it does not primarily bear a
symbolic relation to the Cave of Plato's *Republic*.[2] Although in
language and imagery it does indeed owe a good deal to this
famous passage, it is in fact, symbolically, just another[3] of those
Shelleyan paradises such as we find in *The Revolt of Islam* and
Epipsychidion, and its blisses are but a variation on the blisses of
the Isle and the Temple. Like these it is the destination of a
voyage, for to get there Asia's soul becomes 'an enchanted boat'.
It is, says Prometheus,[4]

> A simple dwelling, which shall be our own;
> Where we will sit and talk of time and change,
> As the world ebbs and flows, ourselves unchanged.
> What can hide man from mutability?

---

[1] III. iii. 10–21, Hutch., p. 246.   [2] 514 foll.

[3] One of the manuscripts of *Prometheus* contains a drawing which seems to
represent an Isle with such a cave. See White, *Shelley*, ii. 88.

[4] III. iii. 22–25, Hutch., p. 246.

He proceeds to tell how they will occupy themselves in this realm of Eternity where they remain, immutable like the One, watching the mutable realm of men where 'the many change and pass':[1]

> And we will search, with looks and words of love,
> For hidden thoughts, each lovelier than the last,
> Our unexhausted spirits; and like lutes
> Touched by the skill of the enamoured wind,
> Weave harmonies divine, yet ever new,
> From difference sweet where discord cannot be . . .

The function of music and verse in the ideal realm is exactly what Shelley was to proclaim for it in *A Defence of Poetry*—a power which takes possession of Man and brings him peace and delight:[2]

> Man is an instrument over which a series of external and internal impressions are driven, like the alternations of an ever-changing wind over an Aeolian lyre, which move it by their motion to ever-changing melody.

This conception may or may not derive, as Professor Grabo[3] believes, from the Plotinian conception of the One as the source of emanations and irradiations such as Divine Thought, the object of all aspirations. More certainly here in *Prometheus Unbound* Shelley had in mind a passage from the *Symposium*[4] in the light of which its application becomes clear. The passage occurs in the speech of Eryximachus[5] and arises out of the subject of 'love and concord' in medicine: Eryximachus draws an analogy from music and refers to Heracleitus' notion that the whole universe is held together by the strain of opposing forces, just as the right use of a bowstring or a lyre depends on opposite tension. Nothing could make clearer the significance of the *double* symbolism of the union of Prometheus and Asia. For this 'strain of opposing forces' is exactly Shelley's own conception in his drama of how the Universal system is kept working: here was 'the subject he loved best to dwell on', namely 'the image of One warring with the Evil principle . . .'. In Prometheus and Asia Mind, as we have

---

[1] *Prom.* III. iii. 34–39, Hutch., p. 246.   [2] Jul. vii. 109.

[3] *Prometheus Unbound, An interpretation*, pp. 68, 90–91, 139.

[4] 187a–b. Though in the *Defence* he was probably writing herein mainly in terms of his own experience of the poetic process. See Ch. 11 and Ch. 12.

[5] This passage in Eryximachus' speech is referred to later by Agathon—O.C.T. 196e, Bipont edn., p. 217—when he allegorizes the relation between Love and Poetry and the other arts. See above, p. 55, n. 4.

seen, is united with love and also with Beauty; in the world of
reality where this double union has happened there reigns a
harmony of which poetry and song are themselves a symbol. Nor
is this all, for Shelley held that poetry was not merely a symbol
of harmony but actually a *cause* of it and, as such, all-powerful
among men:[1]

> Poetry is indeed something divine . . .
>
> A poet participates in the eternal, the infinite, and the one . . .
>
> Poets are the unacknowledged legislators of the world.

It is here that the Veil-symbolism we have been following brings
us to the heart of what is essential in Shelley and what is essential
about him: this is one of the points at which those who would
judge him may rightly pause and do so: here are the conceptions
on which he would himself be judged, believing himself formed
to communicate them—

> . . . the conceptions which result from considering either the moral or
> the material universe as a whole.

Prometheus Unbound represents his major, large-scale attempt at
such communication: Man in the Universe was his subject, and
poetry, as he conceived it, was something exalting Man beyond
mortality. To exalt Man and poetry in combination was the
essence of his climax, and more particularly in the passage that
follows where all his powers are concentrated upon the communication of their combined glory. Of these twenty-three lines,[2]
in which Prometheus continues his description of the world of
peace and harmony in which he will henceforth dwell with the
unveiled Asia, Professor Notopoulos has said[3] that they 'constitute one of the best examples . . . of Shelley's power of trans-
muting Platonic metaphysics into poetry' and 'the clearest
re-expression of Plato's philosophy in English poetry'. Robert
Bridges, whose text I follow here, was at particular pains to
emend their punctuation for his anthology *The Spirit of Man*[4], and
his study of them may be traced in *The Testament of Beauty*: what
Shelley has here conceived might be not inappositely described by
a combination of these two grand titles of the late Laureate's:[5]

---

[1] Jul. vii. 135, 112, 140.   [2] III. iii. 40–63, Hutch., p. 246–7.   [3] pp. 254, 255.
[4] No. 68; the emended lines are 44–62. See Addendum, below, p. 146.
[5] Sir Edward Bridges has kindly permitted me to quote from an unpublished

And hither come, sped on the charmèd winds, 40
Which meet from all the points of heaven, as bees
From every flower aërial Enna feeds,
At their known island-homes in Himera,
The echoes of the human world, which tell
Of the low voice of love, almost unheard, 45
And dove-eyed pity's murmured pain, and Music,
Itself the echo of the heart, and all
That tempers or improves man's life, now free;
And lovely apparitions, dim at first,
Then radiant—as the mind arising bright 50
From the embrace of Beauty (whence the forms
Of which these are the phantoms) casts on them
The gathered rays which are reality—
Shall visit us, the progeny immortal
Of Painting, Sculpture, and rapt Poesy, 55
And arts, though unimagined, yet to be.
The wandering voices and the shadows these
Of all that man becomes, the mediators
Of that best worship, Love,—by him and us
Given and returned; swift shapes and sounds, which 60
  grow
More fair and soft as man grows wise and kind,
And, veil by veil, evil and error fall:
Such virtue has the cave and place around.

The significant change is that the parenthesis which, in all editions since Shelley's of 1820, had begun before 'dim' (in line 49) is made to begin after 'radiant' (line 50) so that the comparison, which ends at line 53, forms the unit demanded by the syntax. One might pause to wonder how often Shelley's difficulty in communicating his conceptions was complicated by problems arising from the mechanics of punctuation. Perhaps Bridges is unduly severe, for Shelley's printed achievement, when compared with his MS., is considerable. Giving to the Platonic tones and terms of the passage something not too far from the rhythm,

letter of his father's to which my attention was drawn by Professor H. W. Garrod. Writing to W. B. Yeats on 7 Oct. 1915, he says, 'Yesterday I had to repunctuate a piece of Shelley's Prometheus, 19 lines. It was nonsense in the received text, or at least unintelligible . . . I consulted the MS. at the Bodleian Library, and found that Shelley's own punctuation was almost worse than nothing.' It is a sidelight on Shelley's MSS. that this particular one of which Bridges complains—contained in three notebooks, Bod. MS. Shelley E. 1, E. 2, E. 3—an 'intermediate fair copy', as Locock has called it—is textually one of his best.

shape, and syntax of a Platonic period, he has contrived, out of his experience as a translator and student of the *Symposium*, together with absorption of kindred ideas from the *Ion, Phaedrus,* and *Republic*, to make a synthesis which is both Platonic and, at the same time, characteristically his own, a totality of rare poetry worthy of its great theme. We must look carefully into the evolution of this synthesis, for there could be few more illuminating points at which to observe the mind of Shelley at work.

Only the first three of these dialogues will be referred to for the present: the *Republic* must await our next chapter. To start with let us take the *Ion*. If we had not noticed a connexion with this dialogue in lines 40–48, we might have been led to look for it by the fact that one of the three notebooks[1] into which Shelley copied *Prometheus* contains also a part of his translation, and there we find the famous simile:

For the souls of the poets, as poets tell us, have this peculiar ministration in the world. They tell us that these souls, flying like bees from flower to flower and wandering over the gardens and the meadows and the honey-flowing fountains of the Muses, return to us laden with the sweetness of melody; and arrayed as they are in plumes of rapid imagination, they speak truth.

It is from Plato's image here of 'the souls of the poets . . . flying like bees' that Shelley conceives (40–46) the idea of Love and Pity reaching Prometheus' Cave from the human world *sped on the charmèd winds . . . as bees*. And it is because Plato's poet-souls 'speak truth' that their poetry can ascend on wings from the human, relative world to the ideal world of reality beyond the Veil.

As we come round once again to the *Symposium*, we may notice in parenthesis what a world of poetry and poetic thought here emerges from that one-word memorandum of Shelley's, the name Diotima: it is in her discourse that the stages are described by which the soul makes its ascent and three passages from this— one preceding her description and two following it—are the chief sources of Prometheus' remaining lines (46–63) about his Cave.

The point at which we pick up Diotima's argument is the point at which we left it in Chapter 4.[2] 'The mortal nature', she has just said, 'seeks so far as it is able to become deathless and eternal', and of this, she says, the ordinary manifestation is the desire to beget children:[3]

---

[1] Bod. MS. Shelley E. 1, ff. 44^r and 45^r; from *Ion* 534a, Jul. vii. 238.
[2] *Symp.* 207d. See above, p. 62.   [3] *Symp.* 208e.

the instinct, however, is one of the soul as well as of the body, and she proceeds to speak of those whose 'souls are more pregnant than their bodies and who conceive and produce things more suitable to the soul'. It was from what follows that Shelley took, used, and coloured Plato's view that the arts are the progeny of Love: it is here that our first passage starts. 'What', asks Diotima, 'is suitable to the soul? τί οὖν προσήκει [sc. καὶ κυῆσαι καὶ τεκεῖν];' She goes on :[1]

φρόνησίν τε καὶ τὴν ἄλλην ἀρετήν—ὧν δή εἰσι καὶ οἱ ποιηταὶ πάντες γεννήτορες καὶ τῶν δημιουργῶν ὅσοι λέγονται εὑρετικοὶ εἶναι· πολὺ δὲ μεγίστη, ἔφη, καὶ καλλίστη τῆς φρονήσεως ἡ περὶ τὰ τῶν πόλεών τε καὶ οἰκήσεων διακόσμησις, ᾗ δὴ ὄνομά ἐστι σωφροσύνη τε καὶ δικαιοσύνη— τούτων δ' αὖ ὅταν τις ἐκ νέου ἐγκύμων ᾖ τὴν ψυχήν, ἤθεος ὢν καὶ ἡκούσης τῆς ἡλικίας, τίκτειν τε καὶ γεννᾶν ἤδη ἐπιθυμῇ, ζητεῖ δὴ οἶμαι καὶ οὗτος περιιὼν τὸ καλὸν ἐν ᾧ ἂν γεννήσειεν· ἐν τῷ γὰρ αἰσχρῷ οὐδέποτε γεννήσει. τά τε οὖν σώματα τὰ καλὰ μᾶλλον ἢ τὰ αἰσχρὰ ἀσπάζεται ἅτε κυῶν, καὶ ἂν ἐντύχῃ ψυχῇ καλῇ καὶ γενναίᾳ καὶ εὐφυεῖ, πάνυ δὴ ἀσπάζεται τὸ συναμφότερον, καὶ πρὸς τοῦτον τὸν ἄνθρωπον εὐθὺς εὐπορεῖ λόγων περὶ ἀρετῆς καὶ περὶ οἷον χρὴ εἶναι τὸν ἄνδρα τὸν ἀγαθὸν καὶ ἃ ἐπιτηδεύειν καὶ ἐπιχειρεῖ παιδεύειν. ἁπτόμενος γὰρ οἶμαι τοῦ καλοῦ καὶ ὁμιλῶν αὐτῷ ἃ πάλαι ἐκύει τίκτει καὶ γεννᾷ, καὶ παρὼν καὶ ἀπὼν μεμνημένος, καὶ τὸ γεννηθὲν συνεκτρέφει κοινῇ μετ' ἐκείνου, ὥστε πολὺ μείζω κοινωνίαν τῆς τῶν παίδων πρὸς ἀλλήλους οἱ τοιοῦτοι ἴσχουσι καὶ φιλίαν βεβαιοτέραν, ἅτε καλλιόνων καὶ ἀθανατωτέρων παίδων κεκοινωνηκότες.

Shelley's translation is best considered piece by piece: we will begin with the first lines, down to the colon (209a):

What is suitable to the soul? Intelligence, and every other power and excellence of the mind; of which all poets, and all other artists who are creative and inventive, are the authors.

It is Plato's thought here, readapted in terms of Shelley's poetry, that emerges in those lines about the propagation from Intellectual Beauty of the

progeny immortal
Of Painting, Sculpture, and rapt Poesy.

For it is the fact of being 'suitable to the soul' that enables Poetry and the other arts to lift the Veil and penetrate to the world of reality symbolized[2] in Prometheus' Cave. Let us note in

[1] *Symp.* 209a–c, Jul. vii. 204–6. No notice will be taken here of the points, irrelevant to the purposes of this chapter, at which Shelley has discreetly adapted the homosexual foundations of the ideal love in Plato.

[2] For the symbolical difference between Prometheus' Cave here (III. iii) and the cave of Demogorgon (II. iv) see pp. 156–7.

passing that Shelley translates the single word ἀρετήν by 'power and excellence of the *mind*'[1]—one might gather that he was out to emphasize the Intellectual character of this Beauty: this is quite in line with the emphasis on mind in Prometheus' speech, where it is mind which grasps at the beauty of the *lovely* apparitions or forms—Plato's τὰ σώματα τὰ καλά. Shelley continues (209a):

> The greatest and most admirable wisdom is that which regulates the government of families and states, and which is called moderation and justice.

'Moderation and justice'—σωφροσύνη τε καὶ δικαιοσύνη—are cardinal virtues inherent in the humanitarian love pervading the poem: Shelley's identification of the Good and the Beautiful makes them part also of the virtues of poetry: hence they are reflected in the idea (61) of the words 'as man grows wise and kind', as well as in the idea that the poetic voice echoes Love and Pity (45–46). Such virtues result from the attainment of Intellectual Beauty: (209b)

> Whosoever, therefore, from his youth feels his soul pregnant with the conception of these excellences, is divine; and when due time arrives, desires to bring forth; and, wandering about, he seeks the beautiful in which he may propagate what he has conceived; for there is no generation in that which is deformed; he embraces those bodies which are beautiful rather than those which are deformed, in obedience to the principle within him, which is ever seeking to perpetuate itself.

That phrase 'Wandering about he seeks the beautiful' [ζητεῖ δὴ ... περιιὼν τὸ καλόν] comprises the whole ideal of the spiritualized Ariadne-quest, its end being, in the phrase of Prometheus (51), *the embrace of Beauty* [cf. ἀσπάζεται] (209b ff.).

> And if he meets, in conjunction with loveliness of form, a beautiful, generous and gentle soul, he embraces both at once, and immediately undertakes to educate the object of his love, and is inspired with an overflowing persuasion to declare what is virtue, and what he ought to be who would attain to its possession, and what are the duties which it exacts.

Such was the Platonic ideal anticipated instinctively or indirectly by Shelley with Harriet: such was the Beauty Shelley so vainly

---

[1] For other examples of Shelley's exegetical renderings from Greek, see above pp. 52, 54, and below, pp. 139, 141, and for an example from Spanish, p. 85, n. 1.

sought 'in many mortal forms' on the near side of the Veil: such
virtue existent beyond the Veil is what Prometheus is declaring
in his speech (63) *Such virtue hath the cave and place around.* Something of the educating is perhaps implicit in the search of Prometheus and Asia together 'for hidden thoughts each lovelier than
the last'. Shelley concludes his translation of this passage thus
(209c):

> For, by the intercourse with and, as it were, the very touch of that
> which is beautiful, he brings forth and produces what he had formerly
> conceived; and nourishes and educates that which thus is produced
> together with the object of his love, whose image, whether absent or
> present, is never divided from his mind. So that those who are thus
> united are linked by a nobler community and a firmer love, as being
> the parents of a lovelier and more enduring progeny than the parents
> of other children.

Here again in ἁπτόμενος τοῦ καλοῦ καὶ ὁμιλῶν αὐτῷ we have *the
embrace of Beauty*: Shelley's translation, 'by intercourse with, and
as it were the very touch...' seems slightly to idealize the original,
as though he were trying to divorce the meaning from suggestions
of the physical. And if we once more take those lines from *Prometheus Unbound* (54 et seq.) about '... the progeny immortal—Of
Painting, Sculpture, and rapt Poesy' and compare them this time
with Plato's phrase about the 'lovelier and more enduring progeny'—ἅτε καλλιόνων καὶ ἀθανατωτέρων παίδων κεκοινωνηκότες—
we find an admirable example in miniature of what Shelley
could do with his borrowings.

In the second and third of the *Symposium* passages we get Plato's
conception, which was likewise Shelley's as symbolized in Prometheus' description, of the world of reality behind the Veil: here
is the second[1] followed by Shelley's translation[2]:

ὅταν δή τις ἀπὸ τῶνδε διὰ τὸ ὀρθῶς παιδεραστεῖν ἐπανιὼν ἐκεῖνο τὸ
καλὸν ἄρχηται καθορᾶν, σχεδὸν ἄν τι ἅπτοιτο τοῦ τέλους. τοῦτο γὰρ δή
ἐστι τὸ ὀρθῶς ἐπὶ τὰ ἐρωτικὰ ἰέναι ἢ ὑπ' ἄλλου ἄγεσθαι, ἀρχόμενον ἀπὸ
τῶνδε τῶν καλῶν ἐκείνου ἕνεκα τοῦ καλοῦ ἀεὶ ἐπανιέναι, ὥσπερ ἐπαναβασ-
μοῖς χρώμενον, ἀπὸ ἑνὸς ἐπὶ δύο καὶ ἀπὸ δυοῖν ἐπὶ πάντα τὰ καλὰ σώματα,
καὶ ἀπὸ τῶν καλῶν σωμάτων ἐπὶ τὰ καλὰ ἐπιτηδεύματα, καὶ ἀπὸ τῶν
ἐπιτηδευμάτων ἐπὶ τὰ καλὰ μαθήματα, καὶ ἀπὸ τῶν μαθημάτων ἐπ' ἐκεῖνο
τὸ μάθημα τελευτῆσαι, ὅ ἐστιν οὐκ ἄλλου ἢ αὐτοῦ ἐκείνου τοῦ καλοῦ
μάθημα, καὶ γνῷ αὐτὸ τελευτῶν ὅ ἐστι καλόν.

[1] *Symp.* 211b–d.   [2] Jul. vii. 206–7.

When any one, ascending from a correct system of Love, begins to contemplate this supreme beauty, he already touches the consummation of his labour. For such as discipline themselves upon this system, or are conducted by another ⟨this is the right approach⟩[1]—beginning to ascend through these transitory objects which are beautiful, towards that which is beauty itself, proceeding as on steps from the love of one form to that of two, and from that of two to that of all forms which are beautiful; and from beautiful forms to beautiful habits and institutions, and from institutions to beautiful doctrines; until, from the meditation of many doctrines, they arrive at that which is nothing else than the doctrine of the supreme beauty itself, in the knowledge and contemplation of which at length they repose. . . .

Here, in Plato, Shelley finds the phrases and symbols to express his lifelong search for Intellectual Beauty and the disappointments he had had from so many of its mortal embodiments: 'transitory objects'—mere καλὰ σώματα, unreal, like everything else on this side of the Veil, real only when the far side is reached:

> . . . lovely apparitions, dim at first,
> Then radiant . . .

as he expresses them in Prometheus' speech (49–50). Here too, in the various stages, are

> . . . the mediators
> Of that best worship love. . . . (58–59)

For Love, we remember, is an 'intermediary spirit'.

Diotima thus goes on[2] and Shelley thus translates her:[3] here is our third *Symposium* passage:

τί δῆτα, ἔφη, οἰόμεθα, εἴ τῳ γένοιτο αὐτὸ τὸ καλὸν ἰδεῖν εἰλικρινές, καθαρόν, ἄμεικτον, ἀλλὰ μὴ ἀνάπλεων σαρκῶν τε ἀνθρωπίνων καὶ χρωμάτων καὶ ἄλλης πολλῆς φλυαρίας θνητῆς, ἀλλ' αὐτὸ τὸ θεῖον καλὸν δύναιτο μονοειδὲς κατιδεῖν; ἆρ' οἴει, ἔφη, φαῦλον βίον γίγνεσθαι ἐκεῖσε βλέποντος ἀνθρώπου καὶ ἐκεῖνο ᾧ δεῖ θεωμένου καὶ συνόντος αὐτῷ; ἢ οὐκ ἐνθυμῇ, ἔφη, ὅτι ἐνταῦθα αὐτῷ μοναχοῦ γενήσεται, ὁρῶντι ᾧ ὁρατὸν τὸ καλόν, τίκτειν οὐκ εἴδωλα ἀρετῆς, ἅτε οὐκ εἰδώλου ἐφαπτομένῳ, ἀλλὰ ἀληθῆ, ἅτε τοῦ ἀληθοῦς ἐφαπτομένῳ· τεκόντι δὲ ἀρετὴν ἀληθῆ καὶ θρεψαμένῳ ὑπάρχει θεοφιλεῖ γενέσθαι, καὶ εἴπέρ τῳ ἄλλῳ ἀνθρώπων ἀθανάτῳ καὶ ἐκείνῳ;

---

[1] I have added these words to Shelley's text: editors of his translation do not seem to have observed that the sentence they print does not construe, or that the words τοῦτο . . . ὀρθῶς are not translated. The error is traceable to Mary Shelley's transcript of the dialogue: Bod. MS. Shelley adds. d. 8, p. 128. No holograph seems to exist. The text of the Bipont Plato contains no discrepancy here from O.C.T.

[2] *Symp.* 211d–212a.   [3] Jul. vii. 207.

What then shall we imagine to be the aspect of the supreme beauty itself, simple, pure, uncontaminated with the intermixture of human flesh and colours, and all other idle and unreal shapes attendant on mortality; the divine, the original, the supreme, the self-consistent, the monoeidic beauty itself? What must be the life of him who dwells with and gazes on that which it becomes us all to seek? Think you not that to him alone is accorded the prerogative of bringing forth, not images and shadows of virtue ⟨but reality⟩,[1] for he is in contact not with a shadow but with reality; with virtue itself, in the production and nourishment of which he becomes dear to the Gods, and if such a privilege is conceded to any human being, himself immortal.

A sidelight on Shelley's methods as a translator, and on the value of his translations in showing us what an original passage signified for him, may be found in the words 'the original, the supreme, the self-consistent', which do not occur in the Greek.[2] But, before commenting on this third passage from the *Symposium* in relation to our *Prometheus* context, it will be desirable to set beside it the two *Phaedrus* passages with which, likewise, the latter is closely related.[3] They come from Socrates' second discourse in that dialogue: he is discussing the nature of the soul. Every soul, he says, has, in the way of nature, known τὰ ὄντα, reality, before it enters the human body—an idea from Plato, which was in Shelley's mind that day when, as an Oxford undergraduate, he stopped a poor woman on Magdalen Bridge to ask whether the baby she was carrying could divulge any information about pre-existence:[4] furthermore to him as to us it must have been familiar from Wordsworth's 'Ode on Immortality'. The strong souls soar aloft, says Socrates, to 'the heaven above the heavens'—ὁ ὑπερουράνιος τόπος—where Zeus leads the array of gods marshalled in eleven bands. Here is the first of the two passages:[5]

[1] To complete the sense and in translation of ἀλλὰ ἀληθῆ I have supplied these two words not found in printed texts of Shelley's translation.
[2] But the idea of consistency is not here interpolated so much as borrowed and transferred from 211b where τὸ καλόν is αὐτὸ καθ' αὑτὸ μεθ' αὑτοῦ μονοειδὲς ἀεὶ ὄν. For a similar borrowing and transference in Shelley's translation from Spanish see p. 85.
[3] 247 c and 250b–c. The two dialogues were together in Shelley's mind in August 1818: he was studying the *Phaedrus* while Mary was in the process of transcribing his *Symposium* translation. [Jones, *Mary Shelley's Journal*, p. 103.] And this was in the period between the completion of the first act of *Prometheus* and the writing of Acts II and III.
[4] Hogg, *Life* (in H. Wolfe's combined *Life*), i. 247–8.
[5] *Phaedr.* 247c.

ἡ γὰρ ἀχρώματός τε καὶ ἀσχημάτιστος καὶ ἀναφὴς οὐσία ὄντως οὖσα,
ψυχῆς κυβερνήτῃ μόνῳ θεατὴ νῷ, περὶ ἣν τὸ τῆς ἀληθοῦς ἐπιστήμης γένος,
τοῦτον ἔχει τὸν τόπον.

There lives the very being with whom true knowledge is concerned
—the colourless, formless, intangible essence visible only to mind, the
pilot of the soul.

Such in Plato is Intellectual Beauty to which the winged soul
can rise, living in the divine realm of reality which is the realm
beyond the Veil: thus for Shelley, when Claire Clairmont sang, the
Veil that covered the ὑπερουράνιος τόπος, the 'cope of heaven',[1]
was rent

> The cope of heaven seems rent and cloven
> By the enchantment of thy strain,
> And o'er my shoulders wings are woven
> To follow its sublime career. . . .

Beyond the Veil only the elect can peer, the elect for Shelley
being poets and philosophers who have the vision; most souls in
fact never come within range of it: they weaken and, as their
wings lose power, they fall back to the mortal, relative world
where are 'mimicked, as with colours idly spread, / All men believed or hoped': of the 'colourless, formless, intangible' things—
the things of reality—copies and images, coloured and distorted,
are all that can be perceived by the weakened vision of these
souls, and then only by a few of them. We come to the second of
our *Phaedrus* passages, where Plato puts all this as follows:[2]

δικαιοσύνης μὲν οὖν καὶ σωφροσύνης καὶ ὅσα ἄλλα τίμια ψυχαῖς οὐκ
ἔνεστι φέγγος οὐδὲν ἐν τοῖς τῇδε ὁμοιώμασιν, ἀλλὰ δι' ἀμυδρῶν ὀργάνων
μόγις αὐτῶν καὶ ὀλίγοι ἐπὶ τὰς εἰκόνας ἰόντες θεῶνται τὸ τοῦ εἰκασθέντος
γένος· κάλλος δὲ τότ' ἦν ἰδεῖν λαμπρόν, ὅτε σὺν εὐδαίμονι χορῷ μακαρίαν
ὄψιν τε καὶ θέαν, ἑπόμενοι μετὰ μὲν Διὸς ἡμεῖς, ἄλλοι δὲ μετ' ἄλλου θεῶν,
εἶδόν τε καὶ ἐτελοῦντο τῶν τελετῶν ἣν θέμις λέγειν μακαριωτάτην, ἣν
ὠργιάζομεν ὁλόκληροι μὲν αὐτοὶ ὄντες καὶ ἀπαθεῖς κακῶν ὅσα ἡμᾶς ἐν
ὑστέρῳ χρόνῳ ὑπέμενεν, ὁλόκληρα δὲ καὶ ἁπλᾶ καὶ ἀτρεμῆ καὶ εὐδαίμονα
φάσματα μυούμενοί τε καὶ ἐποπτεύοντες ἐν αὐγῇ καθαρᾷ, καθαροὶ ὄντες καὶ
ἀσήμαντοι τούτου ὃ νῦν δὴ σῶμα περιφέροντες ὀνομάζομεν, ὀστρέου τρόπον
δεδεσμευμένοι.

So of justice and moderation and those other things which are
precious to souls there is no radiance in our earthly copies, but only

---

[1] Cf. above, p. 97.   [2] *Phaedr.* 250b; my translation.

through dim sense-perception, only with difficulty and by a mere few who have recourse to the images is the real kind of thing beheld which they represent. But Beauty, all-radiant, could be seen, a beatific vision, and those who were with the happy band of Zeus saw it and were initiated into a mystery which may justly be called most blessed, the which we celebrated in a state of innocence, untroubled by evils yet to come, when we were admitted to the sight of apparitions innocent and simple and calm and happy and beheld them shining in pure light, pure ourselves and not bearing the marks of that thing we carry around and call the body, imprisoned in it like an oyster in its shell.

Taking this second passage from the *Phaedrus* side by side with the last of our *Symposium* extracts, we may perceive to start with that they contain not only the general idea of Shelley's Veil sonnet[1] but also certain obvious sources of its phrasing: the *Veil* itself, for instance, is implicit in δι' ἀμυδρῶν ὀργάνων and we compare again

unreal shapes:	εἴδωλα [*Symp.*] εἰκόνας, φάσματα [*Phaedr.*].
mimicked, as with colours	ἀνάπλεων σαρκῶν τε ἀνθρωπίνων καὶ χρωμά-
idly spread:	των καὶ ἄλλης πολλῆς φλυαρίας θνητῆς [*Symp.*].

No less when we make a comparison with our *Prometheus* speech[2] do we find that the two passages contain between them not only most of the thought that Shelley has distilled into it but a good deal of its language-colour:

apparitions (49)	
forms / Of which these are	εἴδωλα [*Symp.*] εἰκόνας . . . φάσματα
the phantoms (51–52)	[*Phaedr.*].
dim at first (49):	δι' ἀμυδρῶν ὀργάνων.

It is from *the embrace of Beauty* (51) (ἀσπάζεται in another *Symposium* passage, as we saw) that the *apparitions / phantoms* become *Then radiant* (50) in

The gathered rays which are reality (53)

and *radiant* and *gathered rays* are a Shelleyan compression of the several Platonic light-images applied to Beauty,

κάλλος δὲ τότ' ἦν ἰδεῖν λαμπρόν . . . μακαρίαν ὄψιν . . . ἐν αὐγῇ καθαρᾷ, καθαροὶ ὄντες [*Phaedr.*]

[1] See above, pp. 122–3.   [2] See above, p. 135.

while *reality* is compressed from

τίκτειν οὐκ εἴδωλα ἀρετῆς, ἅτε οὐκ εἰδώλου ἐφαπτομένῳ, ἀλλὰ ἀληθῆ,
ἅτε τοῦ ἀληθοῦς ἐφαπτομένῳ [*Symp.*].

Out of all the Platonic extracts in this chapter here is the one upon which we must, in the end, most specifically focus our attention: here it is that Plato is talking of the effect of ideal Beauty upon the man who gazes upon it and lives with it: his, he says, is the prerogative of

bringing forth not images and shadows of virtue but reality for he is in contact not with a shadow but with reality. . . .

In the relation of this to Prometheus' speech we have the most vital, essential point of Shelley's beliefs as expounded in *Prometheus Unbound*. On the near side of the Veil lie merely εἴδωλα ἀρετῆς, 'images and shadows of virtue': beyond the Veil lies ἀρετή itself, the ἀρετή τοῦ Ἔρωτος, the virtue and power of (59) *that best worship Love*. We have seen how, out of Ἔρως in the poem, there evolves the concept of a sort of ἀγάπη, a humanitarian love that is the microcosm of the World-love, and this is engendered in Plato by the stages of progress from 'beautiful forms' (i.e. physical embodiments of love on the near side of the Veil, mere illusory εἴδωλα) to 'beautiful habits and institutions', and thence to 'beautiful doctrines': i.e., in the words of the speech (47–48) to

all
That tempers or improves man's life, now free

—all in fact that lies in the reality beyond the Veil. The Shelleyan concept of reality which we find here in *Prometheus Unbound* is not only vital to an understanding of the play but has a significance extending into Shelley's theory of poetry, his hopes of political reform, and the pattern of his own life. The man who gazes on and dwells with Beauty, who thus attains a contact with reality, has contact, Plato goes on, we remember

. . . with virtue itself, in the production and nourishment of which he becomes dear to the Gods, and, if such a privilege is conceded to any human being, himself immortal.

The 'production and nourishment' of this 'virtue' depended for Shelley on the power of art, like it the 'immortal progeny' of love and Beauty. The power, more particularly, of poetry to

regenerate Man by enlightening his opinions was an axiom with
Shelley, unifying in him the reformer with the poet: it was thus
that he wrote in his Preface to the poem,[1] conscious of the process
in his own time:

> The great writers of our own age are, we have reason to suppose, the
> companions and forerunners of some unimagined change in our social
> conditions or the opinions which cement it. The cloud of mind is dis-
> charging its collected lightning, and the equilibrium between institu-
> tions and opinions is now restoring, or is about to be restored.

With the addition of a little touch of scientific metaphor from
Shelley-the-amateur-of-electrical-experiments the great phrase
about the cloud of mind and its collected lightning is, concep-
tually, no more than a reflection of the Platonic light-imagery of
Prometheus' speech, e.g. such phrases as *the mind arising bright . . .*
(50), *the gathered rays that are reality* (53).

In Shelley's life too, as much as his work, the crystallization in
Prometheus Unbound of Platonic notions of reality which went with
the Veil-symbol, marked the turning-point of the pattern, even as,
earlier, a turning-point had been marked by the climax in *Queen
Mab* of his belief in the doctrine of Necessity and the doctrines of
the materialist philosophers. These latter doctrines he was now to
characterize as 'false and pernicious': henceforth, he proclaimed
in his Preface, Plato and Lord Bacon would be his mentors. And
now—such, as always, is the unity of direction in Shelley's
symbols—this chapter leads us as others have done to that final
working out of patterns at Lerici. Trelawny tells us how, on a
trip in his boat to Leghorn, he once observed:[2]

> With regard to the great question, the System of the Universe, I
> have no curiosity on the subject. I am content to see no further into
> futurity than Plato and Lord Bacon. My mind is tranquil: I have no
> fears and some hopes. In our present gross material state our faculties
> are clouded—when Death removes our clay coverings the mystery will
> be solved.

His Platonic allusion here is, most directly, to the *Phaedo*,[3] but in
his σωφροσύνη, that Socratic calm and fearlessness in face of death
which Shelley so frequently displayed, we may detect, no doubt,

---

[1] Hutch., p. 206.
[2] *Recollections* in H. Wolfe's combined *Life*, ii. 199.
[3] 63e–69e.

a colouring of the conviction of his own immortality as a Beauty-seeker 'dear to the Gods', and in addition to this reminiscence from the *Symposium* we may feel that his phrase about the clay coverings is closely germane, at any rate, to the Veil if not to that phrase from the *Phaedrus* about imprisonment in the body 'like an oyster in its shell'. The synthesis of Platonism which went into *Prometheus Unbound*, and most notably into the speech we have been examining, remained a part of Shelley's feeling until the last moments of his life, so that he seems to have been almost impatient for the moment when he would leave the world of Mutability for the world of reality where (62)

> . . . *veil by veil, evil and error fall.*

ADDENDUM (*see above, pp. 134–5*)

The passage so brilliantly emended by Bridges is typical of many in Shelley's MSS. where meaning depends on syntax, syntax on punctuation, and punctuation entirely on editorial resource. The text given here is from the second edition of *The Spirit of Man*, and incorporates adjustments to the punctuation of the first which were made by Bridges on the suggestion of Henry Bradley and others. For its significance in relation to subsequent theories of editing, cf. N. Rogers, 'Punctuating Shelley's Syntax' in *Keats-Shelley Memorial Bulletin*, ed. Dorothy Hewlett, no. xvii, 1966; cf. also Rogers, *The Esdaile Poems*, xxvii, and Preface and Introduction, *passim*.

9. The Cave

SHELLEY's symbols, we have frequently noticed, are not always to be identified precisely or separated analytically: on the contrary they are as likely as not to be fused in his imagination and brought to bear in conjunction upon a point in his poetry. Such a point occurs in the speech we have been examining in our last chapter, where the Shelleyan doctrines of love and Beauty on the one hand and humanitarian idealism on the other are triumphantly fused in a synthesis which comes to its climax in the lines

> And, veil by veil, evil and error fall:
> Such virtue has the cave and place around.

The Veil and the Cave are closely related expressions for closely related conceptions of reality, and the synthesis, generally speaking, corresponds to a fusion of what Shelley the poet was adducing from the *Symposium* and the *Phaedrus* with what Shelley the reformer was bringing in from the *Republic*. The correspondence, however, is only a somewhat rough one, for within the poetical crucible the two symbols become almost indistinguishably blended into the pervading Platonic imagery of darkness and light. The relation of the Cave to the Veil will be found incidental to the subject with which this chapter is principally concerned, namely the implications from the *Republic*[1] which run through the greater part of Shelley's Cave-symbolism and the vital significance of these first in the crucial speech in Act III of *Prometheus Unbound* which we have just been examining—the speech where Prometheus is describing his Cave-Paradise—and then in the philosophical climax of the drama as worked out in that earlier Cave, the Cave of Demogorgon in Act II.

No attentive reader of Shelley's poetry will need to look in *The Shelley Concordance* for evidence that *cave*, *caves*, *cavern*, *caverns*, stand high in the list of his favourite words. The implications are not always Platonic: originally his attraction to the Cave as to the Daemons and other supernatural machinery derived from the

---

[1] Like the *Symposium* and the *Phaedrus* the *Republic* was being studied by Shelley at dates material to the composition of *Prometheus Unbound*. For a comparison of such dates see Jones, *Mary Shelley's Journal*, pp. 217, 224.

imaginings of childhood fostered by his early reading of contemporary horror-fiction; so much he tells us in the 'Hymn to
Intellectual Beauty':[1]

> While yet a boy I sought for ghosts, and sped
>> Through many a listening chamber, cave and ruin,
>> And starlight wood, with fearful steps pursuing
> Hopes of high talk with the departed dead.
> I called on poisonous names with which our youth is fed. . . .

Again there are many places in Shelley's poetry where the Cave
is used merely as a symbol for the human mind without direct
reference to a context[2] so that there will be no need to look for
any special subtleties of nuance: basically, however, the symbol
derives from one particular context in the *Republic* and, where the
derivation is a direct one, it becomes charged with all the subtlety
that Plato can lend or Shelley borrow and adapt.

The subject with which Plato deals in the passage in question[3]
is the progress of the mind from the lowest state of unenlightenment to a knowledge of the Good, and this he illustrates by the
famous allegory in which the world of appearance, in contrast to
the world of reality, is compared to an underground Cave. The
Cave has an entrance open to the light, but the length of the εἴσοδος,
the long passage leading into it from this entrance, is too great to
allow the penetration of daylight. Inside are prisoners, men who
since childhood have been firmly chained in such a manner that
they cannot look behind them where, at some distance away and
higher up, there is a track with a parapet built along it. Behind
the parapet pass people carrying along various artificial objects
including wooden and stone images, which project above it; some
of them are talking, others silent. Since they are unable to turn
the prisoners can see nothing of themselves or of each other; they
can see only the shadows thrown by the firelight upon the wall of
the Cave which is opposite to them. For them in consequence the
passing shadows are the only realities they can conceive, and when
they talk they imagine that their words refer to them: they cannot
conceive that they refer to the objects being carried past behind
their backs. Their ears, like their eyes, are deceived, for when the

---

[1] 49–53, Hutch., p. 531.
[2] e.g. 'Jul. Madd.', 573; 'Ode Lib.' 256 (Hutch., pp. 202, 609).
[3] 514a foll.

people passing behind them speak they naturally believe that these voices, echoed by the Cave, proceed from the shadows passing in front of them. So, if one of them were suddenly unchained and made to turn and face the light, he would be too dazzled to recognize the objects, and would refuse to believe that they were real and that what he had previously believed to be reality was merely meaningless illusion. Still more so if somebody dragged the unchained prisoner up out of the Cave into the outer world of daylight would he be at a loss to distinguish what he saw there: to start with he would find it easiest to make out shadows and then the images of men and things reflected in water[1] before he could make out the things themselves: afterwards it would be easier to watch the heavenly bodies and the sky itself by night, looking at the light of the moon and the stars rather than the sun and the sun's light in the daytime; last of all would he be able to look at the sun itself, not reflected in water but as it is in reality. When he was able at last to do so he would draw the conclusion that it is the sun which produces the seasons and the course of the year and controls everything in the visible world and is in a way the cause of all that he and his companions used to see. As a result he would be happy in his change, and would think with pity of his fellow-prisoners and the standards of judgement which among them had passed for wisdom and the honours awarded among them for their skill in judging by those standards the illusion they saw. Plato goes on to describe what would happen if the man thus enlightened went back to the Cave. Coming out of light into darkness he would find his eyes dimmed, he would be unable to compete with his fellows in delivering opinions on the shadows, and he would then become the object of their mockery, for they would say that it was hardly worth while to make the ascent into the upper world: indeed, if they could lay hands on the man who was trying to set them free and lead them upwards, they would kill him.

In *Prometheus Unbound,* beside the two caves which are sym-

---

[1] Shelley seems to have had this in mind when, viewing an Italian scene in 1821, he took out his pencil and in one of his notebooks recorded the thought on truth and reality which it suggested to him (Bod. MS. Shelley adds. e. 7, p. 236 rev.; Jul. vii. 154). 'Why is the reflection in that canal far more beautiful than the objects it reflects? The colours more vivid yet blended with more harmony; the openings from within into the soft and tender colours of the distant wood and the intersection of the mountain lines surpass and misrepresent truth.'

bolically a part of the drama—those of Demogorgon and of Prometheus—there are various others which receive poetic mention. These, however, are seldom of any philosophical import and their significance is mainly a scenic one. Roughly speaking the Platonization of the Cave follows the Platonization of the drama itself. Its literary origin is Aeschylean and is to be traced to Shelley's reading of the *Prometheus Vinctus* in 1816 and 1817: for the Shelley of the latter year, struggling for his rights against the Lord Chancellor, tortured by a decree which was the punishment for his earlier struggles for human liberty, there was an easily perceptible analogy in the tortured Titan of the Greek play, enchained by celestial tyranny. Here was a subject in which feeling coloured thought, and during the journey to Italy he seems to have brooded on it, if we may judge from the entry he made in Mary's *Journal* on 18 March 1818 at Les Échelles: the Alpine scenery was, he noted,[1]

like that described in the 'Prometheus' of Aeschylus: vast rifts and caverns in granite precipices . . . walls of toppling rocks, only to be scaled, as he describes, by the winged chariot of the Ocean Nymphs.

Such at any rate were the caverns of his first act when he wrote it that autumn at Este: Romantic trappings which, characteristically, his imagination had at once invested with a Grecian significance, Aeschylean to start with. Then, as the subsequent acts developed, the Cave took on a new and deeper meaning, evolved partly through Platonic study but corresponding also with the evolution of Shelley himself. This was the turning-point in his life at which the libertarian was still in the process of being absorbed by the poet: bitter experience had taught him the uselessness of kicking against the pricks by direct political action as in the past: henceforth his fight for liberty would be conducted not by head-on collisions with tyranny but, more subtly, by a campaign to bring to men's minds some of the enlightenment in the face of which, he was convinced, tyranny must fall. What he hoped to do sooner or later was 'to produce a systematical history of what appear . . . the genuine elements of human society':[2] let not his enemies flatter themselves that he would play into their hands as before: he would no longer be the enchained Titan, he would take not

---

[1] Jones, *Mary Shelley's Journal*, pp. 94–95.
[2] Preface to *Prometheus Unbound*, Hutch., p. 207.

Aeschylus but Plato as his model.[1] Out of his experience and, concurrently, as prescribed in the *Symposium*, out of his 'meditation of many doctrines'—Platonic doctrines now—grew his conception of himself not as the hero of Aeschylus' play but as a Platonic man, that man of the *Republic* who had wanted to lead others to the light and whom they, as his reward, had wanted to destroy. It was as such a Platonic man, the apostle of the progress of the mind towards enlightenment, that he projected himself into the poem. As we read it we find that from the second act onwards the Aeschylean echoes in the language are becoming fewer and fewer[2], and that, correspondingly, the caves of the earlier part, mere details of Aeschylean scenery, change and pass into the symbolic cave of Plato. It may be possible perhaps to agree with Professor Notopoulos[3] that we have here an allegory of the freeing of Shelley himself from the captivity and chains of Radicalism, the French Revolution and Godwinism, a process which started in the first place from the Platonism latent in his nature.

To what has been said about the Aeschylus-Plato transition in *Prometheus Unbound* some slight qualification must be added: Shelley would not be Shelley if it were possible to make in his poem an exact distinction of the Aeschylean from the Platonic and of the scenic cave from the allegorical one: indeed, as we shall see, the Cave of the Republic makes its appearance even among the earlier and more predominantly Aeschylean portions. When we return, as now we must, to the scene from the third act which we discussed in the last chapter, we find a characteristic example of how Shelley loved to make the symbolic and the allegorical identifiable with the real and the tangible for here he has taken Plato's Cave and given it a local habitation and a name, not to speak of a description.

If we try to evaluate the contribution made by the *Republic* to the Platonic synthesis in Prometheus' speech in this scene, we find that, whereas in the passages from the *Symposium* and the *Phaedrus* upon which Shelley drew for his Veil-symbolism the search for

---

[1] This was, however, by no means the only point of the preference. See above, p. 65, and below, pp. 153, 160-1.

[2] See A. M. D. Hughes, *Shelley, Poems Published in 1820*, Clarendon Press, 1910. In his notes Professor Hughes carefully records Shelley's echoes of Aeschylean phrases and it is of interest here to notice that whereas in Act I these number 21 there are only 4 in Act II and none in Acts III and IV.

[3] pp. 14-15.

reality is a search for Beauty through Love, the emphasis in the
Cave-allegory of the *Republic* is, rather, on the attainment of
Goodness through Knowledge. But for him the two concepts were
identical : and in the darkness-and-light imagery of his language
they meet and merge, such imagery being indeed, with the slightest
of verbal variations, common to them both as an expression of
the relation between the two worlds, of semblance and reality.
In Prometheus'[1]

> . . . lovely apparitions, dim at first

are combined the 'beautiful bodies' and 'forms' [καλὰ σώματα . . .
εἴδωλα] of the *Symposium* and the *Phaedrus* respectively with the
'images' [εἰκόνες] of the Cave-allegory in the *Republic*: these
apparitions, symbols of Beauty from the first two dialogues and
of Goodness from the third, are *dim at first* both because, in terms
of the *Phaedrus*, Beauty is not clearly apparent on this side of the
Veil owing to men's 'dim sense-perceptions', and because, in
terms of the *Republic*, while Man's mind remains unenlightened
from dwelling in his Cave he cannot at first perceive Goodness :
'Would not his eyes be filled with darkness' [ἆρ' οὐ σκότους ⟨ἂν⟩
ἀνάπλεως σχοίη τοὺς ὀφθαλμούς][2] so that 'at first he would most
easily distinguish shadows' [πρῶτον μὲν τὰς σκιὰς ἂν ῥᾷστα
καθορῷ]?[3] And here is Plato's summary of the allegory as it
relates to Goodness :[4]

> θεὸς δέ που οἶδεν εἰ ἀληθὴς οὖσα τυγχάνει. τὰ δ' οὖν ἐμοὶ φαινόμενα
> οὕτω φαίνεται, ἐν τῷ γνωστῷ τελευταία ἡ τοῦ ἀγαθοῦ ἰδέα καὶ μόγις ὁρᾶ-
> σθαι, ὀφθεῖσα δὲ συλλογιστέα εἶναι ὡς ἄρα πᾶσι πάντων αὕτη ὀρθῶν τε καὶ
> καλῶν αἰτία, ἔν τε ὁρατῷ φῶς καὶ τὸν τούτου κύριον τεκοῦσα, ἔν τε νοητῷ
> αὐτὴ κυρία ἀλήθειαν καὶ νοῦν παρασχομένη, καὶ ὅτι δεῖ ταύτην ἰδεῖν τὸν
> μέλλοντα ἐμφρόνως πράξειν ἢ ἰδίᾳ ἢ δημοσίᾳ.

Heaven knows whether it is true; but this, at any rate, is how it
appears to me. In the world of knowledge, the last thing to be perceived and only with great difficulty is the essential Form of Goodness.
Once it is perceived, the conclusion must follow that, for all things, this
is the cause of whatever is right and good; in the visible world it gives
birth to light and to the lord of light, while it is itself sovereign in the
intelligible world and parent of intelligence and truth. Without having

---

[1] III. iii. 49. See above, p. 135.   [2] *Rep.* 516e.
[3] *Rep.* 516a.   [4] *Rep.* 517b.

had a vision of this Form no one can act with wisdom, either in his own life or in matters of state.[1]

The symbolic unity given to the *Symposium/Phaedrus* passages and these passages from the *Republic* by the darkness-and-light imagery of the language corresponds to common factors in their conception. We have, in both cases, a *progress* conceived as an ascent, in the one case from physical love through ideal love to Beauty-which-is-Reality, in the other from unenlightenment through Knowledge to Goodness-which-is-Reality: in consequence, in the world beyond the Veil Goodness and Beauty are one. It is in the working out of this equation that the essence is to be found of the aesthetic and social teaching expressed in *Prometheus Unbound*: indeed the association and identity of the two is the essence of Shelley's poetical philosophy, for it is when Beauty and Goodness are merged in a common reality that

> . . . veil by veil, evil and error fall

because evil and error are, according to him, mere illusions and must yield to their combined 'virtue and power'—

> Such virtue has the cave and place around.

It is correspondingly that the two terms 'visible' [τὸ ὁρατόν] and 'intelligible' [τὸ νοητόν] applied in the Cave allegory to Goodness are identical with the whole Veil-concept of Beauty, for they apply to the two sides of the Veil, on the one side the mimic world of 'colours idly spread' and on the other the real world, perceptible at last when the senses lose their dimness. Even more of Shelley's aesthetic lies in that reference in the *Republic* to 'the intelligible world' as 'the parent of intelligence and truth': herein is contained that same *Symposium*-derived notion of the creative power of Mind which appears in Prometheus' description of the lovely apparitions as[2]

> the progeny immortal
> Of Music, Sculpture, and rapt Poesy.

The essential form of Goodness, says Plato, is the last thing to be perceived but 'without having had a vision of this Form no one can act with wisdom either in his own life or in matters of state'. Among the things inherent in Shelley's preference of Plato to

---

[1] Cornford, p. 226.   [2] See above, pp. 137 foll.

Aeschylus was just this idea of the regeneration of man. And the identification of the Form of Beauty with the Form of Goodness was the basis of his belief in the regenerative power of poets, 'the unacknowledged legislators of the world'.

So much for Shelley's Platonic synthesis in this speech of *Prometheus Unbound*; it has, as we have seen, implications extending not only into the whole conception of the poem but into his whole conception of poetry. If we stop to consider the implications of his borrowings and adaptations in so far as they cast light upon his working method and poetical development, we should be able to perceive by now that the process involved is not one of deliberate patchwork—a process much less favoured by poets than many modern source-hunters would seem to want us to believe— but rather one of absorption, transmutation, and, in the end, creation—creation of a most original kind. Shelley had read Plato, pondered him, translated him, and drawn his thoughts and his language into his own mind so that he sat there like some resident super-daemon always ready to take a hand in, and indeed to direct when he could, the work that was always astir, enriching it all the time but, so far as he appeared in it, taking from it as much original colour as he lent.

There are numbers of passages where Shelley's use of the Cave symbolism, though based on the *Republic*, shows variations puzzling to those of us who might attempt to interpret it too strictly in the light of its origin. One of these comes early in *Prometheus Unbound*[1], where are lines reminiscent of what Shelley was to say to Trelawny on the Gulf of Leghorn:

> For know there are two worlds of life and death:
> One that which thou beholdest; but the other
> Is underneath the grave, where do inhabit
> The shadows of all forms that think and live
> Till death unite them and they part no more.

What he has done here is to fuse two Platonic notions, firstly the relation of the relative and the eternal world from the *Republic* and secondly the immortality of the soul from the *Phaedo*. And what is confusing about his use of the Cave idea is that for his own dramatic needs he has so far departed from the characteristic notion of the ascent as to make the eternal world 'underneath the

---

[1] I. 195–9, Hutch., p. 212.

grave' a symbol of transcendence *below*: the purpose of the variation here is to lead up to the entrance from among the 'shadows
of all forms' of the 'phantasm' of one of his characters, Jupiter.[1]
Another, and a very fine, variation of Shelley's power to give his
own colour to this Greek imagery comes in the second act[2] where
he views the Earth, by a cosmic extension of the Cave symbolism,
as the shadow of some lovelier spirit, not quite a perfect one, the
pure ἀχρώματός τε καὶ ἀσχημάτιστος καὶ ἀναφὴς οὐσία, but having
none the less a beauty of its own which the Earth acquires by
transference:

> How glorious art thou, Earth! And if thou be
> The shadow of some spirit lovelier still,
> Though evil stain its work, and it should be
> Like its creation, weak yet beautiful,
> I could fall down and worship that and thee.

Throughout the whole of this particular scene the Cave symbol
is predominant, and it ends with the Song of the Spirits exhorting
a descent to a transcendence which, once again, is *below*:[3]

> To the deep, to the deep,
> Down, down!
> Through the shade of sleep,
> Through the cloudy strife
> Of Death and of Life;
> Through the veil and the bar
> Of things which seem and are
> Even to the steps of the remotest throne,
> Down, down!

Shade, veil, things which seem and are—all the usual semblance-
reality terms are here and with them the idea, which will be the
subject of our next chapter, of sleep as a conception related to the
Veil. The Song is, as it were, an overture leading to the fourth
scene of the act, which is laid in the Cave of Demogorgon where
'the veil has fallen'. On the symbolism here hangs the ultimate
interpretation of the problem of evil as conceived in the poem.
Let us give it our most careful attention.

The crux of the problem comes in the long colloquy between

---

[1] The 'lower transcendence' also appears in the somewhat mysterious fragment
'An Allegory', Hutch., p. 624.
[2] ii. iii. 12–16, Hutch., p. 234.   [3] ii. iii. 54–62, Hutch., p. 235.

Demogorgon and Asia, chief speakers in the scene. Dramatically this scene[1] follows the recantation by Prometheus of this curse and the overthrow of Jupiter by the 'virtue and power' of the humanitarian love thus manifested: the proximity of universal regeneration has been symbolized in the opening lines of the Act about the return of spring.[2] But not only has his ἀγάπη-love been operating but also his Shelleyan-Platonic Ἔρως. His aspirations for Asia who is Intellectual Beauty were expressed at the close of the previous Act. Those aspirations have reached her in her Indian vale in the form of a vision of him—'a shade, a shape', the Platonic σκιά, εἴδωλον, or εἰκών—and in the echoes of a voice which have drawn her 'down, down' to the Cave of Demogorgon: these are the echoes of the Cave Allegory in the *Republic*. But the vision and the echoes represent 'a going out of [Prometheus'] own nature, and an identification of [himself] with the beautiful[3] which exists . . . in [a] person'. And to understand the all-important colloquy we must first be as clear as we can about the symbolical relation of Asia to Demogorgon and to his Cave.

Though Shelley's habit of fusing rather than clearly differentiating metaphysical concepts makes it always unsafe to regard any single interpretation of them as exclusive or final, it is my belief that the identification of Demogorgon with Fate or Necessity is fundamentally sound. Professor Grabo's definition[4] may well be quoted again:

> By casting out hate Prometheus has identified himself with the ruling Power of the universe which is Love, and Love commands Destiny or Fate which is Demogorgon.

Demogorgon's Cave is, substantially speaking, the Cave of the *Republic*. Asia comes there to evoke the aid of its mysterious Spirit on behalf of Prometheus. While she is there her preparation takes place for her coming union with the latter, and this is now evolved dialectically. Panthea, who accompanies her, can see only dimly the figure of Demogorgon on his throne: Asia's eyes can see more —'The veil has fallen', she cries. This means, in terms of the Veil-symbol characteristically grafted on to the Cave-symbol, that she can perceive light bursting into the Cave—the radiance, due to the lifting of the Veil by Prometheus' love, is imperceptible to

---

[1] II. iv, Hutch., pp. 236–42. [2] Hutch., p. 227 foll.
[3] See above, pp. 131–2. [4] See above, pp. 55–57.

Panthea. Like the prisoners in Plato she is at first dazzled: her progress towards enlightenment is made through her questionnaire and the answers of Demogorgon. Symbolically this is the progress of Beauty through Knowledge towards Goodness; thereby she, Beauty, will be fitted for her union with and identification with Prometheus[1] who is Mind. This is what is to take place in Demogorgon's Cave which, as far as she is concerned, we might perhaps call the 'Cave of Enlightenment': the culmination of her enlightenment will be her transference to the second cave introduced by Shelley: to this second cave, of which we have had so much to say in the preceding chapter, we might perhaps give the name of 'the Cave of Reality'.

In the questions and answers that follow we have the Education of the Beloved as adapted by Shelley from the idealized παιδεραστία of the *Symposium*: somewhere dimly behind them we catch a glimpse of Shelleyan processes applied to Harriet, Mary, and Emilia. In the gloom she sees what she feels is a living Spirit, but so far it has 'neither limb / Nor form, nor outline' (5–6)—at present she can see only εἰκόνες, images. Demogorgon encourages her and they proceed (7–11):

Demogorgon. Ask what thou wouldst know . . .
Asia. Who made the living world?
Demogorgon.   God.
Asia.   Who made all
   That it contains? thought, passion, reason, will,
   Imagination?
Demogorgon. God: Almighty God.

By 'God', of course, he here means 'the One with its power of consentaneous love, the World Spirit': a reply the meaning of which must be pointedly distinguished from that of his next reply. For when Asia, posing the everlasting theological problem of pain, etc., demands (19)

   And who made terror, madness, crime, remorse . . .?

he only says, somewhat cryptically, three times (28, 31, 33)

                        He reigns.

though his meaning, undoubtedly, is 'Jupiter': he could have helpfully elaborated this in the sense of the poem had he replied 'Jupiter, the "Monarch of Gods and Demons and all Spirits /

---

[1] See above, pp. 131–2.

Save One" . . .'. Therein, in terms of ancient beliefs, is Shelley's view of the conventional God of the Christian churches: a man-made tyrant. Then, in a long, magnificent speech, Asia enumerates the gifts of Prometheus to Jupiter, bestowed on him 'with this law alone, "Let men be free' " (45): his gifts are the gifts of Man's Mind to the world, bestowed with this typical Shelleyan proviso that Mind will work only when liberty exists. Love, Fire, Science, Music, Sculpture, Medicine, Astronomy, and Navigation are all enumerated: a catalogue of the 'progeny immortal' of 'the mind arising bright . . .'. If, she wants to know, these are the powers of man's Mind, *can* man be a slave? And if so who enslaves him? It cannot be Jupiter, for Jupiter trembled at the curse of Prometheus: if not Jupiter, what is the superior power to which, apparently, even Jupiter is a slave? In Demogorgon's answer Shelley states the essence of his belief in free will (110–11):

> All spirits are enslaved which serve things evil:
> Thou knowest if Jupiter be such or no.

Which means that if Jupiter *is* evil and if man serves him, he in turn is enslaved. Asia presses the problem (112):

> Who calledst thou God?

Her enlightenment has not yet progressed to the point of Knowledge where she can apprehend the One, and Demogorgon has to make plain that here he is talking of the only God she knows, the tyrant, the theologians' God:

> I spoke but as ye speak.

The 'ye', of course, implies not only her own but the general inability to make the distinction. But by now her vision is growing accustomed to the light and she begins to perceive that there may be some God beyond this theologians' God: for she asks (114)

> Who is the master of the slave?

by which she means 'if you merely spoke but as I spoke, if you are merely adapting your answers to my limited conceptions, please go ahead and enlarge those conceptions: if it is *not* Jupiter who reigns, who does?' The apparent obscurity of Demogorgon's reply to this has been a puzzle to all who have ever studied *Prometheus Unbound*. Yet, in the light of what we have been discovering in previous chapters about Shelley's Platonic symbolism, perhaps his meaning is not beyond conjecture. His question as to whether Jupiter is evil or no is one about which Asia, faithful friend and watcher over the sleep of his victim Prometheus, can be in no doubt as to the answer. What she does need to know is the answer to another question, the natural corollary of what has preceded: 'if man is ruled by Jupiter only so long as man consents to serve him, who is man's real master?' In other words, 'if Evil, being thus dependent for its existence on the weakness of man's will, is mutable, what is *not* mutable, what is eternal?' The direct and reasonable answer would seem to be 'why, the opposite of Evil, namely Good'. Why does Demogorgon not give this direct answer? There are, I think, two reasons. The first of these concerns Asia, and the second Demogorgon himself.

Asia, according to the terms of Plato's allegory, has not yet *quite* reached the point where she can apprehend the nature of the Good. It is because 'the last thing to be perceived, and only with great difficulty is the Form of Goodness', because, so far, he is not satisfied that her vision is equal to the radiance of the truth of the Good, the Eternal, because her cognition may still be undeveloped beyond that of the Cave-dwellers and therefore unable to perceive more than *images* [εἰκόνες] that he makes the famous answer (116)

. . . the deep truth is imageless.

His answer becomes intelligible, I think, if we interpret it in the light of the passages in the *Republic* which immediately precede the Allegory of the Cave,[1] and where Plato is discussing the stages of cognition; the stages by which progress is made from semblances to reality, from the visible to the intelligible world. The lowest of these stages of cognition is what Plato calls εἰκασία, a word which defies translation but which is etymologically connected with εἰκών 'image' or 'likeness' and with εἰκός 'likely': its meanings embrace the notions of *likeness* (representation), *likening* (comparison), and *estimation of likelihood* (conjecture). What Demogorgon means is that for her, at present, the 'deep truth' (a confusing Shelleyan inversion of what might have been more Platonically expressed, in terms of an *ascent*, as 'the *high* truth') is beyond εἰκασία and if we understand the meanings of this

---

[1] *Rep.* 509d–511e.

Platonic word we can understand the meaning here of *imageless*.
Demogorgon's meaning becomes still plainer perhaps, if we interpret it in the light of the passage, more particularly, where Plato
deals with higher education as a training for escape from the
prison of appearances by training the intellect,[1] first of all, in
mathematics and subsequently in moral philosophy. He speaks
of the visible figures, diagrams and models, etc., which mathe-
maticians use: when, however, we get beyond mathematics into
philosophy, there are truths which cannot be thus represented
diagramatically or by models: i.e. they are *imageless*. Asia, with
her question, is exactly one of those students to whom Plato here
refers[2] τούτοις μὲν ὡς εἰκόσιν αὖ χρώμενοι, ζητοῦντες δὲ αὐτὰ
ἐκεῖνα ἰδεῖν ἃ οὐκ ἂν ἄλλως ἴδοι τις ἢ τῇ διανοίᾳ, 'students seeking
to behold those realities which only thinking can apprehend'.[3]
Διάνοια (meaning *discursive* thinking, or reasoning from one premiss to another) is the penultimate stage of cognition leading to
νόησις (intelligence) or ἐπιστήμη (knowledge). When she is transferred from Demogorgon's Cave of Enlightenment to Prometheus'
Cave of Reality there to unite with Prometheus, who is Mind, her
διάνοια will provide her with the answer. It might almost be said
that Shelley's two Caves correspond to Plato's two worlds,[4] the
visible and the intelligible, τὸ ὁρώμενον and τὸ νοούμενον, and
that Asia's progress to the second Cave by means of her education
in the first corresponds to the Platonic progress of cognition from
one of these worlds to the other.

Again, apart from what we may learn from these places in the
Republic, the answer which Demogorgon seems to evade is inherent
and deducible in the implications of the symbolism which subsequently evolves out of the plot and to which his next words lead
the way (116–20):

> . . . the deep truth is imageless;
> For what would it avail to bid thee gaze
> On the revolving world? What to bid speak
> Fate, Time, Occasion, Chance, and Change? To these
> All things are subject but eternal Love.

The world of semblances, the relative world, is a 'revolving
world' because made up of the cycles of Mutability: it is a world
subject to 'Fate, Time, Occasion, Chance, and Change', things

---

[1] *Rep.* 511b.   [2] *Rep.* 510e.
[3] Cornford, p. 220.   [4] *Rep.* 509d.

themselves which 'change and pass' though 'the One remains':
the images of this world are merely mutable things and 'the deep
truth' is not to be represented among them. When Asia has
passed to the second Cave, the Cave of Reality, and by her
union with Prometheus has attained the fullness of 'eternal Love'
(being at the same time united with Mind), she will be able to
perceive 'the essential Form of Goodness'. Here in the first Cave
she is still in the realm of Fate or Necessity, personified by Demogorgon: she has yet to make the progress from Necessity to love
which Shelley had made between *Queen Mab* and *Prometheus
Unbound* and which corresponds to yet another aspect of his subsequent preference of Plato to Aeschylus, i.e. of the Platonic
Ἔρως to the Aeschylean ἀνάγκη.

So much, in so far as Asia is concerned, for the interpretation
of Demogorgon's answer and the reason for its curious, evasive
appearance. But it must be considered also in relation to Demogorgon himself and his part in the overthrow of Evil, by the
human will. As we saw from his note on the daemon of Socrates
in the *Memorabilia* Shelley's notion was that the operation of the
human will was achieved through the daemon Love. By means
of this daemon Prometheus, who is a δαιμόνιος ἀνήρ[1] in the sense
of the *Symposium*, can 'modify the divine will', i.e. Jupiter's will.
This Love, the ruling power of the universe, operated also, of
course, over all things mutable, one of which is Fate, just named
by Demogorgon, and Fate/Necessity is himself: implicitly, therefore, in the last two lines of his answer, he is admitting his coming
subjection to Love. For he is of the mutable world of semblances
and will fall with Jupiter: while in the Cave of Enlightenment he
is leading Asia to Knowledge she, the idealized Ἔρως, is, at the
same time, working upon him with the virtue and power of the
love she represents to be the instrument of Jupiter's overthrow:
as she progresses towards Reality, the Form of Goodness, the
imageless Truth, he moves ineluctably towards his doom. If we
remember the position which Demogorgon occupies symbolically
at this stage of the poem—caught between the doom ahead of
him and the power of the tyrant to whom for the moment he is
still subject—his riddling replies become even further explicable.
Dramatically, it must be admitted, they do nothing to assist the
scene.

[1] See above, p. 72.

We now come to Asia's transference from the first Cave to the second.[1] She has one more question to ask of Demogorgon: it is to know the hour of Prometheus' triumph over Jupiter. 'Behold', he replies, and she looks where he is pointing to see cars approaching drawn by 'rainbow-wingèd steeds . . .; in each there stands / A wild-eyed charioteer urging their flight'. As the poem mounts to its dramatic and philosophical climax Shelley's symbols mount one upon another. This car with its winged steed is another of those amphibious Shelleyan vehicles which are used as a variation on the Boat-symbol: it is to travel through the 'intermediate space' between divine and mortal realms and its charioteers may be safely identified with these usual 'intermediate spirits', the daemons: the more safely since, in the manner of one of Shelley's drawings[2] of their kindred, 'Their bright locks / Stream like a comet'. These daemons are the Hours, one of which awaits Asia —the Hour which is to unseat Jupiter: they stand for the cyclic succession of Evil by Good and are among the supernatural forces through which the human will of Prometheus can operate over the divine. Watching the strange phenomenon Asia recognizes that it is a practical answer to her final question. She is longing to rejoin Prometheus: her rapture increases as the coursers 'drink the hot speed of desire' and carry her rapidly to the realm of Love and reality. As the fourth scene passes into the fifth they are borne above the mountain-tops and Panthea, who accompanies her sister nymph, cannot understand the sudden radiance which is bursting through the clouds, though the sun has not yet risen: it is the radiance that proceeds from Asia (κάλλος δὲ τότ᾽ ἦν ἰδεῖν λαμπρόν, μακαρίαν ὄψιν) and she finds it almost unbearable. The symbols continue to pile up. Asia is *unveiled* and as they proceed towards the ideal realm, she reflects on the supreme excellence of ideal love and how those who feel it 'Are happier still, after long sufferings, / As I shall soon become'. A Voice in the Air hails her singing: it is, as we know from an uncancelled passage rescued by Locock, the voice of Prometheus coming from her own lips and we must note how, for a particularly magnificent expression of his 'going out' and 'identification with the beautiful', Shelley has invoked the notion of a mystic harmony of Mind and Beauty in terms of music, preceding thereby the

[1] *Prom.* II. iv. 128–II. v. 110, Hutch., pp. 239–42.
[2] See Plate II *b*.

actual union which is to take place in the second Cave. Asia, on her way to achieve that union, is already transformed by the wonders of it: she is 'Life of Life', her 'limbs are *burning* / Through the *vest* which seems to hide them'; she is a '*Lamp of Earth*' and wherever she moves 'Its dim shapes are clad with *brightness*'. Then we have her own answering lyric: her soul is '*an enchanted boat*' moving towards 'Elysian garden *islets*': Love, in the phrase from the *Symposium*, is her 'most beautiful of pilots', and Love now is Prometheus himself, or his effluence,[1] at any rate, which has been projected in that Voice to be with her. Finally she sings (ii. v. 98–110):

> We have passed Age's icy *caves*,
> And Manhood's dark and tossing waves,
> And Youth's smooth ocean, smiling to betray:
> Beyond the glassy gulfs we flee
> Of *shadow-peopled* Infancy,
> Through Death and Birth, to a diviner day.

So does Asia set out on her journey through which, eventually, she is to reach the Second Cave, the Cave of Reality where she will dwell with Prometheus. Thus Beauty, who is also idealized Woman-Love now qualified by preparation in the Cave of Enlightenment, will unite with Mind and be able at last to look upon 'the essential Form of Goodness', the One. All this no doubt, as Professor Grabo points out,[2] is in part at least based upon Neoplatonic notions: the significance of Asia's joy and 'radiance' becomes clear if we interpret her reunion with Prometheus and their subsequent bliss in the Cave of Reality as the return of the spirit of ideal Beauty to the One whence it emanated. But here, as always, what really is of importance is not so much to trace the origins of the notions which Shelley derives and combines together as to notice the total effect constituted cumulatively by the ingredients of his amalgam. Everywhere, in this portion of the poem, we find variety added to variety and then varied again. He has extended Plato's Cave allegory from the *Republic* by the addition of a second Cave; he has used the two

---

[1] See the uncancelled passage printed by Hutch., p. 269. These were among the passages that Shelley translated into Italian for the Platonic enlightenment of Emilia Viviani. Cf. below, pp. 242–3, 342–3.

[2] *Prometheus Unbound: An Interpretation*, p. 89.

Caves to vary from the *Symposium* and the *Phaedrus* Plato's
account of the ascent of the soul; he has varied this at one point
by inverting it to a *descent* towards a downward transcendence; and
now he has introduced another characteristic change. For here in
Asia's lyric he has reversed what Wordsworth did in his 'Immortality Ode' and—introducing perhaps thereby a little touch of
Godwin-perfectibility into the general Platonism of the lines—
he makes Age remotest from Heaven and traces a progress
through Manhood, Youth, and Infancy to the 'divinest day'
which has been lost by Birth and which can only be regained by
Death, a death amounting to a second birth, a rebirth out of the
evil world of Jupiter into the Shelleyan heaven of the third act.
In these last two scenes we have gone the whole round of the usual
symbols: we have had Daemons, the Boat, and the Isle; we have
had the Veil and the Cave with its *shapes*, *dimness*, and *light*; nor
need we doubt that the element across which Asia is making her
voyage is some aërial version of 'the wide Ocean of Intellectual
Beauty'. Now finally Shelley has come round to the New Birth
conception and he proceeds to colour this new heaven of the
reborn with the beauty of the spring: remote from evil this
heaven will be[1]

> A paradise of vaulted bowers,
> Lit by downward-gazing flowers,
> And watery paths that wind between
> Wildernesses calm and green.

Thus his second act ends with the same symbol of regeneration
with which it began: thus, characteristically, making 'thought
Nature and Nature thought', does he herald the sequel to the fall
of tyranny.

Before Asia reaches the second Cave and its poetico-philosophical amenities thus promised, the two main events in the
drama have to take place: the tyrant Jupiter has yet to be overthrown and the hero Prometheus has yet to be Unbound. When
Act III opens Demogorgon is on his way to bring about the first
of these events. From the dramatic point of view this catastrophe
is a failure: the dethronement and surrender take place so suddenly as to be almost ridiculous and give the impression, almost,

---

[1] II. v. 104-7, Hutch., p. 242.

that in the excitement of working out his philosophical climax Shelley had lost interest in the climax of his plot. Jupiter is rejoicing in his conviction that his expected offspring by Thetis will complete his triumph over humanity, incomplete so far because he has never been able to subdue the human will. The car of the Hour arrives and Demogorgon descends: he does not recognize his own son, for it is the way with tyrants to be unaware of the forces they have created for their own destruction. When asked his name Demogorgon replies, with another of his cryptic answers, 'Eternity'. The answer becomes clearer if we understand Eternity to mean 'non-Mutability'.[1] For, according to Shelleyan doctrine, Jupiter is subject to Mutability and so is everything else except love: love alone is eternal; it follows therefore that he is subject to Demogorgon, since the latter is love's instrument—this he has been since Prometheus, by abjuring his curse, cast out hatred and revenge, gaining thereby the 'virtue and power of love' through which he could, in Shelley's phrase, 'modify' him. In addition to the potent effect upon Demogorgon of this ἀγάπη-love of Prometheus, Asia has been working upon him with her own love-influence, the influence of the idealized Ἔρως, so that *both* kinds of Shelleyan love converge upon him at this point and he is doubly the instrument of Eternal love, so that at the moment, functionally, at any rate, he may justly call himself 'Eternity'. Omnipotent as such he immediately prevails over Jupiter; his victory over whom represents the victory of love-dominated Fate. Meanwhile, since he *is* fate, he is himself subject to love and must fall too. Together they sink into the abyss,[2]

> The conqueror and the conquered, and the wreck
> Of that for which they combated.

Thus is Jupiter dethroned. Instead of proceeding directly to the unbinding of Prometheus, Shelley follows this scene with another which, dramatically, is no better: in it he abruptly introduces two new characters, Ocean and Apollo, who awkwardly hold up the action with a somewhat long colloquy descriptive of the last event and its regenerating consequences. To Shelley the philosopher, however, this too was necessary: he could think of no way of showing the universal benefits of liberty than by presenting the

---

[1] Cf. pp. 160–1, above, and for the whole of this interpretation cf. pp. 71–73.
[2] III. i. 78–79, Hutch., p. 244.

Sun-god himself, supreme personification of Platonic radiance,
rejoicing that he is no longer dimmed by the darkness of evil:[1]

> And I shall gaze not on the deeds which make
> My mind obscure with sorrow, as eclipse
> Darkens the sphere I guide. . . .

In the third scene, at last, we come to the unbinding and this too
is very perfunctorily performed, just as if Shelley, impatient to
lead his poem into the philosophical conjunction of Goodness and
Love which is to take place in the second Cave, were anxious to
get it over and done with. Dramatically he might quite easily
have contrived some such simple and more effective device as the
loosening of the hero's chains at Asia's magical touch, but instead
he awkwardly introduces yet another new character, Hercules, to
perform the unbinding: in this perhaps he was anxious to show
symbolically the power of love to command even the personification of strength. To the Cave of Reality Shelley does not take us:
that is to say that he does not set a scene there: he was, however,
willing to peer into futurity at any rate as far as Plato and Lord
Bacon, and so he gives us, through Prometheus' mouth, the wonderful Platonic description so rightly prized by Bridges among
the poetical triumphs of the Spirit of Man. It is the Earth, proprietress of Caves, who puts this second Cave at the disposal of
Prometheus and Asia. In her numerous caverns she houses many
Spirits, some of which have appeared in the first two acts; out of
these—they seem to be 'shapes' mostly, rather than daemons—
she now summons one who, in his likeness of a winged child, takes
on something of the character of a daemon and is to be the intermediary who will guide the pair to their destination. This spirit
is the torchbearer of Earth; in the past he took light from Asia's
eyes and called her mother—we may remember that it was as
'Lamp of Earth' that she was hailed in the previous Act. As usual
the symbols are imprecise but their general meaning is clear:
Earth is welcoming back the radiance of Beauty and Goodness
which can exist only, as Shelley always held, when tyranny has
been banished. All over the earth, meanwhile, liberty is being
proclaimed by that other useful intermediary the Hour. All this
liberty and joy is the result of love and the harmony which love
has brought to the earth extends also to the universe. No better

[1] III. ii. 35–37, Hutch., p. 245.

way for conveying this could have been found than in Asia's words to the Spirit of the Earth:[1]

> And never will we part, till thy chaste sister
> Who guides the frozen and inconstant moon
> Will look on thy more warm and equal light
> Till her heart thaw like flakes of April snow
> And love thee.

The application here to the Moon and the Earth of the 'radiance' and the 'embrace of Beauty' mentioned in Prometheus' description of the second Cave is a magic Shelleyan blend of Platonic imagery with the ideas of modern astronomy.[2]

Thereafter, philosophically, Shelley had no more to add to his poem except a final driving home of the exhortation to his fellow men which it was his intention that it should be, always supposing that there should be a few συνετοί who might be capable of understanding it. Such an exhortation required a final description of the benefits accruing to humanity when Evil has been driven out by love and he put it into the mouth of the Spirit of the Hour who, having proclaimed the reign of liberty to mortals, returns to the divine realm to end Act III with a kind of Greek messenger's speech. Here his poem was to have ended had he not decided later to write a fourth act which should develop lyrically and in a mood of 'boundless, overflowing, bursting gladness' what had been said in the three acts preceding. In the language used in this fourth act caves are not wanting and by way of a final exaltation of Man Shelley resurrects Demogorgon from his abyss and assigns to him the ultimate praise of Prometheus—Necessity owning, and owning proudly, the supremacy of Mind and Love.

Every human mind [wrote Shelley in his 'Essay on Christianity'[3] of 1816–17] has what Lord Bacon calls its 'idola specus', peculiar images which reside in the inner cave of thought.

Few poets have made more use of 'peculiar images' than Shelley and nowhere did he use them with more subtle effect than in

---

[1] III. iv. 86–90, Hutch., p. 251.

[2] Cf. iv. 457 ff., Hutch., p. 265, where the Moon and the Earth are represented as living spirits and their magnetic attraction as the power of love:
> Thou art speeding round the sun
> Brightest world of many a one. . . .

[3] Jul. vi. 241. The reference is to *Novum Organum*, Aphorism 53, and *De aug. scien.* lib. v, c. 4.

Prometheus Unbound. The theme of the poem is the power of the human mind, its imagery, as we are told in the Preface, is 'drawn from the operations of the human mind' and it is in every way characteristic of the mind of the poet who wrote it. It has followed in consequence that in the preceding chapters, more especially the last two, we have had to dwell upon *Prometheus* at some length, for here, essentially, we find his mind in its inner cave: here are the 'peculiar images' which were the mechanism perfected, as far as he could perfect it, for the expression of his thought and feeling; to these, his symbols, we have come along the paths which we picked up from the clues in his working notebooks: these paths—to revert to Shelley's own language in one of the memoranda from which we started—are the threads in Lionel's labyrinth. The mechanism which he sought to perfect in *Prometheus* was one of which he himself was proud, it being, as he said, 'a mechanism never before attempted': this it is in the poem which makes it the culmination of all his previous efforts to 'apprehend minute and remote distinctions of feeling' and the same mechanism of 'peculiar images', allowing as it always did for infinite variation and adaptation, was to serve him through all his later, unremitted efforts 'to communicate the conceptions which result from considering either the moral or the material universe as a whole'.

Shelley's 'cave of inner thought' has several entrances each leading to a fresh view of its secret aspects, and each of them reached by its own special path, a path of symbolism. Before attempting—as we can and shall—to perceive the processes by which his poems grew up within it, we must explore it yet a little further, and in order to do so we must approach it by yet one more of the paths.

10. The Dream of Life

THROUGHOUT Shelley's poetry the idea of *sleep* or *dreams* is one which has the closest kinship with the Veil and the Cave: no better example could be found than the Song of the Spirits which we have had occasion to quote with reference to these last symbols and which begins[1]

> To the deep, to the deep,
>> Down, down!
> Through the shade of sleep. . . .

Together in fact with the Veil and the Cave the Dream of Life makes up a trio of sister-symbols by means of which, using them either singly or collectively, Shelley most notably expressed his Platonically conceived notions of reality. Though from the study of it we shall have little to learn that we have not already learned from our close consideration of the Veil and the Cave, the Dream calls for our attention both by reason of its own fine effectiveness and, even more, for what it adds cumulatively to the effectiveness of its kindred. And since not in symbols only but in a vast accumulated force of *symbolism* lies the strength as well as the difficulty of Shelley's language and thought, we shall take the opportunity in this, the last of our chapters devoted successively to his major symbols, to make something like a final survey of the whole network of symbolism with which the Dream connects.

A convenient preliminary illustration may be seen in a ten-word memorandum written on a page of one of the notebooks of the period 1820–1 :[2]

The story of Zariadres and Odatis being in love in a dream [

When traced to its origin and viewed in the light of its thought-connexions this memorandum proves no less interesting and rewarding than others of its kind. 'The story', which proves to come from Athenaeus,[3] is as follows: Zariadres was king of the country between the Caspian gates and the Tanais. He and Odatis fell in love with each other's images in their dreams. The father of Odatis, who wished her to marry one of his own friends

---

[1] See above, p. 155.   [2] Bod. MS. Shelley adds. e. 9, p. 372 rev.
[3] *Deipnosophistae*, 575b ff.

or near relatives, summoned a gathering of these to a banquet, filled a cup with wine, and bade her hand it to the man she preferred among them. Meanwhile Zariadres, always on the watch for the lady of his dreams and having heard of the banquet, travelled 800 stadia at top speed and arrived in time for a mutual recognition. Odatis handed him the cup at once, whereat he seized her and bore her away in his chariot.

In the light of what we have continually noticed about Shelley's eye for Platonic reflections in all sorts of authors it is not difficult to see what drew him to this story in Athenaeus. Let us turn back to the *Symposium*[1] and see again what Diotima has to say about love and sleep:

> The divine nature cannot immediately communicate with what is human, but all that intercourse and converse which is conceded by the Gods to men, both while they sleep and when they wake, subsists through the intervention of Love: and he who is wise in the science of it is supremely happy, and participates in the daemoniacal nature. . . .

That story he has hit upon might be a mythical extension of Plato's passage and in it together with the Dream notion go most of his favourite symbolical ideas: we have Love the daemon acting in his role of intermediary, Zariadres the δαιμόνιος ἀνήρ who is 'wise in the science of Love' and becomes 'supremely happy'; we have his Ariadne-quest, first inspired, Shelleyan-wise, by a 'lovely apparition dim at first', a καλὸν σῶμα from the *Symposium*, an εἴδωλον from the *Phaedrus*; we have finally the hero's discovery of a concrete, human embodiment of his vision and their flight together—the escape-motif which belongs to the Boat-and-Isle symbolism. Platonically understood the ten-word memorandum amounts to an unwritten Shelley poem. So much symbolism, so much poetry lay suggestible and ready within the Dream idea.

It will have been noticed of the symbols discussed in the preceding chapters that the pattern according to which they evolve is one that hardly varies at all: originating, that is to say, in his youth from some instinctive idea, observation or feeling, a symbol will take colour from his reading—usually in the first place from some indirectly Platonic source; later, as his studies advance, from preferred passages or ideas in Plato—then, while permeating his

[1] 203b, Jul. vii. 198.

maturer poetry, it will somehow acquire a mysterious connexion with his own life and turn up uncannily in his gleanings from other authors; thus reinforced it seems, still more mysteriously and uncannily, to grow to a climax in his mind in the very last period of his life and to be resolved finally in the very manner of his death. An identical pattern of sameness may be traced for the Dream of Life. Its earliest appearance, very probably, is in a poem entitled 'To Liberty' which concludes thus[1]

> ** The pyramids shall fall—
>   And, Monarchs, so shall ye!
> Thrones shall rust in the hall
>   Of forgotten royalty!
> Whilst Virtue, Truth and Peace shall arise,
>   And a Paradise on Earth
> From your fall shall date its birth,
>   And human life shall seem
>   Like a short and happy dream,
> Ere we wake in the daybeam of the skies.**

The manuscript is not dated but the poem seems likely to have been composed some time before 1812, and it is interesting to see the instinctive beginnings of concepts that were later to be developed on a bigger scale. The Dream has not as yet taken quite the shape it was later to have as a semblance-reality symbol but in the context it is closely associated with the consciousness of Mutability and the association is an expression of the triumph of Liberty through ἀρετή, etc.: the whole passage is an anticipation in miniature by the young reformer of that note of 'boundless, overflowing, bursting gladness' with which the mature poet was to end *Prometheus Unbound*. Sleep and waking become recurrently symbolical in *Alastor* (autumn 1815) and the Poet's dream of a veiled maid is a plainly Platonic one. By next year, 1816, Shelley's direct Platonic studies have advanced and his dream symbolism may have absorbed something besides from Wieland's *Agathon* where[2] there is a long discussion of dreams, reality, truth, and madness: Beauty, meanwhile, has taken the place of Liberty as the real centre of the idealist's gravity and in the Hymn where, in

---

[1] Rogers, *The Esdaile Poems*, pp. 21, 41–50.
[2] *The History of Agathon*, by C. M. Wieland, translated from the German original, London, 1773, i. 89 f.

the Platonic terms of light and harmony, he asserts its power over
'Doubt, chance, and mutability' the Dream of Life has a fine
and a prominent place among the symbols there concentrated:[1]

> Thy light alone—like mist o'er mountains driven,
>   Or music by the night-wind sent
>   Through strings of some still instrument,
>   Or music on a midnight stream,
> Gives grace and truth to life's unquiet dream.

Less valuable poetically than the 'Hymn to Intellectual Beauty'
but hardly less interesting as an exhibition, merely, of Shelleyan
symbolism is the poem 'Marianne's Dream'[2] of 1817: here,
brought together within the dream-framework of the poem, we
have the *cope of . . . heaven* (15), later the *stained cope of heaven's
light* (97), the *Boat*—represented by an 'Anchor' (22) and a
'plank' (90)—the Dome (49, 70, 93), and the idea of *veiled vision*
(33, 143): the poem in fact is a sort of blue-print for the maturer
Shelleyan expressions of reality. This is the year, of course, of
The Revolt of Islam, where we find an extended use of the love-
dreaming of *Alastor*. In *Prometheus Unbound* (1818–19) sleep and
waking are again a prominent motif throughout: Prometheus'
dream, his Platonic 'going out' to Asia, has been noticed in the
last chapter.[3] By 1820 the influence of Calderón is being felt—
less noticeably in the symbolic conceptions, wherein Calderón and
Plato are often indistinguishable, than in the style of language; a
case in point is the particularly lovely and effective Conclusion
to 'The Sensitive Plant', where the Dream is used to relate Mind,
Form, and Reality to 'A Lady the wonder of her kind':[4]

> Whether that Lady's gentle mind,
> No longer with the form combined
> Which scattered love, as stars do light,
> Found sadness, where it left delight,
>
> I dare not guess: but in this life
> Of error, ignorance, and strife,
> Where nothing is, but all things seem,
> And we the shadows of the dream,

---

[1] *Hymn to Intellectual Beauty*, 32–36, Hutch., p. 530. For the association with
harmony cf. *Prom.* IV. iii. 36–39; see above, pp. 133–4.

[2] Hutch., p. 536.   [3] See above, pp. 130–2, 156.

[4] III. 118–29, Hutch., p. 596.

It is a modest creed, and yet
Pleasant if one considers it,
To own that death itself must be,
Like all the rest, a mockery.

Here once again, as in the 'Hymn to Intellectual Beauty', the Dream is subtly blended with the Platonic notions of light and harmony but the Calderonian simplicity and delicacy of the wording is very different from the grand, Coleridgean sweep of words which we find in the Hymn. Shelley's symbols by now produce their effect not only from their instinctively apt use and blending but by the variety they acquire from the word-colour and the movement amid which they appear.

Quite a number of the variously dated 'Fragments' which sprinkle the pages of Shelley's poetical works represent the expression of some Platonic or other favourite concept which, as it flitted through his mind, happened to be caught by his pen within the ever ready notebook. One such is the fragment printed under the title 'A Wanderer'. It appears in a notebook of (mainly) the autumn and winter of 1819—on general grounds I think that Mary has erred in dating it '1821':[1]

He wanders, like a day-appearing dream
Through the dim wildernesses of the mind,
Through desert woods, and tracts which seem
Like Ocean, homeless, boundless, unconfined.

Beginning on the next page[2] there follows a longish excursus on the *Agamemnon* of Aeschylus and there can be little doubt that his first line is a translation of line 82 of the play[3]

ὄναρ ἡμερόφαντον ἀλαίνει.

Not many pages away is an excursus on Shakespeare's imagery written for the Preface to *The Cenci*: it was from this that Mary quoted, in her Note on *Prometheus Unbound*, Shelley's passage about Sophocles' line[4]

πολλὰς δ' ὁδοὺς ἐλθόντα φροντίδος πλάνοις

and from this, Platonically dimming them, Shelley seems to have got his 'wildernesses of the mind'. Possibly something of the wildernesses came also from Calderón whose poetry favours them

---

[1] B-H II, *37ᵛ. I give Shelley's punctuation about which he has taken unusual trouble for some reason. Cf. Hutch., p. 659.
[2] B-H II, *38ᵛ-*41ʳ.
[3] The Greek and the English appear on facing pages.   [4] See above, p. 15.

and whom Shelley read that year: possibly the 'desert woods', etc., are the Cascine where Shelley walked and felt the Ocean-stirring might of the West Wind. One way and another the 'day-appearing dream' may be felt to evoke a true enough image of Shelley as he was when, his own mind 'having come by many ways in the wanderings of careful thought', he was at work in *Prometheus Unbound* with 'imagery . . . drawn from the operations of the human mind'.

But it is from 1821 onwards that the Dream of Life seems chiefly to haunt Shelley: evoked anew amid the great surge of Platonic awareness which swept over him at the time of the ill-ness and death of Keats, it moves through his imagination in a steady crescendo till the time of his own death.[1] *Adonais* was written in the first week, or ten days or so, of June and though we have no evidence earlier than 22 October[2] of his reading Plato's *Gorgias*, it is tempting to credit him with earlier knowledge of one most cognate passage:[3]

οὐ γάρ τοι θαυμάζοιμ' ἂν εἰ Εὐριπίδης ἀληθῆ ἐν τοῖσδε λέγει, λέγων
τίς δ' οἶδεν εἰ τὸ ζῆν μέν ἐστι κατθανεῖν
τὸ κατθανεῖν δὲ ζῆν;

καὶ ἡμεῖς τῷ ὄντι ἴσως τέθναμεν· ἤδη γάρ του ἔγωγε καὶ ἤκουσα τῶν σοφῶν ὡς νῦν ἡμεῖς τέθναμεν καὶ τὸ μὲν σῶμά ἐστιν ἡμῖν σῆμα. . . .

For I should not be surprised, you know, if Euripides were right when he says

> But who knows if to live is to be dead
> And to be dead to live?

And perhaps we really are dead: in fact I once heard one of the sages say that we are now dead and the body is our tomb. . . .

Whether or not this directly lent something to *Adonais*,[4] the interest in the dialogue which Shelley felt and mentioned to Hogg must certainly have extended to that σῶμα . . . σῆμα phrase, another neat Greek variant on such later ideas and phrases of his own as appear, for example, in his remark to Trelawny on the Gulf of Spezia,[5] and the idea of the passage had certainly become part of

---

[1] See Ch. 15 *passim*.

[2] Jones, *Letters of Shelley*, ii. 360. In *New Shelley Letters*, ed. W. Scott, Heinemann, 1948, p. 31, the letter is wrongly dated and full of textual errors. See Neville Rogers, 'A Shelley Letter', *T.L.S.*, 25 April 1952.

[3] 492e; tr. N. Rogers.   [4] Cf. *Adonais*, xxxix, Hutch., p. 440.

[5] See above, p. 145, and below, pp. 288–9.

his thinking when he began his last, unfinished poem in June 1822 :[1]

> As in that trance of wondrous thought I lay,
> This was the tenour of my waking dream. . . .

Indeed during those last months of his life, when all his symbols seem to reach a climax in his consciousness, none, excepting the Boat, is more prominent than the Dream of Life. A notable example is the 'Fragments of an Unfinished Drama' which from its opening[2]

> He came like a dream in the dawn of life . . .

to its last lines[3]

>   I too
> Have found a moment's paradise in sleep
> Half compensate a hell of waking sorrow

is a dream-poem: it is a dream-framework that contains the recurrent Boat-Isle symbolism which we discussed in Chapter 6.

Of Shelley's feeling during those final months that human life in general was a dream and his own in particular a dream from which he would shortly wake there are perceptible hints in his manuscripts. It was, for instance, inside the cover of the notebook[4] in which he drafted the 'Unfinished Drama' that he scribbled one of the extracts from Plato which we quoted in Chapter 2. Let us look at it again, for seen in its place in this notebook it not only seems to relate to the meditation of the Indian in the poem but becomes a pointer to the moods and gropings at Lerici:

> Now if a man believes in the existence of beautiful things, but not of Beauty itself, and cannot follow a guide who would lead him to a knowledge of it, is he not living in a dream? Consider: does not dreaming, whether one is awake or asleep, consist in mistaking a semblance for the reality it resembles?

Equally with the *Symposium* passage requoted above in this chapter it might be adduced as a commentary on the story of Zariadres and Odatis: it was one of the first clues to Shelley's symbolism which we picked up and here we find it fitting perfectly with the last besides having fitted, it will be remembered,

---

[1] 'The Triumph of Life', 41–42, Hutch., p. 508.
[2] Hutch., p. 482.   [3] Ibid., p. 488.
[4] Bod. MS. Shelley adds. e. 18. From *Rep.* 476b; tr. Cornford. See above, p. 21.

with a good deal else that has occurred in the intervening chapters. Such is the unity of his symbolic system.

Only a few pages of this notebook separate Shelley's draft of the 'Unfinished Drama' from the draft of his 'Scenes from Goethe's Faust'.[1] When we come to examine the latter we may notice in passing the point at which it makes its start:[2]

Faust

> I had once a lovely dream
> In which I saw an apple-tree,
> Where two fair apples with their gleam
> To climb and taste attracted me.

The Girl

> She with apples you desired
> From Paradise came long ago:
> With you I feel that if required,
> Such still within my garden grow.

This may be mere coincidence but it is an indication of the way Shelley's mind was moving while he was at work in this notebook: the Girl in *Faust*[3] is just one more Ariadne, she is Odatis and the 'guide' of his quotation from the *Republic*: thus dreamed of as a spiritual vision—and sometimes, in some of his lyrics of that time, given human embodiment in Jane Williams—she is Love and Beauty and only by following her can reality be reached.

There is much more in *Faust*, more especially in the 'Walpurgisnacht', which could be seen as fitting into these 1822 thought patterns which, as we shall see later, are astonishingly clear and consistent. But there is a still stronger piece of evidence of their consistency, for as we turn the pages of the draft we suddenly come upon the following twenty-one lines of blank verse:[4]

> **It is a singular world we live in.
> Experience has taught me one thing, that life
> Is made up of strange and unconnected dreams.
> Man thinks he is—and dreams of that he is
> And never wakes to know he does but dream   5
> Some dream they're kings and in a vain delusion
> But tyrannise to serve—and the applauses

---

[1] In Bod. MS. Shelley adds. e. 18. 'Fragments of an Unfinished Drama' end at p. 124 rev. and 'Scenes from Faust' begin at p. 116 rev.

[2] ii. 326–34, Hutch., p. 760.   [3] i. 4127–35.

[4] Bod. MS. Shelley adds. e. 18, p. 60 rev. I give the punctuation of the manuscript.

Of men are written in the clouds, and death
Scatters the breath to less than air, the Miser
Consumes his life in dreaming he is rich   10
His golden dreams but add unto his cares
The poor man dreams he suffers from the scorn
Of the world and calls it misery to live.
And all, to sum up all, dream that they are
None understanding what or why he is.   15
What is this life that we should cling to it?
A phantom-haunted frenzy, a false nature,
A vain and empty shadow, all the good
We prize or aim at only turns to evil—
All life and being are but dreams, and dreams   20
Themselves are but the dreaming of other dreams.**

Several puzzles are at first raised by these lines. In the first place
they are not in the handwriting of Shelley. Comparison with
other manuscripts easily reveals that they were written down by
his constant companion of 1822, Edward Ellerker Williams, but
what of their source and authorship? Are they the work of
Shelley or of Williams? And are they original verses or are they
a translation? The puzzle, it happens, is more easily solved than
many of its kind. Let us tackle the second question first. This is
frequently a wise rule in dealing with unidentified passages in
Shelley's manuscripts, because, whereas in the case of original
compositions we have little to work upon, with a translation on
the other hand if we have evidence of dating, as here, we can
frequently narrow the field from our knowledge of Shelley's contemporary studies. Two things combine to direct our first guesses:
first the remembrance of what Shelley several times mentions as
his favourite studies at Lerici, namely 'Spanish dramas', and
secondly the knowledge of his outstanding tendencies which we
have by now acquired from following his paths of symbolism—
it being his way to discover in one author or literature what he
has discovered in another author or literature—is it not possible
that it may be with the Dream as it was with the Daemons, and
with Ariadne the Guide to Beauty and Knowledge, that is to say
that having encountered it in Greek and German he may be
pursuing it again in Spanish? The guess would be a reasonable
one, even if we did not happen to know of or to have read that
play of Calderón's of which the title itself might supply the answer

—*La vida es sueño*, 'Life's a Dream'. It is, in fact, from a famous speech in the third act that our lines are a translation. For the rest, since there seems to be no evidence that Williams knew the Spanish language while we do know that, with *Hellas*, for example, he sometimes acted as Shelley's amanuensis, there seems to be a by no means unwarrantable supposition that the rendering is Shelley's. Apart from the first two unmetrical lines—possibly due to hasty transcriptions from an illegible Shelley draft—the blank verse is of a better quality than that exemplified in Williams's manuscript play 'The Promise', and the translation, though it is free in some places and in others has missed a line or two of the original, is on the whole good enough for Shelley's. Possibly the initial roughnesses may be due to its being an 'improvise' which Williams took down as he heard it. Here is the Spanish text:[1]

[Es verdad; pues reprimamos
esta fiera condición,
esta furia, esta ambición,
por si alguna vez soñamos;
y sí haremos, pues] estamos   5
en mundo tan singular,
que el vivir sólo es soñar;
y la experiencia me enseña
que el hombre que vive, sueña
lo que es, hasta despertar.   10
Sueña el rey que es rey, y vive
con este engaño mandando,
disponiendo y gobernando;
y este aplauso que recibe
prestado, en el viento escribe;   15
y en cenizas le convierte
la muerte (¡desdicha fuerte!);
[¿que hay quien intente reinar
viendo que ha de despertar
en el sueño de la muerte?]   20
Sueña el rico en su riqueza
que más cuidado le ofrece;
sueña el pobre que padece
su miseria y su pobreza;
[sueña el que a medrar empieza,   25
sueña el que afana y pretende,

---

[1] Aguilar Edition, i. 243. The lines omitted in the translation are enclosed in square brackets. Shelley, of course, may have used an abbreviated text.

sueña el que agravia y ofende,]
y en el mundo, en conclusión,
todos sueñan lo que son,
aunque ninguno lo entiende.   30
[Yo sueño que estoy aquí
destas prisiones cargado,
y soñé que en otro estado
más lisonjero me vi.]
¿Qué es la vida? Un frenesí.   35
¿Qué es la vida? Una ilusión,
una sombra, una ficción,
y el mayor bien es pequeño;
que toda la vida es sueño,
y los sueños, sueños son.   40

Whether the translation is the work, as I think it is, of Shelley or whether it is by Williams or someone else is matter, certainly, of much academic interest. What, however, is of deeper interest is the evidence it affords, when related to Shelley's reading and his converse with Williams, of how his mind was running in 1822. The play may not have been new to him then. His Calderón studies seem to have started at Villa Valsovano in August 1819 under the guidance of Mrs. Gisborne[1] and to have received a further stimulus from the visit of Charles Clairmont, between 4 September and 10 November or thereabouts:[2] for the rest of November, at any rate, he continued them by himself. There seems to be no evidence as to the exact number of plays he read, though we do know that by the end of September—such was his astonishing power of application to a new subject—he had somehow covered twelve and that he considered them 'among the grandest and most perfect productions of the human mind'.[3] Such was the impression the great Spaniard was making upon him during that highly productive autumn and winter, the final period of *Prometheus* and the period of the 'Ode to the West Wind':

[1] Letter to Peacock, 24 Aug. 1819, Jones, *Letters of Shelley*, ii. 114.
[2] Jones, *Mary Shelley's Journal*, p. 123.
[3] Letter to Peacock, 21 Sept. 1819, Jones, *Letters of Shelley*, ii. 120. I have traced only eight plays certainly read: *El mágico prodigioso, La cisma de Inglaterra, El príncipe constante, El purgatorio de San Patricio, La vida es sueño, Los cabellos de Absalón, Los dos amantes del cielo*, and *La devoción de la Cruz*. One must imagine, I think, that Shelley's 'reading' consisted mainly of oral translation by his friends plus interpretative comments of his own. He can as yet hardly have attained the necessary independent competence.

Mary, writing to Mrs. Gisborne on 29 November,[1] noted how the enthusiasm coloured the very style of his conversation: 'Shelley *Calderonized* on the late weather—he called it an epic of rain with an episode of frost & a few similes concerning the fine weather', and Shelley's own letters are full of it, at that time. Now again in 1822 his letters show the same enthusiasm. In so far as *La vida es sueño* is concerned the final enthusiasm is readily understandable. For here, by a chance or a fate which must seem to anybody little short of miraculous, the last of his 'wanderings of careful thought' found their way in and out of a masterpiece which, had it been written by Shelley himself, could hardly have been more closely patterned on Shelleyan concepts of reality and through which run nearly all the paths of Shelleyan-Platonic symbolism that we have been following through his own creative life from the clues which appear in his manuscripts. Let us try to see the play as Shelley saw it.

The first act opens with a mountainous scene in Poland: Calderón, like Shelley, is fond of rocks, wildernesses, or woodland solitudes.[2] On one side of the stage is a lonely tower. Rosaura, the heroine, enters—one of the heroines rather, for there are two. She is dressed as a man, has arrived on a journey from Muscovy and is lost; with her is her servant Clarín, one of those stock, semi-comic *graciosos* whose pedestrian mind acts as a foil in Calderón's plays to the general imaginative development. They look for help towards the tower. Underneath it is a dungeon from which comes the clank of chains and the sound of a voice in lamentation; all is dark within save for the glimmer of a lamp. Out of this Platonic cave emerges the hero, Segismundo, dressed in skins and chained, like one of Plato's prisoners or Shelley's Prometheus. He demands to know why he is so tormented: 'In what,' he asks, 'apart from the crime of being born, can I have so offended heaven that it should chastise me more?' His long, fine speech contains four symmetrical ten-line similes: the bird is free, the beast is free, the fish is free, the rivulet is free, why not himself? He has more soul than the bird, more humane instincts than the beast, a freedom of will not given to the fish, and, finally,

---

[1] Jones, *Letters of Mary W. Shelley*, i. 87.
[2] Cf. the opening of *El magico prodigioso* as translated by Shelley. Hutch., p. 731. 'In the sweet solitude of this calm place,/This intricate wild wilderness of trees...' and the no less Shelleyan phrases of the Spanish: *amena soledad* and *Bellísimo laberinto.*

more life than the rivulet. Each ten lines end with a slightly
varied question the last being

> ¿ y teniendo yo más vida,
> tengo menos libertad?

And I who have more life—shall I have less liberty?[1]

Such were the 'episodes' which Shelley imitated when he
'Calderonized on' the weather: a piece of Spanish poetical
architecture which he borrowed, as we shall see, to contain the
thoughts about freedom which were suggested to him by the West
Wind.[2] Now Rosaura speaks and at first, like Plato's prisoners,
he resents this vision from the outer world and he wants to kill
her because she knows of his sufferings. Then he is smitten by
her beauty: 'Your voice melts me, your presence holds me in
suspense, your look troubles me': his feelings are the feelings of
the lover in the *Phaedrus*. He remembers that though he may seem
a mere beast at present among men and a man among beasts he
has yet a mind:[3]

> y aunque en desdichas tan graves
> la política he estudiado,
> de los brutos enseñado,
> advertido de las aves,
> y de los astros süaves
> los círculos he medido,
> tú sólo, tú has suspendido
> la pasión a mis enojos,
> la suspensión a mis ojos,
> la admiración a mi oído.

Yet even amid my heavy woes I have studied politics, schooled by
the beasts and counselled by the birds and I have measured the spheres
of the fair stars. But you alone have calmed my frenzy, charmed my
eyes and enslaved my hearing.

Like Prometheus and like Shelley he has studied nature and
astronomy, like both he feels at the mere sight of Beauty the
power of 'the mind arising bright'; his gaze grows more and more

---

[1] Tr. N.R., as also the quotations that follow.
[2] See below, p. 226. The chain of similes in 'To a Skylark' also seems to owe
something to Shelley's Calderonizing. See also App. II, pp. 329-33, for Calderón's
Nightingale-Vine-Sunflower episodes and Shelley's translation.
[3] Ag. edn. i. 223.

enraptured. Rosaura is drawn to him and is about to tell him her name and implore his protection when old Clotaldo, the nobleman who is his jailer, rushes in accompanied by soldiers armed with pistols. Segismundo is shut in his cell, and the intruders are disarmed and blindfolded. Clotaldo is agitated at the sight of Rosaura's sword, given her she says by a woman to ensure her protection in Poland: the sword is his own, given long ago to a woman, and he knows Rosaura for his child, his son as he thinks. Like Segismundo on first seeing her he is confused and wonders

> si tales sucesos son
> ilusiones o verdades

—'if these events be illusions or realities'. Here we encounter the Spanish dilemma of conflicting honour, for he is torn between love and paternal duty towards his 'son', come here he learns, to avenge a wrong, and allegiance to his king.

Act II[1] takes us to the palace of the king, King Basilio of Poland. There enter separately Astolfo, Prince of Muscovy, his nephew, and Estrella, Princess of Poland, his niece, the second heroine. Estrella is daughter of the King's eldest sister and Astolfo of a younger sister and they are rivals for the succession, he having no child of his own as heir. Astolfo pays her compliments and offers love; their union, he says, will mean the end of the rivalry. She rejects the compliments and the offer saying that in any case the throne is rightly hers and furthermore that his sincerity is belied by the portrait hanging from his neck. We rightly guess that the portrait, like the sword, is a simple recognition-device and is of Rosaura.

King Basilio now enters with his attendants and is greeted with reverence and compliments. He says he has come to settle their rivalry; first let them listen to what he has to say: it is something he has long had in his mind. In a long speech[2] he refers first of all to the learning for which he has long been famous:

> Esos círculos de nieve,
> esos doseles de vidrio
> que el sol ilumina a rayos,
> que parte la luna a giros:
> esos orbes de diamantes,
> esos globos cristalinos

[1] Ag. edn. i. 226–41.   [2] Ag. edn. i. 227–8.

que las estrellas adornan
y que campean los signos,
son el estudio mayor
de mis años.

Those spheres of snow, those canopies of ice which the rays of the sun illumine and the phases of the moon traverse, those diamond orbs, those crystalline globes which the stars festoon and the signs of the Zodiac beflag—such have been the chief study of my years.

If Shelley had not read this passage when he wrote *Prometheus Unbound*,[1] he must have been very much at home with its sound and colour when he came to it later in 1822. But to Basilio, as to Prometheus, Faust, and Shelley, learning and foreknowledge have brought sorrow. He tells of the birth of his son: the son is Segismundo.

En Clorilene, mi esposa,
tuve un infelice hijo,
en cuyo parte los cielos
se agotaron de prodigios.
Antes que a la luz hermosa
le diese el sepulcro vivo
de un vientre (porque el nacer
y el morir son parecidos),
su madre infinitas veces,
entre ideas y delirios
del sueño, vió que rompía
sus entrañas atrevido
un monstruo en forma de hombre. . . .

By Clorilene, my wife, I had an unhappy son at whose birth the heavens spent themselves in portents. Before he was delivered to the light of day from the living sepulchre of the womb—for birth and death are much alike—his mother many times saw amid the delirious fancies of her dreams a fierce monster in the form of a man who tore through her entrails.

The foreknowledge in a dream is Shelleyan enough and in 'porque el nacer / y el morir son parecidos' Shelley has hit upon an

---

[1] Though he may have read *La vida es sueño* before writing his fourth act he did not learn Spanish till Acts I–III had been written and his own allegorical pattern worked out. The parallels must therefore be regarded not as potential examples of Calderón's influence but as examples of the astonishing skill or coincidence directing Shelley's studies.

almost literal translation of τίς δ' οἶδεν εἰ τὸ ζῆν μέν ἐστι κατθανεῖν / τὸ κατθανεῖν δὲ ζῆν; All this accords well with his opinion in 1822 that it is best to be 'content to see no further into futurity than Plato and Lord Bacon'. For at the child's birth, which occasioned the death of his mother, further omens appeared and King Basilio, having had recourse to his studies, learned that the boy would grow up to be the most cruel of princes and the wickedest of monarchs: his own father would be among those he would trample down. He put it about, therefore, that the child had been still-born and caused him to be imprisoned in a tower in the mountains. But now at last, after many years, his conscience is stirring. Has he any right to deprive Segismundo of liberty? Has he not perhaps been too credulous? At this point the Free Will question enters. Much as Fate or Necessity had been displaced in Shelley's philosophy by the belief in the power of man's mind, so now in the mind of the King belief in destiny begins to yield to a hope that the power of Segismundo's human will may prevail over it. He has made a plan: tomorrow his son shall be released and set on his throne: if he be prudent, wise, and kind, Astolfo, Estrella, and everyone else will benefit from his rule: if he be insolent, reckless, and cruel he shall be returned to the dungeon and his niece and nephew shall marry and reign in his stead. In fact the whole operation of his will depends on his ἀρετή.

All now go out except the King and Clotaldo who detains him and Rosaura and Clarín who are in the background. Clotaldo asks pardon for the irruption into the tower of the stranger, the 'youth'. As Segismundo's imprisonment is about to end in any case this is readily granted: exit the King. Clotaldo returns the sword to Rosaura who reveals her true sex. It is Astolfo, he learns, who has dishonoured her; though betrothed to her he has departed from Muscovy to wed Estrella. 'Alas,' he says, in soliloquy, when she has gone out, 'It is my honour that is wronged, for her problems of honour are her father's', and, meanwhile, Astolfo is a prince, to whom he owes allegiance. 'What a maze', he says, 'Qué confuso laberinto!'

It is at this point that the dramatic allegory really begins to take shape through which Calderón is working out problems of philosophical reality. Clotaldo describes to the King how Segismundo has been drugged, removed from the dungeon, and placed in the royal bed: when he wakes he will be waited on like a king.

All this is in accordance with the commands of Basilio. Clotaldo asks his motives and learns of the moral tests that are to be applied. If they fail, says Basilio as he goes out, Segismundo can be told that his regal state was all a dream—'For', he adds, 'in this world all who live are dreaming.' Clarín comes in to tell Clotaldo that Rosaura, having resumed woman's attire, is now maid of honour to the Princess Estrella. Then we see Segismundo in his new condition: reality is naturally a puzzle to him and he is very ready to believe that his new life is a dream:[1]

> ¿Yo en palacios suntuosos?
> ¿Yo entre telas y brocados?
> ¿Yo cercado de criados
> tan lucidos y briosos? . . .
> Decir que sueño es engaño:
> bien sé que despierto estoy.
> ¿Yo Segismundo no soy?
> Dadme, cielos, desengaño.
> Decidme, ¿qué pudo ser
> esto que a mi fantasía
> sucedió mientras dormía,
> que aquí me he llegado a ver?

I in gorgeous palaces? I among satins and brocades? I surrounded by lackeys in their shining gay livery? To say that I sleep is an illusion: I know well I am awake. Am I not Segismundo? Disillusion me, ye heavens! Tell me, what trick has my fancy played that I should come to behold myself here?

His mood is not unlike the mood of Caliban on waking from his music-induced slumbers, though Caliban speaks from the opposite pole of reality[2]

> . . . then, in dreaming,
> The clouds methought would open and show riches
> Ready to drop upon me, that, when I waked
> I cried to dream again.

With the Shakespearian man-beast, poetically conceived when Calderón was a boy, Segismundo has a certain amount in common, notably that both are victims of the learned arts and the objects of experiments: *The Tempest*, we may remember—a favourite play of Shelley's in his later months—has much to do

---

[1] Ag. edn. i. 233.   [2] Shakespeare, *The Tempest*, III. ii. 149–52.

with dreaming and reality. Clotaldo tries to explain what has happened in the past and Segismundo rounds on him as a traitor and threatens his life. Astolfo intervenes and Clotaldo makes his escape saying, 'Shame on you to show such pride, little knowing you dream'. Then Segismundo proceeds to give a most distressing exhibition of pride and the other qualities which the portents had foretold : he quarrels with the servants, one of whom he throws out of the window for intervening when he makes advances to Estrella, and he threatens Astolfo with death : only with the time-serving Clarín can he agree.

The confrontation of father and son is a close study in free will and destiny as well as semblance and reality. Basilio rebukes Segismundo for the murder of the servant: 'So soon has your coming cost a life! I turn a prisoner into a prince and this is your gratitude.' Segismundo replies that what has been given him is his by right, so that his father ought to be grateful that he asks no more. Such is the situation that has been produced by the King's original, summary attempts to interfere with destiny; his own treatment of his son has made him just the sort of monster he had sought to prevent him from becoming. Basilio warns him to be humble and courteous: this present existence may be merely a dream from which he will wake. Segismundo reflects on this : he knows that he is a creature compact of man and beast—'un compuesto de hombre y fiera'—but he now knows, what he did not know before, that he has a prince's birthright: if he was a prisoner before, this was because he had submitted to his condition but now he will no longer submit. This is Shelley's own view about tyranny as worked out in *Prometheus*, namely that tyranny only exists when the weakness of Man's mind permits it. Shelley's further tenet, as we saw, was that the cultivation of meekness was a necessary part of the power of Man's will: with this Basilio's warning is in line, for until he can become *humilde y blando*,[1] his ἀρετή will be insufficient.

Now comes the confrontation with Rosaura. This vision of beauty, is it real or not? Though she is now arrayed as a woman he is conscious of having seen her somewhere before but wonders if this can have been in a dream. 'But now at last', he says, 'I have found life.' Rosaura says she is merely Astrea, a humble attendant of the Princess Estrella. Playing upon the Spanish meaning of the

---

[1] See above, pp. 53–55.

Princess's name and using a Shelleyan-Platonic image—he all but calls her 'Lamp of Earth'—he replies, 'No, say not so. For you are the sun in whose reflected glory the star lives on your borrowed light.' Here, just where Shelley might, Calderón inserts a hymn to Rosaura which is a hymn to Beauty represented in her: the form, however, is the Calderonian 'episodic' form. In the realm of flowers, says Segismundo, the rose is empress by right of her beauty, among jewels the diamond is emperor by reason of his brilliance, among the planets Lucifer is lord for the same reason: if flowers, jewels, planets are ranked according to their beauty, why then should Rosaura, the equal of rose, diamond, and Lucifer all in one, serve one who is less beautiful? But, as previously with Estrella, he becomes possessive and violent. Clotaldo and Astolfo intervene and he fights with the latter. The King entering, Segismundo insults him and rushes out frenziedly: the King remarks that it is time he was put to sleep again—he has not yet learned humility. Astolfo and Estrella now quarrel about the lady in the locket: he promises to give the portrait to her and goes to fetch it. Rosaura is asked by Estrella to receive it on her behalf. This is a dilemma for her, since she has promised Clotaldo her saviour to remain unknown, he having said that by silence she may win back her honour; against this she is bound by her loyalty to her mistress.

It is the turn of Rosaura and Astolfo to be confronted. She tries to maintain the identity of Astrea but he is not deceived. There is a complicated quarrel about the portrait in the midst of which Estrella returns and she too quarrels with Astolfo.

When Act III opens we have returned to the prison in the tower whither Clotaldo has brought back Segismundo; he is in skins and chained, as before—now his pride ends where it began. He is asleep. Clarín, who has followed and now moralizes hypocritically on his downfall and on the pride by which he had attempted to profit, is put likewise in prison: he knows too many secrets says Clotaldo. Now the King comes into the dungeon and with Clotaldo listens to Segismundo who is muttering in his sleep. 'It is a prince's duty', he says, 'to punish tyrants; Clotaldo shall die at my hands and my father kiss my feet.' Such is *his* reality as he knows it at the moment, though to the listeners the reality is the simple fact that he wants to kill one of his benefactors and humiliate the other. Dreaming of valour and triumph over persecutors Segismundo wakes and at first takes the dungeon for a scene that he is dreaming. But Clotaldo persuades him that he has never left it and has just wakened from a long dream; this he asks him to relate. Segismundo then explains how in his dream Clotaldo had told him he should be Prince of Poland and how this had come true. He had been a master of men and had taken revenge on all but now all his grandeur has faded. One memory alone remains and seems real—the memory of a woman. Deeply moved the King departs and it is here that the speech follows which is translated in Shelley's notebook: it follows directly upon a reminder from Clotaldo that he would have done well to reward his benefactor and tutor since[1]

> ... aun en sueños
> no se pierde el hacer bien.

The good we do is not wasted—even in dreams.

Now there is a sudden irruption of excited soldiers who are looking for their prince: they demand their natural lord; never shall the Muscovite rule over them. At first they take Clarín for the Prince and he, always ready to take what opportunity offers, makes no denial of this identification: when the mistake is discovered he says that as he never claimed what they assumed, the folly and the presumption is on their side, not his. Clarín is the eternal 'little man'; his is the unschooled, unimaginative mind, always calculating chances and ready to profit by them; one of those people who scorn imagination and imaginative people to whom they think they are superior by reason of having their own 'feet firmly on the earth', being at the same time always glad to exploit what they conceive to be the folly of the imaginative. Calderón's use of this minor character—in his day the type of the middle-class, the antithesis of all a nobleman stood for—is a brilliant piece of technique: his aim is what such people like to conceive as 'realism' and he is in sharp contrast to the chief characters who are concerned with *reality*. Nothing could be more effective here than the contrast between the reactions of the pathetic little 'realist' when wrongly hailed as Prince and those of the true Segismundo when the soldiers turn to him. In their assurances that the people want him the latter can see no reality but only illusion and to illusion, this time, he is unwilling to

---

[1] Ag. edn. i. 243.

yield: he has had a vision of kingly state but will base no more upon its baseless fabric which, like an unsubstantial pageant faded, leaves not a wrack behind. Earlier he had prayed for *desengaño*, disillusionment or awareness of illusions, and he now has it:[1]

> ... no quiero majestades
> fingidas, pompas no quiero
> fantásticas, ilusiones
> que al soplo menos ligero
> del aura han de deshacerse,
> bien como el florido almendro,
> que por madrugar sus flores,
> sin aviso y sin consejo,
> al primer soplo se apagan,
> marchitando y desluciendo
> de sus rosados capullos
> belleza, luz y ornamento.

I'll seek no more false majesties, no fantasy of pomp—these are illusions that vanish at the lightest breath of wind like almond-blossoms that wake too soon, imprudent, ill-advised, and perish in the first breath of the breeze, their rosy buds shorn of their beauty, light and ornament.

The soldiers point to the mountains where the people are waiting. Segismundo still believes that he is dreaming and that he will wake at the height of the enchantment; nevertheless he will dare all: 'Atrevámonos a todo!' he cries: man can mock misfortune by meeting it in advance. Such is the power of the human will in him, as in Shelley's Prometheus 'to defy power which seems omnipotent'. Clotaldo fears to be treated as before but Segismundo affectionately reassures him: this time he has learned his lesson, has become 'humilde y blando' and knows that 'the good we do is not wasted even in dreams'. Here again the abjuring of vengeance is a reminiscence of the crisis in *Prometheus Unbound*: love and meekness go to make up the ἀρετή which is to prevail over power.

We return to the royal palace where King Basilio is 'Calderonizing' the prospect of facing an angry mob into three 'episodes' of similes: it is like trying to check a bolting horse, like trying to stay a rushing torrent, like trying to hold up a falling boulder. Astolfo goes out to fight and the King becomes full of reflections: it is by

[1] Ag. edn, i. 245.

his attempts to interfere with fate, he remembers, that he has wrecked his country. Estrella begs him to do what he can to restrain the mob from bloodshed. Clotaldo comes in, does homage, and tells how Segismundo has been set up against his father: he himself has been chivalrously sent by Segismundo to stand at the King's side. Basilio dashes out to fight followed by Estrella who is resolved to fight beside him. Clotaldo is detained by Rosaura, who begs him to save her honour by killing Astolfo. He is caught between loyalty to his daughter and his debt of gratitude to Astolfo for saving his life when he was threatened by Segismundo. There is much argument about these Spanish niceties; finally he agrees to save her honour but not by killing Astolfo; instead he will give her his inheritance and she shall retire into a convent where her honour will be safe. This does not satisfy her at all. She will kill the Prince herself, she says. He appeals in vain to her sense of loyalty to the man who is to be her future ruler: there is a rapier-like thrust and parry of words: 'What', he demands, 'will such an action represent? Mere spite.' 'No,' she replies, 'not spite but honour!' 'Mere folly!'—'No, courage!'—'Frenzy!'— 'No, righteous fury!' Which of these motives, Calderón seems to ask, are semblance and which reality? Here Rosaura, a Shelleyan character in her role of dream-woman to Segismundo, adopts an attitude that is anything but Shelleyan, for she insists on the revenge which, in any eventuality, must ruin her. Clotaldo resolves to perish with her.

The scene changes to the field of battle where we see Segismundo in skins leading soldiers who are on the march; among these is Clarín. Rosaura enters and tells him her unhappy history—how her mother had been betrayed by an 'unknown villain' and how she in turn had been betrayed in Muscovy by Astolfo the Prince, who, having been her husband in all but name, had deserted her to woo the Princess of Poland. She begs him to kill Astolfo, thereby avenging her wrong and securing his own throne. He recognizes her as the woman of what he has now come to believe was his dream-life and says that he will defend her honour: meanwhile he will not look at her, because it is hard to look at her beauty and to look to her honour at the same time. Here, from the Shelleyan-Platonic point of view, is something else that Segismundo has come to learn: the idealization of love has taken the place of previous manifestations of his grosser instincts.

The battle begins. The first casualty is Clarín who, true to his nature, seeks to save himself from danger: a stray shot knocks him dying from his rocky hiding-place. The last words of the poor ignorant fool, the 'realist' who sought to save his life and who fled from the fray in which problems of reality were being fought out, are[1]

> y así, aunque a libraros vais
> de la muerte con huir,
> mirad que vais a morir,
> si está de Dios que muráis.

And so even though you think to save yourself by running, you run to your death, if it is the will of God that you die.

They are a comment on the whole conflict of Fate and Free Will as it is conceived in the play. King Basilio hears them: he who by his science and learning had tried, no less than poor Clarín, to divert the course of Fate and who, no less, has ruined himself, not to speak of his country. He refuses to fly, though the battle has been early lost and he, Clotaldo, and Astolfo are in retreat. Segismundo enters and Basilio prostrates himself. The Prince speaks of the power of Fate and the lesson that has been learned; his father by harshness and injustice had sought to stave off doom: can he succeed where his father failed? No, vengeance never succeeds; he will take none. He raises his father and kneels in his turn. His father forgives him and proclaims him Prince and heir. As in *Prometheus* love and meekness have prevailed.

A few strands of plot and nuance remain to be tidied up. Segismundo bids Astolfo pay his debt of honour to Rosaura by giving her his hand; there is a slight difficulty here for Astolfo's own honour requires that his bride be of unimpeachably noble birth but this is quickly surmounted when Clotaldo reveals her hitherto concealed parentage. Segismundo himself then chooses Estrella for his bride; this transference of his affections from the woman he has called 'the sun' to the woman he has called a mere 'star' seems somewhat abrupt to us, but this part of the dénouement too was required by the Spanish code of honour, according to which it was as important for Segismundo to have an unsullied bride as for Astolfo to have one who was nobly born. All appreciate these arrangements and when, finally, Clotaldo is rewarded for his long

---

[1] Ag. edn. i. 253.

services to the royal house they marvel at the wisdom of their
prince and at the change in him. 'Is it so marvellous', he asks in
his final speech, 'if, being tutored in a dream, I fear to wake and
find myself once more a prisoner? And if this were not so to
dream would be enough, for by dreaming I have learned that all
happiness is but a dream and passes like a dream; henceforth I
will make the most of my own happiness while it lasts, begging
forgiveness for my faults and believing that noble natures are the
most forgiving.'

So, in brief, runs *La vida es sueño*, a play which at every turn is
full of varied subtleties capable of varied interpretations that do
not concern us here. Thus in the great Catholic dramatist of
seventeenth-century Spain did Shelley come to find, mixed up
with the conventions of the honour-code and with such stock
theatrical devices as the business of the locket and the sword, a
good deal of the Platonism which had found its way there out of
the general European tradition, and the effect of this upon a mind
both instinctively inclined to Platonic ideas and, by now, en-
riched with the fruits of intense Platonic study, was quite naturally
a most inspiring one; when we come to discuss his last big poem
'The Triumph of Life' we shall perceive the value of the clue to
his Calderonian moods and thoughts afforded by those lines which
Williams had written into that notebook of 1822. 'Every mind'—
to quote once again[1] what he had written in 1816–17—'has what
Lord Bacon calls "idola specus", peculiar images which reside
in the inner cave of thought . . .' Shelley's own 'peculiar images'
which we have followed through so many paths of his notebook
and his poetry become none the less vivid for his rediscovery of
them gathered into the sleep-allegory of Calderón's 'inner cave'.
Let us turn again for a moment to the 'Fragment of an Unfinished
Drama', the dream-play which, being something of an extem-
porization thrown off in 1822, as Mary tells us, 'for the amusement of the individuals who composed our intimate society', may
be taken as an indication of what was uppermost in his mind:
indeed when the Enchantress makes her spell and she is answered
by a Spirit, the Spirit, though borrowed from Milton's *Comus*[2] as
his opening lines reveal, is at the same time Shelley himself, come
straight from his own 'inner cave' bringing most of its images with
him:[3]

[1] Cf. p. 167 above.   [2] Cf. Milton, *Comus* 1 ff.   [3] *Unf. Dr.*, 15–26, Hutch., p. 483.

Within the silent centre of the earth
My mansion is; where I have lived insphered
From the beginning, and around my sleep
Have woven all the wondrous imagery
Of this dim spot, which mortals call the world;
Infinite depths of unknown elements
Massed into one impenetrable mask;
Sheets of immeasurable fire, and veins
Of gold and stone, and adamantine iron.
And as a veil in which I walk through Heaven
I have wrought mountains, seas, and waves, and clouds,
And lastly light, whose interfusion dawns
In the dark space of interstellar air.

Here, fetched from that 'silent centre' or *cave*, interpenetrating each other and *woven* around sleep we have most of the semblance–reality symbols which were his and Plato's and which he was just then re-encountering in Calderón: the central idea is the contrast between *this dim spot*, the relative world, the world of appearances, and *light*, the light of the real world, the world of eternity. In expressing this idea in his quasi-Miltonic masque it is as a *veil* that he sees his poetry, the bardic vision through which he can catch glimpses, though never more, of 'the moral and material universe as a whole'. One may recall that the *veil* with its wondrous *images* (the εἰκασία of the *Republic*) is less usually an image for poetry than for life itself.[1] But here, it might seem, poetry and life are becoming identified and will attain reality together when the veil is lifted as in his last days Shelley seems to have felt that it soon would be; as he said to Trelawny,[2] 'My mind is made up, I have no fears and some hopes . . .'; his references at the same time to Plato and Lord Bacon look directly back to similar references both in the *Essay on Christianity* of 1816–17 and in the Preface to *Prometheus Unbound*:[3] as regards futurity he would look no farther than these philosophers. Life might be a dream but who knew if a dream might not turn out to be reality? The hopes he had were greater than the fears his more prudent and practical friends sought to instil into him when he went out in his boat: it was not by prudence, the prudence of Clarín, that a philosopher would attempt to oppose fate:[2] 'when

---

[1] e.g. the 'painted veil' sonnet, see Ch. 8, pp. 122–3.
[2] Cf. Ch. 8, p. 145, and Ch. 16, p. 289; see also Ch. 16, for the general subject of Shelley at Lerici.   [3] Hutch., p. 207.

death', he said, 'removes our clay coverings the mystery will be solved'. Here was the 'impenetrable mask' the 'veil in which I walk through Heaven'. And as he so walked, poetically, μεταξὺ θεοῦ τε καὶ θνητοῦ he, the δαιμόνιος ἀνήρ, became the δαίμων, almost. As the daemon he saw himself in more than one way: those last words of what he said to Trelawny on the Boat—itself almost a daemon vessel to his Platonic imagination, as we noticed earlier—are exactly what he said of himself in the lovely lyric in which he appears as another English sprite, no longer Miltonic now but Shakespearian:[1]

> And now, alas! the poor sprite is
> Imprisoned, for some fault of his,
> In a body like a grave. . . .

Shelley's voice of 1822 is, in every sense, the voice of a seer, *non mortale sonans*. Ariel in a sense he had become—not the ballet-fairy Ariel of M. Maurois's popular fantasy but an Ariel endowed with peculiarly Shelleyan attributes: a man half disembodied, half of him a far-flying Platonic daemon, half of him a mortal still having 'no fears and some hopes' about what lay beyond the Veil and ready, like Prospero's servant, to be released from the world of shifting semblances, conscious enough of 'some fault of his' which had made his mortal life so difficult—chiefly, it may be, the fault of letting some of his dreams aspire too absurdly far.

[1] 'With a guitar to Jane', 37-39, Hutch., p. 672.

PART TWO

The wind, the lyre, and the labour

11. Shelley at work: a closer view: 'To a Skylark'

OUR concern in Part I of this book has been with Shelley's mind—with the manner, that is to say, in which, side by side with the evolution of the symbolical system of language by means of which its perceptions and conceptions were communicated in his poetry, its character was shaped out of thought and emotion, study and experience. In Part II we shall be concerned to discover what we can about how, out of a mind thus formed, operating through a system of language thus evolved, his poetry came into being. The basis of the second part of our inquiry, like that of the first, will be his working notebooks through which with the exercise of a little patience it is possible, clue by clue, to follow some of his more significant poems from their generation by thought and emotion to their conception in language and their eventual birth upon his page.

But before we come to individual poems it will be helpful to find out what the notebooks can tell us in a general way about his approach to poetry. This will involve considering, in the first place, how poetry made its approach to him, as it so constantly did whether he would or not. 'Man', he wrote in *A Defence of Poetry*—meaning, of course, Man as represented especially by that specimen of him the Poet whose peculiar gift ('Negative Capability' as Keats[1] called it) made him approachable to poetry:[2]

Man is an instrument over which a series of external and internal impressions are driven, like the alternations of an everchanging wind

---

[1] M. Buxton Forman, *Letters*, p. 82.   [2] Jul. vii. 109.

over an Aeolian lyre, which move it by their motions to an ever-changing melody.

Though here, as in other such passages, we may seem to hear something of the voice of Coleridge it is out of his own *biographia literaria* that he is speaking and he is telling us exactly how he personally experienced the supreme phenomenon in the art of which he was a practitioner. Across a mind sensitive by nature, and trained by the process of controlled evolution we have been studying to[1] 'apprehend minute and remote distinctions of feeling whether relative to external nature or the living beings which surround us', an emotion, an experience, or even a mere idea would sweep, the strings would begin to vibrate and, like opening chords passing into a tune, the poem if it did not dodge conception, as poems will, would be conceived. But generation and conception may both be in vain without the labour which is necessary to bring a poem safely to birth. Of sensibility, powers of apprehension, etc., others of mankind may often have as much as the poet but it is finally his conjoined powers in the hard-learned art of communication which distinguish him from his fellow men and the life and death of a poem depend on what he, the exponent of ποίησις, can *make* of what he has apprehended. This Shelley knew and this is what he was explaining more simply for Medwin when he said that[2] 'the source of poetry is native and involuntary but requires severe labour in its development'. Poetry might approach him like a wind sweeping over an Aeolian lyre but everything then depended on his own approach to the poem. This had to be made by such sheer hard labour as we are about to exemplify.

Let us turn the pages of a notebook particularly full of the variegated stages of ποίησις. A little attentive meteorological observation will easily detect some of the winds that are sweeping through Shelley's mind. Here, for instance, are two facing pages which have frequently been displayed among the Shelley-Rolls treasures in the Bodleian. Let us look first at the left-hand page at which few visitors can have spared more than a glance. At its top we perceive a memorandum in French decipherable, with a little difficulty, as follows:[3]

---

[1] See above, p. 24.   [2] See above, p. 1.
[3] Bod. MS. Shelley adds. e. 12, pp. 62–63. There follow one or two illegible words.

**Rousseau
C'est pourtant lui qui a été la cause de la révolution. Au reste je
ne dois pas m'en plaindre, car j'y ai attrapé le trône**

Underneath is a comment by Shelley:[1]

The sentiment of a rascally Italian cameriere di piazza

There follows, on the same page, part of a much-cancelled draft:

> **Vipers have been bruised and broken
> By the heels which they have stung
> Scorpions made into a token
> Of the danger which is spoken[**

But if the visitor to the Bodleian notices these cryptic scribblings
at all, he does not usually dwell long upon them, for his eye is
caught immediately by the page facing them where words meet
it which have been familiar from schoolroom days, but which
seem the more striking for being set out here in the poet's own
hand, Shelley's copying hand, a very beautiful hand:

> Oct. 25
> Ode to the West Wind
> O wild West Wind thou breath of Autumn's being. . . .

What has the first page to do with the second? Nothing indeed
and yet much, since the contents of both are parts of Shelley and
integral parts. The French quotation I have not yet identified
but there can be no possible doubt as to its purport: it represents
a comment of Napoleon's on Rousseau and what follows is
Shelley's comment on the comment. The draft verses are easily
identifiable by reference to the preceding pages of the notebook:
they are an unpublished, rejected stanza of the poem which Mary
Shelley entitled[2] 'Similes for Two Political Characters of 1819'
and which in the Harvard MS. Fair Copy book are headed 'to
S—th and C—gh', i.e. of course Sidmouth and Castlereagh, the
same statesmen who had been pilloried in *The Mask of Anarchy*
written in September 1819. Now above the opening of the Ode
Shelley has been obliging enough to give us a date—the date, it
proves, of the copying of that portion of it, Stanzas I–III.[3] So,
diverse and unrelated as the three things may *seem* which we have

---

[1] Ibid.   [2] Hutch., p. 573.
[3] Hutch., pp. 577–8; see below, p. 226.

on these pages, we at any rate know for certain that two of them
were in his mind in September and October of 1819. In reality
they do not prove quite so unrelated. We know Shelley's views
about Napoleon: they were expressed as well as anywhere in the
lines which he wrote two years later on the Emperor's death.[1]

> Napoleon's fierce spirit rolled,
> In terror and blood and gold,
> A torrent of ruin to death from his birth. . . .

What Napoleon represented for him was the reign of disorder,
blood, and misery that had spread over Europe: that anarchy
which Shelley feared and hated worse than anything, the one
thing worse than tyranny, the horror that is liable[2] to follow as
Shelley's age had discovered, when men have had recourse to
violent revolutionary methods. It was because tyranny was liable
to provoke men to revolution that Shelley had been so anxious
about the possible results of the 'Manchester Massacre': it was
because they were potential provokers of revolution, the parent
of 'Anarchy, that ghastly birth', that he attacked Sidmouth and
Castlereagh in the *Mask* which was his plea to the working men
of Manchester to adopt not violent but passive methods of resistance in seeking redressal of their wrongs. The point of Shelley's
memorandum may, I think, be safely guessed: 'Here is Napoleon
himself, the Anarch of Anarchs, boasting of the fruits of revolution that they were brought to him, in the end, through the work
of Rousseau the idealist, the man who had sought a better world
than that of eighteenth century tyrannies and who had, in the
end, merely led men towards something worse.' It is a fact that,
although Shelley is still sometimes both praised and blamed as
a revolutionary and even, strangest of all, as an anarchist, he
was, at all times, in favour of governmentary institutions as such
and, except as a last resort—e.g. he could hail with joy the Spanish
and Neapolitan insurrections where peaceful methods seemed to
have failed—he was as opposed to the use of violence against
them as he was to tyrannical violence itself. What he preached
was quite simple: to the rulers the beginnings of reform—reform
was to be a slow process—and to the populace 'Spirit, Patience,
Gentleness': in a word the Platonic virtues of ἀρετή and σωφροσύνη
merging into a near-Christian kind of humanitarian love. This

---

[1] Hutch., pp. 641–2.   [2] See Ch. 16 *passim*.

was what, earlier that year, he had said philosophically in the first three acts of *Prometheus Unbound*. He said it again that autumn not only in *The Mask of Anarchy*, an allegory directly shaped to the Manchester troubles, but also, bringing philosophy into practical political policy, in *A Philosophical View of Reform*. Such were some of his thoughts for humanity which he prayed that the West Wind might drive over the universe. Is it strange that two memoranda concerning them should appear on a page adjacent to a copy of the poem? It was just such things as these, a penetrating comment on modern French history encountered in his reading or news from England of the latest iniquities of Sidmouth and Castlereagh, which could set blowing through his mind that other wind, the ever-changing but seldom-ceasing wind of poetic energy: the chords it awakened might merely die away or they might move it to thought that found much variety of expression both in prose and in verse. How in the Ode poetry made its approach to Shelley we shall see in the next chapter.

The more we look through the notebooks the more we see how many and various were the alternations of the ever-changing poetic afflatus. There were times when, a poem being only partially drafted, it would change direction bearing with it the seeds of another: thus in the midst of his draft for *The Mask of Anarchy* we suddenly come upon these lines:[1]

> *   If the Spade and the plough and the loom
> Could yield ye liberty or peace [*

Both lines were cancelled but the first eventually passed into the last stanza of 'Song to the Men of England'[2] and the pair of them may reasonably be regarded as the germ of the whole piece:

> With plough and spade, and hoe and loom,
> Trace your grave, and build your tomb. . . .

Then, some pages farther on,[3] we come to the third poem, related both to the *Mask* and the Song: one fragment of it, as at present printed, is entitled[4] 'To the People of England'. Readers of the Poetical Works are often conscious of these and other such relationships between poems and fragments of poems: what we become conscious of when we encounter them in the notebooks is

---

[1] B-H II, *36ʳ.   [2] viii. 29–30, Hutch., p. 573.
[3] B-H II, *57ᵛ.   [4] Hutch., p. 573.

the embarrassed struggle of Shelley with the double, triple, or manifold birth which his fertility can give to a single poetical germ-cell, a single feeling or idea. But once one has grown accustomed to this struggle, things that might have appeared strange appear hardly strange at all. It is no surprise to find, for example, in the midst of the British Museum manuscript of *The Mask of Anarchy* some lines which are a rejected version of a passage from *Prometheus Unbound* (iv. 325–7) and which begin

> *Green and azure wanderer
> Happy globe of land and air. . . .*

What has been happening is simply that, revising the *Mask* with Act IV of *Prometheus* still half created in his mind, he suddenly finds that the trochaic movement of the former has started off into rhythmical existence the embryo he already had in his head of a lyric for the latter. But to anyone who stops to reflect upon the interrelation of these varied pieces, large and small, and the way in which they grew up it will be plain enough that, even if the wind which bore their seeds into Shelley's mind does seem to veer and change an occasional degree or two, it is all the time blowing from the same *general* direction: it is the same libertarian wind which was for him at all times one of the most powerful of poetic energies. And should it happen, as it often did, that the seeds blew in more than one direction Shelley would be frequently quite ready to tend them no matter where they fell. Here lies a most important point too often overlooked. When, for instance, Professor G. E. Woodberry was preparing his 1892 edition of Shelley's poems and making use of the Harvard Fair Copy book, the useful textual source which at that time had only recently become available, he deliberately withheld from publication the ballad on a woman driven to prostitution by social conditions, remembering, he has told us,[1] how Captain Silsbee, donor to Harvard of the manuscript volume, had covered the poem with his hand saying that it was 'not quite worthy'. His decision was 'entirely on poetical, not ethical grounds'. Richard Garnett's commendation—Lady Shelley was still vigilantly alive at that time—may have been based on more grounds than one. 'The ballad', he wrote,[1] 'had better remain in obscurity, being

---

[1] *The Shelley Notebook in the Harvard College Library*, reproduced with Notes and Postscript by George Edward Woodberry, Cambridge, Mass., 1929, p. 22.

what you describe it to be. Is it really Shelley's, do you think? If so it must be one of his attempts to compose poetry in a popular style as an aid to political agitation about 1819.' One must allow perhaps for the fact that the general Victorian public as well as the Shelley enthusiasts required the 'divine bard' legend to invest a poet and for the suppression of the ballad on grounds of expediency there may well have been justification. What, however, is both striking and regrettable is the point-missing attitude of both Woodberry and Garnett especially as reflected in the latter's last sentence. Quite apart from the failure of that keen Shelleyan to perceive that the whole of Shelley's political writing of 1819 was directed to a purpose the opposite of inflammatory he failed to perceive not merely the nature but the existence as a unifying force in the poet of the libertarian energy we have spoken of. But neither Garnett nor Woodberry had an opportunity of freely examining, as we now may, the notebook now in the Shelley-Rolls Collection at the Bodleian in which Shelley threw off the *draft* of his ballad. This is the notebook of which we listed the main contents in Chapter 1.[1] A reference to these and a comparison with the Bodleian version of the ballad itself will reveal, in fact, three points: first the amazing ability for self-diversion displayed in his power to turn aside right in the midst of composing so much fine stuff as he has drafted nearby in order to write an efficient and quite moving 'popular piece'; secondly how it carries on into 1820 (Garnett's date is almost certainly wrong) the zeal of 1819 for political versifying; and thirdly how easily and naturally this political zeal may be integrated with such other contents of the notebook as the notes on sexual ethics in Plato and Sir Humphry Davy's work on agricultural chemistry. So much for home affairs —meanwhile the revolution in Spain inspired the 'Ode to Liberty' which is drafted throughout the book. Out of all this emerges a Shelley of whom the ballad is as typical a part in its own way as *Prometheus Unbound*, a Shelley too often disintegrated and underestimated both by his admirers and his enemies and who, when we see him at work, never fails to be doing his best to justify his claim that he is 'formed to communicate the conceptions which result from considering either the moral or the material universe as a whole' or to illustrate his conception of the human mind as something 'wide as the universe'. Too often has he been made the

[1] See above, pp. 7–9.

object of judgement based on a focal point that is not his own. For him the pathetic heroine of his ballad, victim of 'Young Parson Richards', was a figure demanding treatment in verse for exactly the same reason as Beatrice Cenci, another victim of injustice and oppression: her wrongs might be different and different treatment might be required but the point was the same. Prostitution was no more his *theme* in the ballad than incest in *The Cenci*: the theme in both was oppression and female sufferings: this, precisely, was the point missed by Garnett and Woodberry when they deemed the ballad 'not worthy' of Shelley. Had they realized that, basically, his theme in the despised ballad might even be regarded as an adaptation for a less select class of readers of much that was inherent even in the general libertarianism of *Prometheus Unbound*, they would have better understood his approach to poetry—they would, in fact, have seen their poet as a robust and active spirit and not merely a divine bard dreamily waiting for a breeze to stir the lyre or a mischievous child who must be made clean and tidy before appearing in public.

It was, as a rule, when Shelley was less active than usual, or paused from his communication of the more serious consideration of things and could bring himself back to the people and concerns of his own life, that he wrote those lovely, much-anthologized little lyrics which have been so much admired: on these poems like everything else he spared no labour, though as far as their conception went they came to him, it is true, most easily of all and among the pages of his notebooks they seem to spring up like wild flowers. At times we may even see the seeds a-blowing. We have seen how on one occasion his metre took him from the *Mask* into *Prometheus*: another good instance of this kind of transition is found in the notebook where, being busy on a left-hand page with those lines for his *Faust* draft beginning[1]

> Through the mossy sods and stones,
> Stream and streamlet hurry down . . .

and having it in his heart to present Jane Williams with a compliment as well as a guitar, he lets his thoughts stray from his translating to be borne in the same trochaic gust past an intervening right-hand page—which happens to be occupied by a

[1] Bod. MS. Shelley adds. e. 18, 107 rev., 106 rev., 105 rev. 'Scenes from *Faust*', II. ii. 51 ff., Hutch., p. 753.

fine nautical sketch—to take root and flower upon the next left-hand page:[1]

> Ariel to Miranda:—Take
> This slave of Music, for the sake
> Of him who is the slave of thee. . . .

More often it is not a rhythm but an idea which transfers itself, e.g. when he has drafted the third stanza of 'Music'[2] ('I pant for the music which is divine . . .') which ends thus

> And the violet lay dead while the odour flew
> On the wings of the wind o'er the waters blue—

he has hit on a new notion that he appears to find attractive, so, after another four lines, away flies the original idea leaving his first poem to lie dead (or at least unfinished: Mary Shelley later rescued what there was[3]) while the new notion is experimented with

> **It was and is not—let this be
> Thine epitaph and mine poor flower
> Our fortunes are alike poor blossom
> My place and thine together
> For from the time we left her bosom
> We both began to wither**

Those who like to make a closer examination of the germination of a well-known lyric may compare these hitherto unpublished lines with the final version, subsequently printed, into which they emerged on Shelley's very next page[4]

> The odour from the flower is gone
> Which like thy kisses breathed on me. . . .

Music, we know, was more than once the inspiration of lyrics: a famous case is the fragment 'My spirit like a charmèd bark doth swim' inspired by Claire Clairmont's singing at Marlow—the notebook[5] proximity of 'Prince Athanase' suggests that the terza

---

[1] Hutch., p. 672.
[2] Bod. MS. Shelley adds. e. 12, pp. 111–14, Hutch., p. 657.
[3] Mary dates the poem 'Music' 1821 and 'On a Faded Violet' 1818. The manuscript of the second poem is certainly a first draft and I suspect that both poems belong to 1819. Unfortunately this notebook is a particularly difficult one to date accurately.
[4] Hutch., p. 553. See above, p. 50 and n. 3.
[5] MS. Shelley E. 4.

rima may represent another metrical transition. Another is the 'Indian Serenade', which is known to have been inspired by the aria 'Ah perdona'[1] from Mozart's *La clemenza di Tito*, and it is interesting to notice at the head of the draft[2] of this poem a number of curious little vertical pen-marks which seem to correspond to the opening beats of the tune. Similar marks appear in the manuscript of the 'Ode to Naples'[3] and here they are elaborate enough to suggest that Shelley had actually sketched out the rhythmic shape of the first stanza in this odd, idiosyncratic form of prosodic notation: this he did still more elaborately for 'O world! O life! O time!'[4] using another notation system, 'na na, na na na na / na'. Yet another system, 'Hum, humb um Haumb haum aum',[5] is invoked with a fragment we shall have occasion to mention in connexion with *Epipsychidion*, 'The beauty hangs about thee . . .'.

Like certain other poets, and painters and composers as well, Shelley often found that his notebooks came in handy as a kind of 'bottom drawer' in which he could rummage for such odd remnants as might be incorporated into a poem of the moment. Those lines, for instance, in terza rima which proceeded in 1817 out of Claire's singing at Marlow[6] broke away all too soon but the feeling of them, preserved in Shelley's notebook,[7] grew warm again two years later in Italy when he was writing Asia's lyric in *Prometheus Unbound*.[8]

> My soul is an enchanted boat,
> Which, like a sleeping swan, doth float
> Upon the silver waves of thy sweet singing. . . .

It was, in much the same way, at some time previous to the composition of *Adonais* that he had written those lines printed by Sir John Shelley-Rolls and Roger Ingpen[9]

> *Panther-like spirit beautiful and swift. . . .*

Whatever may have been their original connexion they were

---

[1] See H. Buxton Forman in *The Athenaeum*, 31 Aug. 1907.
[2] Bod. MS. Shelley adds. e. 7, p. 144.
[3] Bod. MS. Shelley, adds. e. 8, p. 4.   [4] B-H II, 9ᵛ.
[5] Bod. MS. Shelley, D. 1, f. 104.   [6] See above, p. 98.
[7] Bod. MS. Shelley, E. 4, f. 34ʳ. See Neville Rogers, 'Music at Marlow', in the *Keats-Shelley Memorial Bulletin*, no. v, pp. 20–25.   [8] II. v. 72 ff., Hutch., p. 241.
[9] *Verse and Prose*, p. 42. Bod. MS. Shelley adds. e. 6, p. 18. Cf. above, pp. 12, 264, 272.

there in the notebook when *Adonais* was being planned in it and very little change was needed to evolve from them the stanza beginning[1]

> A pard-like Spirit, beautiful and swift. . . .

Another striking incorporation of a stray fragment became noticeable to me as a result of my long inability to identify a recurrent and somewhat unusual drawing of Shelley's:[2] it seemed, more than anything else, to resemble a cat-o'-nine-tails, or alternatively a comet. Investigating comets I discovered that there was indeed a comet, Winnecke's comet, visible in July 1819, at the time when the notebook was in use, and this reminded me belatedly of the news given by Shelley to Peacock on 6 July 1819[3] of the discovery of the comet by the Shelleys' English maid, Amelia Shields: 'She will make a stir', he added, adapting Wordsworth,[4] 'like a great astronomer.' And so she did, in a way, for down in the same notebook,[5] a little further on, went the lines

> Thou too, O Comet beautiful and fierce

which two years later were incorporated in *Epipsychidion*.[6] Nor was this the only traceable effect upon Shelley's imagination of the blazing astral body to which his attention was called by sharp-eyed Milly for, to say nothing of its possible stimulus to his astronomical imagery in the fourth act of *Prometheus*, it is drawn, amongst other places, upon the page where he has recorded Plato's epigram Ἀστὴρ πρὶν μὲν ἔλαμπες . . . ('Thou wert the morning star among the living . . .') which was to stand at the head of *Adonais*, and thence in the course of time it passed into the Platonic imagery of the poem as

> The soul of Adonais, like a star.

In such ways from Shelley's untidy notebooks can we see his imagination at work making[7] 'Nature thought and thought Nature, the internal external and the external internal', which, said Coleridge, 'is the mystery of genius in the fine arts'.

---

[1] Cf. below, p. 260.
[2] e.g. Bod. MS. Shelley adds. e. 9, p. 314 rev.
[3] Jones, *Letters of Shelley*, ii. 100.
[4] Cf. 'To the Small Celandine': 'Little Flower—I'll make a stir/Like a sage Astronomer.' [5] Bod. MS. Shelley adds. e. 9, p. 196 rev.
[6] 368 ff., Hutch., p. 419. [7] See above, pp. 24–25.

But it is time to cease multiplying general instances of one kind and another and to take a particular example of how poetry worked upon Shelley and Shelley in turn worked upon a poem. An admirable one is afforded by that occasion in the summer of 1820 when Shelley taking a stroll with Mary across the plain of Pisa amid 'the wild fertility of the foreground and the chestnut trees' heard, as Professor Blunden has put it,[1] 'his old friend the skylark carolling overhead as in Buckinghamshire and up sprang his poetry to meet the lark'. The lyric which ensued has become so familiar that we are liable to take for granted the rhythmical ease and spontaneousness of feeling which combine to give it its charm. An unusual glimpse into the hidden workings of genius is afforded by the record we possess[2] of some of the 'severe labour' which could go towards the perfection of a Shelley poem even when it happened to be one of those lyrics which flowed most easily from their 'native and involuntary source'.

Two manuscript versions of 'To a Skylark' are extant. The first, with which we shall be chiefly concerned, occurs in one of the Shelley-Rolls Notebooks; it is a mere fragment consisting of a single page only, the succeeding pages having been torn away: it is exceedingly rough and confused and it bears all the appearances of one of Shelley's first drafts. There seems a reasonable enough likelihood that this was the page that first lay open before him as he sat listening on that summer evening near Leghorn. A tree, perhaps a chestnut, which he has sketched in pencil near the top right-hand corner, might seem further to relate it to the scene. The second of these versions is a facsimile of the fair copy made by Shelley in one of the Harvard Notebooks; this, a complete version, forms the basis of the printed text. It is neatly written but it contains a few corrections and these we shall need to collate with the draft.

Attempts have often been made to reproduce deciphered in print the erasures and counter-erasures in Shelley's drafts but these are not very instructive in themselves: what is important is to discover, if we can, what were the poet's first thoughts and what, in something like their significant order, were the stages of emendation through which embryo lines and stanzas grew towards maturity. Such disentanglement is by no means easy, but it is not impossible. We may notice, for instance, that what he first

[1] *Shelley*, pp. 230-1.   [2] Bod. MS. Shelley adds. e. 6, p. 97 rev.

III

Draft for opening of 'To a Skylark'

wrote normally runs in a direct line across the page, distinct from the jagged tiers of corrections: a guide, too, may often be found in the state of his quill or the variations of his ink—here, in the draft we are examining, it is noticeable that, whereas the original lines are written with a sharp quill in a dark black ink, the corrections have been superimposed in a brownish ink with a very much blunter quill. It should be mentioned that in what follows I have omitted, for the sake of space and clarity, two or three very minor details of the draft; they are without significance but those who wish will find them reproduced in facsimile in Plate III.

At the top of our page of the draft and to the left of the pencilled tree appears the embryo of three lines subsequently incorporated into what is now the sixteenth stanza of the printed text of the poem:

> Heaven is all above
> Yet that in thy joyance
> Languor cannot be[

Below the tree we find the birth of what I believe to be the first two stanzas conceived: they correspond in the printed text to the first stanza and the seventh, but I shall refer to them, in their original order, as stanzas 1 and 2. As they reach their final form lines and phrases will be italicized. Here then, stripped of emendations, is what Shelley first wrote:

1

> What art thou blithe spirit
>   For bird thou hardly art
> That from blue Heaven or near
>   Dost pour from thy full heart
> Such sweet sounds   art

2

> Ah, what thou art we know not
>   But what is like to thee
> From the   star flow not
>   Clear   to see
>   The silver
> As from thy presence showers rich
>   melody

The draft is characteristic. Impulse, which he never lacked, would run madly ahead leaving where he stumbled a blank, a hieroglyph or the indication of a rhyme or an idea; his difficulty, at all times, was to get a line or a stanza completed upon the page before its successors came crowding in; later, if he were moved and had time, he would return to his blanks, etc., art and intelligence joining with newer inspiration to fill them up. All too frequently, alas, he failed to return to them; hence so many of the numerous lacunae which his editors have been obliged to reproduce.

The general feeling of the poem is already apparent in these first beginnings and the stanza form, too, is roughly felt, though the four short lines are limping and the fifth line, in spite of its evolution from a mere shadow to a promising pentameter, has yet to find its measure. A stroke of the pen through syllables which the meaning can spare and the rhythm soon picks up:

> What art thou blithe spirit
> Bird thou hardly art
> That from Heaven or near
> Dost pour thy full heart. . . .

Other improvements to these lines quickly follow. The rhetorical question with which the stanza has opened is changed to an invocation by which the whole poem is helped into motion:[1]

> *Hail to thee blithe spirit. . . .*

Then in the second line 'art' must be avoided since the word is reserved as a rhyme-basis below in line 5. One of Shelley's useful and effective half-rhymes comes in very handily and with it a firmer negation that further strengthens the opening:

> *Bird thou never wert*

It is to be remarked that adjustments of rhyme are rare in Shelley's drafts: whatever else he may have to alter his first rhyming is usually confident and final. With this in view, together with the evidence from stanza 2 that his rhyme-scheme for the poem was already decided, we may safely assume that the omission of 'it' in the third line was due to haste; the word is duly found in the Harvard fair copy and we may conveniently anticipate it here while recording at the same time his elimination of the false accent 'dost pour':

---

[1] With this example of what Shelley could do with a slight touch may be compared the change into question-form of the last line of the 'Ode to the West Wind'. See below, p. 228.

That from Heaven or near it
Pourest thy full heart

Lines 1–4 being completed the stanza proceeds no further in the draft: line 5 is left unfinished though by the erasure of 'Such sweet sounds . . .' and the addition of 'In these . . .' its syntactical shape is prepared.

Now, in stanza 2, redundant syllables, similarly, are chiselled away:

What thou art we know not
What is like to thee

(In the fair copy another change was made to emphasize the various similes which by then had been invented to follow:

What is most like thee).

To emend the next few lines drafted Shelley needs to be something more than a skilled mechanic: it is here that he begins to wrestle with the stuff of poetry itself. His intention is plain: something flowing from some universal source is to be named as a likeness for the song of the skylark. What is that source to be? Line 3 in the draft demands careful scrutiny. A comparison of my transcription on p. 207 with the facsimile on the opposite page will reveal that I have omitted the word 'morning' which appears between 'the' and 'star'. I cannot bring myself to believe that, once he had got a simple metre swinging, any practised verse-writer, let alone Shelley, would be capable of writing

From the morning star flow not . . .

What seems most likely is that he left a space before 'star', as he often did before a noun, to be filled up later when the right adjective appeared: then, after adding 'morning' cancelled 'star' so that the line read, for the moment

From the morning flow not . . .

Soon 'morning', in its turn, was to be cancelled. But although when, in due course, the second stanza of the draft became the seventh stanza of the finished poem, both words had been jettisoned, they, or the idea of them, were to reappear in the fourth and the fifth stanza together with the word 'silver'.

The pale purple even
Melts around thy flight;
Like a star of Heaven,
In the broad daylight . . .

> *Keen as are the arrows*
> *Of that silver sphere,*
> *Whose intense lamp narrows*
> *In the white dawn clear . . .*

Some, including, formerly, myself, have wrongly supposed the 'silver sphere' to be the moon. But the pointed reference to the 'star of heaven' makes plain that Shelley has the planet Venus in mind.[1] The light of Venus does narrow to a pin-point at dawn, while the moon remains the same size and is easily visible. The arrows are not Diana's but Cupid's, a fine Shelleyan nuance: 'Love in the Universe'. But, to return to our draft, stanza 2: Shelley is still juggling with the suggestions of 'liquescence' and 'radiance' suggested by the birdsong. *Clouds*, symbolizing electrical light and energy, were dear to him both as a Platonist and as an amateur of science. Next, I think, we get, for lines 3–4

> From the *clouds* there flow not
> Beams so sweet *to see . . .*

'Beams' does not please him: he vacillates with 'Drops' and 'dewdrops': then finally comes line 4 as we know it

> *Drops so bright to see.*

Clouds may be good, but he is still not satisfied. After trying 'From the clear moon flow not' he finds something very much better:

> From the *rainbow* flow not . . .

With its associations of colour as well as liquescence, the rainbow brings, at the same time, a suggestion of calm after storm, joy after sorrow, etc., exactly suited to the poet's mood and here, in the draft, Shelley was content to leave it. But after writing out the Harvard fair copy he managed, by a brilliant last-minute correction, to pack in his clouds as well:

> *From rainbow clouds there flow not*
> *Drops so bright to see.*

Now, reviewing his stanza as it stands, he gives his attention to the makeshift 'rich'. Something is needed which will add finally to the associations accumulated in *clouds* or *rainbow*, *drops* and *showers*; something, too, which will loosen the rhythm of the line. Instinctively, then, it comes to him—that superb Alexandrine which is to send each stanza soaring with the lark:

> *As from thy presence showers* a rain *of melody.*

[1] For this correction I am most grateful to Mr. Desmond King-Hele.

12. Shelley and the West Wind

WIND, that ancient symbol of life-animating forces, had a peculiar attraction for Shelley. With his passage about wind and the Aeolian lyre we may compare another passage from *A Defence of Poetry*:[1]

. . . the mind in creation is as a fading coal which some invisible influence, like an inconstant wind, wakens to transitory brightness.

This too appears very apt if applied to the processes of his own mind in creation as revealed in his notebooks. When the process chances to be a straightforward one—e.g. when the beauty of the lark's song evokes a lyric which has more in it of momentary joy than deeply centred thought or emotion—a single page of draft may be enough, as we have just seen, to show the stages by which poetry emerges. But there are other times when the creative process is something more than can be described by the fading coal image and might be better described as the firing by some sudden, accidental spark of a vast magazine of accumulated thought and feeling. Such an accumulation had taken place in 1819 when one day in October the poet chanced to take a walk and it was set ablaze by the sudden beauty of 'a woodland near Florence'. For the great 'Ode to the West Wind' which was then generated did not begin with one famous walk in the Cascine: nor indeed did it end there. Its deeper origins and its relationship to the last six months generally of that *annus mirabilis* of 1819 are very revelatory both of its true meaning and of the manner in which poetry could most characteristically come to Shelley. It happens that there is plenty of manuscript evidence to show not only how the fire was lit but how it was kept alive: to show, in fact, how poetry worked upon Shelley and he in turn upon the poetry that came. So extensive is the evidence that we must examine this time not a mere draft or drafts but the results of a careful search through no less than six notebooks. These, for convenience, I shall number from 1 to 6.[2]

[1] Jul. vii. 135.
[2] The notebooks referred to in this chapter are: 'Notebook 1'—B-H II. 'Notebook 2'—Bod. MS. Shelley adds. e. 15. 'Notebook 3'—B-H I. 'Notebook 4'—Bod. MS. Shelley adds. e. 12. 'Notebook 5'—Bod. MS. Shelley adds. e. 6. 'Notebook 6'—The Carl Pforzheimer Notebook.

Shelley's feelings that autumn were sad ones, both when he considered 'the moral and material universe as a whole' and on his own account. By the time he left England in March 1818 his political disillusionment, begun in 1812 at the time of his experiences among the Irish, had been completed by the personal disaster of 1817 when the Lord Chancellor had ruled that owing to his views he was unfit to bring up the two children of his first marriage. From then on the poet in him, somewhat overlaid in the past by the political and theological inquirer, began to come into his own and into the poetry now went the crusading zeal formerly diverted into over-ambitious or quixotic attempts at practical social reform. The change, corresponding as it did to the absorption or superseding in his mind of Godwinism and other eighteenth-century doctrines by Platonism, corresponded to developments we have already traced within his own *Prometheus Unbound*, namely the transition from an Aeschylean to a Platonic tone involving, notably, the introduction of the Platonic notion of love in a form amounting closely to the Christian humanitarian ideal. The Prometheus who triumphs over tyranny after abjuring vengeance is the Shelley of late 1819, bowed beneath his sorrows yet recovering his courage secure in the conviction that good can triumph over evil and love over hate and tortures and that so long as the human will remains strong the hour of triumph will come round just as the seasons come round in turn.

He himself had plenty of opportunity just then for the exercise of his power of will. 1818 had been a year of ill health and sorrows, including some sorrows of which we do not know the real nature and which culminated the mood reflected in the 'Stanzas written in Dejection near Naples'.[1] It had been a year too in which his major creative projects seemed to wither: *Prometheus Unbound*, the chief of them, which had been begun in the autumn, was laid aside till the March and April of the following year. It was the beauty of Rome and 'the vigorous awakening spring' of 1819 which inspired the second and third acts, and that same spring happiness inspired the beginning of *The Cenci*. Then suddenly the happiness was shattered by a blow the more fearful because it fell upon hardly healed wounds. Of the three children born to Mary one had died in England and it was partly a fear of losing the other two to the Lord Chancellor as Harriet's children had been

[1] Hutch., pp. 561–2.

lost that had caused the departure to Italy; a vain precaution it had proved in the case of little Clara whose death at Este had been among the sorrows of the previous year. Now, quite without warning, three-year-old William, delight of his parents, fell ill of an intestinal disorder and died too. A two months' gap in the records of Mary's journal and a medical prescription in Shelley's hand headed[1] τεκνου σκωλεκες [*sic*] are eloquent of the tragedy.

It is during that summer that 'Notebook 1'[2] comes into use. From its record of Shelley's work can be traced the events and the thoughts behind it. These lines, for instance, must undoubtedly refer to William:[3]

> *A swift & hidden spirit of decay
> Which made its victim, as declining day
> Grows beautiful ere darkness [*

In another fragment Shelley tries to look above and beyond the death of his child at the whole vast problem of life, death, and reality which had been occupying him philosophically in *Prometheus Unbound*: echoes of passages in the drama and of a sonnet of 1818, show once again that the Veil symbol was as prominent in his private thinking as in his consideration of the universe.[4]

> *What hast thou done then Lifted up the veil
> Which between that which seems & that which is
> Hangs on the scene of life? With shapes uncertain
> Confusedly oerwrought—tombs palaces
> Baths [?*

The 'tombs palaces / Baths' held intolerable associations for the Shelleys and that sudden breaking off seems somehow a reminder how, three days after the child's death, they left what had been their beloved Rome and set out for Leghorn. Then, some pages on, we find the pathetic lines beginning 'My lost William'[5] which likewise—*bis patriae cecidere manus*—come to a sudden end

> Let me think that through low seeds
> Of sweet flowers & sunny grass

[1] Abinger MS.
[2] The fragments quoted from 'Notebook 1' and 'Notebook 3' were transcribed and privately printed by H. Buxton Forman: see above, p. 15, n. 4.
[3] B-H II, *23^r.
[4] B-H II, *24^r. Cf. above, pp. 122–3. Perhaps the 'painted veil' sonnet may be connected with the death of Clara Shelley.
[5] B-H II, *45^v, *46^r. Hutch., p. 581.

> Into their hues and scents may pass
> A portion [

At the foot of the first page of the draft is noted a funeral inscription Shelley had seen on an urn in Rome μνήμη τῶν ἀγαθῶν ἀει-θαλής.[1] The feeling of both was to be rekindled by Keats's burial near William under the cypresses and oleanders of the Protestant cemetery in Rome: 'He is a portion of the loveliness / Which once he made more lovely.' What concerns us more for the moment is the kinship of the feeling with the regeneration of nature motif which was to provide a climax in the autumn to the 'Ode to the West Wind'. And let us notice how this feeling and the attempt in the preceding fragment to seek Platonic universals show us Shelley, once again, practising his poetical aspiration to 'make thought Nature and Nature thought' even where Nature involved personal emotions centred around matters of life and death. 'I always seek in what I see', he had written to Peacock in the previous year,[2] 'the manifestation of something beyond the present and tangible object.' Beyond present sorrows, beyond the present and tangible beauties of Nature, lay something universal his search for which was to find triumphant expression in the Ode.

But William died in June and thought and feeling had to pass through much varied poetical manifestation before reaching the Ode in October. In July and August Shelley tried to lose his personal sorrows in his labour on *The Cenci*. In early September came news by which his thoughts were switched to more topical sorrows of humanity: this was the news of 'Peterloo', the so-called 'Manchester Massacre'. For Shelley-the-Crusader, a being no longer independently active since being merged in Shelley-the-Poet yet none the less vocal for that, here was a chance not to be missed for exercising the poetical function, dear to both, of preparing men's minds for an improvement in their condition: the case of 'trampled France' had shown him how the horrors of anarchy can ensue when men know their needs but not how best to attain them nor how, in the end, to profit by them. Perhaps the opening dream owes something to the Calderón studies begun in the previous month:[3]

[1] I print the last word from Liddell and Scott. Cf. 'Notes on Sculptures', Jul. vi. 313, where the inscription reads ΤΩΝ ΑΓΑΘΩΝ Η ΜΝΗΜΗ ΑΕΙ ΘΑΛΗΣ which Shelley translates 'The memory of the good is ever green'.

[2] 7 Nov. 1818, Jones, *Letters of Shelley*, ii. 47.

[3] B-H II, 7ʳ. Hutch., p. 338. The idea and title of the poem may have arisen,

As I lay asleep in Italy
There came a voice from over the Sea,
And with great power it forth led me
To walk in the visions of Poesy.

Thus, roused from such a poetic dream, do we see him dashing into action near one end of 'Notebook 1': beginning his *Mask* indeed with 'great power'. Above these lines on the page are others not hitherto perceived, I think, to concern this dream-approach of Poetry.[1]

> *O sudden & inconstant light which shinest
> On us who wander through the night of life
> Whereby we see the past . . . O Power divinest,
> O Knowledge*
> Come thou awakener of the spirit's Ocean
> Zephyr, whom to thy cave or hollow cloud
> No thought can trace . . . feed with thy gentle motion [

The theme on which he has started is the power of Poetry and the dissemination of Knowledge: unable, in Keats's phrase, to 'curb his magnanimity' he breaks down defeated by the sheer grandeur of his conceptions. It was, in fact, the very theme of *A Defence of Poetry* and a comparison with the fading coal passage shows a remarkable similarity in the language: the 'sudden and inconstant light', for instance, is merely a variation on 'transitory brightness' and (as likewise in the Aeolian lyre image) the animating, evocative power is *wind*. But his prose-treatise was not to be written till well over a year later and poetically, long before that, he was to return to his theme when a West Wind, physically felt, evoked from him an Ode in which the *Cloud* and the *Ocean* too were to have their proportionate shares.

Meanwhile, more immediately, he descends from abstractions and it is with his feet more firmly planted on the earth, and his powers well under control that, laying aside his invocation, he sallies in to attack Castlereagh and Sidmouth and to exhort the working classes. We have already noticed how his doctrine of passive resistance forms a common factor between this poem and *Prometheus Unbound* and how, in places, the manuscripts of the two

perhaps, out of Petrarch's *Trionfo della Morte* which Shelley read aloud on 17 Sept. 1819. See Jones, *Mary Shelley's Journal*, p. 124.

[1] Hutch., p. 660, prints the last three lines of this fragment but, like Rossetti whom he follows, omits 'hollow' before 'cloud' and has 'speed' for *feed* in the last line.

poems overlap; it may well be that it was the Manchester affair which inspired him into starting in mid-September an additional fourth act for the latter and one or two additional lyrics for the earlier acts, among them the 'down, down' lyric, the last lines of which

> Resist not the weakness,
> Such strength is in meekness

are found drafted in 'Notebook 1' among pages[1] bearing the draft of the *Mask*—nothing strange here for, as we observed earlier, they exactly echo its main theme that Tyranny is weak because of the eventual inability of tyrants to withstand knowledge and thought:

> Science, Poesy and Thought
> Are thy lamps . . .

was what he preached to humanity for its improvement, salvaging something at least for these lines from his tumbled-down invocation, to Knowledge: it was against them, we may remember, that he drew the paddle-steamer[2] with which he was hoping to start his steamboat service between Leghorn and Marseilles. Metaphysically, meanwhile, Science was coming together with Poetry and Thought[3] in the fourth act of *Prometheus* where enthusiasm for the new developments in astronomy and electricity shine through the whole texture of the imagery and the Platonic symbolism. The conception we find in his broken invocation of Knowledge and the power of mind as something electrical in quality, something lurking in some aerial 'cave or hollow cloud', some elemental power directing all mankind, comes out in his Preface where he says 'the cloud of mind is discharging its collected lightning'.[4] When the clouds found their way into the Ode they were 'angels of rain and lightning'—symbolical of Knowledge and, at the same time, conveyors, physically, of energy: to give the word its Greek sense 'messengers', evangelists almost, of 'Science, Poesy and Thought'.

In October 1819 Shelley and Mary, now near the end of a new pregnancy, moved from Leghorn to Florence where they installed themselves in Via Valfonda near Santa Maria Novella.

---

[1] B-H II, 24^v and 25^r.   [2] B-H II, 16^v. Cf. above, pp. 93–95.
[3] e.g. characteristically, on 22 Sept. 1819, Mary notes 'Shelley reads Calderón and talks about the steam engine', Jones, *Mary Shelley's Journal*, p. 124.
[4] The combination of the Platonic and the scientific is to be noted in this phrase.

In mid-October something happened that fanned the smouldering fire in Shelley's mind—going one day into Delesert's reading-room he came upon the number of the *Quarterly* which contained a bitter attack upon *The Revolt of Islam*. Outwardly he proceeded to show amusement rather than annoyance. 'The only remark worth notice',[1] he wrote on 15 October to his publisher Ollier, 'is the assertion that I imitate Wordsworth.' There was much of Wordsworth's work that he admired and remembered but he deprecated the older poet's secession from the Radicalism of his youth and his apparent opinions just then that 'ignorance and force were the best allies of purity and virtue' and before the month was out he had filled what I am calling 'Notebook 2' with the draft of *Peter Bell the Third*, his gay and witty satire of Wordsworth's recently published *Peter Bell*:

> *A very heroic* poem

he called it to Hunt on 2 November.[2] Mary was then busy copying it out:

> I suspect [he wrote, and his italics need to be noted] the last thing she will do before the *new birth*.

In the same letter he added that Southey, he was sure, was 'the perverse-hearted writer of these calumnies'. 'Notebook 1' contains a fragment making fun of both poets, together with Coleridge, as political renegades, able, like Proteus of ancient legend, to change their shapes at will, impossible to grasp.[3]

> *Proteus Wordsworth who shall bind thee
> Proteus Coleridge who shall find thee
> Hyperprotean Proteus, Southey,
> Who shall catch thee who shall know thee
> Hecate & the Trinity
> Are but feeble types of thee
> Thou polyhedric polyglot
> And polymorphic I know what
> Hundred-headed Imp of change
> Never
> Aristaeus Menelaus [*

---

[1] Jones, *Letters of Shelley*, ii. 127.   [2] Ibid. ii. 135.

[3] B-H II, *27ᵛ. This fragment may, conceivably, be the germ of *Peter Bell the Third*: cf. in the Dedication (Hutch., p. 346) 'Peter is a polyhedric Peter, or a Peter with many sides. He changes colours like a chameleon, and his coat is like a snake. He is a Proteus of a Peter. . . .'

But he could not laugh away the deeper anxiety. What was the use of his *Mask*, of his *Prometheus*, what was the use of struggling to spread Knowledge if nobody listened? Were the children of his mind to suffer 'a swift and sudden spirit of decay' like the children of his body?—a thought much with him as he wondered about the child so soon to be born. And as far as personal sensitivity went Shelley was not very different from the rest of us in matters concerning his reputation. We may well connect with the attack of the *Quarterly* the lines printed under the title 'An Exhortation'[1] which went down in 'Notebook 1' ('My lost William...' is drafted on the preceding pages).[2]

> Chameleons feed on light and air:
> Poets' food is love and fame....

For him, as for others, some degree of fame was necessary for survival. Yet what concerned him more than a personal survival was the perpetuity of what he wrote. Certain phrases of the review stuck in his memory, one in particular: 'like the Egyptians of old the wheels of his chariot are broken, the "path of mighty waters" closes in on him behind and a still deeper ocean is before him.' He found it difficult to conquer the doubts raised in him by such an attack: might not a poet just as well abandon his struggles to teach humanity 'Spirit, Patience, Gentleness', as he had been trying to do in the *Mask*, if he were to be eclipsed by the apostles of 'ignorance and force'? But even if men thus obscured his light he must continue to show it: otherwise he would offend against the light of Intellectual Beauty itself of which he is the representative, his poetry being its microcosm. He roughly sketches an eclipse and, astronomic imagery mingling typically with, once again, the Platonic symbol of light—that 'sudden and inconstant light', that 'transitory brightness' of his inspiration which must be kept alive at any cost, he sets down his resolve.[3]

> *Hold—divine image
> Eclipsed Sun—Planet without a beam
> Wilt thou offend the Sun thou emblemest
> By blotting out the light of written thought [?*

The manuscript position of this fragment is worth noticing: it

[1] B-H II, *47^v, *48^r.   [2] B-H II, *45^v, *46^r. Hutch., p. 579.
[3] B-H II, 25^r.

occurs immediately above those lines for *Prometheus*, 'Resist not the weakness / Such strength is in meekness' which, as we have seen, come right in the midst of the draft of *The Mask of Anarchy*.

Between the writing of his letter to Ollier referring to the *Quarterly* and his letter to Hunt referring to his satire on Wordsworth Shelley had worked himself by a mixture of courage and humour into a mood in which he could practise what he had preached in *Prometheus* and the *Mask*. We find yet another laugh at the 'apostle of ignorance and force' for his conception of Carnage as God's daughter:[1]

> *A poet of the finest water
> Says that Carnage is God's daughter
> This poet lieth as I take
> Under an immense mistake
> As many a man before has done
> Who thinks his spouse's child his own.*

Then, one day when he was walking in the Cascine woods, he came across a fountain representing Narcissus and copied into a notebook—'Notebook 3'—an inscription upon it about the death of that celebrated self-lover of antiquity:[2]

> *Eterno monumento in questo loco
> generosa pietà fonda a Narciso
> che vagheggiando al fonte il proprio viso
> morì consunto d'amoroso foco.*

Noble pity set up in this place an everlasting monument to Narcissus who admiring his own face within the fountain perished in the fire of love.

He remembered very readily how easily one might fall into self-love through that very self-pity to which he was at the moment a prey. Should he yield to it and perish like Narcissus? Then he remembered the rest of the myth and how after the death of the boy the nymph Echo had pined away into a sound. Incongruously, in his mind from which he was seeking to banish hatred in accordance with his precepts, the nymph became a reviewer whose passion, unlike his in being a hate-passion instead of a

---

[1] B-H II, *51ᵛ. The offending line ('Thanksgiving Ode', 1816, xii. 23), 'Yea Carnage is God's daughter', was mocked at also by Byron (*Don Juan*, viii. ix). Wordsworth removed it from other editions published in his lifetime.

[2] B-H I, *8ʳ.

love-passion, had at least this resemblance that being equally unreciprocated it was equally without hope. Therefore, he says in conclusion to his 'Lines to a Reviewer', not without a smile at himself:[1]

> Of your antipathy
> If I am the Narcissus, you are free
> To pine into a sound with hating me.

Having his little say first about Wordsworth and then about the reviewers had been a κάθαρσις for Shelley. He would not be like the former, at once a turncoat-chameleon and an 'apostle of ignorance and force': he would not hate the latter, his enemies, but would show them 'what strength is in meekness'. The poem for which he was all ready would be, not least, an assertion of such strength.

Shelley's capacity for seeking, and finding, in what he saw 'the manifestation of something beyond the present and tangible object' is admirably illustrated by the use to which he put the Italian inscription. Then, five or six pages away[2]—the fruit of his new Spanish studies—we come across three lines from Act I of *El Príncipe Constante*[3] with a translation appended.

> *A florecer las rosas madrugaron
> y para envejecerse florecieron
> cuna y sepulcro en un botón hallaron

The roses arose early to blossom & they blossomed to grow old & they found a cradle & a sepulchre in a bud.*

Calderón's lovely little nature-image, being so apt to Shelley's own favourite symbol of the regeneration of the seasons and at the same time to the bitter consciousness that summer had brought him of the proximity of the cradle and the grave, passed easily into the thoughts that were with him on his autumn walks. The perishing things of Nature made him think again of the doom that seemed to lie heavy on the creations both of his mind and of his body:[4]

> If I walk in Autumn even
> While the dead leaves pass
> If I look on Spring's soft heaven,—
> Something is not there which was.

---

[1] B-H II, *28ᵛ. Hutch., p. 625.   [2] B-H I, *11ᵛ. Cf. also above, p. 50.
[3] Ag. edn., i. 927.   [4] B-H I, *13. For textual variants cf. Hutch., p. 659.

> Winter's wondrous rain & snow,
> Summer clouds, where are they now?

Everywhere here, in leaves, clouds, and the passing seasons themselves, he could 'seek the manifestation of something beyond': Narcissus-like introspection began to disappear. What we discover on the page following these lines—they are in the same notebook, 'Notebook 3', as the Italian quatrain and the lines of Spanish—is a substantial preliminary version of the 'Ode to the West Wind'.

In the composition of the Ode five stages are discernible.

> This poem [runs Shelley's footnote[1]] was conceived and chiefly written in a wood that skirts the Arno, near Florence. . . .

The first three stages are found in 'Notebook 3': roughly speaking the word 'conceived' may be interpreted as referring to Stage One and Stage Two and the phrase 'chiefly written' to Stage Three, though if we wished to apply the biological metaphor more strictly we might describe Stage Two by itself as the stage of conception and regard Stage One as representing the preliminary process of generation which actually took place in the Cascine.

Stage One begins with desultory, descriptive fragments about the walk. It was perhaps as he walked along the Arno from Via Valfonda that, with his usual attraction to reflections in water—we have seen their Platonic significance for him—he paused to note down lines which might have a 'bottom-drawer' usefulness like other generalities so collected[2]

> *Within the surface of the fleeting river
> The wrinkled image of the   lay
> Immoveably unquiet; it[*

Extended by a Wordsworth reminiscence[3]

>   and for ever
> It trembles but it cannot pass away

they did indeed come in handy twice: once for the 'Ode to Liberty'[4] and once for the poem about evening at Pisa.[5] For the 'Ode to the West Wind' they were rejected, or rather, it may be,

---

[1] Hutch., p. 577.   [2] B-H I, *3r.
[3] Cf. 'Elegiac Stanzas Suggested by a Picture of Peele Castle in a Storm', 7–8: 'Whene'er I looked thy Image was still there; / It trembled but it never passed away.'   [4] Hutch., p. 603.   [5] Hutch., p. 654.

changed, to suit the reflections in Baiae's bay in the third stanza.
Soon Shelley reached the wood :[1]

> *A lone wood walk, where meeting branches lean
>   Even from the Earth, to mingle the delight
>   That lives within the light.*

He tells us the date and something of his mood—gay to start with
then yielding to the sombre autumn scene. His metres too are
changeable and the broken lines and lacunae are typical of the
pauseless speed of his composing[2]

> *'Twas the 20th of October
>   And the woods had all grown sober
>   As a man does when his hair
>   Looks as theirs did grey & spare
>   When the dead leaves
>   As to mock the stupid
>   Like ghosts in ⟨?⟩ [*

We learn something too of the weather and the time. Once more
we notice wind, and cloud and leaves keep recurring :[3]

> *The gentleness of rain is in the Wind
>   But all the earth & all the leaves are dry*

> *Now the day has died away
>   And the clouds are cold & grey
>   And their shapes grow undefined [*

Already, in the first two fragments relating to the wood, come
anticipations of actual phrases in lines of the Ode-to-be

meeting branches	*tangled boughs* (16)
dead leaves	*the leaves dead* (2)
like ghosts	*like ghosts* from an enchanter fleeing (3).

And when we come in the next fragment to 'wind . . . all the
leaves are dry' if we remember that numbers of those dry leaves
would be borne in the air and that a remark about *chariots* was
very close to the surface of Shelley's mind and sensitivity the hint
of lines 5–8 becomes a distinct even if a distant one

>   *O thou,*
> *Who chariotest to their dark wintry bed*
> *The wingéd seeds, where they lie cold and low,*
> *Each like a corpse within its grave. . . .*

---

[1] B-H I, *3[r].   [2] B-H I, *7[v].   [3] B-H I, *2[r], 10[r].

And, at the same time, the *seeds* in their *bed*, which is also a *grave*, seem to have derived something from the cradle-sepulchre of Calderón's buds. Then Shelley watched the waters of the Arno as they were whipped by the wind and his mind ranged from the river to the ocean. Very soon, though the form is not yet their final one, we come upon whole lines which are to find their place in the Ode:

> *Lulled by the silence of his crystal streams*
>
> *At whose voice the Atlantic's battling powers
> Band themselves into*

In the final version of line 31

> Lulled by the coil of his crystàlline streams

Shelley gives a magnificent exhibition of his revisionary sleight-of-hand. He gives another in his amendment of lines 37–38:

> *Thou*
> *For whose path the Atlantic's level powers*
> *Cleave themselves into chasms. . . .*

It is tempting to wonder whether here that other phrase from the *Quarterly* about the Egyptians and 'the path of mighty waters' may not have risen up in Shelley's recollection so that the cleaving into chasms owed something to Exodus xiv. 21 where 'the waters were divided'.

So much for Stage One in which 'present and tangible objects' are observed and transmuted and more is added to them out of inner depths. So far there has been no *major* manifestation of 'something beyond'; so far the poem has been given no shape or direction.

In Stage Two (continuing in 'Notebook 3') we pass from words, phrases, and their suggestions into the realm of ideas, and these coalesce into the preliminary poem referred to above. The loose blank verse, etc., of Shelley's first thoughts now settles into a promising terza rima[1]

> *And what art thou presumptuous who profanest
> The wreath to mighty Poets only due

[1] B-H I, *14^r, *14^v, *15^r. These lines were first properly assembled by H. Buxton Forman in *Shelley Notebooks*. Hutch., pp. 660–1, follows Mary Shelley in splitting them into two separate fragments incomplete and incorrect in themselves: such is the usual printed version. The usual date, '1821', is certainly wrong. I have not amended punctuation.

Even whilst, like a forgotten name thou wanest
  Touch not those leaves which for the eternal few
Who wander oer the Paradise of fame
  In sacred dedication ever grew—
One of the crowd thou art,—without a name
  Ah friend 'tis the false laurel which I wear
And though it seem like it is not the same
  As that which bound Milton's immortal hair
Its dew is poison, and the hopes which quicken
  Under its chilling shade, though seeming fair
Are flowers which die almost before they sicken
  And that I walk thus proudly crowned withal
Is that I know it may be thunderstricken
  And this is my distinction, if I fall
I shall not creep out of the vital day
  To common dust nor wear a common pall
But as my hopes were fire, so my decay
  Shall be as ashes covering them. Oh, Earth
Oh friends, if when my   has ebbed away
  One spark be unextinguished of that hearth
Kindled in [*

With Stage Two the poem, in this preliminary form, has reached conception: time and much labour are required to shape it and bring it to birth. What here is most instructive is to notice the point at which the terza rima has broken down. In substance it is an assertion by Shelley of his power, presumptuous, he realizes, as such an assertion may be on his part: is *his* to be the laurel which grows to adorn the brows of the 'eternal few', the select band of real poets? Religious searchings enter. Like Milton he is a rebel but unlike Milton he does not seek to justify God's ways to men: his attitude, on the contrary, is rather that of Amphitryon in the *Hercules Furens*, sceptical through persecution and railing against the power that permits the existence of such sorrows as his—ἀμαθής τις εἶ θεὸς ἢ δίκαιος οὐκ ἔφυς—'a rather stupid god or else unjust'.[1] Can it be the lack of religious sanctity that poisons his laurel so that it is fatal to him and his work? Yet he will wear it, he will be true to poetry and even if it does kill him he will not 'creep out of the vital day / To common dust'. His hopes are fire: for the moment they may be reduced to

---

[1] See above, p. 19.

smouldering ashes, yet out of these very ashes something shall arise. The boldness of the assertion is weakened in its effect by the fact that with it is combined a refusal—a running away from what the poet most feels the need of, namely the need for prayer. To the Christian God[1] he will not pray, and yet he longs to pray to *some* power to kindle and keep alight the 'sudden and inconstant light' of his poetry, the 'spark' as it has become in the poem. What kindles sparks? The answer was all around him driving through the Florence woodland, the force that was preserver as well as destroyer. And the reason why the poem is abandoned at this particular point is that Shelley has suddenly perceived what he must do—reshape it into the form of a *prayer*. By so doing he can satisfy his need, restore the boldness lost to his assertion by his running away, and mitigate his presumptuousness. An impossible undertaking? It might well seem so did we not have the evidence that Shelley achieved it. We will now trace the way he worked towards that achievement. But before we leave Stage Two we must not fail to notice that he already has in mind the climax towards which the poem will move—its invocation involving the *light* of poetry, that 'sudden and inconstant light', the 'light of written thought' generated by what is later to be called 'the mind . . . a fading coal' and what is here to be called an *unextinguished hearth*—

> Scatter, as from an unextinguished hearth
> Ashes and sparks, my words among mankind!

Very apposite just here is that remark of Shelley's to Trelawny which has been quoted already: 'When my brain gets heated with thought it soon boils and throws off images and words faster than I can skim them off. In the morning, when cooled down, out of the sketch (as you so justly call it) I shall attempt a drawing.' If we were to think of Stage One, the stage of generation, as the 'boiling-brain' stage and Stage Two as the 'sketch' wherein we have just found the poem's conception we might think perhaps of Stage Three as the 'drawing'. It is here and in the succeeding stages that the poem at last comes to birth. Stage Three—we are

---

[1] Something of Shelley's religious searchings may be seen in the fact that immediately after 'Lines to a Reviewer' [B-H II, *29ʳ, *29ᵛ] he had started to make a tabular comparison of statements in the gospels.

still in 'Notebook 3'—consists of a pencil draft of the first three stanzas of the Ode very much as we know them.[1] The stanzaic form is a highly original invention consisting of fourteen lines (four tercets and a couplet) wrought out of the preliminary terza rima so that while each moves along with the swift and supple movement given by that measure to the poem as a whole each, in itself, has the strength and compactness of a sonnet. Inside this architecture, of Italian design and materials, the substance of the poem is arranged symbolically on the plan of Calderonian 'episodes'. Señor Madariaga long ago pointed out[2] that the first three stanzas might be entitled respectively 'the leaf', 'the cloud', 'the wave'—symbols, be it noted, all derived from 'the present and tangible objects' noted at Stage One, through which, here at Stage Three, Shelley can now see 'the manifestation of something beyond'. Next, in 'Notebook 4', comes the beautifully penned fair copy of stanzas I–III referred to in the last chapter. The date at its head, 'Oct. 25',[3] shows that five days separate it from the beginnings of Stage One on 'the 20th of October'. Of the actual intervals and brain-cooling between the first four stages there seems nothing measurable that we can deduce.

It may well be that a number of days, or even a longer time, elasped before Shelley came to Stage Five, the drafting in 'Notebook 5' of the last two stanzas, there having been, meanwhile, an intermediate drafting of stanza IV in 'Notebook 4'. In stanza IV, Calderón-wise, the three elements leaf, cloud, and wave,[4] the subjects of the first three stanzas, are drawn together and shown as symbols of himself, Shelley the Poet, and in stanza V he ends, in true Shelley fashion, by a final piling-up of symbols: to the light/fire symbol for Knowledge which now at last reaches its climax in *ashes . . . sparks . . . unextinguished hearth* he adds two

[1] The story 'Una Favola' has been drafted on top of this.
[2] *Shelley and Calderón*, Constable, 1920.
[3] In 'Notebook 2', Bod. MS. Shelley adds. e. 15, p. 2, Shelley notes: 'I am no proficient in the knowledge of the human heart if there is not something in the scene of to-night deeper than what seems.' Above this is the date. 'Oct. 25, 1819'. And Mary Shelley's *Journal* notes under the same date: 'A great fright with Charles Clairmont.' Herein lies a biographical mystery which may or may not have some connexion with this stage of the composition of the Ode. About Charles Clairmont's visit to the Shelley's (4 Sept.–10 Nov.) this much, however, is certain: first that with his habits of money-borrowing and philandering he was an additional strain upon Shelley's emotional tension, and secondly that he was a help with Shelley's Spanish studies.
[4] The fine use of *dome* in stanza II needs noticing.

more symbols: for the Poet he prays (cf. once more the anticipation of *A Defence of Poetry*) 'Make me thy *lyre* . . .' and, with a last image of all to bring the poem back to the Florence woodland, he prays for his poetry—and it is, at the same time, a prayer for all poetry—

> Drive my dead thoughts over the universe
> Like withered leaves to quicken a new birth!

'New birth', as we know, was a phrase very near the top of Shelley's consciousness in those late October days of 1819: Mary's child, the future Sir Percy Florence Shelley, his second name not lightly given, was born on 12 November and, just as a new child had come to defy the 'swift and sudden spirit of decay' which had taken William, so Shelley's poetry would re-arise, regenerated in time as 'Earth's decaying leaves' were regenerated by the Seasons. With his voice, the voice of truth and ἀρετή, identified now with the strength of the Wind, he can defy the Power to which he will not submit—ἀρετῇ σε νικῶ θνητὸς ὢν θεὸν μέγαν—

> By my virtue-and-power I, a mortal, vanquish thee, a mighty god

was his private defiance,[1] jotted on a page of the draft, to possible stupidity and injustice from above. By 15 December the mood of defiance had been confidently extended to his particularly stupid and unjust enemies on earth, those reviewers who had compared his fate to that of the Egyptians of old:[2]

> They say that 'my chariot wheels are broken'

he wrote to Ollier, his publisher:[3]

> Heaven forbid! My chariot, you may tell them, was built by one of the best makers in Bond Street, and it has gone several thousand miles in perfect security.

---

[1] See above, pp. 18–20, 54, and below, pp. 289–99.
[2] The mood of defiance and the application of the line from Euripides can be traced to his letter to Ollier, written on 15 Oct., five days before the Ode began, referring to the *Quarterly* article. Jones, *Letters of Shelley*, ii. 128. 'It describes the result of my battle with their Omnipotent God; his pulling me under the sea by the hair of my head, like Pharaoh; my calling out like the devil who was *game* to the last . . . pretending not to be drowned myself when I *am* drowned; and, lastly, *being* drowned.' A cruel comment on the prophetic irony might be found in an announcement in *The Courier* in 1822: 'Shelley the writer of some infidel poetry has been drowned; now he knows whether there is a God or no.' (See Sylva Norman, *Flight of the Skylark*, p. 37.)   [3] Jones, *Letters of Shelley*, ii. 163.

The draft of stanzas IV and V, which bears the line from Euripides, is very rough and there must have been a later one embodying the final touches with, among them, the magnificent amendment of what was to have been the final assertion[1]

> When Winter comes Spring lags not far behind

into a question which was a challenge having behind it all the defiance of Shelley and of the Wind[2]—all the power of man's mind to bring round the cyclic succession of evil by good. No manuscript either of this or of a complete fair copy of the poem seems to have survived.

I have mentioned a sixth notebook. In truth all that 'Notebook 6' contains of the Ode is one note, that note quoted above about the occasion of its composition: what, however, is significant is the link of this note with the contents of the notebook for these, apart from a few scraps including some lines for the last act of *Prometheus*, consist almost wholly of the draft of *A Philosophical View of Reform*. Herein is found once again the invariable unifying, libertarian energy. In its context the 'Ode to the West Wind' is more than a personal prayer and assertion: it comprises something like a philosophical view of poetry of which Shelley himself is the representative, the symbol. Such presumptuousness as may appear in his invocations 'Drive my dead thoughts', etc., may appear less if we remember how busy he was at that time in setting out thoughts that might be worthy of dissemination. Over and above his other occupations of those immensely busy months of 1819— *The Mask of Anarchy* (mid-September), *Peter Bell* (finished about 24 October), the fourth act of *Prometheus* (finished by Christmas), magnificent letters to Reveley about the steam-boat project (28 October and 17 December), a huge letter to Hunt about the legal defence of Carlile the printer (sent off on 2 November)— over and above time found for numerous smaller political pieces and time taken up by the troubles of Godwin, etc., he was planning for the guidance of his contemporaries, as he explains in the Preface to *Prometheus*,[3] 'a systematical history of what appear to me to be the genuine elements of human society'. Such, it is considered, was to have been his 'Philosophical View' which remains unfinished and was never published till 1920, by which

---

[1] Bod. MS. Shelley adds. e. 6, p. 138.
[2] Cf. above, pp. 19, 33, 126.   [3] Hutch., p. 207.

time the 'ineffectual angel' legend had long taken root. The poet of *Prometheus* might be conscious of a confusion between 'things which seem and are', but there was, none the less, another Shelley ready to face whatever lay on this side of the Veil and concerned with the practical problems of reform. 'Our business', he wrote,[1] 'is with the unbending realities of actual life . . . it becomes us with patience and resolution to apply ourselves to accommodating our theories to practice.' *Prometheus* had been addressed to 'the highly refined imaginations of a select class': here he was addressing himself to the less refined imaginations of practical reformers and even the working-classes, telling them that the need was for a[2] 'limited *beginning*' and that[3] 'the broad principle of political reform is the natural equality of men not with relation to their property but to their rights', and that[4] the people must have time to 'become habituated to exercising the functions of Sovereignty'. Here, in practical form, was what Shelley had referred to in the Preface to *Prometheus* as 'the equilibrium between institutions and opinions'—a principle[5] that lay within all the thoughts he cast upon the Wind and in accordance with which, rather than by revolution, his countrymen have long since carried out almost all of the reforms[6] he advocates. It is the principle which is more than ever the basis of our Western civilization now that other seeds are blowing from the East.

[1] Jul. vii. 43.   [2] Ibid. 46, Shelley's italics.   [3] Ibid. 42.   [4] Ibid. 46.
[5] Traceable perhaps to the τὸ ὀρθὰ δοξάζειν of *Symp.* 202a. Cf. pp. 59–60.
[6] Professor White, *Shelley*, ii. 144–53, gives an admirable summary of *A Philosophical View of Reform*.

13. Italian Platonics and *Epipsychidion*

FROM a poem inspired by Nature we pass to a poem inspired by love. Here again we shall see how poetry lurking in deep reserves of thought and feeling was stirred up in Shelley by a situation; here too we can identify the exact moment at which it burst into blaze and here too the necessary afflatus was at first a libertarian breeze. The situation of Emilia Viviani, immured in a Pisan convent pending the choice of a husband by her family, was just the thing to attract the Lockeian liberator; very soon it involved the Education of the Beautiful One in accordance with the ideas of Wieland, Rousseau, Mary Wollstonecraft, and, above all, Plato. Hence came hours of 'studious zeal or love's delight' in which Emilia grew to be the supreme Ariadne, the culminating Woman-symbol of Intellectual Beauty. It is now possible to piece together some unprinted and, in part apparently unnoticed, manuscript scraps relating to Emilia, to Shelley's Italian studies, and to his manner of Platonically enlightening the Beloved which cast much new light on the beginnings of *Epipsychidion*.

Before we can apprehend the 'minute and remote distinctions of feeling' involved in the delights and torments of this particular Platonic love, we must try to be clear about the Platonic basis of Shelley's general views on the sex matters involved. His purpose here was to broaden the basis of contemporary sex-morality by adding to it the best of what he found applicable in Plato. In his *Discourse on the Manners of the Ancients Relative to the Subject of Love*, a good deal of which is still inaccessible to most readers, he makes quite clear his views about the chief obstacle, Greek homosexuality.[1] So far as personal feelings went, although he realized the ennobling effects of deeply affectionate relationships between members of his own sex, they formed no part of his own aspirations, and towards what he called the 'operose and diabolical machination . . . usually described' his feelings were of horror not unmingled with incredulity. His rejection of these ancient 'manners' was, however, not based on his personal prejudice

[1] Cf. Jul. vii. 223–9 and the full text privately printed (100 copies) by R. Ingpen in 1931.

against them or on a modern moralist's desire to sit in judgement—
could anything, he asked, call as much for condemnation as contemporary prostitution with its attendant diseases? It was based
on the practical fact that they could have no place in modern
life, having their origin, as he saw it, in a society where 'one
half of the adult population', i.e. the women, were in a condition of slavery. Yet herein something might yet be learned
from the Greeks: why should not the more spiritual ideals of love,
as described by Plato for men and youths, be adapted to man-
and-woman relationships? This, with the implied improvements
in men's attitude to women, was Shelley's ideal.[1] It was not a
new idea: it had appeared in Wieland whose Agathon and
Psyche—the Platonic philosopher and the ideal embodiment of
Beauty—are found thus translating their loves into a brother-
sister relationship. The frequency of the brother–sister motif not
only in Shelley but in other Romantic writers of various countries[2]
may be better understood if we realize that it represents an
adaptation of the brother–brother aspect involved in the *Symposium* ideal of what Freudian jargon would call 'sublimated'
homosexual affection. These are matters which Shelley was
anxious to have understood even though he did not in the end
print certain lines[3] which he had drafted to expound them, pre-
ferring to let the poem speak for itself:

> And as to friend or mistress, 'tis a form;
> Perhaps I wish you were one. Some declare
> You a familiar spirit, as you are . . .
> And others swear you're a Hermaphrodite. . . .[4]

---

[1] **‘ἀνδρὸς καὶ γυναικὸς ἡ αὐτὴ ἀρετή’** notes Shelley inside the cover of a notebook [Bod. MS. Shelley adds. e. 10] containing part of the *Laon and Cythna* draft (he
would seem to have remembered the title of a work by Cleanthes listed by Diogenes
Laertius). And according to *Symposium* notions the ἀρετή nurtured in women by
'a correct system of loving' (so Shelley translates τὸ ὀρθῶς παιδεραστεῖν) might grow
from an individual to a civic virtue. Plato *Rep.* 445b–471c may be compared.

[2] This is of a piece with contemporary, and later, movements for intellectual and
social emancipation of women arising, likewise, from the gradually spreading
effects of eighteenth-century German Hellenism.

[3] *Ep.* Frags. 45–57. Hutch., p. 427.

[4] Cf. 'The Witch of Atlas', 321 foll., where the creature, more beautiful than
Pygmalion's image, which the Witch creates to assuage her loneliness, is a Herm-
aphrodite. Its bisexuality symbolizes the harmonizing power of love and Intellectual
Beauty, which she has acquired by her reading and by her trance-like immersion
in the well of love. And it is in a notebook containing drafts of *Epipsychidion* that
we find the strange hermaphroditical figure shown in Plate IIa, perhaps representing some generic form of the Beloved pursued by a κακοδαίμων.

In another rejected passage[1] he bids the inquisitive find in Shakespeare's sonnets 'a whetstone for their dull intelligence', and refers also to Diotima, Socrates, and the speech of Agathon. The point at issue is the unimportance, since the love is entirely a spiritual one, of knowing, for the appreciation of the poem, whether the object of it is wife, mistress, or friend, male or female. Shelley's use of the word 'friend', both in poems and in correspondence addressed to women, is exactly in correspondence with the spiritualized conception of the word which he understood to be present in Shakespeare's sonnets. In the Sonnets indeed may be found much to assist our understanding; we need only look at the last six lines of Sonnet **XXXI**:

> Thou art the grave where buried love doth live,
> Hung with the trophies of my lovers gone,
> Who all their parts of me to thee did give:
> That due of many now is thine alone:
> Their images I loved I view in thee,
> And thou, all they, hast all the all of me.

which is exactly what Shelley has to say:[2]

> In many mortal forms I rashly sought
> The shadow of that idol of my thought.

Emilia, the culmination of the series of women pursued in his quest, is hung with the trophies of her predecessors: he refers to them cryptically in the poem but it does not really matter, for instance, what woman of the past was the 'Comet beautiful and fierce'[3] nor who had the voice which was 'venomed melody':[4] Emilia now comprehends them all. She is the symbol of love itself.

To Shelley's Italian studies we have paid little attention so far. They went, in fact, far deeper than his studies in Spanish and German. As far back as the period of *Alastor* (written in 1815) he had translated Dante's sonnet to Cavalcanti, 'Guido vorrei che tu e Lapo ed io', 'Guido, I would that Lapo, thou, and I . . .',[5] and probably about the same time Cavalcanti's sonnet to Dante, 'Io vengo il giorno a te infinite volte . . .', 'Returning from its

---

[1] *Ep.* Frags. 99–100, Hutch., p. 428.   [2] *Ep.* 267–8, Hutch., p. 417.
[3] *Ep.* 368, Hutch., p. 419.   [4] *Ep.* 256, Hutch., p. 417.
[5] Hutch., p. 725.

daily quest, my Spirit . . .',[1] and he read much Italian habitually. Not unnaturally the years in Italy increased his sensitiveness and enthusiasm for Italian poetry and he was quick to pick from it, as he had done from Calderón and Goethe, those threads of Platonism which had been woven into it out of the general European tradition or such indigenous notions as could be Platonically related. In Dante, Cavalcanti, and other early Italian poets he was especially delighted with the all-prevalent conception of the *fino amore* which harmonized perfectly with his own notion of spiritualized love, and which in *Epipsychidion* became blended with the Platonic and the Shakespearian elements.

Closely related, more especially, to *Epipsychidion* is the First Canzone from Dante's *Convito*[2] which Shelley translated: directly or indirectly his translations usually connect somehow with his compositions. To the relevance of this Canzone he himself gives us a clue both by printing in his Advertisement its first line, 'Voi che 'ntendo il terzo ciel movete . . .',[3] and by setting at the head of his own poem his translation of its *envoi* or *tornata*. It is always instructive to see what Shelley borrowed and how he adapted what he took. In form Dante's poem, as he tells us in the *Convito*, consists of three parts, an Invocation, the Conflict (i.e. the emotional conflict), which forms the body of the poem, and the *tornata*. In his own longer, looser poem Shelley finishes (592 ff.) with a *tornata* of his own and duly begins with an Invocation: the Invocation, however, quickly becomes a series of Invocations and these are not finished before the Conflict has begun to work its way among them. But it is Shelley's use of the *substance* of the Canzone that is really interesting. Its central thought, that of the soul of the lover going out to meet the beloved, appears in the fourth stanza and Shelley thus translates it:[4]

> Thou art not dead, but thou hast wandered,
> Thou Soul of ours, who thyself dost fret, . . .

This thought—which, incidentally, also occurs in some form or

---

[1] Hutch., p. 731. That Cavalcanti's sonnet is of roughly the same date may be fairly assumed from the fact that Shelley's Sonnet to Wordsworth, also published with *Alastor*, owes a good deal to his rebuke to Dante.

[2] Hutch., p. 726. The title *Convito*, as used by Shelley, will be adhered to here. For Shelley's use of this title in place of the *Convivio* commonly preferred to it see App. V (*a*).

[3] 'Ye who intelligent the Third Heaven move.'   [4] Hutch., p. 727.

other in more than one of Shakespeare's sonnets, e.g. in the lines quoted above from Sonnet XXXI—appears very similarly in *Epipsychidion* when he asks the winds[1]

> Whither 'twas fled, this soul out of my soul.

We shall see in a minute how it found its way there, being not so much a deliberate borrowing but an absorption, a Dantean feeling,[2] which in the heat of his own emotion rose to the surface of Shelley's mind demanding from him the new poem he proceeded to construct to contain it.

We come to the Conflict itself. In Dante this is between the two ladies of the Canzone, Beatrice in heaven and the 'Lady of the Window', to give her the name she is commonly known by from her appearance in the *Vita Nuova*[3]—the lady who came to comfort him after the death of Beatrice. Now as a sub-motif to his main purpose in writing the *Convito*, namely his enthusiasm for the study and promulgation of philosophy, he is trying hard to allegorize some of his real odes of passion by asking his readers to accept the identification of this second lady with The Lady Philosophy. In the end he came to realize, as Wicksteed says,[4] that if we are to dissociate ourselves from our past we must do so not by trying to allegorize it away but by purgatorially living ourselves out of it. Here it was that the *Convito* broke down: this was the point in Dante's life at which thought began to deepen into the stuff of the *Commedia*. What makes this immensely interesting is that Dante's problem here is the old one which always troubled Shelley—the pursuit of love on two planes at once. Later on he was to confess where the error lay—θνητὸς ὢν μὴ θνητὰ φρονεῖν.[5] But for the present he was too carried away to tackle the problem in Dante's way, by an attempt to distinguish between Beauty/Philosophy and its mortal embodiment: for the moment Emilia *is* Truth, Philosophy, and everything else:[6]

> I love you!—Listen, O embodied Ray
> Of the great Brightness; I must pass away
> While you remain. . . .

---

[1] *Ep.* 238, Hutch., p. 417.

[2] Closely akin is Plato's notion of the soul as a 'daemon' 'which resides in the very summit of the body, elevating us from the earth to an alliance with the heavens'. This Shelley knew (see above, pp. 75–76) and it may well have been known to Dante from the *Timaeus*.

[3] Ch. 6.   [4] *The Convito of Dante*, Dent, 1908, p. 435.

[5] See above, pp. 75–77 and below p. 303.   [6] *Ep.* Fr. 38 ff., Hutch., p. 426.

She is in fact the symbol of the One with all its Platonic radiance;
she is hung not merely with the trophies of earlier Ariadnes but
with all the trappings of Shelleyan symbolism: in the language
of the Cave she is, as we have just seen, the *shadow* of the *idol*[1]
of his thought; in the language of the New Birth of Nature and
thought she is 'like incarnate April, warning, / With smiles and
tears, Frost the Anatomy / Into his summer grave';[2] at the same
time she is 'the Vision *veiled* from me / So many years'[3] and,
according to the dream-allegory, 'the shadow of some golden
dream'—no less than dreamed-of Odatis to Zariadres when he had
discovered her 'Youth's vision thus made perfect'.[4] From the
Dantean vision Shelley steals her away and installs her in his own
Shelleyan-Platonic one,[5]

A Splendour
Leaving the third sphere pilotless,

to become not only, according to his brother–sister notion,[6]

Spouse! Sister!

on the Elysian isle to which he will bear her in the Spirit-Boat
but also a Dantean

Angel!

and, in Plato's phrase, a κυβερνήτης ἄριστος,[7] the most excellent

Pilot of the Fate
Whose course has been so starless.

With this fusion of concepts, untrammelled by the greater
subtlety of the distinctions made by Dante, he addresses himself
more directly, more passionately to his Lady, not needing as
intermediaries those angels 'who intelligent the third heaven
move'. And indeed he has stolen too from Dante that very 'third
sphere' itself, cosmographically incorporating it with Emilia's
Isle.

In a notebook containing much of the draft of *Epipsychidion*
is found a page and a half of notes on the *Convito* together with
page references to Shelley's copy;[8] these notes are given in

[1] *Ep.* 268, Hutch., p. 417.
[2] *Ep.* 121–3, Hutch., p. 414.   [3] *Ep.* 343–4, Hutch., p. 419.
[4] *Ep.* 42, Hutch, p. 413. For Zariadres and Odatis see above, pp. 169–170.
[5] *Ep.* 116–17, Hutch., p. 414.   [6] *Ep.* 130–1. Hutch., p. 414.
[7] See above, pp. 55–58.
[8] Bod. MS. Shelley adds. e. 8, pp. 168 rev., 167 rev. For bibliographical details
of Biscioni's edition which Shelley used see App. V (*a*).

Appendix V (*a*) together with a collation of the quotations and references with the Oxford text of Dante. Not all of his comments are noticeably relevant to *Epipsychidion*, but taken together they do have the wider interest of showing the mind of Shelley at work on his Dante studies, ranging far and wide and picking up on his way and adapting things that attracted him, whether new ideas, ideas cognate to his own, or ideas in keeping with what he had already discovered in other authors. Some of these we have touched upon in earlier chapters, e.g. existence of spirits employed in the government of the universe (we seem to see him identifying Dante's angelic figures as his own intermediary daemons), the refusal to retaliate against tyrants, immortality of the soul, the heavenly bodies as portents and symbols. One passage quoted from the *Convito* (see App. V) is most relevant to *Epipsychidion* and I translate it here:

Love . . . is nothing else but a spiritual union of the soul and the thing loved, by which union the soul, in virtue of its own nature, runs swift or slow.

Behind *Epipsychidion* too lay much of the conception of love in the *Divina Commedia* and the *Vita Nuova*. Other Italian poetry as well flowed with Dante's into the Platonic mainstream: Petrarch's, for instance, with its devotion to Laura, and a direct verbal contribution has been traced between his

Spirto gentil che quelle membra reggi[1]

and Shelley's opening[2]

Sweet Spirit! Sister of that orphan one,
Whose empire is the name thou weepest on.

---

[1] Canzone VI.

[2] On a page of one of the manuscripts of *The Mask of Anarchy* are found the lines

Anima dolce chi [*sic*] sei la sorella
Di quella orfana anima che regge
Il nome e la forma mia.

If they were written, like the *Mask*, in 1819 they must be Shelley's earliest attempts at verses in Italian and must have been drawn out of the 'bottom drawer' in 1821: it seems more likely, however, that what he did in 1821 was just to make use of an old manuscript page. It was Adolfo de Bosis, Shelley's fine Italian translator, who pointed out that the 'orphan one' is not Mary, as often supposed, but the spirit of Shelley. He makes the suggestion that it was the strange Christian name of Shelley, 'mio adorabile Percy' as Emilia called him, which provoked from her the question, ingenuous, sorrowful, or jesting, '*Persi*? Lost?'. See *Bulletin and Review of the Keats-Shelley Memorial*, no. 2, 1913, pp. 14–19.

Then there is Brunetto Latini, a precursor of Dante: from his *Tesoretto*, a poem full of poetic journeyings and allegorical personages, Shelley translated the lines entitled by Garnett 'Love, Desire, Hope and Fear'; his translating, as we have said, was no barren pastime and they too made a direct if slight contribution to *Epipsychidion*.[1] More considerable was the influence of Guido Cavalcanti whose description of love in the famous *Canzone d'Amore*, 'Donna me prega . . .', has recently been summarized as follows:[2]

> In Cavalcanti's thought love is a human psychological phenomenon amenable to scientific analysis and exposition. . . . The love with which he is concerned is, of course, 'fine love'. He maintains that love may exist continuously in the mind as the cherishing of an ideal image of feminine beauty; that it becomes active emotionally when a man cherishing such an image beholds, and is beheld by, a woman who seems to him to be the counterpart of the ideal image in his mind; that he then seeks responsiveness, being in a deathlike distress until it is attained, or, if it is withdrawn; and that the active phase of love ends whenever—typically as a result of tensions inherent in the experience itself—the ideal and the real images cease to coincide in the lover's mind.

Nothing could better summarize, at the same time, much of what we noticed in Chapter 4 about Shelleyan love in general and nothing could be more applicable to the moods which preceded, accompanied, and followed the writing of *Epipsychidion*.

So much for the general thought and feeling and the poetic fires, Platonic, Dantean, etc., which were ready to be stirred up at the time when Emilia Viviani made her appearance in the life of Shelley-the-Emancipator. We now approach more closely to inspect the stages by which Emancipation turned to Instruction and love stirred Instruction into poetry.

Though Trelawny was wrong in believing that *Epipsychidion* was originally composed in Italian, his error can now be shown to be a very understandable one; indeed had he said that the poem was *conceived* in Italian, he would have been very nearly correct.

---

[1] Cf. these lines Hutch., pp. 724–5, with *Ep.* 379–82. Hutch., pp. 419–20.

[2] E. Hatch Wilkins, *A History of Italian Literature*, O.U.P., 1954, p. 30. Very Shelleyan too are the *spiriti*—fanciful personifications of psychological faculties or special psychological phenomena—which people Cavalcanti's poems: perhaps *Adonais* owes something to these. It is to be noticed that the *Canzone d'Amore* is much concerned with 'the virtue and power of love', *sua vertute e sua potenza*.

For Shelley did indeed think and write a good deal in Italian concerning Emilia and of this there still remain in his notebooks:

> (*a*) fragmentary drafts of letters,
> (*b*) a prose fable,
> (*c*) attempts at verse composition,
> (*d*) translations from his own poetry.

Of this (*a*) at any rate seems hitherto to have wholly escaped notice and neither (*b*), (*c*), nor (*d*) have been examined in the light of their real significance, which did not emerge until the notebooks were subjected to systematic analysis on the lines described in Chapter 1.

The two notebooks in which Shelley drafted letters to Emilia contain also parts of his draft for *Epipsychidion*. Many pages have been torn out, and it is mostly from mere stubs that I have rescued the fragments that remain. Tantalizing and incomplete as they are, they are sufficient at any rate to show the Shelley of *Epipsychidion*, first strengthening acquaintance with Emilia, then making arrangements for her comfort and welfare and, finally, warming to his mood of love and poetry. Their Italian text—which I have deciphered only with the greatest difficulty since Shelley's writing is at its very wildest, his punctuation non-existent, and his unreliable grammar a further complication—is given in Appendix V (*b*) together with the manuscript references. I give them here in the best translation I can manage and in a sequence which, for want of dates, must necessarily be an arbitrary one. In the first letter the Emancipator is pointing out his qualifications as a sympathizer.[1] Reference to the Appendix will show that in all these letters he makes use in Italian of the second person singular, the 'familiar' form of address:

**] no influence [with the rich and noble.] Having been an open enemy to all tyranny, political and domestic, I have all tyrants against me. And is not the world dominated by tyrants? I would offer you what I have and what I can—would that I had more!

Think of everyone and everything. May points and arguments come into your mind. Never despair and do believe that I shall have no regard for danger to my own country but only for your good in every plan or every means of assistance I am able to devise for you.**

[1] See App. V (*b*), no. 1.

Next he enlists a friend, perhaps Lady Mountcashell or Jane Williams.[1]

I have spoken to a friend about you and in order to interest her the more in your most unhappy fate I have shown her your last letter (forgive the translation for which I must make my good intention my excuse). Eventually she promised me that she would write to the Prior of St. Nicholas at Pisa telling him of your unhappiness and asking him to call on you and to employ every possible means of inducing your father to give you a husband.

Already, after an acquaintance of *pochi giorni*, we find him warming to a friendship which he explains in terms of poetry. The poem he quotes is Dante's sonnet to Cavalcanti which he had himself translated and I give his own rendering of the lines.

You had asked [

he starts, but neither cancels the words nor finishes the sentence. He starts again[2]

**Here we are then, bound by ⟨? our⟩ few days' friendship, gathered together by some strange fortune from the ends of the earth to be perhaps a consolation to each other. Let my wish for you and for us be, in the words of Dante, that we

> 'Led by some strong enchantment might ascend
> A magic ship, whose charmèd sails should fly
> With winds at will where'er our thoughts might wend,
> So that no change, nor any evil chance
> Should mar our joyous voyage . . .'

and I would add this also: 'Would that

>   each were as content and free
>   As I believe that thou and I should be.'**

Dante in his sonnet wishes that he and his friends Guido Cavalcanti and Gianni Lapo might take a pleasure-voyage together with 'Vanna and Lagia and my gentle love' (i.e. Beatrice).[3] There are two feelings here which concern *Epipsychidion*, first the

---

[1] App. V (*b*), no. 2.

[2] App. V (*b*), no. 3. *Eccoci dunque tu e noi,* literally = 'here we are then you and we': i.e. presumably, Emilia, on the one hand, and Shelley and his family and friends on the other, 'Marina, Vanna, Primus, and the rest'. See below.

[3] Shelley's translation has 'Vanna and *Bice*' according to the text he used: modern texts agree upon *Lagia*.

idea of the soul-flight symbolized by the Voyage in the Boat[1], and secondly the old Shelleyan hope (it had been so fatal with poor Harriet) of making his Ariadne[2] of the moment the microcosm of a wider love in which his friends and their own loves shall share: the voyage is to be a sort of select ἀγάπη party. On the previous page an uncancelled false start for this piece of the draft reads: 'Here we all are then, people whom some Spirit has gathered. . . .' The Spirit is a truly Shelleyan fancy; whether he be by origin the Spirit of love from the fourth stanza of the First Canzone in the *Convito* or a Platonic daemon, he is all ready to fly into a new poem. Now Shelley is becoming lovingly enthusiastic, hovering, we may feel, on the verge of a lyric[3]

You, Emilia, who were lovelier to behold than the white lily on its green stem and fresher than May when [

One lyric from this mood was discovered by Sir John Shelley-Rolls and Roger Ingpen.[4]

> *Thy gentle voice, Emilia dear,
>   At night seems hovering o'er mine.
> I feel thy trembling lips—I hear
>   The murmurs of thy voice divine. . . .*

In what follows the mood is still more apparent though Shelley, ἁπτόμενος τοῦ καλοῦ (or rather τῆς καλῆς) καὶ ὁμιλῶν αὐτῷ (or rather αὐτῇ)[5], seems to feel that he is straying a little too far beyond pure Platonism and *amore fino*, for he cancels what he has written with a diagonal swirl of his pen—such at that moment is Love's 'virtue and power' which can confound the evil daemon in conflict with it:[6]

**Your form, visible to my mind's eye, surrounds me with the gentle shadow of its divine beauty. Many times you thus ⟨?⟩ me. Your dark eyes, ever most beautiful, are above me. I seem to feel your hand on mine and your lips—but then I close my eyes ⟨*MS. continues in a different ink*⟩ until you cease to love it—then it will be quenched like a flame which lacks fuel.[7] I have suffered much in health today⟨?; no longer

---

[1] Cf. *Ep.* 407 foll.: 'Emily, / A ship is floating in the harbour now . . .' and references in Ch. 6, especially pp. 102–3.

[2] In a notebook of the period [Bod. MS. Shelley adds. e. 9] Shelley *sketched* his Ariadne complete with her maze. See Plate I *b*.   [3] App. V (*b*), no. 4.

[4] *Verse and Prose*, p. 5.   [5] Plato, *Symp.* 209c. See above, pp. 137–9.

[6] App. V (*b*), no. 5. For the idea of death-with-the-Beloved cf. the early Mary poems: see above, p. 38.

[7] An echo from Petrarch, *Trionfo della Morte*, 157–62. See App. V, p. 342, n. 1.

have I been very happy.⟩ Your sweet eyes are smiling within me. I no longer think of death: I believe that the soul that is loved by you cannot [**

But here at the same time thought and feeling, leaping beyond the merely lyrical mood, are characteristically reaching out into universals, and the climax of *Epipsychidion* itself is forecast:[1]

> Two overshadowing minds, one life, one death
> One Heaven, one Hell, one immortality. . . .

'Una favola', the fable written in Italian for Emilia,[2] would seem to have been an attempt on Shelley's part at an allegorical exposition of his notions of love. Its connexion with her, if not known, might be deduced from its notebook proximity to the lyric 'Madonna wherefore hast thou sent to me', referring to a gift of flowers she had made: its general feeling and some of the substance of its allegory may be traced in *Epipsychidion.* Emilia herself, reciprocally, wrote an essay on love which was printed by Medwin, and one sentence of this was set by Shelley at the head of his 'Advertisement' to the poem.[3] Since 'Her own words', of which he thus emphasized the significance, are seldom translated, even if they are noticed at all, I repeat and translate them here

L'anima amante

she wrote—and we may note that with the 'gentle voice' went a considerable power of expression in her lovely Tuscan tongue—

si slancia fuori del creato, e si crea nell' infinito un mondo tutto per essa, diverso assai da questo oscuro e pauroso baratro.

The soul that loves is hurled forth from the created world and creates in the infinite a world for itself and for itself alone, most different from this present dark and dismal pit.

The notion of the Soul–Voyage, Platonic and Dantean, and the whole Shelleyan Boat–Isle symbolism have been perfectly apprehended and perfectly summarized. Apt pupils, even without beauty, can inspire their teachers: here is Shelley's *anima amante* once more doing its broken best in Italian—trying, now, to versify:[4]

---

[1] *Ep.* 585–6, Hutch., p. 424.   [2] See above, p. 3.   [3] Hutch., p. 411.
[4] Jul. iv. 90 where, however, Ingpen wrongly reads 'Sciogleró' ('I will loose'). The notebook from which he transcribed these and other fragments of Shelley's Italian verse composition is badly damaged by water. See above, pp. 11–13.

*lontan di ogni pena
Scieglerò un ⟨   ⟩ sul purpureo Oceano [cielo]
Un quieto asilo, che ⟨   ⟩ quando[

. . . far from all pain I will choose a ⟨   ⟩ on the purple Ocean
[heaven,] a quiet refuge, which ⟨   ⟩ when[*

In choosing what is to be[1]

A Solitude, a Refuge, a Delight

he hesitates, we may notice, between the words 'Ocean' and
'heaven', and the hesitation speaks for the amphibious nature of
the Boat which we described in Chapter 6. But he apologizes for
his Italian which he calls[2] 'clothing true affection in barbarous
accents' ('Cosi vestivo in barbari accenti / Il vero affetto . . .').

Medwin perceived[3] that Shelley's love for Emilia was of the
Symposium[4] kind, 'desire of generation in the Beautiful', and
quotes[5]

Love is like understanding, that grows bright,
Gazing on many truths. . . .

Some of Shelley's translations into Italian of passages of his own
poetry are in a notebook[6] presented to the Bodleian in 1893
by Lady Shelley and have long been known as an interesting
curiosity; nobody, however, as far as I know, has inquired into
the reason for these performances. Of the reason there can now
be no doubt: it is that he wanted Emilia to gaze on the Platonic
truths which he had crystallized in his own verse. The passages
chosen are five in number:

1. The song of the Voice in the Air from *Prometheus Unbound*, II. v.
   48 ff. :[7]

   'Life of Life! thy lips enkindle . . .'

2. Asia's continuing lyric, II. v. 72 ff. :

   'My soul is an enchanted boat . . .'[8]

3. Lines 1–90 of *Prometheus Unbound*, Act IV.[9]
4. Stanzas 1–13 of the 'Ode to Liberty'.[10]
5. Stanzas 1–3 and part of stanza 4 of *The Revolt of Islam*, Canto II.[11]

---

[1] *Ep.* 64.   [2] Jul. iv. 90.
[3] *Revised Life*, p. 285.   [4] 207d. See above, pp. 62–63 and 136–9.
[5] *Ep.* 162–3.   [6] Bod. MS. Shelley D. 1.
[7] Hutch., p. 241. And cf. above, pp. 162–3.
[8] Hutch., p. 241.   [9] Hutch., p. 254.
[10] Hutch., p. 603.   [11] Hutch., pp. 40–41.

It will be noticed at once that of these the first two are concerned
with Platonic love, the first being sung by Spirits cognate to Plato
and, no less, to the Duecento; the third, similarly, is a Chorus
of unseen spirits, Forms, Shadows, etc., and the fourth and the
fifth relate to the theme of Liberty. In Appendix V (*c*) are given
samples from each of these translations. Parallels between the
passages in question and *Epipsychidion* have been noted before:
we need only note in passing

Lamp of Earth! where'er thou movest[1]	Veiled Glory of this lampless Universe ...
Its dim shapes are clad with brightness ...	*Ep.* 261
Prom. ii. v. 66–67	
... o'er the Aegean main / Athens arose ...	The blue Aegean girds this chosen home ...
Ode. Lib. 60–61	*Ep.* 430
... Tyrants dwelt side by side, And stabled in our homes ...	... the sightless tyrants of our fate
Rev. Isl. 695–6	*Ep.* 240

About such parallels, of which the list might be considerably
extended, the point of real importance is the manner in which
they occurred, for what they represent is the passing of some of
Shelley's earlier poetry into *Epipsychidion* through the medium of
the translations of it which he made for Emilia Viviani. We have
seen him, in at least one of his letters, caught in the conflict between the good daemon and the bad, the earthly love and the
spiritual: we have seen him prevailing by his philosophic virtue
over the κακοδαίμων pursuing him. All this while he has been
trying to carry out the technique from the *Symposium*[2] of Educating the Beloved and ascending, in *Symposium* fashion, from particular beauties to Beauty itself. It is exactly here that his mind
behaves most characteristically by taking just that 'imaginative
leap'—to borrow once more the apt and useful phrase of Professor Notopoulos[3]—which it took when the beauty of the Swiss
Alps moved him to his 'Hymn to Intellectual Beauty'. Characteristic of this 'imaginative leap', as Professor Notopoulos points

[1] Cf. also in Shelley's letter to Emilia the notion of a *lamp* which lacks fuel.
[2] 211c and see above, pp. 138 foll.
[3] See above, pp. 40–42.

out, is its 'little distinction between emotion and idea', a point
well illustrated above in what we have noticed about Shelley's
departure in *Epipsychidion* from the distinction made by Dante
in the *Convito* between, on the one hand, Philosophy and pure
Beauty and, on the other hand, their human embodiment,
Emilia. It is at this most vital moment in the Shelley–Emilia
relationship that we fall in with another of those strange pieces of
luck with which the notebooks now and then present us. What
has happened—and Medwin's comment proves to come very
close to the mark—is that any success Shelley has had in van-
quishing physical desire has resulted in the diversion of love's
'virtue and power' into 'desire of generation in the beautiful',
i.e. the generation of poetry. And as we turn the pages on which
he made his translations, we come upon clear manuscript evidence
of the precise point at which imagination lifted the Emancipator
and Educator into the writing of *Epipsychidion*. As he translates
from *Prometheus*, raking over the embers of these old fires for
Emilia, new sparks begin to fly, and there on the page separating
these two translations the flow of Italian writing is interrupted by
the beginnings of an English poem.[1]

> The death-knell is ringing
> The raven is singing
> The earth worm is creeping
> The mourners are weeping
>   Ding dong, bell—

This fragment, discovered by Locock, has not yet been associated,
I think, with *Epipsychidion*. More directly it should be associated,
I do not doubt, with 'The Fugitives',[2] which appears in another
notebook drafted close to part of the *Epipsychidion* draft. But a
tiny vehicle like 'The Fugitives', being quite inadequate to contain anything on the scale of what Shelley had to say about the
Boat-flight, it remained itself unfinished while he went back to his
translating. Meanwhile, as we have seen from a letter he drafted,
thoughts of death had vanished. Some pages farther on, between
his version of the opening of *Prometheus*, Act IV, and his version

---

[1] Hutch., p. 662. The feeling is strangely anticipative of *Ginevra*, though *Epipsychidion* was written in Jan.–Feb. 1821 and Shelley does not seem to have known
the Ginevra story till later. See Ch. 14.

[2] For the connexion of 'The Fugitives' with *Epipsychidion* see above, pp. 93, 102.
For *Epipsychidion* as an example of a 'multiple birth' poem see below, Ch. 14.

of the second canto of *The Revolt of Islam,* another fragment of
English stands out amid the Italian:[1]

> Thy beauty hangs around thee like
>   Splendour around the moon—
> Thy voice, as silver bells that strike
>   Upon [

It is very little but it shows us where we are moving. Already
Emilia is the vision of Platonic radiance necessary to a major
Shelley poem: we may note once more the mention of her *voice*:
the impact of one of the most beautiful of languages upon one of
the most sensitive of ears must have had no little to do with the
Italian origins of the poem that is just ahead. By now it is apparent that lyrical beginnings are useless: no lyric can contain the
proportions of the poem that is evolving out of the brother–sister
love of Laon and Cythna, the many ideas of *Prometheus,* the
Voyage notion, Shelley's persecutors and Emilia's, and the whole
wide concept of Intellectual Beauty: as with the 'Ode to the West
Wind' he devises a form of his own and does it, as we have seen,
by a loose adaptation from the *Convito* Canzone. Meanwhile
Shelley is wrestling with his usual problem of too much inspiration and too many ideas. It is as he is seeking for a title that will
catch and bind together what is careering around his mind that
imagination takes its leap: it is here[2] that we see, triumphantly
and clearly written across the page in all the *arriviste* pride of its
doubtful philological lineage, the word **Epipsychidion.** A strange
word? To Shelley, thinking in Italian, a language rich in expressive diminutives, it may perhaps have seemed less so. He liked
new song-names: to Leigh Hunt, talking about Love-songs, he
remarked that he saw no reason why there should not be Hate-
songs[3] as well. And so if you may have an *Epinikion* for a Triumph-
song and an *Epithalamion* for a Marriage-song why should you not
have an *Epipsychidion* for a Soul-song? So, I think, his mind worked,
and the fact that ἐπιψύχη did not exist in Greek need not have
troubled him in his excited determination to write what would *be*
an Epipsychidion. Like Dante's soul in the *Convito* his soul had
fled to his lady's feet and his poem would be the song that would

---

[1] Bod. MS. Shelley D. 1, f. 104ʳ, rev. Hutch., p. 662.
[2] Bod. MS. Shelley D. 1, f. 103ʳ, rev. See above, pp. 40–42 and cf. below, p. 267.
[3] W. M. Rossetti, *P.W.* 1870, iii. 522.

herald it. On the very next page[1] the poem is off and away, together with the draft preface containing the significant Greek phrase to which we have often referred. As Locock correctly guessed[2] it began with its ending. Here are the first words to be written: they are printed with their cancellations as they appear in the manuscript —

[the feelings]
On wings of   soul
[Inflamed] words on which my [heart] would pierce
Beyond the [height] of Love's rare universe
        depth
              which upon its fiery flight
Are [lead] chains of lead [upon its flight of]
I sink

'L'anima amante si slancia fuori del creato'—Shelley's 'soul within his soul' (having naturally the wandering tendency of Dante's in the First Canzone of the *Convito*, and having also, to pull it upwards, the resident daemon from the *Timaeus*[3] of Plato) had already been carried aloft to the world in the infinite, a world long ago created by his imagination: it lay far across the 'intermediate space'[4] μεταξὺ θεοῦ τε καὶ θνητοῦ and you reached it in an amphibious Boat piloted by that κυβερνήτης ἄριστος,[5] Emilia, *vice* the daemon Love: somewhere or other you rent and passed the Veil that separated reality from illusion, whichever was which, and somewhere further on—onwards and upwards— you reached 'the cope of heaven', the ὑπερουράνιος τόπος[6] of the *Phaedrus*, the 'heaven above the heavens'. Somewhere here in

the height of Love's rare universe

(which was also Dante's Third Sphere) you would come to Pindar's 'festival of the Hyperboreans',[7] to which Shelley had given his own local colouring: this was the Elysian islet which was to be Emilia's: in the past it had been the home of Cythna, Asia, and the whole company of her Ariadne-predecessors and it was hung with the trophies of these lovers gone. Its conception was very familiar to Shelley and even its topography, which

---

[1] Bod. MS. Shelley D. 1, f. 102ᵛ, rev. ff.
[2] *An Examination*, p. 3.
[3] Cf. above, pp. 75–77.
[4] Cf. above, pp. 59–61.
[5] Cf. above, pp. 55–58.
[6] Cf. above, pp. 97, 142.
[7] Cf. above, p. 100.

he had sketched as we saw; his soul could always get there when imagination could take that leap. But for a poem to accompany it? That was more difficult. Once more composition, not inspiration, was the trouble: 'When composition begins', he was to say in *A Defence of Poetry*, 'inspiration is already on the decline': thus, now too, his winged words found their very wings too heavy and chainlike and for long refused to take flight. But at last his Soul-song is finished and he gives it its *envoi*

> Weak Verses, go, kneel at your Sovereign's feet. . . .

His sovereign is Love: here, I think, the World-love, identifiable with Beauty itself to which he, the Platonic lover, had ascended from loving the latest of his particular beauties. His *Epipsychidion*, his herald, would bear his salutations: it would then call up its sisters, the rest of Shelley's poems, and with them tell us about 'the world beyond the grave': the world of reality with which Shelley's poetry is symbolically concerned. So would the *Epipsychidion* survive Shelley himself. It had still another, a third, mission and this was to bid Mary, Jane, and Williams love one another so that with him they might become guests beyond the Veil in the rare Universe ruled by Love on high.

For all its nobility and beauty, many may still feel that the poem finally remains chain-weighted from an excess of symbolism; for, link by link, tangled at times in knots, there hangs upon it the whole system of symbols through which Shelley was wont to express his poetico-philosophical apprehensions. He himself was never happy about it. His final revulsion, to which we have referred and must refer again,[1] had to do with his revulsion against Emilia and was emotional in origin. But he may have had artistic misgivings: it may be, for instance, that his prefixing to it of the lines translated from the *Convito* are as much an apology to the reader who 'cannot conceive [his] reckoning' as a complaint of his dullness. And quite possibly he was aware of the basic difficulty of trying to think more Platonically, θνητὸς ὤν, than he was able to feel. Hogg's comment, 'very droll and wicked',[2] he calls it, was 'Tantum de medio sumptis accedit honoris'. This, referred to its context in Horace[3] and taken with what there precedes it, 'tantum series iuncturaque pollet', I take to mean

---

[1] See below, pp. 253–4.   [2] Jones, *Letters of Shelley*, ii. 434.
[3] *Ars Poetica*, 242–3.

'such is the power of order and arrangement: with such high language may ordinary things be clothed'. An apt description of Shelley's way with relationships, as with imagery, of adopting their style from the Greeks while he 'gifted [them] with that originality of form and colouring which sprang from his own genius',[1] but it might refer drolly and wickedly, as Hogg no doubt intended, to the way such relationships tended to become shaped, eventually, by his own too human nature.

Shelley neither expected nor wished for many readers for this poem:

'The Epipsychidion', he wrote to Gisborne, on 22 October, 1821,

is a mystery—As to real flesh & blood, you know that I do not deal in those articles,—you might as well go to a gin-shop for a leg of mutton, as expect anything human from me. I desired Ollier not to circulate this piece except to the Συνετοί and even they it seems are inclined to approximate me to the circle of a servant girl & her sweetheart.—But I intend to write a Symposium of my own to set all right.

The passage has been more often quoted than understood. He is, of course, using 'mystery' in its Greek sense of 'mystical, something for initiates only'—Συνετοί.[2] What he means is 'if it's meaty sex-poetry you want, don't come looking for it at the spiritual liquor-shop of Plato, Dante, Shelley & Co.' What he says about the difficulty which average minds will always find in understanding *Epipsychidion* applies to the greater part of his major poetry. But if we understand these highly significant comments, set them beside his comments to Godwin of 11 December 1817,[3] and thence follow the Platonic trail that starts from his notes on Plato's *Symposium*,[4] we may not remain among the wholly uninitiated—we may even attain something like that understanding which his own, unwritten, 'Symposium' was to have given us.

---

[1] With the whole of this chapter cf. Ch. 4, *passim*. Cf. also special references to *Epipsychidion* in Ch. 5, pp. 75–77, Ch. 6, pp. 102–4, Ch. 8, pp. 127–8. For the Ascent to Beauty through Education of the Beloved cf. Ch. 8, pp. 136–42. Cf. also much of Ch. 9, especially pp. 162–4.

[2] Shelley's appearance as a ναρθηκοφόρος in *Adonais* is in exactly the same vein of classical banter.

[3] See above, p. 24.   [4] See above, p. 44.

14. 'Ginevra': Emilia to Keats

WHEN Shelley's inspiration was in full flood—if we may thus, to adapt Mary's phrase, 'Calderonize' upon it, adding a third 'episode' to his own similes of the lyre and the fading coal—it did not always flow forward in a single stream. It was thus, we have seen, that in 1819, out of the same common fund of thought and feeling there proceeded such different works as *Prometheus Unbound*, *The Mask of Anarchy*, the 'Ode to the West Wind', and *A Philosophical View of Reform*, besides a number of minor tributary poems. The same happened in 1821: Emilia Viviani, the source of *Epipsychidion*, was also the source of two other poems, 'Fiordispina'[1] and 'Ginevra',[2] as may be seen in the notebook[3] in which their drafts at times are so closely intermingled as to be distinguishable only with difficulty. 'Fiordispina' was a stream which dried up before it got very far, but 'Ginevra', despite shoals and sandbanks, persisted in its course until finally it was diverted into a greater river that had come along to meet it. The causes and nature of the diversion are to be discerned in the manuscripts.

'Ginevra', says Mary Shelley,[4] was 'founded on a story to be found in the first volume of a book called *L'Osservatore Fiorentino*.' The book is a guide to antiquities and is by M. Lastri, and the story[5] is as follows: Ginevra degli Almieri, or Amieri, a Florentine girl of good family, was in love with one Antonio Rondinelli but was forced by her father to marry Francesco Agolanti. Antonio was heart-broken, and still more so Ginevra whose decline of health culminated after four years of marriage in a swoon so deep that she was taken for dead and conveyed to the family vault in the Cemetery of the Duomo, near the Campanile. Awakening at night from her swoon, Ginevra managed to emerge from the vault and to take the shortest way back to the house of her husband. He, however, believing her a ghost, refused her admission. Being

[1] Hutch., p. 630, wrongly placed by Mary in 1820.
[2] Hutch., p. 649.   [3] Bod. MS. Shelley adds. e. 8.
[4] *Poetical Works*, 1839, p. 124.
[5] Given by H. Buxton Forman, *Poetical Works*, 1876. For a fuller account of what follows see Neville Rogers in the *Times Literary Supplement*, 12 Feb. 1954 and 5 Nov. 1954.

similarly repulsed at the houses of her father and uncle she turned in her despair to her faithful Antonio, who duly took her in and in a few days she was restored to health. Later, in spite of the fact that her husband was still living, the ecclesiastical court proclaimed that by reason of her own 'death' the marriage had been dissolved—the implied eagerness of the Church to welcome her 'resurrection' as a miracle was a point that Shelley would not have missed. These events are supposed to have taken place in the last decade of the fifteenth century.

It may be safe to guess that Shelley read *L'Osservatore Fiorentino* at about the same time as Mary, viz. 10–14 April 1821.[1] The tale, probably a piece of plague lore, which had interested the antiquarian Lastri chiefly as an explanation of a street name, 'Via della Morte, ossia della Morta', struck special chords in him. It was a bare two months from the writing of *Epipsychidion*, visits were still being paid to Emilia Viviani in her convent, and the emotional impulse of the friendship was by no means spent. Emilia's marriage was being planned and although, as he wrote to Claire on 29 April,[2] that event would take 'a great and a painful weight' off his mind—'Poor thing! she suffers dreadfully in her prison'—he knew very well that she would have no more say than Ginevra in the choice of her husband. In Ginevra therefore lay a theme very close to his thoughts. Taking most of his details from Lastri—a notable exception being the name of the husband whom he rechristens Gherardi—and telescoping much of the story into a single day, he sets his scene with great dramatic effect: there at once is the bride 'Wild, pale and wonder-stricken . . .' returning from the altar; she reaches the garden 'now her own' and 'Suddenly / Antonio stood before her, pale as she'. The draft, as I have shown elsewhere,[3] is in two parts. It is here at line 48 that the first part, written in a notebook of 1821,[4] breaks down; in the second part, written in a notebook of 1822,[5] the fine confrontation scene is finished. Ginevra goes to rest in the late afternoon and after she has been found apparently dead the manuscript fragments, rather less than 200 lines in all, come finally to an end with the dirge of the mourning women.

[1] Jones, *Mary Shelley's Journal*, pp. 151–2.
[2] Jones, *Letters of Shelley*, ii. 288.
[3] *Times Literary Supplement*, 23 Feb. 1954.
[4] Bod. MS. Shelley adds. e. 8.
[5] Bod. MS. Shelley adds. e. 18.

What did Shelley plan? That he would have continued to follow Lastri seems likely from the ring incident:[1]

> . . . she with patient look
> The golden circle from her finger took,
> And said—'Accept this token of my faith,
> The pledge of vows to be absolved by death. . . .'

The 'vows', of course, were her own vows to Gherardi, and 'to be absolved by death' seems to anticipate that Shelley's poem would have come round again to her divorce on these grounds: such a dénouement would have been fully in accordance with such views on marriage as he had expressed, for instance, in his note in *Queen Mab*, v. 189. But as often as not, as we know, he liked to give an original twist to a borrowed tale and he might well have done so with 'Ginevra', especially since, apart from its relation to Emilia, its dramatic possibilities and its possibilities as a vehicle for his feelings on the whole subject of marriage, female liberty, etc., there is something else in the story which he could hardly have failed to develop, namely the 'dream-of-life' allegory offered to him by his heroine's strange 'death'. Why did he fail, not once but twice, to finish such a promising poem?

With his first failure may be connected what he remarked to Claire in the letter of 29 April just referred to: 'I do not write anything at present. I feel incapable of composition.' The mood may have been partially due to the beginnings of his doubts about Emilia, but this was not all. Something else had come upon him that April to render him 'incapable of composition' and at the same time to stir those depths of thought and feeling out of which a major Shelley poem was to emerge. Not only thought and feeling but, as we shall see from its manuscript relics which will appear in the next chapter, all his kindred powers of study, all his 'spirit's Ocean' had been thrown into turmoil by a recent piece of news. This news, which had reached him not later than 16 April,[2] was of the death of Keats representing, he believed, a triumph of the reviewers in 'blotting out the light of written thought'. The mood was the mood of 1819 but with a difference. For himself he had then been content with passive resistance— '. . . you are free / To pine into a sound with hating me'—secure in his own courage and in his prayer to the Wind, 'Drive my

---

[1] 72–75, Hutch., p. 650.   [2] See below, pp. 259–60.

dead thoughts over the universe', but in his concern for the dead thoughts of Keats this was not enough, and we are to see, in 1821, the passive resister of 1819 turning once more into the old crusader of 1812. Then before taking up his lance and buckler the crusader keeps vigil in reflective study. With his usual flair for hitting upon something related to the context of his thoughts—neglecting where necessary the context of an author—he finds things in Pindar[1] which, interrupting the first part of his 'Ginevra' draft,[2] he jots down on the next page[3]

> **νῦν δ' αὖ μετὰ χειμέριον ποικίλων μηνῶν ζόφον
> χθὼν ὥτε φοινικέοισιν ἄνθησεν ῥόδοις
> δαιμόνων βουλαῖς**

Once again, after the wintry gloom of the many-coloured months the ground, as it were, has blossomed anew with scarlet roses by the will of the daemons

which looks straight back to the conclusion of the 'Ode to the West Wind', and possibly forward to the forty-ninth stanza of *Adonais*: 'A light of laughing flowers along the grass is shed.' Again (almost as if in the last words Pindar were translating his 'unextinguished hearth' motif) we find[4]

> **τοῦτο γὰρ ἀθάνατον φωνᾶεν ἕρπει,
> εἴ τις εὖ εἴπῃ τι· καὶ πάγ-
> καρπον ἐπὶ χθόνα καὶ διὰ πόντον βέβακεν
> ἐργμάτων ἀκτὶς καλῶν ἄσβεστος αἰεί.**

For whatsoever one has said well goes forth with a voice immortal; and thus over the fruitful earth and across the sea has passed the light of noble deeds, unquenchable for ever.

Here, in brief in fact, is what Shelley was to say of Keats, as soon as he became less 'incapable of composition', in fifty-five stanzas: in the first of them, as he thought of what Keats had 'said well', it was Pindar's words, almost, which were to go forth in the voice of Shelley:[5]

> . . . his fate and fame shall be
> An echo and a light unto eternity!

---

[1] *Isthm.* iv. 19–21.   [2] Bod. MS. Shelley adds. e. 8, 133 rev.   [3] Ibid. 132 rev.
[4] *Isthm.* iv. 44–47. Here, as often, a quotation seems to be used without much reference to context: cf. p. 63, n. 1, and p. 100, n. 2. With Pindar's ἄσβεστος αἰεί should be compared also the phrase 'unextinguished Spirit' in the Preface to *Adonais*, Hutch., p. 431.   [5] *Adonais*, 8–9, Hutch., p. 432.

Nor are other notes towards *Adonais* wanting in this notebook, so frequently referred to in Chapter 14, to show the diversion into it of the 'Epipsychidion'-'Ginevra' mood. What is of significance is the diversion of the Ariadne-quest, for in turning to *Adonais* he was getting further away from Emilia, the 'mortal image' in which he had tried, erroneously, to find 'the likeness of what is immortal' and turning to Keats, the dead bard, the symbol of pure Intellectual Beauty, wherein was true immortality.

From Pindar Shelley returns straight away to 'Ginevra' for a few pages, and then the 1821 part of the draft comes to an end. If his resumption of it in 1822 cannot be securely explained, it may be reasonably guessed to have something to do with his speculations—never finally resolved before his death, as we shall see in connexion with 'The Triumph of Life', about the whole vast problem of semblance and reality; these we shall discuss in Chapter 17. His ultimate failure had something to do, no doubt, with the failure of the Viviani relationship. By 18 June 1822 he could write to John Gisborne concerning *Epipsychidion*:[1]

... the person whom it celebrates was a cloud instead of a Juno; and poor Ixion starts from the centaur that was the offspring of his own embrace.

So much, as far as Emilia was concerned, for the 'desire of genera-tion in the beautiful': and he cannot have enjoyed returning to the 'Ginevra' drafts, bred themselves in the stables of the centaur. And meanwhile when he returned to his dream-symbolism, e.g.[2]

> ... in our night
> Of thought we know thus much of death,—no more
> Than the unborn dream of our life before
> Their barks are wrecked on its inhospitable shore

he found himself vainly trying to recall his own spirit's bark which, following the soul of Adonais, had vanished, 'burning through the inmost veil of Heaven': Keats, nearer to Intellectual

---

[1] Jones, *Letters of Shelley*, ii. 434. Professor White, *Shelley*, ii. 325, somewhat oddly, sees in this passage the power of Shelley's revulsion 'to turn the beautiful Emilia into a centaur' although in terms of ancient legend Ixion, of course, was himself, Emilia the cloud in Juno's shape, and the poem the outlandish monster that had resulted from his infatuation.

[2] 'Ginevra', 157–60, Hutch., p. 652.

Beauty than any of its womanly embodiments, had given him a greater theme on which he could employ the dream-symbolism unmixed with mere dramatic effects :[1]

> Peace, peace! he is not dead, he doth not sleep—
> He hath awakened from the dream of life. . . .

[1] *Adonais* 343–4, Hutch., p. 440.

15. *Adonais*: Keats to Intellectual Beauty and the One

To Shelley, who thought in symbols, the Poet was many things but above all a *light*:[1]

> **Hold—divine image
> Eclipsed Sun—planet without a beam
> Wilt thou offend the Sun thou emblemest
> By blotting out the light of written thought?**

Thus he had exhorted himself when in 1819 death took his child and the reviewers threatened his poetry, and in the end, strong in his ἀρετή, he had prevailed over despair and continued to write. In 1820–1 together with a personal affection for Keats went a sense of Keats's symbolical significance and, projecting his own moods on to his notion of his friend, he came easily to credit a man who in health was robust in mind and spirit with a nature more vulnerable than his own. Hence—and this explains the depth of the feeling as well as the intellectual power of *Adonais*— Keats gradually became aligned in his mind with himself; already by May 1820[2] he wrote of him as a poet ready 'like the sun, to burst through the clouds', and the very metaphor contains the essentials of the eclipse-image. Thenceforward the Platonic opposition of the light of Poetry to the darkness that threatened to enfold it is constantly present in his words and thoughts about Keats. Despite Keats's courteous refusal in August of his invitation of 27 July he continued to hope to see him, more especially after reading the *Lamia* volume which reached him some time[3] in October: his praise of 'Hyperion' at the expense of the other fine poems may perhaps be partly accounted for by his characteristic delight in the allegory of the Sun-god and it may be fair to suspect that this too merged into the general colour of his thinking, as for instance in *Adonais* XLIV, about splendid things and people who may be eclipsed rather than extinguished. Late in

---

[1] See above, p. 218.   [2] Jones, *Letters of Shelley*, ii. 197.
[3] Jones, *Mary Shelley's Journal*, p. 139: 'Oct. 18 . . . Shelley reads "Hyperion" aloud.'

the month, he told Mrs. Hunt, he was anxiously expecting Keats in Italy:[1]

... I intend to be the physician both of his body and his soul, to keep the one warm and to teach the other Greek and Spanish. ...

By 'Greek and Spanish', there is no need to doubt, he meant, more specifically, 'Plato and Calderón'. The entrancing prospect of discussing Platonic and Calderonian imagery and concepts of reality with the author of 'Hyperion' was a visionary variant on the 'desire of generation in the beautiful', quite characteristic of Shelley albeit to Keats, as in the past, to have his 'own unfettered scope' in poetical thinking would have seemed more desirable than all the prospects of the Shelley-begotten ideas that might have resulted from such intercourse.

In November Shelley drafted to Gifford[2] a letter in which he sought to save Keats's new volume from the treatment that had been given to his *Revolt of Islam*: about his own wrongs he spoke with restraint and with a smile once more at the Pharaoh-simile,[3] then, after objective comments on *Endymion* and with a reference to Keats's health, he laments that the composition of 'Hyperion', a piece 'in the very highest style of poetry', had been 'checked by the review in question'. By now Keats and Shelley were standing together in Shelley's mind in firm resistance to the powers of darkness: the fact that he realized the hopelessness of an attempted appeasement and did not send the letter marks the passing into active crusading of his 'resist not the weakness' or passive resistance policy several months, if dates can be relied on, before the death of Keats. The beginnings of the crusade are again perceptible in a pair of embryo dialogues, one referring to himself and the other to Keats: they lie on adjacent pages. The first, which begins[4]

A strange fellow that Lionel but there is a kind of method in his madness . . .

was quoted in Chapter 2 and has been frequently referred to in subsequent chapters. Here is the second:[5]

[1] Jones, *Letters of Shelley*, ii. 240.
[2] Ibid., ii. 251.
[3] Cf. above, pp. 218, 223, 227, n. 2.
[4] Bod. MS. Shelley adds. e. 8, pp. 70–71. Quoted above, pp. 16–17.
[5] Bod. MS. Shelley adds. e. 8, pp. 72–73.

**—I think that is *Keats's* new volume I see before you—
— [Yes] It is—a new knot of abortions engendered by vanity upon [credulity] idleness.
—You are too severe, or rather you are totally unjust. The three first pieces in the volume are, I acknowledge, very inadequate to what we should have a right to expect from the mature and disciplined powers of the writer. But the last Poem, the fragment,—you have not read it?
—Yes, a diseased curiosity [to see what was coming urged me] to the end:—
—[Will you say what think you of [those verses] that poem: and what think you of the blighting influence which, as the Publisher informs us, checked the conception of the majestic [design and execution of the astonishing] stream of a strain of poetry of the purest and the deepest hue] Well are there no passages in this fragment which [. . .?**

Shelley's depreciation of 'the first three pieces', 'Lamia', 'Isabella', and 'The Eve of St. Agnes', is little short of extraordinary: two of these poems, as we shall note below, were eventually to be felt in stanzas of *Adonais*, though for the moment he seems to have been dazzled by the 'fragment', i.e. *Hyperion*. But what we should notice chiefly here is the anticipation of some of the substance and manner of the Preface to *Adonais* and the connexion, by that phrase 'checked the conception', with his letter to Gifford of the preceding November. There can be little doubt that both dialogues belong to the period just preceding the composition of *A Defence of Poetry*, i.e. late January or early February 1821. The next three pages[1] bear two small fragments printed by Garnett and others as 'probably connected with the *Defence*' together with a large one which Garnett[2] guessed to be 'a part of the original exordium'. A comparison of the printed text of the *Defence* establishes the latter identification at once, and if we look at the second, comparing it with the Lionel dialogue,[3] we shall see that both contain similar phrases about 'the disciples of a certain mechanical and superficial philosophy'. It is clear enough what Shelley's intentions were and what has happened to them: having planned originally a discussion in dialogue form—a good-humoured reply couched, just conceivably, in Peacock's own idiom, not only to 'The Four Ages of Poetry' but also to the portrait in *Nightmare Abbey* of Scythrop, the 'transcendental eleutherarch'—he has

---

[1] Ibid. 74–77. [2] *Relics of Shelley*, pp. 88–89; Jul. viii. 117.
[3] See above, pp. 16–17.

reshaped his theme into a long essay, surveying past and present history and demonstrating the philosophical status of poetry for the future.

From all these connexions we can chart quite clearly the stream of inspiration which went into *Adonais*. It is in fact not a single stream but two separate, confluent ones. Starting in 1819 from the attacks of reviewers upon *The Revolt of Islam*, the first stream runs into the New Birth mood of the 'Ode to the West Wind'. Full of thoughts of the power and immortality of great verse, it flows through 1820 and into 1821, becoming broadened as events unlock floodgates at three points: first—and this is where the abortive dialogues appear—where Shelley begins to see Keats's health and poetry as the victims of the reviewers, secondly where Peacock produces his essay, and, thirdly—here the stream becomes a cataract—when Shelley hears of the death of Keats. Just above the second of these points, i.e. before Peacock's essay had elicited Shelley's *Defence*, comes the writing of *Epipsychidion*. This is the point where the second stream, that inspiration drawn from love and Intellectual Beauty which had wound its way so circuitously and often brokenly throughout his whole life and poetry, falls into the first. Henceforth the two themes of the immortality of poetry and the quest for pure Beauty have become a single, swollen torrent which, loosed at last at the third point, rushes into *Adonais*, as the Serchio, in Shelley's poem, 'rushes to the Ocean'. Into *Adonais*, borne along by the general current, much was swept that Shelley's mind had gathered both for *Epipsychidion* and for the *Defence*. In one notebook,[1] where he drafted much of the latter, are to be found his verse translations of the Platonic epigrams he had culled from Diogenes Laertius—they were printed in his Bipont Plato. 'Eagle why soarest thou . . .',[2] with its image of the soaring soul of Plato, was there in the bottom drawer when he came to his elegy and all ready to blend into his general vision of the soul of Adonais: there too was 'Thou wert the morning star . . .'[3] which, in the Greek, he was to set at its head. How the *Defence* marked a point in his course is well seen in the letter which he wrote to Peacock on 15 February,[4] telling him how he had 'excited [him] to a sacred rage, or *caloethes scribendi*' by the 'anathemas against poetry itself'; as if he were

[1] Bod. MS. Shelley adds. e. 8.   [2] Bod. MS. Shelley adds. e. 8, p. 147 rev.
[3] Bod. MS. Shelley adds. e. 8, p. 142 rev.   [4] Jones, *Letters of Shelley*, ii. 261.

partially making a specific defence of Keats he then asks if the anathemas included *Hyperion*. *A Defence of Poetry* was dispatched to Ollier on 20 March. Presumed to be roughly contemporary with this is the letter Shelley drafted but did not send to him: in it he wrote of Peacock's essay[1]

> So dark a paradox may absorb the brightest rays of mind which fall upon it. . . . He would extinguish Imagination which is the Sun of life, and grope his way by the cold and uncertain and borrowed light of the Moon which he calls Reason.

The imagery in which he writes of poetry is, we may note, the same light-and-darkness imagery in which he continues to think of Keats. The Platonic mind is attuned and the crusader's lance is ready for the moment when the sad news comes to him. Keats died on 23 February 1821.

The moment when Shelley received the news is easier to guess than its origin. A biographical source here is the correspondence between John Gisborne at Leghorn and that curious English eccentric 'the Rev. Col. Finch'. Among the huge collection of his papers which Finch bequeathed to the Bodleian is a letter from Gisborne, dated 30 May 1821. In this he says[2]

> I did not reply to your letter of the 7th April as I thought that you might very soon after that be on the move for Florence . . . I had heard before your letter reached me of the death of poor Keats. . . .

In her interesting life of Finch[3] Miss Elizabeth Nitchie prints this letter but omits the first sentence. What we may now learn from it is, first, that Finch was not, as has sometimes been wrongly supposed,[4] the original informant of the Gisbornes and secondly that the news must have reached them before his letter, i.e. before, say, 9 or 10 April. That it had not reached Shelley by 13 April seems tolerably certain, for there is no mention of it in his letter to Claire of that date,[5] although Keats's illness was a subject on which he had previously written to her with much concern. From 6–18 April inclusive there is, apparently, no Shelley–Gisborne correspondence, but Mrs. Gisborne's son, Henry Reveley, dined with the Shelleys on the 14th and 15th[6] and the presumption that

---

[1] Jones, *Letters of Shelley*, ii. 273; non-significant anomalies in the MS. have been adjusted here.   [2] Bod. MS. Finch, d. 2, pp. 234–5.

[3] Elizabeth Nitchie, *The Reverend Colonel Finch*, New York, Columbia Press, 1940, p. 186.

[4] e.g. Neville Rogers, *Times Literary Supplement*, 5 Nov. 1954.

[5] Jones, *Letters of Shelley*, ii. 281.   [6] Jones, *Mary Shelley's Journal*, p. 152.

he brought the news seems therefore a fair one. That he was the Gisbornes' informant rather than they his is suggested by Mary Shelley's mention to Mrs. Gisborne of Keats's death on 19 April as a thing about which 'Henry will have told you perhaps'.[1] On 28 March he had returned from a fifty-day holiday in the Maremma[2] and it seems possible that having somehow picked up the report he had anticipated Finch by bringing it back to Leghorn. That Shelley had had it by 16 April is certain from his letter to Byron:[3] that it reached him on the 13th or 14th seems more than likely.

It would be interesting if we possessed manuscript evidence to show the stage-by-stage evolution of *Adonais*. What we have is disappointingly incomplete. There seems to be no extant fair copy, and for much of the poem, including the first three and the last nine stanzas, there are no drafts either: drafts of the remainder are furiously scribbled throughout four notebooks on pages, as often as not, left vacant amid drafts for *Epipsychidion* or the *Defence*. Nevertheless, from the *disjecta membra* of the drafts, together with related memoranda and scraps of prose and verse, it is not impossible to attempt a reconstruction, at any rate of its beginnings.

The first of these four notebooks, which for convenience of reference[4] I shall number from 1 to 4, contains a stanza beginning[5]

> Pantherlike Spirit! Beautiful and swift
> Thou desolation clothed with loveliness. . . .

This, perhaps one of the earliest stanzas to be drafted, has a cancelled heading 'To —' which, oddly enough, shows that in origin it had nothing to do with *Adonais* but was merely pulled out of the 'bottom drawer' for adaptation into stanza XXXII as a description of Shelley himself. In the same notebook comes a very relevant memorandum from Pindar:[6]

> **ἐπάμεροι. τί δέ τις; τί δ' οὔ τις; σκιᾶς ὄναρ
> ἄνθρωπος. ἀλλ' ὅταν αἴγλα διόσδοτος ἔλθῃ,
> λαμπρὸν φέγγος ἔπεστιν ἀνδρῶν καὶ μείλιχος αἰών.**

---

[1] Jones, *Letters of Mary W. Shelley*, i. 139.
[2] Bod. MS. Finch, d. 8, f. 230.   [3] Jones, *Letters of Shelley*, ii. 283.
[4] 'Notebook 1'—Bod. MS. Shelley adds. e. 6. 'Notebook 2'—Bod. MS. Shelley adds. e. 8. 'Notebook 3'—Bod. MS. Shelley adds. e. 20. 'Notebook 4'—Bod. MS. Shelley adds. e. 9.   [5] Cf. above, p. 204.
[6] Bod. MS. Shelley adds. e. 6, p. 143 rev. *Pyth.* viii. 95–97.

Ephemeral creatures, what *is* any one? What is any one not? Man is but a dream of a shadow: but when a god-given ray of sunshine comes a radiant light rests on men, and a gentle life too.

Hence we may pass to 'Notebook 2'. An embryo form of stanza xxix is the only portion of *Adonais* proper[1] that it contains:

> **The sun rides forth and many reptiles spawn
> He sets and each ephemeral insect then
> Flows   to death without a dawn
> So is it in this world of living men
> A mighty spirit in their sunless heaven [**

Can these lines be the real start of the poem? They certainly contain its initial idea, the light of thought, its procreative powers, and the blotting out of light by darkness: here was not only a symbol of the blotting out of Keats's 'light of written thought' by the darkness of ignorance and prejudice, but a microcosm also of the whole Shelleyan conception of good and evil. The guess is an attractive one, though without manuscript confirmation we can say no more than that they fall easily, at many points, into the moving stream of Shelley's thinking as it can be traced through the previous and the succeeding months. Once again we notice how he discovers a Platonic notion in Pindar and blends it in his lines. With that use of the word 'ephemeral', by which we are instantly struck, one cannot help connecting Mary's description of the Pisa canal:[2]

... By day, multitudes of ephemera darted to and fro on the surface; at night, the fireflies came out among the shrubs on the banks. . . .

On 14 April she records 'A divine evening', and on 15 April 'A divine day. The evening somewhat clouded':[3] it is on this latter day that 'Henry Reveley dines and goes to Leghorn with Shelley and Williams'.[3] On the 16th there comes the boating accident during their return by the Pisa canal, one of two subjects fresh in Shelley's mind that evening when he is writing to Byron; the other is the death of Keats. 'Notebook 3',[4] the water-stained volume long known as 'Shelley's Last Notebook', is crammed with *Adonais* draftings; if, as I believe, it had its 'ducking' that day and not in

---

[1] Bod. MS. Shelley adds. e. 8, p. 112.
[2] 'Note on the Poems of 1821', Hutch., p. 663.
[3] Jones, *Mary Shelley's Journal*, p. 152.
[4] Cf. above, pp. 11–13.

1822, he must have worked very hard on the preceding day or two, though by no means uncharacteristically so. Though documentary evidence does not add up to a full picture of Shelley at work on the first drafts, we may not be far wrong if we allow ourselves to perceive him with his open notebook somewhere by or on that canal, busy, on pages not taken up by the remains of *A Defence of Poetry* in 'making thought nature and nature thought', seeing before him a persistent image not only of Keats and himself but of the whole multitude of humanity ('numerous as gnats upon the evening gleam')[1] in the darting ephemeridae whose life and death could be measured in terms of that 'divine day' and the 'evening somewhat clouded'. But which was which—which reality and which semblance? Then, even then, as imagination rushed beyond and above the boat that was a Neoplatonic symbol of his own soul seeking for Adonais beyond the Veil, bad watermanship came all too near to supplying the answer.

It would seem that *Adonais* was not finally finished till early June.[2] 'Notebook 4' contains more of the draft including many rejected stanzas. Never did Shelley strive harder to conquer the monsters of his own thought, to concentrate the inspiration of his too-far-ranging mind: it was as if he were trying to show Keats that he could achieve his recommendations—'you might curb your magnanimity and be more of an artist and load every rift of your subject with ore'[3] as if he were trying to show the reviewers that Lionel *had* a 'method in his madness'. Into it went all his vision, all his craftsmanship, and the fruits of all the years of thought and study of which his notebooks remain the tangible token. In form it is an imitation of the Greek Bucolic poets: lines of Moschus (echoed in stanza XXXVI) stand at its head, the first words are Bion's—αἰάζω τὸν Ἄδωνιν—and lines of his lament for Moschus are here and there interwoven. Shelley had translated lines from both these poets, and the poem generally is deeply rooted in the results of his practice of translation. But never for a moment does it leave us in doubt how very much more it is than an exercise. Above all—and this it becomes in the very first stanza—it is a Platonic relation one to another of the two realms of Keats's

---

[1] Cf. 'The Triumph of Life', 46, Hutch., p. 508.
[2] Letter to the Gisbornes, postmarked 16 June 1821, Jones, *Letters of Shelley*, ii. 299, and letter to Ollier, 8 June 1821, Ibid. ii. 297.
[3] Forman, *Letters of John Keats*, pp. 505–6.

life, the temporal and the eternal. Herein it owes much to the
Phaedo and the *Republic*: Keats's death becomes an ascent from
the world below where, like the man in Plato's cave, he is a prey
to blindness, ignorance, and falsehood, to a world where he will
become one with the true essence of Intellectual Beauty. Beyond
Plato and the Bucolic poets the other sources are multiple and
out of them Shelley makes an amalgam of original, cumulative
magnificence. Professor White[1] has shown the close parallels with
the *Trionfi* of Petrarch which interpret Laura's death in terms,
Platonic themselves, wherein human life is visualized as a shadow-
procession passing before the light of eternity. Through *Adonais*
passes the full panoply of symbolism which we have examined in
the first part of this book: the New Birth, the Daemons—who
are many and various including 'Wingéd Persuasions and veiled
Destinies'; Urania too is a Daemon, owing to 'The wonderful
description of Love' her own description in stanza xxiv—the
Veil, the Boat, and the Dome. Then come reminiscences of Keats:
of 'Isabella' in stanza vi and of the nightingale in stanza xvii:
with this should be connected 'The Woodman and the Nightingale'[2] which is drafted in 'Notebook 2' and is certainly a Keats
allegory despite Mary Shelley's odd ascription of it to 1818.
Again in stanza xxi the character of the verse reveals a distinct
awareness both of the 'Ode on a Grecian Urn' and of 'The Eve
of St. Agnes'. It is noticeable that all the references are to Keats's
poetry and not to Keats the man. Similarly he rejects personal
touches concerning his own feeling: in 'Notebook 4' he had
jotted down, for instance, a few lines about the Protestant
Cemetery for his Preface:[3]

**. . . My beloved child is buried there. I envy death the body far
less than the oppressor the mind of those whom they have torn from
me.**

He was right so to 'curb his magnanimity' for his poem was not
a man's lament for a dead friend: it was a poet's lament for the
blotting out of a sun of poetry: nor was the memory of the Lord
Chancellor at all relevant now: he must save his barbs for the
reviewers. So in stanza xliii he transfers to Keats the feeling
of his broken poem to William of 1819,[4] 'He is a portion of the

---

[1] *Shelley*, ii. 294, 373, 631.   [2] Hutch., p. 562.
[3] Bod. MS. Shelley adds. e. 9, p. 314 rev.   [4] Cf. above, pp. 213–14.

loveness', and William enters into his elegy only to bring a touching simile about 'that spot of green access

> Where like an infant's smile, over the dead,
> A light of laughing flowers along the grass is spread.'

When he himself appears he is merely an odd, impersonal, allegorical figure, tricked out from a second-hand, refurbished stanza, a 'pard-like spirit' armed, again rather oddly, with the lance which in 'Notebook 3' he had sketched himself bearing against Peacock[1]—it is a 'light spear' now, ceremonially 'topped with a cypress cone'. Yet the poem is by no means without emotion and very personal emotion as in stanza XXI:

> Alas! that all we loved of him should be,
> But for our grief, as if it had not been,
> And grief itself be mortal! . . .

Few lines have ever penetrated more sensitively into the pathology of the moods which follow loss. Well did Shelley know them.

Among the variegated memoranda which traceably belong to the poem is a note of the selection of dead bards who might mourn Adonais or whose souls might welcome him 'the Vesper of their throng'. It is followed by a kind of 'short list' which he further shortens by cancelling some names:[2]

It were difficult to assign any order of precedence except that founded on fame. Thence ⟨why *written above*⟩ the S⟨criptures⟩ excepted ⟨?⟩ Virgil, [Ana⟨creon⟩], Petrarch, Hom⟨er⟩ [Sop⟨hocles⟩] Aesch⟨ylus⟩, Dant⟨e⟩, [Pet⟨rarch⟩] [Virgil] Lucretius Calderon, Shaks⟨peare⟩ Milton.

In the end only Milton, out of all these, was included: he gets very distinguished mention in stanza IV. Intended for *Adonais*, I am sure, was the fragment[3] 'I dreamed that Milton's spirit . . .': it occurs among the drafts in 'Notebook 4' and is remarkable for its fifth line which, to rhyme with *took* and *shook*, ends in the incredible but clearly-written archaism *quook*. And on the subject of Milton it is interesting, incidentally, to find in 'Notebook 4' a confirmation of Professor White's belief that the musical qualities of Urania, not found in Plato, are added from his conception of her in *Paradise Lost*[4] as 'mistress of celestial song'. For here[5] the first two lines of stanza IV read

---

[1] Cf. above, p. 12; and below, p. 272.
[2] Bod. MS. Shelley adds. e. 9, p. 24.   [3] Ibid., 333 rev., Hutch., p. 634.
[4] vii. 1.   [5] Bod. MS. Shelley adds. e. 9, p. 25.

> Most musical of mourners, weep again!
> Lament anew, *great poetry*. . . .

With the single touch of the revising hand which substituted 'Urania' for 'great poetry', Shelley thus changes his mourner from a colourless abstract to a *symbol* and at the same time to a *character*, a fusion of a Platonic daemon with Milton's Muse who will have dramatic value later, as a speaker: her early appearance here serves to steer the poem at once into Platonic waters. It may be recorded also of this stanza that the draft is headed 'spirits of the 18th century' which would suggest that 'magnanimity' before it was 'curbed' extended to a procession of libertarians—Rousseau, perhaps, and Locke and Godwin and others. Among those believed to be represented in some of the rejected stanzas are Napoleon, Horace and James Smith, and Sir Walter Scott.[1]

Shelley's flair for rediscovering in an author concepts which he had already discovered in another author or in several authors is a thing we have many times noticed. After a while, when study of his manuscripts has brought familiarity with this flair, and it becomes possible, as one reads in the light of his symbolic system some of the extracts copied into his notebooks, to see them as he did, their connexion with his poetry ceases to be a puzzle. For example, it is hardly surprising, in view of the darkness–light imagery that is the essence of *Adonais*, to find as we turn the pages of 'Notebook 4' that he has written out the famous prophecy from Isaiah, 'The people which sate in darkness saw great light'.[2] And indeed to Goethe, Dante, Calderón, and the many in whom he found Platonic concepts we must certainly add the Scriptures. Under the Isaiah extract he has noted the Beatitudes from St. Matthew, Chapter 5, adding after the blessing of the poor in heart 'the persecuted, the reviled, and the calumniated': correspondingly *un*blest, we remember, were such as the 'most base and unprincipled calumniator' mentioned in the Preface to *Adonais*. Still more interesting, if we can see it with Shelley's eyes, hardly atheistical eyes now, is an extract made in 'Notebook 2' from the Book of Wisdom, Chapter 7:[3]

**For Wisdom is more moving than any motion: she passeth and goeth through all things by reason of her pureness.

[1] *Verse and Prose*, pp. 38, 39, 40.
[2] Bod. MS. Shelley adds. e. 9, p. 210,—sic.
[3] Ibid., e. 8, pp. 161 rev.–160 rev. Text as given by Shelley.

For she is the vapour of the power of God, & a pure stream flowing from the glory of the Almighty; therefore can no defiled thing fall into her.

For she is the brightness of the everlasting light, the unspotted mirror of the power of God and the image of his goodness.

And being but One she can do all things and remaining within herself she maketh all things new and in all ages entering into holy souls she maketh them friends of God and prophets.

For God loveth none but him that dwelleth with wisdom. For she is more beautiful than the sun and above all the order of the stars, being compared with the light she is found before it.

For after this cometh night but vice shall not prevail against wisdom.**

The virtue and power of 1819, the vision of *Prometheus* and the 'Ode to the West Wind', working their way towards *Adonais* picking up kindred concepts as they go, have here collected something from the Apocrypha which Shelley finds leading him, hardly less Platonically than Plato, towards an all-comprehensive vision of the One.

'My least imperfect poem' was Shelley's own description of *Adonais*. He may well have felt that it aimed highest and, being less weighted with superincumbent trappings than, say, *Epipsychidion*, reached the highest places. The simple and effective structure is a help. Two themes are announced in the first stanza:

> I weep for Adonais—he is dead

and

> . . . his fate and fame shall be
> An echo and a light unto eternity.

These correspond to the two worlds of semblance and reality divided by the Veil. Twenty-two Spenserian stanzas express not only the poet's desolation at the death of his brother-poet but the grief of the natural forces and the daemons of the imagination which had been made beautiful by the poetry of the latter. Seven more express the same sorrow as felt by Urania, at once the Muse of Poetry, as we have seen, and the daemon—here a Shelleyan *woman*-daemon—Love: her voice is the voice of Love and Beauty, as these are known beyond the Veil. Her speech passes from her adoration and grief for Adonais to 'the herded wolves' his enemies and ends with that stanza (stanza XXIX) about darkness and light, the passing on earth of ephemeral creatures and, in contrast, symbolizing one of the processes of immortal thought, the lighting by godlike minds of kindred lamps. In the next six stanzas we have the procession of some of these 'kindred lamps', Keats's contemporaries: Byron and Moore—a selection, in so far as it implied admiration of Keats, based chiefly on wishful thinking—Shelley himself and Hunt. Three stanzas, XXXVI, XXXVII, and XXXVIII, return finally to the reviewer and Shelley's earthly curse is added to Urania's heavenly one: well does he wield his lance:

> Live thou, whose infamy is not thy fame!
> Live! fear no heavier chastisement from me,
> Thou noteless blot on a remembered name!
> But be thyself, and know thyself to be!

'Blessed are the meek' as far as Keats is concerned: in stanza XXXVIII he passes from the 'most base and unprincipled calumniator' whose

> ... cold embers choke the sordid hearth of shame

—in notable verbal contrast to that 'unextinguished hearth' which in 1819 he had proclaimed was his and which, in 1821, is Keats's too—to Keats himself who

> ... wakes or sleeps with the enduring dead.

Here it is that the poem passes from the realm of the temporal to the realm of the eternal: here it is that Shelley's philosophical imagination takes its leap[1]—a leap of leaps indeed. Good-bye now to Bucolic conventions: from here onwards the stanzas are pure Shelley and not a whit the less original for the fact that the mind of genius from which they emerge has been exercised in the study of every kindred mind of genius that it could. 'Wakes or sleeps?' Here is the old, ultimate problem of reality which always faced him—'τίς δ'οἶδεν εἰ τὸ ζῆν μέν ἐστι κατθανεῖν / τὸ κατθανεῖν δὲ ζῆν;' ... 'porque el nacer / y el morir son parecidos'.[2] He grasps it firmly at once (stanza XXXIX):

> Peace, peace! he is not dead, he doth not sleep—
> He hath awakened from the dream of life—

From the night-blackness of the Cave below where men 'keep / With phantoms an unprofitable strife' the poem shoots upwards

---

[1] Cf. above, pp. 40–42 and 243–4.
[2] Cf. above, pp. 174, 183–4, and Ch. 10 *passim*.

to the realms of Light. Here is the home where Adonais has already arrived, the home prepared by Coleridge for the creative imagination, where substances are thinned to shadows and shadows deepened to substances. Long before Keats's death it had been designed by Shelley's imagination and it stood always, as we have seen, before his mind's eye: it lay on an isle which had to be reached in a Boat across a 'wide ocean of Intellectual Beauty':[1] he had sketched some of its physical features in a note-book and described others in *The Revolt of Islam*: here was the Dome he had constructed for those lovers, with its columns and halls where[2]

> Beneath, there sate on many a sapphire throne,
>   The Great, who had departed from mankind,
>   A mighty Senate. . . .

They it is, together with 'the inheritors of unfulfilled renown . . . And many more whose names on earth are dark / But whose trans-mitted effluence cannot die', who are welcoming Adonais (XLVI):

> 'Thou art become as one of us', they cry . . .

and they have a special 'wingéd throne' awaiting him. In imagina-tion Shelley had been there many times as we have seen, not only with the creatures of his poetry but with the Shelleyanized souls with which in his own life he had endowed a long series of women: unfortunately these woman-souls all proved errors of his imagination—'the error', he was soon to say of Emilia, 'con-sists of seeking in a mortal image the likeness of what is perhaps eternal'. But what he had not been able to find in the souls of living women he had found in the soul of the dead poet, symbol of the immortality of verse, 'an echo and a light unto eternity'. At this point imagination, so often in Shelley on the heels of prescience, overtakes and becomes identified with prescience itself. Darkly, fearfully—now, indubitably, on no mortal plane of love—he is borne in his enchanted boat far across a sea of pure abstract, universal beauty to where the soul of Adonais—here at last is his Guide: 'some truth as fair as Ariadne'—is beckoning him. On he goes, towards the realm beyond the Veil where Mutability is no more and where there is no more weeping for envy-smitten bards, they being eternal with the One (LII):

---

[1] See pp. 41, 92, and Ch. 6 *passim*.

[2] *Rev. Isl.*, 604–6, Hutch., p. 52. See above, pp. 116–19.

The One remains, the many change and pass;
Heaven's light for ever shines, Earth's shadows fly;
Life, like a dome of many-coloured glass,
Stains the white radiance of Eternity,
Until Death tramples it to fragments.—Die,
If thou wouldst be with that which thou dost seek! ...

The first four lines, over-familiar from quotation, have come to be regarded as a typical example of spontaneous Shelleyan inspiration, a fine specimen of the shining *vers donnés* which Francis Thompson's[1] *enfant terrible* could always bring home by merely dabbling his fingers in the day-fall and allowing a few friendly meteors to nuzzle their noses in his hand. In truth, however, they form an excellent illustration in miniature of the truth of Shelley's own description of his elegy (his italics) as 'a highly-wrought *piece of art*'.[2] In his indispensable chapter on *Adonais* Professor Notopoulos classes them as 'the best epigrammatic expression of Platonism in English poetry'. Epigrammatic is exactly what they are, though so cunningly woven into the substance of the stanza as to be hardly distinguishable as such. Professor Notopoulos[3] explains how this is achieved: the first line briefly states the doctrine, the second restates it in the usual imagery, translating the One into Heaven and the Many into Earth, symbolized by its shadows; then, chiastically, in the third and fourth lines, 'Heaven's light' is restated as 'the white radiance of eternity', placed last for emphasis, and 'Earth's shadows' is restated as 'a dome of many-coloured glass' which stains the radiance. It is interesting to note that an example of the technical effectiveness of chiasmus lay ready to Shelley's hand in Plato's epigram to the boy Aster:

Ἀστὴρ πρὶν μὲν ἔλαμπες ἐνὶ ζωοῖσιν Ἑῷος·

νῦν δὲ θανὼν λάμπεις Ἕσπερος ἐν φθιμένοις.

If we compare the translation drafted in 'Notebook 2',[4] noting his arrangement of the words,

... morning star ... living

... having died ... Hesperus

we can see him practising the device:[4]

---

[1] *Shelley*, p. 3.   [2] Jones, *Letters of Shelley*, ii. 294.
[3] p. 298.   [4] MS. Shelley adds. e. 8, Hutch., p. 720.

> Thou wert the morning star among the living,
>   Ere thy fair light had fled;—
> Now, having died, thou art as Hesperus, giving
>   New splendour to the dead.

Nor does he borrow without, as usual, making some adaptation: the recalcitrant English, he finds, requires a *second* chiasmus

. . . having died . . . Hesperus

. . . New splendour . . . to the dead.

And, knowing how carefully Shelley pondered over such things, one is tempted to wonder whether it could possibly have been as a 'doodling' reminder of a useful technical trick that he boldly penned four times the Greek letter *chi* which gives it its name.[1]

Such is the briefest of glimpses into a little of what went to make up the *form* of these famous lines. For the rest they are a translation into visual imagery by an imagination that had delighted in kaleidoscopes and solar microscopes of the vision in the *Phaedrus* of the things of reality to which, if philosophers, we attain[2]

καθαροὶ ὄντες καὶ ἀσήμαντοι τούτου ὃ νῦν δὴ σῶμα περιφέροντες ὀνομάζομεν. . .

. . . being pure ourselves and not bearing the mark of that thing we carry around and call the body.

For most of us this vision of[2]

. . . the colourless, formless, intangible essence

cannot be seen because we are *not* ἀσήμαντοι so that the stains of life come between us and its pure whiteness: only to the light of Mind is it visible. [ἡ γὰρ ἀχρώματός τε καὶ ἀσχημάτιστος καὶ ἀναφὴς οὐσία ὄντως οὖσα . . . μόνῳ θεατὴ νῷ.] The way to the vision lies through Shelleyan Intellectual Beauty, a concept much akin at times to the state of the soul which Socrates in the *Phaedo* called φρόνησις and to that Wisdom as well for which the writer in the Apocrypha found imagery more concrete than the Greek:

---

[1] Bod. MS. Shelley adds. e. 8, pp. 142 rev. and 143 rev. Each time the letter has had smaller letters added to make up the word ἔχουσιν which bears no relation to anything nearby.

[2] Cf. above, p. 142.

. . . the unspotted mirror of the power of God and the image of his goodness.

Out of all these and many kindred, overlapping concepts, out of much translucent imagery subtly fused and concentrated into the image of the Dome, Shelley's imagination constructed one of the most arresting, memorable, and at the same time apparently spontaneous images in our poetry: an overarching image of immortality which in the context, where the concern is with universals and nothing less, becomes an ultra-dimensional temple of Poetry enshrining one poet, Keats, the symbol of all poets, of light outshining darkness, of light that can attain to the unstained, unspotted reflection of the power of the One. All his powers of vision, of thought and study, of hard-practised modes of utterance are brought to bear upon the rearing of this vast edifice. Then, at the point where the great image fades and the epigram is merged in the stanza, Shelley gives us his answer to the whole universal problem of reality, the problem into which so many have searched and will continue to search—it is contingent now to Keats (LII):

> . . . Die,
> If thou wouldst be with that which thou dost seek!

Do we notice that 'die'—which means 'live'—is in sharp antithesis to the earlier injunction to the reviewer—'Live! . . . Live! fear no heavier chastisement from me . . .'? A reader may well miss the nuance, but of this no matter anyway for the reviewer has been forgotten, the poem has swept past him—upwards from the 'noteless blot' lost in nether darkness to the realm of the One where the 'remembered name' of Adonais is for ever an echo and a light.

To this vision at length has Shelley arrived, 'having come by many ways in the wanderings of careful thought'. Starting from Platonic philosophy, 'that universal system of which Lionel is a disciple', taking from it what he could, blending with it what he took from other studies and with the thoughts and feelings that came from experience, he has attained finally—*tantum series iuncturaque pollet*—to a synthesis amounting to a vision, nothing less, of the power of God. It is here that the poem begins to run away with him: on he goes, following the beaconing soul of Adonais, his 'guide' by now, enfolded, as he is well aware, in his own bardic vision (LV):

The breath whose might I have invoked in song
Descends on me; my spirit's bark is driven
Far from the shore. . . .

We cannot tell how far, over and above, a certain knowledge of
the occasionally thespesian quality of his powers, Shelley could
perceive what, in thought or otherwise, was lying ahead of him.
What did he mean by 'breath'? Was it simply the divine afflatus
of poetry, that wind which appears symbolically in *A Defence of
Poetry*? Or was it that Wind which he had invoked in the Cascine
and had since become almost a symbol of that force of thought
and feeling which had been blowing through his mind since 1819,
driving him eventually towards Keats? Here we may do what
nobody could have done when *Adonais* appeared in 1821—we
may allow our own imagination to take a leap forward to the
afternoon of 8 July 1822 when Dan Roberts, through his spyglass,
stood watching Shelley's boat disappearing into a veil of Tyrrhenian mists and shortly afterwards, Trelawny tells us, a wind
began to blow from the south-west.

ADDENDUM *(see above, p. 264)*

For the 'cypress-cone' cf. Plato, *Phaedo*, 69d:

εἰσὶν γὰρ δή, ὥς φασιν οἱ περὶ τὰς τελετάς, ναρθηκοφόροι μὲν πολλοί, βάκχοι δέ τε παῦροι.

Socrates' context, like Shelley's, is the after-life; he is talking about the
reception of the 'elect' among the gods. Put within the framework of
Adonais this means 'There are plenty who run around with the outward
trappings (ναρθηκοφόροι, thyrsus-bearers) but not everybody is an authentic
bard, one of the "elect".' Shelley cannot be sure that, like *Adonais*, he will
have a sure place among the immortals, but he modestly enters as a thyrsus-
bearer. Here, once again, we have his concern with the Συνετοί[1] and with
the possible presumptuousness of a poet who aspires too far.[2] No less relevant,
as Professor Notopoulos has pointed out to me, is Shelley's identification of
himself, as a thyrsus-bearer (290), with the figure of Pentheus in Euripides'
Bacchae, a play which he knew well.[3] Like Shelley Pentheus is a 'man with
a mission' who appears to some a destroyer of evil, to others a blasphemer;
like Shelley he is now hunter, now hunted by critics; finally when he joins
the cult he has sought to extirpate he is torn to pieces—the *disjecti membra
poetae*. If, like Euripides' play, the symbolism gives no hint as to what we
are to conclude, that may well be because Shelley's views were not yet
conclusive—because, like Pentheus, he ranged from disbelief to doubt in
his own disbelief.

[1] Cf. above, p. 75, and n. 1; also p. 248, Addendum.
[2] Cf. above, p. 224.   [3] Cf. *Prom.* iv. 473-4.

16. From *Hellas* to 'The Triumph of Life'

'NNo missing manuscript in our poetry', says Professor Blunden, 'would be better worth finding than that which Shelley was about to write at the end of June, 1822.'[1] None of the extant notebooks, unfortunately, contain material for 'The Triumph of Life' and though the tortured Bodleian manuscript, written on loose sheets, offers material for valuable verbal emendations, we must still, it seems, account the rest as something that 'Shelley was about to write'. What, precisely, were his conceptions for the poem and how they would eventually have taken shape must consequently lie beyond any such answers as a new editor could supply. For light upon the riddle we are thrown back upon what we have discovered about Shelley's thought-patterns, and how they shaped his writings as a whole.

By good fortune we are in possession of several valuable, if at first cryptic-seeming, clues, given to us by Shelley himself, about the general directions in which his mind was moving in the summer of 1822. Writing to Horace Smith on 29 June, nine days before his death, he half-opens the door of a tightly-packed storehouse of thought, and thought of a kind most certainly relevant to the major poem upon which he was then at work:[2]

It seems to me that things have now arrived at such a crisis as requires every man plainly to utter his sentiments on the inefficacy of the existing religions no less than political systems for restraining & guiding mankind. Let us see the truth whatever that may be.—The destiny of man can scarcely be so degraded that he was born only to die: and if such should be the case, delusions, especially the gross & preposterous ones of the existing religion, can scarcely be supposed to exalt it.—if every man said what he thought, it could not subsist a day. But all, more or less, subdue themselves to the element that surrounds them, & contribute to the evils they lament by the hypocrisy that springs from them.—England appears to be in a desperate condition, Ireland still worse, & no class of those who subsist on the public labour will be persuaded that *their* claims on it must be diminished.

---

[1] *Shelley*, p. 294.   [2] Jones, *Letters of Shelley*, ii. 442.

But the government must content itself with less in taxes, the land-holder must submit to receive less rent, & the fundholder a diminished interest,—or they will all get nothing, or something worse {than} nothing.—I once thought to study these affairs & write or act in them —I am glad that my good genius said *refrain*. I see little public virtue, & I foresee that the contest will be one of blood & gold two elements, which however much to my taste in my pockets & my veins, I have an objection to out of them.

Here, in a sense, we find Shelley continuing at a point where he had left off in *Adonais*. Granted that reality lay in the world beyond the veil, it was not enough merely to say to the seeker after truth 'Die, / If thou wouldst be with that which thou dost seek . . .' : in life too there was a truth to be sought and not shirked —'The destiny of man can hardly be so degraded that he was born only to die . . .'. Therefore, although he had requested of Trelawny the prussic acid[1] which might at any moment enable him to follow the philosophic conclusion of his elegy, he would not deliberately, as yet, seek reality through death. Thus, nine days before death came to him, we find him, as usual, *facing* some-thing—life.

In facing life we see him turning, as in his youth, to the sorrows of humanity, a subject about which he was as ready as ever to 'utter his sentiments' when a crisis required them. What they were can be partly deduced from what he says, and does not say, of how he intended to utter them. His mention of the Irish is a reminder that he was no longer the starry-eyed young reformer of 1812 : indeed it was the campaign for their emancipation which had taught him the futility of trying, as he had done, 'to act in' these affairs : he had learned that patriots may be as ignorant, intolerant, selfish, and grasping as tyrants, and that genuine, lasting enlightenment was more a matter for the future than he had supposed. When, in consequence, in his great period of 1819 he sympathetically deserted 'the odorous gardens of literature',[2] as he 'Calderonized' it, 'to journey across the great sandy desert of Politics', what he had preached in *A Philosophical View of Reform* was the need for 'a limited *beginning*' ; the ending of that treatise, with its condemnation of violent methods, is of a piece with his dread in 1822 of 'the contest of blood and gold'. Manuscript notes

[1] 18 June 1822, Jones, *Letters of Shelley*, ii. 432.
[2] Letter to the Gisbornes, 6 Nov. 1819, ibid. ii. 150.

and references to Hume on the Civil War[1] give an illustration of
how he had recently sought to study libertarian affairs, and a new
and a different kind of attempt 'to write in them' had been made
in his drama on Charles I to which he refers later in this same
letter of 29 June: disillusionment had, however, arisen from the
beheading of the king which made him see the despot as the
victim and Cromwell the 'patriot' as something even more despotic than he;[2] he had in consequence turned away from his
libertarian drama when he found that philosophical problems
intermingled with human sympathies had begun to outweigh the
purely dramatic element. (This, as we saw, had happened with
'Ginevra', though the cases are not quite analogous, the problems
there having been life *beyond* the Veil, whereas what obsessed him
now, as his letter shows, is the present, nearer world and the
problems of flesh-and-blood humanity.) Yet in turning away
from his drama he had not been drawn towards another prose-
work, such as his *Philosophical View*, but towards a poetical inquiry
about the truths necessary 'for restraining and guiding mankind'.
Not didactically—'didactic poetry is my abhorrence', he had
written in the Preface to *Prometheus Unbound*—but, as always,
in terms of allegory and symbolism he would 'seek the truth
whatever it may be'. Such, I think, was the general scope
of 'The Triumph of Life' which, following the answer given
in *Adonais* to the problems of death and eternity, might have
dealt with the complementary question of Man's destiny in
this transitory human existence. In the fragment which Shelley
left behind him, life is depicted as a chariot in a procession
which never reaches 'the cope of heaven' because its charioteer
is a symbol of the taint and corruption of mankind. It does not
go far enough to tell us either the answer to the final question,
'What is life?' or in what manner he conceived life as a triumph.
What we learn in the first instance from his letter to Horace
Smith, is that the two main subjects on which he wanted to
seek philosophical truths 'for restraining and guiding mankind', were 'the inefficacy of existing religions' and 'the political
system'.

Though much has been written concerning Shelley's attitude

---

[1] Bod. MS. Shelley adds. e. 7, pp. 255 rev.–237 rev.
[2] Medwin: see H. B. Forman, *Revised Life*, pp. 340 ff.

to matters of religion, the prevailing notions about it still tend, in one way or another, to be distorted by over-simplification. It is important here to see the difference between the Shelley of Oxford and the Shelley of Lerici.

If we look at the title-page of *The Necessity of Atheism*, that over-magnified Oxford pamphlet of 1811, we find there an Advertisement which begins[1]

As a love of truth is the only motive which actuates the Author of this little tract . . .

and ends

. . . Through deficiency of proof,

AN ATHEIST

Underneath the challenging title and form of the pamphlet the viewpoint is that of an intelligent adolescent inquirer, a younger edition of the same inquirer who at twenty-nine was still writing 'Let us seek the truth whatever that may be'. Throughout the intervening years there had been an unending quest for 'some truth as fair as Ariadne' which we have been tracing in chapter after chapter. Shelley's opposition, basically, was to the manifestation of contemporary religion and, even when writing *Queen Mab*, where he allows his fury to carry him into an attack on its founder, he vacillates in his notes between scorn and respect. It is to be doubted if he was ever naturally a denier of religion, although like many young men he was liable to deny anything, and to do so with ever increasing vehemence, once somebody else had denied his right to question it. Professor Koszul[2] has pointed out how he subsequently moved from the pamphlet, which in its form if not in its substance is certainly a positive denial, and which he caused to be widely circulated in 1811, through a negative *Refutation of Deism* privately printed in 1814 for a select few, to the project in 1817 of an Essay in Favour of Polytheism. Even this was a considerable stride for the great scorner of Paley and Warburton. Thereafter he came progressively nearer, by two paths, to a religious faith.

First of all, Christ as a reformer and lawgiver held a personal

[1] Jul. v. 205.
[2] *Shelley's Prose in the Bodleian*, Oxford, 1910, p. 125.

attraction for him. Hence came the astonishing vision in *Prometheus Unbound* of[1]

> . . . A woful sight: a youth
> With patient looks nailed to a crucifix.

and one of the furies who come from

> Kingly conclaves stern and cold,[2]
> Where blood with gold is bought and sold . . .

voices thus the tormenting tragedy of life as he saw it on this side of the Veil:[3]

> Behold an emblem: those who do endure
> Deep wrongs for man, and scorn, and chains, but heap
> Thousandfold torment on themselves and him.

Such, for instance, had been Rousseau whose efforts at liberating man had, in the end, helped on the Napoleonic tyranny:[4] such, among many others, himself. Shelley it is who, in the voice and person of Prometheus, feels not only the physical horror of the vision but also the irony and the *lacrimae rerum*:[5]

> Remit the anguish of that lighted stare;
> Close those wan lips; let that thorn-wounded brow
> Stream not with blood . . .
> > Thy name I will not speak,
> It hath become a curse. I see, I see
> The wise, the mild, the lofty, and the just,
> Whom thy slaves hate for being like to thee,
> Some hunted by foul lies from their heart's home,
> An early-chosen, late-lamented home . . .
> Some . . .

Prometheus continues with the tale of those who strive for humanity and learn, for their reward, what it is to be hunted and to have their teaching misrepresented. What this meant Shelley himself knew well. Perhaps had he finished his 'Triumph' he would have placed himself among those whom, like Rousseau and Plato, he considered to have fallen short of their ideal and whom he shows in consequence as chained to the car of Life. Perhaps he would have placed Christ with Socrates in the poem,

---

[1] *Prom.* i. 584–5, Hutch., p. 221.   [2] *Prom.* i. 530–1, Hutch., p. 219.
[3] *Prom.* i. 594–6, Hutch., p. 221.   [4] Cf. above, pp. 196–9.
[5] *Prom.* i. 597 ff., Hutch., p. 221.

thereby setting the two men above the rest of mankind, as Keats had done in a letter[1] where the former is recognized as pre-eminent for 'his Mind and his sayings and his greatness', although (says Keats) his history was 'written and revised by Men interested in the pious frauds of Religion'.

Second, side by side with his attraction to Christ as a reformer, Shelley was drawn philosophically, as we have seen, towards monotheistic religion. There can be no doubt that progress in that direction was helped by his reading of the Bible, a constant source of thought and poetical inspiration which he sought to synthesize with the idea of the World Spirit and whatever else he had drawn from Platonic and other sources. His invariable readiness to check conclusions, his everlasting search for 'proof' appeared in the tabular comparison of statements in the Gospels[2] which he began to make amid his soul-searchings of 1819, and other Biblical extracts in his notebooks are frequent and sometimes extensive. How close to Christian thinking he could come by such means has been seen in the synthesis of Scriptural and Greek images of immortality and the One[3] which he made in *Adonais*.

Two things follow from this later attitude which are relevant to the puzzle of what he might have said in 'The Triumph of Life' about 'the inefficacy of existing religions'. The first is that, living in a day when men 'contributed to the evils they lamented by the hypocrisy that sprang from them', and when it was too often the business of the Church, terrified by the French Revolution, to invoke the name of God in justifying social conditions which threatened, so he thought, a similar succession of violence and anarchy in England, Shelley felt himself to be on the same side as Christ, in fighting against a state of affairs which, while being the reverse of Christian, was upheld by those false followers of Christ, through whom his name had 'become a curse'. In the meantime, while abuses in the world at large had made him a reformer, the inner world of thought—here is the second point—had been giving him something approaching a creed in addition to a moral ideal. Through Platonism he had so far advanced from professions of atheism as to have attained the doctrine of the One. Again, through Platonism and out of the search for his own

---

[1] M. B. Forman, *Letters*, p. 317.   [2] B-H II, 295, 29^v, 30^r.
[3] See above, pp. 265–6.

particular brand of "Ερως, the ideal Beauty and Truth that would extend to love of mankind, one's fellows, he had evolved, for the purposes of our life on this side of the Veil, ideals which are almost identical with the ideals taught and practised by Christ :[1]

> To suffer woes which Hope thinks infinite;
> To forgive wrongs darker than death or night;
> To defy Power, which seems omnipotent;
> To love, and bear, . . .

What Demogorgon here has to say by way of conclusion to *Prometheus Unbound* is what is frequently proclaimed in our Christian churches with much rhetoric, although seldom so well.

But here we must pause. Though Shelley may have come close to the fundamentals of much Christian idealism in so far as he could relate it to practice, a great gulf continued to separate him from the popular contemporary expressions of Christianity. To him the essence of Paley's famous definition of virtue

. . . The doing of good to mankind in obedience to the will of God and for the sake of everlasting happiness

would never have been anything but unacceptable. The 'doing of good' was Shelleyan enough, but the goal of 'everlasting happiness' was far from being so : for this heaven of Christian believers he had substituted the immortality of thought. Then again, in place of the 'passive obedience to the will of God'—a dangerous concept inseparable from the interpretations of priestcraft—he believed that his mission was to prepare and prepare actively for what Professor White has admirably phrased as[2]

A rendezvous between a destined Hour and a human spirit made ready for it by a courageous resistance to evil.

We may not be far wrong if we guess that Shelley's last poem was to have envisaged mortal life as a procession moving towards that Hour. The movement of the car of Life may very well have been an elaborate variation, based on Petrarch's *Trionfi* and bas-reliefs of Roman triumphal processions, of the movement of the car in *Prometheus Unbound* which transferred Asia from the first Cave to the second.

---

[1] *Prom.* iv. 570 ff., Hutch., p. 268. Cf. also below, p. 296, n. 1.
[2] *Shelley*, ii. 125.

To pass for a moment from 'existing religions' to political anxieties: it will have been noticed above that that striking phrase 'blood and gold', which he uses to describe that nature of the political affray which he expects to be a hell-on-earth in 1822, is almost identical with a phrase we have quoted from *Prometheus Unbound* referring to the hell-on-earth which is the home of one of the Furies. This phrase is, in fact, so frequently used by Shelley, and always in a telling context, that it becomes the equivalent of a symbol. If we look at some of these contexts, we shall find that they tell us a good deal about one aspect of what *triumphs* signified for Shelley. It occurs, for instance, in the 'Lines on hearing of the Death of Napoleon Bonaparte',[1] a fine, original poem written in the summer of 1821 which, as Professor Blunden has said,[2] may be 'a pointer to the kind of work towards which Shelley would have turned had his time been longer'. The bright Italian morning causes the poet to marvel at the heartlessness of Earth, who can be thus cheerful when so mighty a spirit has just passed from here, and Earth replies (the italics are mine in this and the following quotations):

> 'Ay, alive and still bold', muttered Earth,
>   'Napoleon's fierce spirit rolled,
>   In terror and *blood and gold*,
> A torrent of ruin to death from his birth.
> Leave the millions who follow to mould
> The metal before it be cold;
> And weave into his shame, which like the dead
> Shrouds me, the hopes that from his glory fled.'

Here was the post-war mintage Shelley feared in the Europe of 1821; even after the death of the arch-tyrant there were millions to follow in his wake, their greedy ambitions moulding the ruinous torrent of revolution and anarchy. It was a similarly 'desperate state' of affairs in England about which he wrote his fears from Lerici. When Napoleon comes into 'The Triumph of Life' Shelley's feelings about him are in the same key exactly:[3]

> . . . I felt my cheek
> Alter, to see the shadow pass away,
> Whose grasp had left the giant world so weak

---

[1] Hutch., pp. 641–2.   [2] *Shelley*, p. 253.
[3] 'Tr. of Life', 224–32, Hutch., pp. 512–13.

That every pigmy kicked it as it lay;
And much I grieved to think how power and will
In opposition rule our mortal day,

And why God made irreconcilable
Good and the means of good. . . .

The conflict between 'power and will' is, of course, the old conflict which always haunted Shelley, the conflict between the power of the rulers and the will of the people, which in the Preface to *Prometheus Unbound* he had called 'the equilibrium between institutions and opinions', and in consciousness of which he had exhorted the people in *The Mask of Anarchy* to passive resistance and patience in awaiting 'The Hour' when the weakness in evil must bring about its decay. Perhaps in connexion with this Shelley would have tackled the theological problems arising from the irreconcilability of 'Good and the means of good'.

How the mood of *The Mask of Anarchy* persisted in 1822 may be seen from one of the fragmentary scenes of 'Charles I', where the comments of the citizens on Strafford and Laud might be those of Shelley himself on Sidmouth and Castlereagh. It is of Laud that the Second Citizen uses the phrase we are watching for:[1]

He looks elate, drunken with *blood and gold*.

It is observable too that the scene is headed 'The *Masque* of the Inns of Court' and the procession, watched by the Citizens, may not be a wholly unrelated predecessor in Shelley's mind of the 'sad pageantry' of 'The Triumph of Life'. Let us now look at four stanzas of *The Mask of Anarchy* itself:[2] the relevance of these will be clear at once from the words which I am italicizing:

XIII

O'er fields and towns, from sea to sea,
Passed the *Pageant* swift and free,
Tearing up, and trampling down;
Till they came to London town.

XIV

And each dweller, panic-stricken,
Felt his heart with terror sicken
Hearing the tempestuous cry
Of the *triumph* of Anarchy.

---

[1] 'Charles I', i. 60, Hutch., p. 490.   [2] Hutch., p. 339.

XV

For with *pomp* to meet him came,
Clothed in arms like blood and flame,
The hired murderers, who did sing
'Thou art God, and Law, and King.

XVI

'We have waited, weak and lone
For thy coming, Mighty One!
Our purses are empty, our swords are cold,
Give us glory, and *blood and gold* . . .'.

'Pageant' . . . 'pomp' . . . *triumph*—we can see that the phrase *blood and gold* (it comes again in stanza LXXII) is closely associated in Shelley's mind with the connotation of these words. The varied contexts in which it is used leave no doubt as to its significance for him: it was a symbol, almost an Apocalyptic one, for the wealth which oppressed humanity together with the wars which generated it: 'blood is the seed of gold' runs a phrase in *Hellas*,[1] which forms almost an explanatory comment. Here lay the centre of Shelley's horror for the contemporary world. What of his hopes for the future? From the pessimism of the fragment that remains to us some have argued that the 'triumph' of Life in the poem was to have been a paradoxical one, and his 'blood and gold' phobia certainly seems to lend colour to the argument. Yet it must, I think, be dismissed on a number of purely negative grounds, notably that it is out of key both with all we know generally of the endings of his major poems and, more particularly here, out of key with the hopeful assertions of Man's destiny which he was making to Horace Smith. Nor do we lack positive evidence too to show that Shelley had hopes as well as fears for humanity. To show the nature of those hopes a ready example may be found within 'The Triumph of Life' itself. This is the figure of Plato, which illustrates the way in which the dangers may be avoided that Shelley feared, namely by fidelity to the ideals of Intellectual Beauty. That this, in his view, was a major virtue far outbalancing minor human weaknesses is seen in the fact that, although Plato has to be condemned and chained to the car of Life because of the weakening in his ἀρετή which went with a non-Platonic love[2] for the boy Aster, the 'star' of his

[1] 248, Hutch., p. 458.

[2] love without 'virtue and power' (see pp. 52 f.); loss of *Wirksamkeit* (see pp. 302, 306).

epigrams, he treats him with sympathy for his imperviousness to worse corruptions.[1]

> The star that ruled his doom was far too fair,
>
> And life, where long that flower of Heaven grew not,
> Conquered that heart by love, which gold, or pain,
> Or age, or sloth, or slavery could subdue not.

First named, we note at once, of the weapons whereby Life, the conqueror, gains her triumphs, is *gold* to which the succeeding word *pain* may again convey to us, at least partially, the sense of the normally concomitant word *blood*. In contrast to the sympathy for Plato who, in his own way, was merely a case of θνητὸς ὢν μὴ θνητὰ φρονεῖν, comes the condemnation of the 'sceptre-bearing line', the monarchs who[2]

> . . . spread the plague of *gold and blood* abroad.

It is in this contrast that we may detect the clue to Shelley's hopes, for they lay in his belief that the wealth which oppressed humanity, the gold that grew from field of blood, was an evil that could be counterbalanced by the generation of liberty through regeneration of thought. Such had been his belief in 1819, and he had in no way departed from it in the year 1822.

Concerning his beliefs generally in that year we have much to learn from *Hellas*. Inspired in the autumn of 1821 by the Greek insurrection against the Turks, it comes, in the succession of his major poems, midway between *Adonais* and 'The Triumph of Life'. Like both of them it is full of accumulations from past poetical moods and, at the same time, as we have already had occasion to observe from a striking instance, its language often reveals symbolically a thought-connexion with the mood of the following June. We shall see now that in other respects too this thought-connexion is a far closer one than at first might ever have seemed likely, and the philosophical conclusions which are worked out in it may be regarded as having much potential significance to the conclusions which his last, uncompleted poem might have had.

In *Hellas*, as in the latter part of Adonais, the keynote is one of the highest philosophical exultation: we pass from 'blood and

---

[1] 'Tr. of Life', 256–9, Hutch., p. 513.

[2] 'Tr. of Life', 287, Hutch., p. 514.

gold' to hope, and from hope to radiant joy. Its final chorus is a vision hailing the regeneration of newly-liberated mankind :[1]

> The world's great age begins anew,
>   The golden years return,
> The earth doth like a snake renew
>   Her winter weeds outworn. . . .

Such language, with its New-Birth-of-Nature symbolism, suggestive of the 'Ode to the West Wind', at once again takes us back to the Shelley of 1819; the regeneration which he conceives is one based on the ἀρετή of the contemporary heirs of ancient Greece, and through it once more runs the belief in the immortality of thought which was Shelley's substitute for the Christian belief in immortality. But then Shelley's vision, as it was liable to do more and more in the last year of his life, starts to run away with him, and the Byronic numbers carry him along to a point where into the Shelleyan-Platonic interfusion of beauty and freedom merges a notion, a Christian notion, it may be, of the One:

> Saturn and Love their long repose
>   Shall burst, more bright and good
> Than all who fell, than One who rose,
>   Than many unsubdued:
> *Not gold, nor blood* their altar dowers,
> But votive tears and symbol flowers.

Yet, once again, if the morality is Christian, Shelley's theology, though even nearer now to Christian orthodoxy, has still to go a very considerable way before reaching it. In this chorus, as he explains in a note[2] on a chorus which occurs earlier in the poem,[3]

> The popular notions of Christianity are represented . . . as true in their relation to the worship they superseded . . . without considering their merits in a relation more universal.

Thus, if we can follow him, Shelley tells us his antithesis to 'blood and gold'—'votive tears and symbol flowers'. By 'symbol flowers', I do not doubt, he meant 'pansies for remembrance', for thus he had used these flowers in the last stanza of the lyric 'Swifter far than summer's flight'[4] where, very pertinently, the context is concerned with his *hopes* and *fears*: by 'votive tears' he meant,

[1] *Hell.* 1060 ff., Hutch., p. 477.   [2] Hutch., p. 478.
[3] *Hell.* 197 ff., Hutch., p. 457.   [4] Hutch., p. 643.

presumably, 'verse memorials' such as *Adonais* had been to the immortality of Keats's thought, and such as *Hellas* was to have been to the immortality of the whole of mankind's Hellenic heritage: such immortality—it went along with general freedom and happiness—resulted from the pursuit of Intellectual Beauty, as it had been pursued by Plato, for instance; Keats too.

Thus far it may be agreed at any rate that, according to Shelley's notions of June 1822, if 'the destiny of man', in the sense of life in the mortal world, were not to be 'so degraded' that death was the only thing to look forward to, if mortal life were to triumph in any real sense, it must combat the dangers symbolized by 'blood and gold' which threatened all that was represented by Keats, still more by the Greeks of whom Keats, Shelley, and the whole of western civilization were the heirs: defence must lie in the ἀρετή needed by civilization for the struggle and in the ideal of an Ἔρως sublimated on the one hand into the quest for Intellectual Beauty and on the other hand into the equivalent of the Christian ἀγάπη.[1] Herein lay hopes by which his fears might be outbalanced.

But before we come to speculate more closely on what *Hellas* has to tell us about these hopes of his for the future, let us take a look at him as he was at Lerici, and try to discover something of what the *present* signified for him in that lovely, ominous summer.

At Lerici Shelley led two lives, distinct yet indisseverable, the one careless and happy, the other dark and full of urgency. In the first he had the most marked 'tendencies to happiness and preservation':[2]

I still inhabit this divine bay, reading Spanish dramas and sailing and listening to the most enchanting music . . . my only regret is that the summer must ever pass . . .

So he wrote to Horace Smith on 29 June 1822; then, by a characteristic transition the letter passes on into his second life, that inner world of anxious thought and entirely contrary tendencies into which we have been inquiring. Persistent and incongruous moods were no new thing for him: one remembers, for instance, the time at Naples when in 1818, as Mary has told us,[3] he was miserable all unknown to her. Now in 1822 the two lives were

---

[1] Cf. above, pp. 55–57.   [2] Jones, *Letters of Shelley*, ii. 442–3.
[3] 'Note on Poems of 1818', Hutch., p. 570.

merged in an all-pervading mood of disillusionment, an emana-
tion, it might almost seem, from the *desengaño*[1] of Segismundo and
other characters in the Spanish dramas he was reading. (What
was life . . . '*pompas* no quiero / fantásticas, ilusiones . . .'. So much,
said Calderón, of its *triumphs*.)

What above all seems to have obsessed him was a haunting
sense of time. On 18 June, eleven days before he wrote to Horace
Smith, he revealed in a letter to John Gisborne yet a little more
of the odd, inescapable urgency besetting him : somehow he must
try to conceive the present in its right relation to the past and the
future :[2]

> If [he wrote] the past and the future could be obliterated, the pre-
> sent would content me so well that I could say with Faust to the
> passing moment 'Remain thou, thou art so beautiful'.[3]

The place, it may well be, contributed to the mood. Even today
in the modern Lerici, where the twinkling of the keen stars has
been rivalled by neon lighting and the music of Jane's guitar
supplanted by the blare of a dance-band, there are moments when
it is still possible to feel that strange sense of a place suspended in
time. In its wild condition of 1822, when the sea roared up to the
door of Casa Magni, so that, as Mary says,[4] 'we almost fancied
ourselves on board ship', the feeling must have been very easily
caught. Never in fact did Shelley live more in that region μεταξὺ
θεοῦ τε καὶ θνητοῦ. It was as if he were suspended with 'the monster
of his thought' somewhere in the Platonic mid-space between
transience and eternity, semblance and reality, and as if the
present were suspended with him : meanwhile the past, it seemed,
with its history of 'blood and gold', was pursuing him urgently
and, no less urgently, he was being somehow mysteriously drawn
towards a future beyond the Veil. The practical Shelley, as happy
with nautical as with metaphysical experiments and busied in
such occupations as organizing the reception in Italy of Leigh
Hunt and his huge family or obtaining a sufficiency of ice when
his wife's life was threatened by a haemorrhage, a feat not easily
to be imitated at Lerici even today—this Shelley was firmly
enough attached to the earth. But there was at the same time a
second Shelley, one can hardly avoid this conclusion, who was

---

[1] Cf. above, p. 189. [2] Jones, *Letters of Shelley*, ii. 435–6.
[3] Goethe, *Faust*, 1700. [4] 'Note on Poems of 1822', Hutch., p. 677.

perfectly conscious of a mysterious attraction elsewhere: it was as if his corporeal self were detached from and in conflict with another self, a daemon-self. This conflict on one occasion was shaped by his imagination, and it seems also by something he had read, into a vision where his own figure seemed to be asking him 'How long do you mean to be content?'[1] Jane too once perceived the figure of a second Shelley when the first was known not to have been present: Edward Williams likewise, when on another occasion Shelley had a vision of a naked child arising from the sea, admits in his *Journal* (6 May 1822)[2] to 'confirming his sensations by confessing he had felt the same'. These were shrewd and sensible people, not given to hallucinations or exaggerated story-telling, and their evidence seems to suggest that not only was Shelley's imagination straining forward into another world but that his imagined world, the world of phantasms, images, 'shapes', 'forms', was coming forward to meet him and over-lapping with his world of physical existence and those who dwelt in it. One is reminded again of what he had written of Christian miracles about 1814:[3]

> They may have been produced by a peculiar agency of supernatural intelligences, analogous to what we read of animal magnetism and daemons good, bad and indifferent who from caprice or motives inconceivable to us may have chosen to sport with the astonishment of mortals.

Now, in 1822, long after, he was driven to seek comfort in Jane's gifts of 'animal magnetism'. Unfortunately the hypnotic cure for his curious mental condition was only a temporary one: Jane, as he tells us in a poem,[4] had to go to bed and

> . . . soon, the guardian angel gone,
> The daemon reassumed his throne.[5]

It was all as if Shelley were waiting for some κακοδαίμων, some spirit of evil in that solitary place to 'wake a tumult on the sapphire ocean' like the Demon in *El mágico prodigioso* which he had recently translated. All we know of the events at Lerici,

---

[1] Jones, *Letters of Mary W. Shelley*, i. 143.
[2] Frederick L. Jones, *Gisborne and Williams, Journals and Letters*, p. 147.
[3] Cf. above, p. 67.
[4] 'Lines Written in the Bay of Lerici', 27–28, Hutch., p. 674.
[5] Cf. 'The Magnetic Lady to Her Patient', Hutch., p. 667.

together with all that Shelley and those who were with him have recorded of their feelings, combines to convey to us their common consciousness of supernatural forces gathering momentum, and this consciousness, deepened everywhere by Shelley's peculiar personal prescience, remarkable at all times and now more sensitive than ever, seems to hang like a shadow over his conceptions in 'The Triumph of Life'. His obsession with time emerges vividly in a pathetic little snatch of verse which we find scribbled in pencil on a page of the manuscript[1]—'Werd' ich zum Augenblicke sagen: / Verweile doch du bist so schön!'—[2]

> **The hours are flying
> And joys are dying
> And hope is sighing
>   There is
>   Far more to fear
>   In the coming year
>   Than desire can bear
>   In this**

Above the lines is a date, 'July 4'.[1] Shelley had four more days to live. He and Williams were then at Leghorn, where they had gone to welcome the Hunt family. On the very same day Williams too, once again, seems to have become specially conscious of the gathering power of hidden forces for, after watching 'sad pageantry' of a kind with which Shelley too must have been extremely familiar in Italy, he wrote in his *Journal*[3]

Fine. Processions of Priests & religiosi active in their prayers for rain—but the Gods are either angry or Nature is too powerful.

Beautiful as might be the passing hour, conscious as he might be of its unceasing flight and that with it joys were dying and hopes were sighing, he was neither more nor less careless about his physical safety than he had been six years before in the storm at Geneva: through his *desengaño* ran a σωφροσύνη transcending ordinary human courage. His remarks to Trelawny in the boat must be quoted again:[4]

---

[1] Bod. MS. Shelley adds. c. 4, f. 37. The date suggests that just possibly the manuscript of the poem went with Shelley on his last voyage and was subsequently salvaged: it is, however, equally possible that it was left with his friends at Pisa or Leghorn.

[2] Goethe, *Faust*, 1700–1. For Shelley's reference to this see above, p. 286.

[3] Jones, *Gisborne and Williams, Journals and Letters*, p. 156.   [4] Cf. above, p. 145.

With regard to the great question, the System of the Universe, I have no curiosity on the subject. I am content to see no further into futurity than Plato and Lord Bacon. My mind is tranquil; I have no fears and some hopes. In our present gross material state our faculties are clouded—when Death removes our clay coverings the mystery will be solved.

To look from this to the passage about Plato and Bacon in 'The Triumph of Life' (255–73) is to have a 'close-up', as far as such a thing is possible, of Shelley's mind at work in his last days. 'A strange fellow that Lionel. . . .' So he well might seem to those who did not, or do not, aspire to a like unity of Platonic theory with Platonic practice. Symbolic of his views, and symbolic of the direction in which his own mortal life was moving, is Trelawny's memorable little picture of him[1] sailing across the bay, one hand on the tiller in casual control of present enjoyments, the other holding a volume of Plato through which he was endeavouring to relate life in this mortal world to the futurity beyond the Veil: further than Plato he did not wish to see—'Ist dir es nicht Geleit genug?'—and perhaps at times his own bardic vision took him further than he liked so that his *desengaño* caused a momentary ruffling of the Socratic calm. Out of all this was growing a poem in which Shelley was to have told us his fears and hopes for humanity. Much of it, we know, was written on the water[2] and we may conceive it as proceeding very much out of his concern for Truth in preference to the claims of the tiller and from his Faustian preoccupation with time. It was impossible not to obliterate the regret 'that the summer must ever pass': the hours as they flew—such was the old, inexorable law of Mutability—were already turning into the past, and present joys died all too soon: no less impossible was it to obliterate the consciousness of the future and its problem, 'could hope be reconciled with the flight of the hours'. But the personal was only a microcosm of the universal for, like the hours of Shelley, swift and short, so were the years of mortal life. *Was* 'the destiny of man . . . so degraded that he was born only to die'? If not—the question passes from the letter to the poem—

'Then what is life? I cried.'—

[1] *Recollections* (in H. Wolfe's combined *Life*), ii. 209–10.
[2] 'Note on Poems of 1822', Hutch., p. 677.

Let us return to *Hellas* where, in the semichoruses, he had faced the same question with enthusiasm:[1]

Semichorus I

Life may change, but it may fly not;
Hope may vanish, but can die not;
Truth be veiled, but still it burneth;
Love repulsed,—but it returneth!

Truth, Life, and *Hope, flying* and *dying*: these words and concepts are, in fact, almost identically, those he was to be playing with in June 1822, though *Love,* we may note, is an important addition: that special Platonic love which is the basis of all his philosophical answers or beliefs. *Truth,* we may note, is *veiled,* but—like the soul of Adonais and other symbols of Truth and Beauty—it is *'burning through the veil'.* The *Hellas* passage goes on:

Semichorus II

Yet were life a charnel where
Hope lay coffined with Despair;
Yet were truth a sacred lie,
Love were lust—

Semichorus I

                    If Liberty
Lent not life its soul of light,
Hope its iris of delight,
Love its prophet's robe to wear,
Love its power to give and bear.

The transience of individuals and the immortality of thought are Shelley's concern here, as they were to be at the time of his last poem and, at the same time, these stanzas look back to *Adonais* in language as well as thought (cf. '*We* decay / Like corpses in a charnel...').[2] Again, as Professor White has pointed out,[3] if 'Poetry' were substituted for 'Liberty'—no very violent change as we have seen from the genesis of so much of Shelley's own poetry—this passage might have been versified from parts of *A Defence of Poetry. Hellas* does in fact derive from the depths of all that is characteristic in the essential Shelley and, from this passage in it as from passages already quoted, we may detect strong indications of an unbroken consistency of thought and an accumulating force

---

[1] *Hell.* 34, Hutch., p. 453.   [2] *Adonais,* 348–9, Hutch., p. 440.
[3] *Shelley,* ii. 278.

of feeling moving towards 'The Triumph of Life'. Out of this we may discover a pattern of fairly systematical symbolism that passes from one poem to the other and of which the observable beginning must in consequence be accounted most relevant to the general contours of the unknown final shape.

The plot of *Hellas* is of the slightest. Mahmud, the despotic Sultan of Turkey, is full of fears for the future of his rule, and his fears are increased when four messengers in turn bring him news of disastrous battles on land and sea: he seeks hope from an old and learned Jew, Ahasuerus, who is gifted with power to see into the future; the Jew puts him in touch with the founder of his line and he learns that its end is near. But what had significance for Shelley was not the plot itself but the conflict that it represented—a conflict between East and West, barbarism and civilization—all that was symbolized in *darkness* and *light*. As with *Prometheus Unbound* the dramatic content, originally Aeschylean (inspired by the *Persae*), very soon took second place to the interwoven philosophical implications.

Almost identical with Shelley's time-obsessions when he was writing 'The Triumph of Life' is the concern of Mahmud in *Hellas* with 'the unborn hour'. His motives, however, are the exact antithesis. For whereas Mahmud sought amid the cycles of time a hope based on the regeneration of *evil*—the regeneration which was to come through 'blood and gold'—Shelley sought hope in the regeneration of *good* through Liberty, synonymous, of course, for him with Poetry or Intellectual Beauty. In Ahasuerus, the man condemned to a weary immortality and himself forming a bridge across time, Mahmud has a well-qualified counsellor for his particular problems. As a character the Jew was an old friend of Shelley's, across whose life and thought too he represents something like a bridge. It is interesting to see him taking shape across the years. In 1810, starting as a stock, legendary figure he is the subject of a 1,500-line poem.[1] Two years later, in *Queen Mab*, he seems to have taken on something of the qualities of Prometheus and of Shelley in his ἀρετῇ σε νικῶ mood[2] and we find him[3]

> Mocking [his] powerless Tyrant's horrible curse
> With stubborn and unalterable will,
> Even as a giant oak. . . .

[1] Jul. iv. 351 ff.   [2] Cf. above, pp. 18–20, 53–57, 227–8.
[3] *Q. Mab.* vii. 257–9, Hutch., p. 792.

By 1814 in *The Assassins* he has become a benevolent figure and by 1821, in *Hellas,* he is[1]

> . . . an adept in the difficult lore
> Of Greek and Frank philosophy. . . .

To the love of Rousseau and Voltaire which he acquired from Shelley in 1812 he has now added Shelley's Platonism and, like Shelley, he is steeped in philosophic studies of reality:[2]

> . . . 'tis said his tribe
> Dream, and are wise interpreters of dreams.

To some extent he comes into *Hellas* as a personification of thought and, unlike ordinary mortal beings (cf. '*We* decay / Like corpses in a charnel . . .'), he is[3]

> . . . so old
> He seems to have outlived a world's decay

and, Mahmud learns, he[4]

> . . . dwells in a sea-cavern
> 'Mid the Demonesi, less accessible
> Than thou or God. . . .

The usual symbolism duly follows. Anyone wishing to interrogate the sage must take a Boat to the Isle where he lives in his Cave: the Boat is vaguely related by a 'gilt prow' to Cythna's 'boat of rare device', and in it he must sail 'At sunset. . . . When the young moon is westering . . .'. Then 'When the omnipotent hour . . . shall compel' (the 'inevitable hour' of Destiny, cf. Demogorgon's) the Jew will appear. Ahasuerus, in time, is duly brought before Mahmud. In what follows Shelley now develops the central metaphysical theme of the poem, which is the Platonic distinction between the temporal and the eternal, that same distinction which had run through *Adonais* though, instead of a single poet it is the whole of ancient Greece, viewed in terms of thought, that he takes as a symbol of the eternal. The dialogue between Mahmud and Ahasuerus is in effect a Platonic one, in which the Sultan is given the propounding of Shelley's problems and Ahasuerus is furnished with the answer to them. Mahmud is extremely conscious of the powers claimed of the Jew—this

---

[1] *Hell.* 741–2, Hutch., p. 470.   [2] *Hell.* 135–6, Hutch., p. 456.
[3] *Hell.* 137–8, Hutch., p. 456.   [4] *Hell.* 163–5, Hutch., p. 456.

incarnation of accumulated Shelleyan philosophy—and loses no time in challenging them on the subject of Time.[1]

> Thy spirit is present in the Past, and sees
> The birth of this old world through all its cycles
> Of desolation and of loveliness. . . .

> I honour thee, and would be what thou art
> Were I not what I am; but the unborn hour,
> Cradled in fear and hope, conflicting storms,
> Who shall unveil? Nor thou, nor I, nor any
> Mighty or wise. I apprehended not
> What thou hast taught me, but I now perceive
> That thou art no interpreter of dreams;
> Thou dost not own that art, device, or God,
> Can make the Future present—let it come! . . .

Ahasuerus replies, in a speech which deals with life in its most cosmic aspect,[2]

> Sultan! talk no more
> Of thee and me, the Future and the Past;
> But look on that which cannot change—the One,
> The unborn and the undying. Earth and ocean,
> Space, and the isles of life or light that gem
> The sapphire floods of interstellar air,
> This firmament pavilioned upon chaos,
> With all its cressets of immortal fire,
> Whose outwall, bastioned impregnably
> Against the escape of boldest thoughts, repels them
> As Calpe the Atlantic clouds—this Whole
> Of suns, and worlds, and men, and beasts, and flowers,
> With all the silent or tempestuous workings
> By which they have been, are, or cease to be,
> Is but a vision;—all that it inherits
> Are motes of a sick eye, bubbles and dreams;
> Thought is its cradle and its grave, nor less
> The Future and the Past are idle shadows
> Of thought's eternal flight—they have no being:
> Nought is but that which feels itself to be.

The Sultan cannot at once comprehend :[3]

> What meanest thou? Thy words stream like a tempest
> Of dazzling mist within my brain. . . .

[1] *Hell.*, 745 ff., Hutch., p. 470.   [2] *Hell.* 766–85, Hutch., pp. 470–1.
[3] *Hell.* 786–7, Hutch., p. 471.

If anything is dazzling here it is the sheer power of great blank verse, in its total effect none the less characteristically Shelley's for such glitterings from Lucretius, Shakespeare, Calderón, and others as may catch the eye. The meaning is anything but misty. 'If ', the Jew is saying, 'an understanding is ever to be found to the problem of the nature of life, that understanding must be sought not, as Mahmud seeks it, in hopes based on the illusory world of time and space but through an appreciation of Platonic reality.' 'The One', 'the unborn and the undying', 'light', 'shadows'— once again we have the language of *Adonais*: once again in 'Atlantic clouds', 'tempestuous workings', etc., and in 'Thought is its cradle and its grave' (adapted from the Calderón quotation[1] jotted down in 1819) we are taken back to the language and thought-materials of the 'Ode to the West Wind'. But if these are backward-pointers, we have a forward-pointer too in the likening of things temporal to a vision and 'all that it inherits'—language which shows that already, when he was writing *Hellas*, Shelley's imagination was working upon the play of Shakespeare's which became a favourite at Lerici:[2]

> Our revels now are ended. These, our actors,
> As I foretold you, were all spirits and
> Are melted into air, into thin air:
> And, like the baseless fabric of this vision,
> The cloud-capped towers, the gorgeous palaces,
> The solemn temples, the great globe itself,
> Yea, all which it inherit, shall dissolve
> And, like this insubstantial pageant faded,
> Leave not a rack behind. We are such stuff
> As dreams are made on, and our little life
> Is rounded with a sleep.

If we add all this up—the accumulation from the past of Shelley's Platonic thought and feeling, a present mood of *desengaño* already underlying the enthusiasm of the poem, and, blending into it from Shakespeare and Calderón, a kindred conception of life (*la vida es sueño*, 'We are such stuff / As dreams are made on...')— we find that we have in *Hellas* a Shelley already attuned to 'that trance of wondrous thought' out of which a few months later his own vision of human existence as an 'insubstantial pageant faded' began to emerge as 'The Triumph of Life'.

[1] See above, p. 220.   [2] *The Tempest*, IV. i. 148–58.

The Jew continues. First—starting with a further fine adaptation of Calderón's cradle/grave image into an expansion of the New-Birth-of-Nature symbol—he relates the Present to the Past and the Future; then, finally, he comes to the question about Futurity propounded in the words of Mahmud:[1]

> Mistake me not! All is contained in each.
> Dodona's forest to an acorn's cup
> Is that which has been, or will be, to that
> Which is—the absent to the present. Thought
> Alone, and its quick elements, Will, Passion,
> Reason, Imagination, cannot die;
> They are, what that which they regard appears,
> The stuff whence mutability can weave
> All that it hath dominion o'er, worlds, worms,
> Empires, and superstitions. What has thought
> To do with time, or place, or circumstance?
> Would thou behold the Future?—ask and have!
> Knock and it shall be opened—look, and lo!
> The coming age is shadowed on the Past
> As on a glass.

The things of Futurity are the things of the world of *reality*, the things that are eternal, namely 'Thought . . . and its quick elements', here specified as 'Will, Passion, / Reason, Imagination': things which endure through the cycles of Mutability and can pass even beyond the Veil—the Veil which 'mutability can *weave*'. With these real, eternal things, with a verbal concatenation Shakespearian in its power, Shelley contrasts

>   . . . worlds, worms,
> Empires, and superstitions . . .

over which 'mutability . . . hath dominion': a grim vision of the 'insubstantial pageant faded' through which we find ourselves looking straight into Rousseau's nightmare-picture in 'The Triumph of Life' of the dead and gone systems:[2]

>   . . . The old anatomies
> Sate hatching their bare broods under the shade

[1] *Hell.* 792–806, Hutch., p. 471.
[2] 'Tr. of Life', 500–5, Hutch., p. 519.

> Of daemon wings, and laughed from their dead eyes
> To reassume the delegated power,
> Arrayed in which those worms did monarchize,
>
> Who made this earth their charnel. . . .

'Delegated power . . .', 'worms', 'monarchize'—when we look back to *Hellas* from 'The Triumph' it is plain that, together with a main concept, some of the original language has been carried over verbally or nearly so. Another place from which a concept seems to have been verbally transferred is those last three lines of the speech of Ahasuerus:

> Knock and it shall be opened—look, and lo!
> The coming age is shadowed on the Past
> As on a glass.

Though here, as in an exalted moment of *Adonais*, certain Scriptural overtones[1] seem to be sounding in the language, the imagery is primarily Platonic, a variation, in fact, of the 'dome of many-coloured glass'. Still more finely is it varied in 'The Triumph of Life' to suggest the coloured fragility of individual lives:[2]

>   'Let them pass,'
> I cried, 'the world and its mysterious doom
>
> 'Is not so much more glorious than it was,
> That I desire to worship those who drew
> New figures on its false and fragile glass
>
> 'As the old faded.'—'Figures ever new
> Rise on the bubble, paint them as you may;
> We have but thrown, as those before us threw,
>
> 'Our shadows on it as it passed away. . . .'

So much, in 'The Triumph', for 'Imperial Rome' pouring out her 'living sea', for Napoleon, Voltaire, Frederick and Paul, Cathe-

---

[1] Cf. Matt. vii. 7, 'Knock and it shall be opened unto you', and 1 Cor. xiii. 12, 'For now we see through a glass, darkly; but then face to face: now I know in part; but then shall I know even as also I am known'. Though I have not discovered any memoranda concerning this passage Shelley can hardly have failed to notice it and, over and above this *Hellas* context, St. Paul's words are an admirable summary of the ultimate Shelleyan-Platonic notion of reality. Verse 13 continues 'And now abideth faith, hope, charity, these three; but the greatest of these is charity [ἡ ἀγάπη]'. This verse, and indeed the whole chapter, might be said to summarize a good deal of *Prometheus Unbound*.

[2] 'Tr. of Life', 243-51, Hutch., p. 513.

rine and Leopold, and others who, doubtless, might have been named later: so much for the 'empires' of poor 'monarchizing worms' to whom, no doubt, would have been added names of religious leaders with their 'superstitions'. Here, implicitly, is one answer to the question 'What is life?'. It is that for each of these people life had been a mere shadow cast on a bubble-world.

But 'the destiny of man could hardly be so degraded that he was born only to die', and Shelley would hardly have been Shelley had he conceived no other answer for his last poem. If we look again to *Hellas*, we may find a clue to what the alternative answer might have been in the early chorus where he talks of bubble-worlds. What he says of them may be taken, *a fortiori*, to be symbolically applicable at the same time to the shadows cast on them:[1]

> Worlds on worlds are rolling ever
> From creation to decay,
> Like the bubbles on a river
> Sparkling, bursting, borne away.

In a note he tells us that with these bubble-worlds (to which we may add the human lives which are their *shadows*), with 'the transience of the noblest manifestations of the external world' it is the purpose of his chorus to contrast[2]

... the living and thinking beings which inhabit the planets, and to use a common and inadequate phrase, *clothe themselves in matter*. . . .

It is in terms of the very chariot-imagery of 'The Triumph of Life' that the chorus goes on to allegorize the contrast:[3]

> But they are still immortal
> Who, through birth's orient portal
> And death's dark chasm hurrying to and fro,
> Clothe their unceasing flight
> In the brief dust and light
> Gathered around their chariots as they go;
> New shapes they still may weave,
> New gods, new laws receive,
> Bright or dim are they as the robes they last
> On Death's bare ribs had cast.

[1] *Hell.* 197–200, Hutch., p. 457.   [2] Hutch., p. 478.
[3] *Hell.* 201–10, Hutch., p. 457.

Here, as usual, we have come to the regular Shelleyan-Platonic
tenet of the immortality of thought and art. Swift as the car of
life may move—in *Hellas* the hurrying of 'The World's eyeless
charioteer / Destiny'[1] again allegorizes both the final query of 'The
Triumph of Life' and that phrase about Man's destiny in his letter
to Horace Smith—Man may yet have time to make his progress
something better than a degradation, always provided that he be
not only a *'living'* but a THINKING being: with the mere 'shadows'
on 'the bubble' are contrasted those who

> Clothe their unceasing flight
> In the brief dust and LIGHT. . . .

The way in which his bright-robes image looks back to *Prometheus Unbound*[2] shows yet again how little Shelley's ideas about
Man's life and his mind have changed since 1819. That they would
have changed very much in the months between *Hellas* and 'The
Triumph of Life' seems to me unlikely. Though he might have
found an infinite number of ways of gifting Platonic imagery with
'that originality of form and colouring which sprang from his own
genius' he could hardly, I think, have done more with the subject
of the nature of life than to find an alternative expression, and
he could hardly have found a more magnificent one, for its two
elements, Matter and Mind—'dust and light'.

What was the 'Triumph' that life was to have had in Shelley's
last poem? If we continue to examine *Hellas* in relation to his
Lerici mood and his general thought-patterns it will suggest a
rough answer to this question too.

Hardly has Ahasuerus finished his exposition when Mahmud
begins to hear sounds of the invading forces which are to overthrow him :[3]

> and now more loud
> The mingled battle-cry,—ha! hear I not
> "Ἐν τούτῳ νίκη!"[4] 'Allah-illa-Allah!'?

---

[1] *Hell.* 711, Hutch., p. 469.

[2] Cf. iv. 412–14, Hutch., p. 264, 'All things confess his strength. Through the
cold mass/Of marble and of colour his dreams pass;/Bright threads whence mothers
weave the robes their children wear'.

[3] *Hell.* 827–9, Hutch., p. 472.

[4] 'In this is victory': a version of the 'hoc signo vinces' accompanying the vision
of a fiery cross seen by Constantine the Great before he defeated Maxentius in 312;
the cause, say some, of his conversion to Christianity. See Eusebius, *Life*, i. 28.

Since his motives are the exact opposite of those of Shelley in
1822 his defeat represents the triumph of Shelley's ideals. The
cycles have run round, and good is triumphant over evil: Greek
thought and the power of the Greek virtues have overthrown the
despotism of 'blood and gold'. Mahmud has been overthrown as
Jupiter was overthrown by Prometheus, and the oddly Christianized war-cry ἐν τούτῳ νίκη that is ringing out is Shelley's cry of
1819:[1]

> ἀρετῇ σε νικῶ θνητὸς ὢν θεὸν μέγαν.

Now 'the sulphurous mist is raised', and through it Mahmud sees
his ancestor, Mahomet: Ahasuerus says[2]

> The Past
> Now stands before thee like an Incarnation
> Of the To-come.

In Mahomet the tyrant sees[3]

> How cities, on which Empire sleeps enthroned,
> Bow their towered crests to mutability.

He is permitted to speak with the Phantom, who explains the
operation of Mutability:[4]

> A later Empire nods in its decay:
> The autumn of a greener faith is come,
> And wolfish change, like winter, howls to strip
> The foliage in which Fame, the eagle, built
> Her aërie, while Dominion whelped below . . .
> The Anarchs of the world of darkness keep
> A throne for thee, round which thine empire lies
> Boundless and mute; and for thy subjects thou,
> Like us, shalt rule the ghosts of murdered life.

Mahmud, in fact, is to join 'the old anatomies' as they are called
in 'The Triumph of Life'. When he came to write the latter poem
Shelley added a few specific names to the list—somewhat oddly
chosen ones—and continued (in a passage which seems to become
almost a continuation from *Hellas*) :[5]

> —'Dost thou behold,'
> Said my guide, 'those spoilers spoiled, Voltaire,

---

[1] Cf. above, pp. 18–20, 53–57, 227–8.   [2] *Hell.* 852–4, Hutch., p. 472.
[3] *Hell.* 845–6, Hutch., p. 472.   [4] *Hell.* 870 ff., Hutch., pp. 472–3.
[5] 'Tr. of Life', 234–40, Hutch., p. 513.

> 'Frederick, and Paul, Catherine, and Leopold,
> And hoary anarchs, demagogues, and sage—
>   names which the world thinks always old,
>
> For in the battle Life and they did wage,
> She remained conqueror.' . . .

Such are the people, mere shadows on a bubble, who are the captives in the contest: the others, the true conquerors, those who are on the side of Life, do not appear. But from the reverse of the medal, as we have it in *Hellas*, a little can be gleaned. Mahmud asks:[1]

>   but say,
> Imperial shadow of the thing I am,
> When, how, by whom, Destruction must accomplish
> Her consummation!

And the Phantom, replying, completes another Shelleyan pattern[2]:

>   Ask the cold pale Hour,
> Rich in reversion of impending death.

Victorious voices from without interrupt the Phantom, and he vanishes in the midst of a speech on the broken cycles of evil. Reality breaks upon Mahmud:[3]

> What sound of the importunate earth has broken
> My mighty trance?

and the voices from without reply:

>   Victory! Victory!

Here, in *Hellas*, we have Shelley's notion for another, non-illusory, non-paradoxical Triumph for Life. The 'cold pale hour' comes round, the 'mighty trance' is broken, 'The curtain of the Universe / Is rent and shattered', and the Past (incarnate in the 'Phantom of Mahomet') brings in the Future, hitherto but 'shadowed on the Past / As on a glass'. Then Mutability completes the cycle of evil, and despotism falls before regenerated thought, which is for Shelley Poetry, Liberty, and Intellectual Beauty: Ἔρως indeed, in its most sublimated form, mingles with ἀγάπη into a strong, triumphant ἀρετή.

---

[1] *Hell.* 899–902, Hutch., p. 473.   [2] *Hell.* 902–3, Hutch., p. 473.
[3] *Hell.* 913–14, Hutch., p. 473.

Such, in *Hellas*, is the Triumph: the triumph over the material world of the world of thought, symbolized by the legacy of ancient Greece. Even so it had been symbolized in *Adonais* by the soul of Keats. These two poems, I think, may be regarded as the arrowhead of a pointer of which the rest is formed of the whole of Shelley's preceding philosophy: it seems to me to point directly towards 'The Triumph of Life'. I find it hard to believe that he would have departed from the fundamentals of his notion. How he would have developed it is another matter.

When, in 1946, it became known that Shelley's drafts for 'The Triumph of Life' were included among the Shelley-Rolls manuscripts in the Bodleian there was, naturally, a good deal of romanticized speculation. The preceding paragraphs of this chapter were written after I had examined it and formed the view that, despite its textual value, it would not, in itself, offer an easy solution to the mystery. In 1961, some years after their publication, Mr. G. M. Matthews printed a fine new deciphering[1] followed, next year, by an interpretation of the poem[2] which attracted much attention, less by its reasoning than by its main premiss; this was that a marginal scribbling, close to the line (541)[3] where Rousseau refers to those who 'fell as I have fallen', constituted a 'wry admission' by Shelley that he had sexually 'fallen' with his friend's wife. That *Epipsychidion* would invite such popular theorizing he had himself foreseen,[4] and its extension to another metaphysical 'mystery' had been accepted as 'proof' even by one of the most discerning among the συνετοί,[5] when Mr. Donald H. Reiman, who has since published a magnificent transcription of his own,[6] re-examined the crucial scribbling[7] (read by Mr. Matthews as 'Alas I kiss you Jane') and found that the last word was 'Julie'. Herein lies a most valuable clue to the Rousseau-Platonic thought-strand.

To understand it we must first get away from out-of-period interpretations of certain words and ideas. 'Fell', in line 541, did not have for Shelley its Victorian connotation of a moral lapse: it simply meant 'became outdated', just as it does in his

---

[1] *Studia Neophilologica*, vol. xxxii, no. 2.
[2] *Review of English Studies*, N.S. xii.
[3] Hutch., p. 520.   [4] See above, p. 248.
[5] Paul Butter, *RES*, N.S. xiii, 1962.
[6] *Shelley's 'The Triumph of Life'. A Critical Study*. Univ. of Illinois Press. 1965.
[7] *Publications of the Modern Language Association*, lxxviii. 3, 1963.

Note on *Hellas*, 1090,[1] where he refers to the gods who 'fell', and in the 'Letter to Maria Gisborne', 198,[2] where Godwin is described as 'fallen'. Again,[3] in 274–5,

> See the great bards of elder time, who quelled
> The passions which they sung . . .

we must be careful to avoid a modern narrowing of the meaning of 'passion'. What matters in the context is not the nature of a passion but its effect; for Shelley the word 'implies', as he wrote to Hogg, on 2 June 1811,[4] 'an incapacity for action, otherwise than in unison with it's dictates'.[5] Passion might be sexual, or it might not: if it was, the significance lay not in the sexuality but on how it reacted on what, looking ahead to Matthew Arnold, he might well have called 'effectuality'.

Concern with functional effectuality—*Tätigkeit*, or *Wirksamkeit* as it is called in Goethe—was universal among the great writers of Shelley's day, and it extended, beyond individuals, to the operative power of social forces, of forces in the Universe and, indeed, of the creative mind itself, whether God's or that of the artist. Out of the *fear* of becoming an 'ineffectual angel' comes the strength of the 'Ode to the West Wind'.[6] Great odes by Keats, Wordsworth, and Coleridge grow out of the same fear. All, alike, are deeply concerned with the vital problem of managing the creative process: how far should the imagination be allowed to operate upon 'wise passiveness', or 'Negative Capability', and when should active composition begin? What I have called above 'Shelley's two lives at Lerici' correspond with these two levels, the active and the passive, of the creative mind. The letters of his last year are full of references to his failure to compose, and his concern with his effectuality extends to that of his publisher. Peacock's comments on his 'want of reality',[7] and Mary's concern with his lack of popularity[8], extend the picture still further. References to Mary during this time are full of tender

---

[1] Hutch., p. 480. Cf. *Keats-Shelley Memorial Bulletin*, no. xvi, ed. Dorothy Hewlett, London, 1965, pp. 12–20, where, in a fine, independent examination of thought patterns, Professor A. M. D. Hughes rightly emphasizes the relevance of these Notes to 'The Triumph of Life'.

[2] Hutch., p. 367.   [3] Hutch., p. 514.   [4] Jones, *Letters of Shelley*, i. 95.

[5] Cf. *OED*, *Hamlet*, II. ii. 65–70, and Rogers, *The Esdaile Poems*, no. 4, 'Passion', pp. 5–7, and nn. p. 119.   [6] See above, Ch. 12.

[7] *Memoirs of Shelley*, in H. Wolfe's combined *Life*, ii. 359.

[8] Hutch., p. 388.

concern and, if there was sadness at home, her health and her reciprocal concern for him and his work might well be enough to explain them. The quotation in the letter to Gisborne of 22 October 1821 is both typical and significant:[1]

> Dem Herrlichsten, was auch der Geist empfangen
> Drängt immer fremd und fremder Stoff sich an.

Its meaning, in his context, is 'Every time I get hold of some fine conception little irrelevant things keep bursting in'. His problem was the reverse of that of Coleridge. So far was *his* 'shaping spirit of Imagination' from deserting him that it often drove him too hard, so that before a conception could be completed on paper another would come tumbling out of his head: hence the many fragments starring his Notebooks, ranging from abortive words and phrases to pieces as considerable as 'Ginevra' and 'Fiordispina';[2] hence too the majority of those organically perfect lyrics which meant so little to him professionally and which still provoke such extremes of praise and depreciation. The inky mess in which 'to Jane' ('The keen stars were twinkling')[3] dropped upon a page of the 'Triumph of Life' manuscript is typical of the 'fremder Stoff' which kept bursting into his mind at Lerici. Jane herself was 'fremder Stoff'—a charming diversion, straight from Porlock.

Now let us follow the 'Julie' clue. It leads us first to Shelley's talks with Byron in 1816, by Julie's lake,[4] and thence to those lines, in the third canto of *Childe Harold*,[5] about the 'passion' of the 'self-torturing sophist, wild Rousseau':

> His love was passion's essence:—as a tree
> On fire he was with lightning, with ethereal flame
> Kindled he was and blasted . . .

So much for the way Rousseau confesses in 'The Triumph of Life': 'I was overcome / By my own heart alone . . .' And with his confession that his words contained 'seeds of misery' we may put Shelley's contemptuous memorandum[6] noting how they had led to the Napoleonic tyranny. This too is explained by Byron.[7] What Rousseau represented for Shelley was the effectuality

---

[1] Jones, *Letters of Shelley*, ii. 364; from Goethe, *Faust*, 634–5. Shelley's textual errors are not preserved here.   [2] See above, p. 249.

[3] Hutch. p. 673, see below, p. 329.

[4] See above, pp. 44–45.   [5] 725, 734–6.

[6] See above, p. 197.   [7] *Childe Harold* III, 779–87.

in his day of the Platonic ideal, the ‘Shape all light’ (352). For[1]

> . . . his was not the love of living dame,
> Nor of the dead who rise upon our dreams,
> But of ideal beauty . . .

> *This* breathed itself to life in Julie, *this*
> Invested her with all that’s wild and sweet;
> This hallowed, too, the memorable kiss . . .

Julie’s kiss—or was it that of the Comtesse d’Houdetot?—does not get into Shelley’s poem, but scribbled in the margin of his manuscript it takes us to the meaning of the ‘triumph’ in which Rousseau and others, ‘All but the sacred few’, are captives—life sweeps on and the effectuality of today becomes the ineffectuality of tomorrow.

Much has been made of the reference (256) to the boy Aster: here too I doubt whether Shelley would have been concerned so much with the nature of sexuality as with its relation to effectuality. Plato’s ‘fall’ refers, presumably, to the collapse of his political ideals in the Sicily of Dion and Dionysius I and II. There were stories of his emotional involvements, and perhaps the ‘star’ is just a symbol of *his* tendency, whereby effectuality was diminished, towards ‘seeking in a mortal [male] image the likeness of what is perhaps eternal’.

The final question to which all this leads is the final question of the poem—‘if life is just a fierce, triumphal procession, bearing away captive all those who were powerful in their day, what *is* real, lasting, effectual? Is life mere Mutability, after all?’ If not

> ‘Then, what *is* life? I cried.’[2]

The italics are mine; their emphasis, I am sure, is Shelley’s. And if the manuscript cannot whisper Shelley’s answer, his works at least proclaim its pattern: ‘Why, the thoughts and the beauty emanating from the human mind, lovelier and more enduring progeny,[3] than the fruits of physical love—here is the “life” that will rise up, new and effectual in every generation, like Nature in the spring.’ As he had put it in *Hellas*.[4]

> Thought
> Alone, and its quick elements, Will, Passion,
> Reason, Imagination, cannot die.

---

[1] *Childe Harold* III, 738–40, 743–6.   [2] ‘Tr. of Life’, 543, Hutch., p. 520.

[3] See above, p. 139.   [4] 795–7, Hutch., p. 471.

CONCLUSION

17. Poetry and the Power of Mind

Thought
Alone, and its quick elements, Will, Passion,
Reason, Imagination, cannot die. . . .[1]

The great writers of our own age are, we have reason to suppose, the companions and forerunners of some unimagined change in our social conditions or the opinions which cement it. The cloud of mind is discharging its collected lightning, and the equilibrium between institutions and opinions is now restoring, or is about to be restored.[2]

SHELLEY is, above all things, the apostle of the power of Mind. Poetry for him was the highest manifestation of that power known to mankind. The personal power of which he was conscious was not, he felt, unequal to the poet's task: he was formed if for anything[3]

. . . to apprehend minute and remote distinctions of feeling, whether relative to external nature or the living beings which surround us, and to communicate the conceptions which result from considering either the moral or the material universe as a whole.

Believing at the same time that this power of his 'exist[ed] very imperfectly in his own mind', he struggled to perfect it by 'the agony and bloody sweat of intellectual travail'.[4] His notebooks are the record of how, in the course of that travail, thought gave a pattern to what feeling had apprehended, and the evolution of this pattern comprises a history of his mind and of the course of his poetry. What gives it coherence and unity is the way in which he took Plato's theory of Knowledge and applied it to Beauty. Beauty was truth, reality, goodness, and its efficacy depended on the virtue and power of love, which could 'bind together the whole universe of things'.[5] Love, in its Platonic ascent from individual beauties towards 'Beauty itself . . . a knowledge of it',[6] starting from a basis broadened and Christianized by Shelley into

---

[1] See above, p. 295.
[2] Preface to *Prometheus Unbound*, Hutch., p. 206.   [3] See above, p. 24.
[4] Mary Shelley's Note on *The Revolt of Islam*, Hutch., p. 158.
[5] See above, p. 59.   [6] See above, p. 21.

811649   X

a desire to 'love mankind the more',[1] took in 'beautiful institutions'[2] and, since institutions are formed by opinions, 'to have a
right opinion'[3]—which was something 'between ignorance and
understanding . . . between divine and mortal'—was an aspiration after Beauty to be striven after by the poet's intellect. Such a
view of the scope of poetry, an intellectual one based on a view of
man's mind as something 'wide as the Universe'[4], and formed in
a mind which sought to be its microcosm, could find the stuff, the
function and the inspiration of poetry in subjects as widely diverse
as the cloud, the skylark or the wind, the singing of Claire or the
speech of Emilia, a line of Calderón or Sophocles, or a whole host
of matters, such as the 'Manchester Massacre', concerned with
the inefficacy for 'restraining and guiding mankind'[5] of 'the existing religions' and the existing 'political system'. 'Wide as the
universe', such a view could rise at the same time to heights that
were correspondingly limitless: once at least, and that was where
the loss was concerned of his fellow-poet Keats, it could carry
Shelley with his poem to the very 'heaven of heavens', the ὑπερουράνιος τόπος[6] beyond the Veil, where the power of poetic mind
approximates to, and seems merged in, the World-mind itself.

Though Shelley did not live to write the metaphysical essays
which, Mary tells us,[7] 'would have served to explain much of
what is obscure in his poetry' we are not, fortunately, without
clues to his patterns of thought, and these it has been our business
to trace and to illustrate in the foregoing chapters. It will be
helpful in conclusion to look yet once again at that striking phrase
from *Hellas*, printed at the head of the present chapter, in which
he refers to the four constituents of thought. Among the fragments
connected with *A Defence of Poetry* is a sentence—connected also
with the 'Lionel dialogue' we have quoted so often—which will
serve as a useful commentary :[8]

It is by no means indisputable that what is true, or rather that which
the disciples of a certain mechanical and superficial philosophy call
true, is more excellent than the beautiful.

What Shelley is referring to is the belief, which many of his contemporaries derived from Locke, that the mind is a mere recorder

[1] See above, p. 39.   [2] See above, p. 140.
[3] See above, p. 59.   [4] See above, p. 15.
[5] See above, p. 274.   [6] See pp. 97, n. 3, 142, 266–72.
[7] 'Note on *Prometheus Unbound*', Hutch., p. 272.   [8] Jul. vii. 107.

of impressions, 'a lazy looker-on on an external world'. Though in both theological and political matters he was so far from considering Locke's philosophy to be 'superficial' as to have frequent recourse to it in argument, in matters of aesthetic theory he did indeed dispute some of its arguments and with much vigour, it being his conviction, as we have just said, that his own mind was formed not merely to 'apprehend' but also to 'communicate', a conviction which, as we saw earlier, is to be related to his, and Coleridge's, more general conviction that[1]

To make the external internal, the internal external, to make Nature thought and thought Nature—this is the mystery of genius in the fine arts.

Such communication when it followed the apprehension of Beauty—Beauty which was truth, or reality, and which was beyond the reach of mere 'mechanical philosophy'—was poetry, ποίησις or creation, the faculty for which sets the poet alone beside the Creator of the World.[2]

Such was the power of thought in general which Shelley with one of his 'remote and subtle distinctions' conceives as having 'four quick elements': 'Will, Passion, / Reason, Imagination.' Let us consider these elements.

The important place held in Shelley's general scheme of thought of the doctrine of Free Will has been observed in our earlier chapters: we saw how it led him from Necessity towards his doctrine of love,[3] how he allegorized its power in *Prometheus Unbound*, and how, later on, it brought him, the 'atheist', into paradoxical proximity to the Jesuitical climax of Calderón's *El mágico prodigioso*[4] as well as to the climax of the first part of *Faust*:[5] 'Will', for Shelley, was the quality of man's mind which enabled him to triumph over evil. 'Passion', in the context, may easily be misunderstood. Of the seven senses of the word which were detected in Shelley's poetry by the editors of the *Concordance* the one assigned to it here, 'ardour, enthusiasm, vehemence', is, I think, the correct one: this sense would cover the idea of ardour of *emotion*, emotive force or energy which appears in a line of *Queen Mab*—'Untainted Passion, elevated Will'. Here once again, we note, it is conjoined with *Will*, and there is another passage in

---

[1] See above, p. 24.   [2] See above, pp. 95–96.   [3] See above, pp. 29–36.
[4] See above, pp. 85–90.   [5] See above, pp. 80–81, 85–90.

the same poem which shows it linked, as in *Hellas*, to the quality of *reason*. We shall not go far wrong if we conceive Shelley as using the word to cover mainly the quality in man's thought exemplified by that restless energy of his own: the quality of the Shelley who said 'I always go on until I am stopped'[1] and who took the West Wind as the symbol of his power. With this its main meaning go subsidiary meanings which might seem to bring into the company of the four thought-constituents the quality of feeling, the vital faculty of sensitive apprehension which must operate before poetry reaches the stage of communication. About 'Reason' and 'Imagination' Shelley himself has much to say in *A Defence of Poetry*, where their relationship is his first point of all:[2]

> Reason is the enumeration of quantities already known; imagination is the perception of the value of those quantities, both separately and as a whole. . . . Reason is to imagination as the instrument to the agent, as the body to the spirit, as the shadow to the substance.

In these and other definitions he is again opposing himself to the yard-rule notions of poetry proceeding from the 'mechanical' philosophies which had often suited his theological and political dialectics. He goes on to say that

> Poetry, in a general sense, may be defined as 'the expression of the imagination'. . . .

In his own poetry, certainly, imagination is a vital power: we have seen its operation not only at supreme moments of inspiration where, in *Epipsychidion*[3] for instance, and in *Adonais*,[4] it takes that sudden 'leap' which is so characteristic of him, but as a sustained, hard-driving energy casting upon his mind permanent or semi-permanent images and symbols, some of them vivid enough to be represented in a pen-sketch,[5] others having a three-dimensional solidity which renders them actually too lifelike for such representation.

'Belief in the imagination', says Sir Maurice Bowra of the Romantic poets, 'was part of the contemporary belief in the individual self.' But herein the attitude of the English poets was different from that of the German, in illustration of which Sir

---

[1] Trelawny, *Recollections* (H. Wolfe, combined *Life*, ii. 194).
[2] Jul. vii. 109.   [3] See above, p. 245.   [4] See above, p. 267.
[5] See above, pp. 105 ff., and Plates I and II.

Maurice quotes from a letter written by Novalis to Caroline Schlegel:[1]

> I know that imagination is most attracted by what is most immoral, most animal; but I also know how like a dream all imagination is, how it loves night, meaninglessness, and solitude.

Such a conception of the imagination, it might be commented, is anything but a philosophical one, and it is quite remote from Shelley's. Like Blake, Coleridge, Wordsworth, and Keats, he believed it to be a faculty essentially related to truth and reality, and his whole poetical life was a quest for such reality. He saw too—witness the passages just quoted from *Hellas* and *A Defence of Poetry*, to look no further—that reason must be somehow related to imagination, and he decided, unlike Wordsworth, that its special function was to analyse the given and to act as an instrument for the imagination, which uses its conclusions to create a synthetic and harmonious whole. Corresponding in practice to the intellectual control which he conceived theoretically to be the function of reason among the other constituents of Mind, is the intellectual travail of which his notebooks are the evidence: the process of analysis is to be seen on almost every page: here is the instrument getting all things ready for the moment when the agent begins to operate. We may well feel here that Shelley himself underestimated the function of intellectual control in effecting the poetico-philosophical synthesis of his poetry. If this is so the explanation may be that, his conception of the sublimity of poetry being what it was and his own intellectual powers what they were, he tended to take intellectual travail for granted, to regard it in fact as something which though essential was not, on the highest levels of creation, to be considered of the same degree of importance as imagination.

Such an underestimation would be consistent at once with the observation of Edward Williams, that modesty in Shelley amounted to a fault, and with the impression of Trelawny, everywhere confirmed by the manuscript records of his study and composition, that 'his intellectual faculties completely mastered his material nature'. It might seem paradoxical then that he has so frequently been regarded as the very antithesis of a poet of the mind, a dreamy sensualist in fact, a creator of lovely but

---

[1] *The Romantic Imagination*, p. 4.

meaningless fantasies, the products of a life in which sensualism made him a rebel against conventions. But if this is paradoxical it is not surprising. It did not *always* seem to his contemporaries that his intellectual faculties had the mastery of his material nature. Striving 'to have a right opinion' and to act upon it in the circumstances of his life, leading the peculiar spiritual existence that he did 'midway between ignorance and wisdom', striving θνητὸς ὢν μὴ θνητὰ φρονεῖν[1]—'being a mortal to aspire after immortal things'—and finding himself uncomfortably poised at the same time μεταξὺ θεοῦ τε καὶ θνητοῦ,[2] between the things of the earth and the things of the world of spirit, he could hardly fail to encounter situations where neither his actions nor their motives appeared the same to others as they did to him. Such a situation arose over Harriet and Mary. Peacock, who knew and understood its still unexplained mysteries better than anybody, affords in *Nightmare Abbey* what might appear to be some hints that part of the explanation is to be sought in the psychological dualism of Shelley's of which we are speaking. Characteristic is the scene where Scythrop, who is Shelley—author of 'Philosophical Gas, or a Project for Illuminating the Human Mind'—invites to his tower the young lady whom he is proposing to rescue 'from an atrocious persecution' : 'You may rely', he says,[3] 'on the honour of a transcendental eleutherarch.' To Scythrop, as to Shelley, never doubting the highest motives of reason and benevolence actuating his conduct, there seemed nothing odd or questionable in such a guarantee. The heroine, a sophisticated young person with no illusions, does not doubt its dubiousness : 'Call me "Stella" ', says she, revealing by her allusion to the heroine of Goethe's that Scythrop in her view was no better than Goethe's hero Ferdinand, who has relations with 'three incomparable beings, made miserable by me—miserable without me!' Thus too to poor Harriet most of Shelley's assurances must have seemed no better than so much Philosophical Gas. The romance of being the rescued captive of Clapham had had time to fade, and maturity had had time to discover many possibilities more attractive in a young woman's life than the processes of Educating the Beloved, etc. When therefore the Transcendental Eleutherarch, the 'Liberator-

---

[1] See above, pp. 75 ff.   [2] See above, pp. 59–60.
[3] *Nightmare Abbey* in *The Novels of Thomas Love Peacock*, ed. with Introduction and Notes by David Garnett, Hart Davis, 1948, p. 404.

in-Chief', found an apter pupil in Skinner Street in the daughter of Mary Wollstonecraft and William Godwin, and when philosophical reasoning, more Godwinian at that time than Platonic, argued according to the tenets of *Queen Mab* that 'cohabitation for one moment after the decay of their affection would be a most intolerable tyranny',[1] it became difficult for him to understand how conduct which he saw as dictated by reason could appear to Harriet and the Westbrooks to proceed out of the depths of selfish feeling. The truth would seem to be that, just as in his writings he tended to underestimate at times the function of intellectual control, so in the situations of his life he tended to overestimate it and to ignore or be unaware of the overmastering power of feeling both to himself and in others. Towards the end of his life he was to learn his lesson : 'The error consists', he wrote, 'in seeking in a mortal image the likeness of what is perhaps eternal.'[2] Over and above its immediate context in 1822 the remark seems to imply the culmination of a gradual awareness that in human life there *might* perhaps be limitations to the power of the human mind. To make possible, for example, a *ménage à trois* of the kind which Shelley had proposed some eight years earlier, the combined minds of Harriet, Mary, and himself would certainly have had to take on a more than mortal likeness. And so, ironically, with all his imaginative idealism he came to appear almost as Byronic at times as Byron who had none and who—hence his continental reputation—approximated so much more closely to the earlier German prototype of a Romantic poet than to the contemporary English one.

When we read *Nightmare Abbey* we are transported into the remote and unusual atmosphere of humour and learning in which Shelley and Peacock moved together. Peacock, whose intellectual perceptiveness was of a range and kind perhaps more nearly akin to Shelley's own than that of any of his other friends, saw deeply into his mind and what he saw there is everywhere complementary with the totality of what is revealed in his notebooks. We need look no farther here than that phrase 'transcendental eleutherarch'. The noun, aptly coined in the best Shelley-and-Peacock manner in reference to the 'Eleutheri', a secret society of libertarians in Hogg's novel *Alexy Haimatoff*, itself covers that whole range of Shelley's activities which extended from the rescue and

[1] 'Note on *Q. Mab*', v. 189, Hutch., p. 806.   [2] See above, p. 79.

enlightenment of Beautiful Beings to the promulgation generally
of Beautiful Institutions 'for restraining and guiding mankind',
but it becomes even apter, in conjunction with its epithet, for what
distinguishes the Shelleyan type of Liberator is the transcendental
nature of his thought. Peacock's own contemporary definition of
transcendentalism[1] is 'discovery of the difference between subjective and objective reality'; this goes far to sum up the Shelleyan
thought that is centred around, for instance, the concept of the
Veil, the Cave, etc., and if we take Dowden's later definition of
a transcendentalist, 'one who seeking the supernatural everywhere loses sight of it as such', we have an additional connotation
comprising the daemons, the 'intermediate space', the moods at
Lerici, etc. We have seen how carefully Shelley was reading
Coleridge at the time of his intimacy with Peacock at Marlow
in 1817: Coleridge, the 'Mr. Flosky' of *Nightmare Abbey*, saw
post-Kantian movements as a return to Greek philosophy, and
Peacock, who was making a stand against undesirable German
influences in English literature, deprecated, as Shelley's Platonic
mentor, the thought that he should become addicted either to the
gloom-and-grandeur meaninglessness of German romanticism
(see Novalis's comment above) or that he should aspire like
Scythrop to imitate 'the divine Kant who delivers his oracles in
language that none but the initiated can comprehend'.[2]

Shelley was very much a man of his time, and it is important to
see him in relation to it. 'Poets', he wrote[3] in the Preface to *Prometheus Unbound* (continuing the subject of the 'cloud of mind
and its collected lightning'), 'not otherwise than philosophers,
painters, sculptors, and musicians, are, in one sense, the creators,
and, in another, the creations, of their age'. In double illustration
of this one might adduce to start with a poet whom Shelley read
and discussed with Byron, and of whom there is a description by a
modern critic which might be a description of Shelley himself:[4]

A man subject to grim nightmares in his personal life: persecuted by
an unknown god driving him to what might be equally the fury of the
poet or the fury of the tyrannicide, making him appear to his contemporaries new and strange and *ex se natus*.

---

[1] *Melincourt* in *Novels*, p. 280. These definitions by Peacock and Dowden are
cited in the *Oxford English Dictionary*.

[2] *Nightmare Abbey* in *Novels*, p. 363.   [3] Hutch., p. 206.

[4] Tr. from Umberto Calosso, *L'anarchia di Vittorio Alfieri*, seconda edizione, riveduta, Bari, Laterza, 1948.

Between Alfieri (1749–1803), a 'forerunner' in time rather than a 'companion', and Shelley there are as many points of difference as affinities: what is relevant here is their common possession of a boundless libertarian zeal, actuated by a supernatural energy. Hölderlin (1770–1843) was chronologically both 'companion' and 'forerunner' to Shelley, though in respect of his creation it had ceased before Shelley's began, since in him the supernatural energy resulted, first in a dualism in some ways comparable to Shelley's, and then in a schizophrenia which rendered him a lunatic for more than forty years. Hellenic liberty and the power of Hellenic thought were prominent motifs in his poetry as in Shelley's: a common bond of Platonism is discernible in the fact that he wrote poems to a beloved woman friend under the name of 'Diotima' and his friendship with Schelling, Hegel, and Fichte brings his transcendentalism into the general Shelley-Coleridge cloud of poetic mind. Again nothing could have been more like a Peacockian fantasy about Shelley than the story of Hölderlin and his youthful *Dichterbund* who washed their hands and faces in a 'Philosopher's Spring', sang Schiller's 'Ode to Joy' over a bowl of steaming punch, and danced round a 'tree of Liberty'.[1] About Schiller (1759–1805), a libertarian contemporary with Alfieri, to whom in many respects he was temperamentally akin, and whom Coleridge translated and Shelley read and admired for his treatment of Christianity as mythology, it is interesting to remember that the words of that same 'Ode to Joy':

> Freude, schöner Götterfunken,
> Tochter aus Elysium,
> Wir betreten feuertrunken,
> Himmlische, dein Heiligtum! . . .

were later to be immortalized by Beethoven in the choral finale of his Ninth Symphony, which was being written at about the same time as *Prometheus Unbound*. When we remember too how close its aspirations for universal brotherhood come to Shelley's in the fourth act of his drama—added likewise as a kind of choral finale—we seem to be aware ourselves of the operation of something like a collective contemporary mind discharging an energy for which lightning is no exaggerated likeness. Comparable in

[1] *Selected Poems of Friedrich Hölderlin*, the German text, translated with an Introduction and Notes by J. B. Leishman, 2nd edn., Hogarth Press, 1954, pp. 12–13.

Spain to Shelley's eleutherarchical aspirations and to Hölderlin's *Dichterbund* was the secret society called *Los Numantinos* organized by Espronceda (1808–42), a libertarian poet whose lot was exile, like that of so many of his contemporaries; Shelleyan motifs are not wanting in his poems.[1]

These and other analogies are less startling if we remember that belief in the power of mind was quite general in the movements of the late eighteenth and early nineteenth centuries, and that other poets besides Shelley thought of themselves as both the creators and the creations of their time. Victor Hugo, for example (1802–85), conceived himself, in a famous passage[2] where the image is reminiscent of Shelley's Aeolian lyre simile,[3] as placed 'au centre de tout comme un écho sonore' and at the same time, since a poet must function not only passively but actively, as a magus, leading men to truth by the light of the star which he has seen in the sky. Hugo perceived Romanticism as 'liberalism in art' and the French Romantics as a whole (who within the field of literature itself were 'eleutherarchs', being innovators in matters of theory and technique) felt themselves to be precursors of liberalism in a wider sphere, some, indeed, took part in liberal politics. In the post-war Europe of the early nineteenth century there went with the collective thinking of poets a conception, midway between a longing and a hope, of a world somewhere just ahead, where the disillusionment that went with war and deflated political ideals would give way to freedom, and the beauty which was truth: the age was an age of visionaries. But with the exception of Hölderlin, who broke his heart with his visions of Hellenic idealism in Germany, none of the Continental poets just mentioned had the same quality of vision as their English contemporaries: 'a visionary insight into a superior order of being'.[4] Hugo, for instance, allowed his great poetical gifts to expend themselves in a wearisome, reverberant didacticism, and with

---

[1] e.g. his 'Canción del Pirata' with its refrain

> Que es mi barco mi tesoro,
> que es mi Dios la libertad,
> mi ley la fuerza y el viento,
> mi única patria la mar.

'For my boat is my treasure, Liberty is my God, strength and the wind are my law, the sea my only homeland.'

[2] *Les Feuilles d'Automne*, 'Ce siècle avait deux ans'.

[3] Cf. above, pp. 195–6.

[4] Bowra, *The Romantic Imagination*, p. 272.

others their dreams of something like the Beethoven-Schiller ideal became little more than a poetic convention. To the company of Blake, Wordsworth, Coleridge, and Keats, visionaries whose imagination had a far more creative quality, came Shelley having a bardic vision all his own, an inquiring intellect that sought for universals and a gospel of beauty and love. If we are to understand him in relation to his age we must endeavour to see its institutions, as he did, in symbolic relation to his Platonic gospel. The paradox that his attempts to practise philosophic reason in his private life have made him appear selfishly unreasonable is no greater than that the application of his gospel of love to public concerns should have made him appear a hater: Shelley-the-Revolutionary and Shelley-the-Atheist are two well-known embodiments of hatred, which still inspire extremes of horror and admiration in those, respectively, who uphold or would destroy existing institutions. The truth is apt to pass unnoticed that the monarchy and the Church, the two institutions which for Shelley symbolized most of the evil of his times, have been so transformed, at any rate in his own country, as to symbolize in some ways the exact opposite, the lines on which they have been transformed or are in process of transformation being lines which he would have approved. Elsewhere in places where these two institutions have been abolished by revolution, institutions have arisen which he would have found symbolical of worse evils. This too is in accordance with Shelley's belief (cf. *A Philosophical View of Reform*) that social progress is achieved *not* by the violence of revolution but by gradual methods and the adaptation of men's minds to them.

In Shelley's day, and later, it must certainly have been difficult enough not to see him as a revolutionary. 'Monarch' and 'King' come second only perhaps to 'Anarch' among his terms of opprobrium, a characteristic example being his wish in the 'Ode to Liberty'[1]

> Oh, that the free would stamp the impious name
> Of KING into the dust! . . .

not to speak, in particular, of his hatred for King George III, 'An old, blind, mad, despised and dying king', and for the Prince Regent his son. Yet what Shelley hated was what George III, the

---

[1] 211–12, Hutch., p. 608.

Prince, and kings in general symbolized—namely the rule of 'blood and gold', the restriction of freedom of mind and, in brief, the exact antithesis of that 'equilibrium of institutions and opinions', founded on the public 'virtue and power of love' which made for the 'unimagined changes' of the Shelleyan vision. That as early as 1817 he had had a presentiment that changes might come around appears in his *Address to the People on the Death of the Princess Charlotte*. There can be no doubt about his own share in the public sorrow:[1]

...A beautiful Princess is dead:—she who should have been the Queen of her beloved nation, and whose posterity should have ruled it for ever.

Thence he passes to the execution of Brandreth, Turner, and Ludlam, three poor labourers believed to have been trapped by *agents provocateurs* of the government:[1]

...LIBERTY is dead...*man* has murdered Liberty.... Let us follow the corpse of British Liberty slowly and reverentially to its tomb: and if some glorious Phantom should appear, and make its throne of broken swords and sceptres and royal crowns trampled in the dust, let us say that the Spirit of Liberty has arisen from its grave and left all that was gross and mortal there, and kneel down and worship it as our Queen.

It is difficult to read this without feeling that Shelley's mind is mysteriously reaching out to 'unimagined changes' which should make Queen and Liberty synonymous in men's minds. He could not know that, as a result of the death of the Princess Charlotte, the Duke of Kent would leave his mistress, marry and beget another royal child, and that that child would be a princess who, like the Princess Charlotte,[1] 'loved the domestic affections, and cherished arts which adorn, and valour which defends', and who just twenty years later, would take the place of 'her who should have been the Queen...'. Two years later, in 1819, in one of his moods of disgust at the doings of Sidmouth, Castlereagh, and others, he reverted in 'A New National Anthem'[2] to this same idea of Liberty as something murdered and at the same time as a queen. But the distressed Eleutherarch, who thus gave what seemed a new and very ironical meaning to the prayer 'God Save the Queen', could not have realized that autumn as he walked in the Cascine, finding in nature's changes an image of the cyclic

[1] Jul. vi. 82.   [2] Hutch., p. 574.

regeneration of all things human, that that very spring now past, the spring which had revived his own spirits and inspired two acts of *Prometheus Unbound,*[1] had in a sense brought the answer to his prayer for it had seen the birth of the Princess Victoria. Had he lived, as just possibly without accidents he might, till 1887—the Shelleys were a long-lived race—he might have heard her acclaimed by the Brandreths, Turners, and Ludlams of that day with an enthusiastic devotion of which most of his 'New National Anthem' would have been a no longer ironical and a hardly hyperbolical expression. Then, and still more, if by any chance he could have lived on into this present century, he would have seen in place of the British monarchy he had known and deplored, a phantom the more symbolic of Liberty for being throned among the débris of other European monarchies, ruined, he might have felt, because reforms had not been effected according to his philosophical views. He would have seen that the cycles had come round.

But here, lest these hypotheses should appear to be presenting Shelley as a potential monarchist or a potential Victorian, we may recollect first that, until quite lately, examples of the kind of monarchy he knew were plentiful, and secondly the likelihood that, his optimism being always limited by the realization that just as spring and summer do not last for ever so the cycles may turn round yet once more, he would have perceived behind the Victorian triumph, with its imperialistic ideals and the complacency they often cloaked, such signs of the decay of ἀρετή as he usually detected among men and believed to be the cause of the decay of what was good in human affairs.

What the word 'priest' meant for Shelley is clearly demonstrated by the context in which it appears in another stanza from the 'Ode to Liberty':[2]

> Oh, that the wise from their bright minds would kindle
> Such lamps within the dome of this dim world,
> That the pale name of PRIEST might shrink and dwindle
> Into the hell from which it first was hurled. . . .

'Bright mind . . . lamps . . . dome'—the array of symbols set in antithesis convey with great precision exactly what the hated word meant to Shelley: something risen from the realms of

[1] See above, p. 26.   [2] 226-9, Hutch., p. 609.

darkness for which there was no place in the temple of Intellectual Beauty. In the Ballad 'Young Parson Richards', the priest is, again, essentially symbolical. The implication is not, as the Victorian editors seem to have thought, that as a seducer and betrayer he is characteristic of the English clergy; what he does however symbolize is the responsibility in England of the Church as a whole for such wilful neglect of social conditions as led to starvation and prostitution. Shelley's views of priests seem to have been permanently coloured by the views of Diderot and other French writers whom he read in his youth, and it cannot be held that in the first quarter of the nineteenth century the Church in England was anything like the menace to social progress it had been in pre-Revolutionary France: it was responsible, in fact, for a good deal of philanthropy. Shelley, however, could not get his mind away from some of the narrow, Calvinistical tenets in which he had been brought up and according to which, God being above all judges and kings, the poor must endure such misery as came to them on the assumption that it came from the hand of God. Such tenets were sometimes cherished even by reformers: Wilberforce, for instance, the great emancipator of negroes, voted on these grounds in favour of almost every restrictive measure. Such a God was the God described by Ahasuerus in *Queen Mab*, the God who, despite his attraction to Christ and his philosophical leanings towards monotheism, became joined in Shelley's mind as a symbol with the priests: the Jupiter of *Prometheus Unbound*:[1]

> Cruel he looks, but calm and strong,
> Like one who does, not suffers wrong.

As the poor prostitute reminds Young Parson Richards, this God, the God of the theologians, is a far remove from the true God of the New Testament:[2]

> *Priest, consider that God who created us
> Meant this for a world of love—
> Remember the story of Lazarus
> You preach to the people of—*

The truth about Shelley-the-hater, whether considered as a revolutionary or as an atheist, is that what he hated in people and in institutions was lack of ἀγάπη, 'charity', humanitarian love

---

[1] i, 238–9, Hutch., p. 213.   [2] Jul. iii. 154.

which was preached by Christ. His quarrel with religion was that its upholders lacked both hope and charity, of which he had an abundance, while the faith which they considered a sufficient substitute for both was one which his inquiring mind would not accept. When he wrote 'The Triumph of Life' he was in a mood in which he seemed more conscious of the disasters threatening his country through weakness in both 'existing religions' and 'the political system' than confident in the ultimate power of mind to rectify them. And yet his earlier consciousness proved prophetic. Abroad the principles of the Holy Alliance were to give way to the ideals of Liberalism and the Risorgimento, and Eleutherarchical energy and imagination were gradually to transform the face of Europe. At home the Victorian age was to see social changes succeeding one another with a rapidity unimaginable in any previous century. Some of these, as Shelley foresaw, were due to physical science. How the railway transformed not only the face but the mind of England has been well shown in a recent study of the eighteen-forties:[1] the pioneer of steam-boats would have been delighted by both the social and the poetical aspects of the application of steam-power to land travel:[2] the poetical aspects of electricity as a power in the universe had filled the imagery of the last act of *Prometheus Unbound* and Faraday's discoveries would have delighted him no less. The survival we have just imagined for him would have brought him in measurable distance of aeronautical experiments, including those of his own great-nephew Sir John Shelley-Rolls, and he would have been glad that in this and the matter of the internal-combustion engine the general fund of Shelley mind still proved that it had a quota of energy to discharge. There will be no need to name here those others whose 'Will, Passion, Reason, Imagination' later contributed to the social reforms of the nineteenth century in England: writers, politicians, philanthropists; men and women of every class and kind. Nor was the Church, more particularly the evangelical section, wanting in its contribution.

'But', it might be objected, 'all this is no more than an imaginative excursion.' Yet if we are to see Shelley in perspective, we must

[1] Kathleen Tillotson, *Novels of the Eighteen-Forties*, Clarendon Press, 1954, pp. 105–8.
[2] See above, pp. 93–96. 'A visionary scheme', said the *Quarterly* in 1831, 'unworthy of notice.'

try to imagine him, as he saw himself, in relation not merely to his own time but to the Past and to the Future. Such was his conception of mind as it manifested itself in poetry: poets and their work were but 'episodes in that great poem which all poets like the cooperating thoughts of a single mind have built up since the beginning of the world'.[1] Imagined against other time-settings Shelley becomes a clearer and more credible figure. Among the ancients the *vates sacer* was a familiar and generally accepted phenomenon, and in medieval times his vision and his humanitarian zeal might have made him the founder of some reforming sect, possibly even within the fold of the Church itself, for the mystical flavour of medieval Christianity might well have attracted the transcendental side of him for which no scope was allowed by the ugly, Calvinistic beliefs and observances amid which he was brought up. But here again we must pause: we cannot by any means make a churchman of Shelley. For though, if he were alive today, he would undoubtedly applaud the modern churches for their greater charity and their present resistance to newer tyrannies, there are still attitudes within it—to divorce for instance—to which the Eleutherarch could never have subscribed. 'Saepe noster', said Tertullian of Seneca, and this, perhaps, is the most, after all, that the Church could claim of Shelley.

Times there are—witness the feeling of suspension between wisdom and ignorance, divine and mortal, past and present—when Shelley's transcendental vision seems to be overleaping a good deal of the sceptical individualism of the nineteenth century to fall into line with Jung's notion of the Collective Unconscious:[2]

The unconscious is anything but a capsulated personal system; it is the wide world, and objectively as open as the world . . . a boundless expanse full of unprecedented uncertainty, with apparently no inside and no outside, no above and no below, no here and no there, no mine and no thine, no good and no bad. It is the world of water, where everything living floats in suspension; where the kingdom of the sympathetic system, of the soul of every thing living begins, where I am inseparably this and that, and this and that are I; where I experience the other person in myself, and the other, as myself, experiences me.

The language of modern psychology here comes very close to the

---

[1] *A Defence of Poetry*, Jul. vii. 124.

[2] Carl G. Jung, *The Integration of the Personality*, tr. Stanley M. Dell, London, 1949, p. 70.

old, mystical World Soul and to the Shelleyan-Platonic conception of the 'intermediate space'; we may even perceive in it
something of Shelley's language when he is writing to Reveley
and his thoughts leap from the Ocean of Water to the Ocean of
Ether. This is a reminder that just as Shelley concerned himself
with boats for travel on the sea so J. W. Dunne, the apostle of
Serialism, was an early designer of craft to travel through the
ether. The word Serialism itself implies something very close to
Shelley's notion of cycles in history or 'episodes' in poetry. Again,
Dunne's theory of limited determinism is much the same as
Shelley's notion of the ability of the human will to help on the
cycles of good and evil. But if we are able to see Shelley's thought
thus leaping ahead through time, we must be as careful to notice
his prophetic limitations as he was to determine them. He was no
Nostradamus and did not aspire to foreknow events: what he
sought was the difference between objective and subjective reality
and beyond the Veil he was 'content to see no further than Plato
and Lord Bacon'.[1]

We have had in our own day one notable example of a poetical
'episode' on the Shelley pattern. This was the career of Lauro de
Bosis, 1901–31, son of his Italian translator. Chief of his works is
the verse-drama *Icaro*, the theme of which is flight. Here is Daeda-
lus, the incarnation of creative Mind, who sees his flying apparatus as a means of escape from the tyranny of his master Minos:[2]

> Tiranni e libertà passano entrambi;
> crollano i regni e crollano gli dei.
> Solo il pensiero vigilante avanza
> e inalza un tempio, la scienza, a fronte
> di cui l'impero de la terra è nulla.

Tyrants and liberty both pass away; kingdoms decay and gods are
overthrown. Thought alone advances, ever vigilant, and raises a
temple, knowledge, compared to which the kingdom of the earth is
nothing.

Not only have we here the general Shelleyan conception of the
collective mind and the unimagined changes that are to come, but
with it we have even the image of the Temple, or Dome. No less
Shelleyan, to take another typical passage, is the speech where

---

[1] See above, p. 145.
[2] *Icaro*, by Lauro de Bosis. With a translation from the Italian by Ruth Draper
and a Preface by Gilbert Murray, O.U.P., New York, 1933, pp. 26, 27.

Icarus the poet tells of his dream and how he hopes to translate it into reality. Every poet, he says, is a messenger between two worlds; from ours he lifts the heart to the harmonies of the ether but from them he carries the sparks to impregnate our fertile earth,[1]

> e quel che oggi è sogno
> per virtù del poeta si fa viva
> forza operante, una terrena cosa;
> da cui altri poeti spiccheranno
> il volo un giorno, verso nuovi sogni,
> che oggi non pur sfiorano la mente.

... and what today is a dream becomes by virtue of the poet a living, working force, an earthly thing from which other poets will one day take flight towards new dreams that today do not even touch the mind.

No comment will be required on this accumulation of characteristic Shelleyanism. Like Shelley, and like his hero Icaro, de Bosis, whose vision had early seen through the mind-darkening menace of Fascism, sought to translate the dreams of poetry into the reality of action and through his imagination and his poetry runs a strange Shelleyan strain of personal prescience. It seems hardly less than logical that at Shelley's exact age he should disappear Shelleywise in his aeroplane into the mists of the Tyrrhenian Sea, after dropping leaflets in which he besought the King of Italy to remember what the Italian monarchy[2] had symbolized and could symbolize and the Italian people not to remain 'servile slaves' but to meet tyranny with a programme of non-violent resistance which he skilfully outlined.

De Bosis's conviction about such tyrannies as Fascism was that their primary danger lay in men's unreadiness to take them seriously,[3] and in their consequent unwillingness to risk their lives against what they believed would automatically perish of its own rottenness. Put in Shelley's terms, what this meant was that they had a dangerous faith in the efficacy of Necessity in place of a realization that evil could only be driven out by a practical exercise of Free Will and the power of Mind. This was the view likewise, independently formed, which was preached in the later

---

[1] *Icaro*, pp. 38–39.

[2] Lauro de Bosis, *Storia della mia morte e ultimi scritti*, prefazione di G. Salvemini, Torino, Francesco di Silva, 1948, pp. 178 ff.

[3] *Storia della mia morte*, pp. 176–7.

thirties and the forties of the twentieth century by George Orwell (1903–50), an Etonian Eleutherarch who had much of Shelley's vision though he was, with the exception of some hard-hitting verse-satire, a prose writer, and he did not move on the same transcendental plane as either Shelley or de Bosis. An example to recall the warning of the latter is to be found in the schoolmaster in one of his novels, who refuses to take Hitler seriously, referring glibly and pompously whenever his name is mentioned to the crumbled empires of Cambyses and Sardanapalus. With this again one might compare the manner in which, before he realized that hopes were empty ones which were placed in Necessity and Mutability alone, Shelley too referred to Sesostris, Caesar, and others. In an article which appeared after the greater part of the present volume had been written, a recent critic has made some further observations about Orwell which, with one or two minor qualifications, are admirably descriptive of Shelley :[1]

... his two major preoccupations [were] the quest for a faith and the obsession with truthfulness. These two made awkward bedfellows; all his life he longed for something to believe in, and yet his policy of absolute candour made it impossible to join those people who adhere to some set of doctrines, such as those of Christianity, for social or personal reasons rather than because they are actively convinced that the doctrines are true. This attitude Orwell ... condemned as a cowardly and destructive surrender of freedom. The alternative was to lie down on the spikes, and he lay on them all his life.

    Orwell, in fact, lived by Christian ethics while brushing aside the claims of Christianity to be literally true.

The same critic goes on to refer to the manner in which Orwell, an avowed Socialist, found himself in frequent conflict with Socialism and points out that

... He was the native English type of Socialist whose politics are based on a version of Christianity. His tradition was that of Owen and Morris, a tradition which is nowadays on the defensive—naturally, because it claims more freedom and dignity for the individual and the

[1] John Wain in the *Observer*, 2 Jan. 1955. As regards the 'obsession with truthfulness' this is applicable to Shelley wherever philosophical or ethical truth was concerned: it needs qualifying, however, by the recollection that like another idealist, T. E. Lawrence, he was liable at times in small matters (e.g. when recounting an incident, cf. p. 168 above) to allow his creative imagination to run away with him.

whole tendency of modern politics, which is geared to industrialism, is to allow people less of both.

The reference to Robert Owen and to William Morris is a reminder of the more direct ways in which Shelley's thought influenced those who followed him, for these reformers, as likewise, in England, the Chartists, and in Germany the leaders of the movements of 1848, regarded *Queen Mab* as something like a testament.

Living in an age when the cycles of revolution and world-war had turned more often than they had in Shelley's, so that men's idealism had become frayed by the reiteration of historical experience, Orwell did not feel the same hope and confidence as Shelley.

. . . He saw that the object of modern tyranny is to succeed by robbing people of their instinct for freedom. In the past, tyrannies had been overthrown because 'human nature' wanted freedom: very well, we will change human nature.

With modern resources of science and technology a tyrant is in a far better position to perpetuate his tyranny than any tyrant of Shelley's day. And under a modern tyranny, which is in fact, first and last, an institution for the destruction of opinions, the old idealistic belief, that as a last resort Man's mind can remain untouched, is no longer tenable: not even this remains to Winston, the crushed eleutherarch of *Nineteen-Eighty-Four*. Knowing this Orwell, a libertarian himself, attacked those sections of advanced English political opinion which derived from the Continent and which, while aiming at liberty and equality for all men, seemed to him to be doctrinaire, anti-human, and subversive themselves of liberty. Shelley has a word on the subject:[1]

. . . We have more moral, political and historical wisdom than we know how to reduce into practice. . . .We want the creative faculty to imagine that which we know; we want the generous impulse to act that which we imagine; we want the poetry of life: our calculations have outrun conception; we have eaten more than we can digest. The cultivation of those sciences which have enlarged the limits of the empire of man over the external world, has, for want of the poetical faculty, proportionally circumscribed those of the internal world; and man, having enslaved the elements, remains himself a slave. . . . From what

[1] *A Defence of Poetry*, Jul. vii. 134.

other cause has it arisen that these inventions which should have lightened, have added a weight to the curse imposed on Adam?

Nothing could be more typical, not only of the far-sightedness of Shelley's thought but also of its coherency and consistency, than that a passage of this kind of practical worldly wisdom should appear in an essay which defends poetry. Today the frontiers of thought and of the meanings of words have shifted, and it is a sufficient illustration of his meaning that the very word 'science' has come to signify no more than those particular sciences 'which have enlarged the empire of man over the external world'. The effect of 'science' of this restricted kind, where 'calculations have outrun conceptions' may be seen in the language in which nine eminent scientists recently launched an appeal to their fellow human beings on the subject of the danger of certain 'scientific' inventions to human existence itself:[1]

. . . We want you to consider yourselves only as members of a biological species which has had a remarkable history and whose disappearance none of us desire.

If this reads, as it might seem to do, like the 'scientific' thought of George Orwell's *Nineteen-Eighty-Four* it is because its drab unimaginativeness would seem to leave no room for any belief in the individual self, its rights and its responsibilities. Shelley, for whom Science meant not one branch of knowledge but all knowledge, all that proceeds from those 'quick elements / Will, Passion, Reason, Imagination' to fill Man's mind and make it the symbol of the universe, conceived Man as something more exalted, less easily calculable, the creator and the creation of a heritage of love and beauty. And here, for an example in Man of 'the creative faculty to imagine . . . the generous power to act', this inquiry into Shelley's own mind as he reveals it to us at work has led us round once again, for the last time, to its reflections in *Prometheus Unbound*.[2] Earth is speaking, speaking of Man:

> Man, oh, not men! a chain of linkèd thought,
> Of love and might to be divided not,
> Compelling the elements with adamantine stress;
> As the sun rules, even with a tyrant's gaze,
> The unquiet republic of the maze
> Of planets, struggling fierce towards heaven's free wilderness.

[1] The *Daily Telegraph*, 11 July 1955.   [2] iv. 394 ff., Hutch., pp .263–4.

Man, one harmonious soul of many a soul,
 Whose nature is its own divine control,
Where all things flow to all, as rivers to the sea;
 Familiar acts are beautiful through love;
 Labour, and pain, and grief, in life's green grove
Sport like tame beasts, none knew how gentle they could be!

 His will, with all mean passions, bad delights,
 And selfish cares, its trembling satellites,
A spirit ill to guide, but mighty to obey,
 Is as a tempest-wingèd ship, whose helm
 Love rules, through waves which dare not overwhelm,
Forcing life's wildest shores to own its sovereign sway.

 All things confess his strength. Through the cold mass
 Of marble and of colour his dreams pass;
Bright threads whence mothers weave the robes their children
                wear;
 Language is a perpetual Orphic song,
 Which rules with Daedal harmony a throng
Of thoughts and forms, which else senseless and shapeless were.

 The lightning is his slave; heaven's utmost deep
 Gives up her stars, and like a flock of sheep
They pass before his eye, are numbered, and roll on!
 The tempest is his steed, he strides the air;
 And the abyss shouts from her depth laid bare,
Heaven, hast thou secrets? Man unveils me; I have none.

APPENDIXES

APPENDIX I

'The wonderful description of Love' (Ch. 4, pp. 44, 47, 48)

S H E L L E Y ' s references to Vol. X of his Bipont Plato[1] collated with the Oxford Classical Text and with his translation of the *Symposium* as printed in the Julian Edition, Vol. VII.

Bipont	O.C.T.	Tr., Shelley
p. 214 [ἀπα]λός to οὐ γὰρ οἷός τ' ἦν (linea ultima) line 8 starts περὶ Ἔρωτα ὅτι ἁπαλός	195d 196a 195e	'He is young . . . moist and liquid', pp. 189–90. 'The same evidence', p. 189.
p. 215, line 7 οὐκ ἐνίζει Ἔρως . . . line 10 ἱκανὰ, καὶ ἔτι πολλὰ λείπεται	196b 196b	'For the winged love . . . unsaid', p. 190.
p. 218 ἐπειδὴ δ' ὁ θεὸς to ξυμπάντων τε θεῶν καὶ . . .	197b 197e	'But so soon as . . . gods and men', pp. 191–2.
p. 228, to line 15 Ἡ καὶ μὴ ἂν σοφὸν to οἵ φασιν αὐτὸν	202a 202c	'Do you not perceive . . . a God at all', pp. 196–7.
p. 231, line 5 [ἀκό]λουθος καὶ θεράπων	203c	'Love is therefore the follower . . .', p. 196.
p. 233 [ἀναγ]καῖον Ἔρωτα to ὁ ἐρῶν	204b 204d	'. . . so that Love is of necessity . . . seek from it', p. 199.
p. 236 οὔτ' ἐρασταί to Ἔρως ἐστίν	205d 206b	'nor are called lovers...the general definition of Love', pp. 200–1.
pp. 239–40 [καί πο]τε ἤρετο to ταὐτὸν πάσχει	207a 208a	'in addition, she enquired . . . the same revolution', pp. 202–3.

[1] The full title of the Bipont Plato is Πλάτων | *Platonis Philosophi* | *Quae Extant* | *Graece ad Editionem Henrici Stephani* | *Accurate Expressa* | *Cum Marsilii Ficini Interpretatione* | *Accedit Varietas Lectionis* | Studiis Societatis Bipontinae | Biponti | Ex Typographia Societatis, 12 vols., 1781–7.

APPENDIX II

The temptation of Justina (Ch. 5, pp. 85–87)
Calderón's 'episodes' (Ch. 10, pp. 180–1, Ch. 12, p. 226)
Shelley as a translator

THE following extract from *El mágicoprodigioso* is given here, principally as a convenient example of the 'episodic'[1] form imitated in the 'Ode to the West Wind' and 'To a Skylark': in order, however, that it may afford a glimpse at the same time into Shelley's quality as a translator the Spanish text has been printed facing his rendering of it. Translation provides an important aspect of Shelley at work. Though his reason for the practice may sometimes have been merely 'a want of spirit to invent', as he tells us in a statement[2] recently discovered by Professor Jones—its value to his composition proved considerable;[3] examples of this in connexion with his Greek and Italian studies have been noted in various chapters of this book. See Appendix III for an example of some fruits borne by his German translation, and Ch. 13 for his translation of Italian poets.

ADDENDUM

A simple and perfect example of the 'episodic' form is the four-stanza lyric,[4] 'The keen stars were twinkling'. Shelley is sitting in the *light* (A) of the stars and moon and listening to *music* (B). In Stanza I he feels the sweetness of Jane's voice, as it repeats the guitar-phrase, a *feeling* which we may call 'C'. In Stanza II the *feeling* (C) in the voice seems to give a *soul* (D) to the strings. In Stanza III the natural world about him (symbolized by the unshaken leaf) seems immobilized and overpowered by the voice. In Stanza IV the three episodes, A, B, and C, are drawn together: he entreats Jane for more of B because B reveals something of a world beyond ours (a D world) where music (B), moonlight (A), and feeling (C) are one.

This analysis has seemed worth while because of the difficulty which some critics have experienced with the lyric subtlety that can thus combine Platonic imagery with the Calderonian pattern; one has written of it: 'Shelley *attempts* [my italics] a synthesis', and another remarks that 'Shelley's lyrics are mechanical rather than organic'. The manuscript (see above p. 303) shows that this organically perfect poem is also a miracle of spontaneous composition.

[1] Cf. below the 'episodes' of the Sunflower, Vine, and Nightingale.

[2] In a postscript to a letter from Mary to Maria Gisborne written on 19 July 1820: he is referring to his translation of the Homeric 'Hymn to Mercury'. See F. L. Jones, *Studies in Philology*, Jan. 1955. The reason does not apply here. Cf. Ch. 5, p. 79.

[3] e.g. again, for a good instance, the relation of the 'Hymn to Mercury' to 'The Witch of Atlas' written a month later.   [4] Hutch., p. 673.

Calderón, *El mágico prodigioso*, III. v[1]

Una voz.	¿Cuál es la gloria mayor de esta vida?
Coro. (Dentro.)	Amor, amor.

[*Mientras esta copla se canta, se va entrando* EL DEMONIO *por una puerta y sale por otra,* JUSTINA *huyendo.*]

Una voz.	No hay sujeto en que no imprima el fuego de amor su llama, pues vive más donde ama el hombre, que donde anima. Amor solamente estima cuanto tener vida sabe, el tronco, la flor y el ave: luego es la gloria mayor de esta vida ...
Coro. (Dent.)	Amor, amor.
Justina.	Pesada imaginación al parecer lisonjera, ¿cuándo te he dado ocasión para que desta manera aflijas mi corazón? ¿Cuál es la causa, en rigor, deste fuego, deste ardor, que en mi por instantes crece? ¿Qué dolor el que padece mi sentido?
Coro. (Dent.)	Amor, amor.
Justina (sosegándose).	Aquel ruiseñor amante es quien respuesta me da, enamorando constante a su consorte, que está un ramo más adelante. Calla, ruiseñor; no aquí imaginar me hagas ya, por las quejas que te oí, cómo un hombre sentirá, si siente un pájaro así; mas no: una vid fué lasciva que buscando fugitiva va àl tronco donde se enlace,

---

[1] Text from Aguilar Edition, i. 1088–9, slightly adapted, to face the English text.

Shelley: 'Scenes from Calderón', III. 24–78[1]

A voice within.	What is the glory far above	
	All else in human life?	
All voices within.	Love! love!	25

[*While these words are sung the* DAEMON *goes out at one door and* JUSTINA *enters at another.*]

The first voice.	There is no form in which the fire	
	Of love its traces has impressed not.	
	Man lives far more in love's desire	
	Than by life's breath, soon possessed not.	
	If all that lives must love or die,	30
	All shapes on earth, or sea, or sky,	
	With one consent to Heaven cry	
	That the glory far above	
	All else in life is—	
All.(within)	Love! oh, Love!	
Justina.	Thou melancholy Thought which art	35
	So flattering and so sweet, to thee	
	When did I give thee[2] liberty	
	Thus to afflict my heart?	
	What is the cause of this new Power	
	Which doth my fevered being move,	40
	Momently raging more and more?	
	What subtle Pain is kindled now	
	Which from my heart doth overflow	
	Into my senses?—	
All. (within)	Love! oh, Love!	
Justina (calming herself).		
	'Tis that enamoured Nightingale	45
	Who gives me the reply;	
	He ever tells the same soft tale	
	Of passion and of constancy	
	To his mate, who rapt and fond,	
	Listening sits, a bough beyond.	50
	Be silent, Nightingale—no more	
	Make me think, in hearing thee	
	Thus tenderly thy love deplore,	
	If a bird can feel his so,	
	What a man would feel for me.	55
	And, voluptuous Vine, O thou	

[1] Text from Hutch., pp. 743–5, slightly adapted, to face the Spanish text.
[2] Hutch, has 'the', leaving *te* untranslated.

Calderón, *El mágico prodigioso*, III. v (*cont.*)

siendo el verdor con que abrace
el peso con que derriba.
No así con verdes abrazos
me hagas pensar en quien amas,
vid; que dudaré en tus lazos,
si así abrazan unas ramas,
cómo enraman unos brazos.
Y si no es la vid, será
aquel girasol, que está
viendo cara a cara al sol,
tras cuyo hermoso arrebol
siempre moviéndose va.
No sigas, no, tus enojos,
flor, con marchitos despojos;
que pensaran mis congojas,
si así lloran unas hojas,
cómo lloran unos ojos.
Cesa, amante ruiseñor;
desúnete, vid frondosa;
párate, inconstante flor,
o decid, ¿ qué venenosa
fuerza usáis?

Coro. (*Dent.*)   Amor, amor.

Shelley: 'Scenes from Calderón', III. 24–78 (*cont.*)

Who seekest most when least pursuing,—
   To the trunk thou interlacest
   Art the verdure which embracest,
And the weight which is its ruin,—   60
No more, with green embraces, Vine,
   Make me think on what thou lovest,—
For whilst I thus thy boughs entwine,
   I fear lest thou shouldst teach me, sophist,
How arms might be entangled too.   65
Light-enchanted Sunflower, thou
Who gazest ever true and tender
On the sun's revolving splendour!
Follow not his faithless glance
With thy faded countenance,   70
Nor teach my beating heart to fear,
If leaves can mourn without a tear,
How eyes must weep! O Nightingale,
Cease from thy enamoured tale,—
Leafy Vine, unwreathe thy bower,   75
   Restless Sunflower, cease to move,—
Or tell me all, what poisonous Power
   Ye use against me—

All.   Love! Love! Love!

APPENDIX III

'A Midsummer Night's Dream Poem' (Ch. 5 *passim*)
Sussex, Goethe, and Rousseau (Ch. 16 *passim*)

THE sixty-five lines which follow are roughly drafted in a notebook of 1822[1] and appear to fall into two distinct fragments, the first consisting of lines 1–51 and the second, which follows it consecutively, of lines 52–65. It is my belief, however, that the two fragments are unwelded portions of a single poem, one of those poems in which, like Goethe and Calderón whom he was then reading, Shelley swung with the poetical mood from metre to metre; so, accordingly, have I printed them.

'A Midsummer Night's Dream Poem'—not previously printed except privately by H. Buxton Forman[2]—has relevance to a great deal in the preceding chapters, more particularly to Shelley's obsession with dreams and the supernatural and to his general moods in 1822. Through Goethe, Calderón, and Plato the poet is looking back through the wrong end of a telescope and perceiving his daemons in the form in which he first knew them: the goblins and fairies of his childhood's imaginings at Field Place.

In what follows I have used H. Buxton Forman's transcription of the very much vexed draft—referred to as 'F' in the notes that follow—together with a microfilm of the manuscript in the Henry Huntington Library. I have had the benefit also of some notes—referred to as 'B' below—made by Professor Blunden to whom, likewise, I am indebted for his suggestion of a title.

> *Ye goblins black & great ghosts white
> Fairies all green & spirits blue
> Through the white mist on Midsummer's night
> Hither come hither over the dew
>> Not a snake   5
>> In the brake
>> Shall awake
>>> With you
>> But a snail
>> With his trail   10
>>> Shall you
>>> Pursue
>> To the cave
>> And the grave
>> And the wave   15
>> Bid adieu.

---

[1] B-H III, *6r–*7v.   [2] *Shelley Notebooks*, iii. 108–111.

The bat & the owl like barn-door fowl
Are asleep in the tower & hollow tree
On a willow doth sit with a mazed wit
The nightingale nodding drowsily   20
Only the brook below in the glen
Is awake & singing—
          halloo, halloo
Who are these quaint ones?
   The fairies are we
Over the covert & meadow we tripped all free   25
Singing so free across mountain & sea
Our sweet & inaudible wanderings—
      The bees horn
      In the morn
      To our scorn   30
        Made a tune
        Then was blown
        With a moan
        By the drone
         His at noon.—   35
The gnats with their hum
Made us both deaf & dumb
In their dance on the glance of the evening sun
   But we passed on the wave
   Of the vapours which pave   40
The regions of day till our journey was done
   Though our feet were well shod
   Yet the sunbeams we trod
Were too sharp & too hard for our delicate palms
   But there fell from aloft   45
   A carpet more soft
When twilight was cast on the Ocean's calms
And when we came where the spirits of night
Were ⟨minding⟩ the roses with mild moonlight
   And the shooting stars fell   50
   O there we sped well [

            ⎧ in a fir-tree
A schoolboy lay ⎨ in a nut-tree   copse
            ⎩ near a pond in a
   Blackberries just were out of bloom
   And the golden bloom of the sunny broom . . .
The pine cones they fell like thunder drops   55
   When the ⎰ lazy noon breathed so hard in its trance
            ⎱ languid
That it wakened the sleeping firtree tops.—
   Under a branch all leafless & bare
He was watching the motes in their mimic da⟨nce⟩

Rolling like worlds through the de⟨wy air⟩
And he closed his eyes at last to see
   The network of darkness woven inside
   Till the fire-tailed stars of the night of his brain
Like birds round a pond did $\Big\{$ flutter & glide
                           quiver
And then he would open them wide again.[¹*   65

In lines 1–51 Shelley seems to be anglicizing and adapting to Sussex some of the atmosphere of Goethe's Walpurgisnacht. This appears in the movements of the opening lines if we compare them with the Witches' Chorus in *Faust* (3956 ff.) and with Shelley's translation of 'Scenes' (ii. 146 ff.).

> Die Hexen zu dem Brocken ziehn,
> Die Stoppel ist gelb, die Saat ist grün. . . .

> The stubble is yellow, the corn is green
> Now to the Brocken the witches go. . . .

Similarly we may feel in lines 5–15 ('Not a snake / In the brake . . .') something of another movement from Shelley's 'Scenes' (ii. 70 ff.).

> . . . A salamander in the brake!
> Every root is like a snake. . . .

Then when, in line 17, the movement changes again to 'The bat & the owl like barn-door fowl . . .' we are still close to *Faust* (3968–9) and to the translation of the 'Scenes' (ii. 162 ff.): Shelley's owl is but awaiting his invocation to awake like Goethe's:

¹ The following are the main departures here from the text as given in *Shelley Notebooks*:

Line 1. Alternative readings, preferred by F., are *goblins*] *devils*; *great ghosts*] *spectres*. F. says that Shelley has 'for some occult reason written *goths* over *devils*'. The suggestion of B. 'that Shelley's substituted word was really *goblins*' is borne out by the microfilm of the manuscript.

Line 49. minding: a doubtful reading but preferable, I think, to F.'s 'mending'.

Line 52. All three versions are uncancelled in the draft.

Line 54. There seems to be an anacoluthon needing Shelley's revising hand.

Line 55. F. reads 'thunder-claps', a noise which seems 'too loud for the occasion and not quite a Shelleyan mis-rhyme'. [B.]

Lines 59–60. A tear in the manuscript, as indicated by the pointed brackets, reduces the ending of both lines to a matter of conjecture. In line 59 F. reads 'onion copse'. The manuscript seems to yield 'mimic' equally well for the first word, and 'dance', which I would refer to Sir Humphry Davy's 'dance of matter', known to Shelley, gives at the same time a rhyme for 'trance', whereas 'copse' as a rhyming word is redundant. In line 60, for want of any greater certainty, I have adopted 'dewy air' from B.

Stimme.	Welchen Weg kommst du her?
	Uebern Ilsenstein!
	Da guckt' ich der Eule ins Nest hinein.
	Die macht' ein Paar Augen!...
A Voice.	Which way comest thou?
	Over Ilsenstein;
	The owl was awake in the white moonshine;
	I saw her at rest in her downy nest,
	And she stared at me with her broad, bright eyne.

Again in line 22 the 'halloo, halloo' may be borrowed from the 'Uhu! Schuhu!' of *Faust* (3889) and in lines 36–38 'the gnats with their hum' seem to be a sort of Zauberchor (*Faust* 3993–5) bringing from Goethe their 'dance on the glance of the evening sun':

> Im Sausen sprüht das Zauberchor
> Viel tausend Feuerfunken hervor.

Meanwhile, over and above their Anglo-German origins, these mid-summer fairies with their 'delicate palms' are related as well to 'the wonderful description of Love' in Plato.[1]

In lines 52–65 something else seems traceable. Writing of Rousseau Professor Hughes[2] rightly says that his influence upon Shelley, early and late, was 'elemental and unmeasurable' and among passages of 'the confessional or imaginative writing [where Shelley] must have fancied he saw his own face' he goes on to cite the following from the Letter to Malesherbes, 26 January 1762.[3]

> The gold of the broom and the purple of the heather smote my eyes with a richness that touched my heart; the majesty of the trees that covered me with their shade, the astonishing variety of the plants and flowers—these held my spirit with a continual alternation between study and wonderment. ... Soon I lifted my thought from the face of the earth to all the being of Nature, to the universal system of things, to the incomprehensible Being who encompasses all. Then, my mind lost in that immensity, I was not thinking; I felt with a kind of voluptuousness that I was overwhelmed by the weight of that Universe ... I would have liked to soar out into the Infinite ... I cried out in the excitement of my transports: 'O great Being! O great Being!'

Although the supposition lacks confirmatory evidence, the general tenor of this passage, together with much of the wording, comes so close to the schoolboy reverie of Shelley's self-recollecting that, if he did not read or somehow recollect it in 1822, the coincidence would seem to be

---

[1] See above, Ch. 4, pp. 44–45.

[2] A. M. D. Hughes, *The Nascent Mind of Shelley*, Clarendon Press, 1947, pp. 206, 207.

[3] The English version is given here, as quoted by Professor Hughes from *A Citizen of Geneva* by Charles William Hendel, Oxford, 1937, pp. 213–14.

a remarkable one. Possibly, hidden away somewhere here, are thoughts that might have gone into the dénouement of 'The Triumph of Life'—Shelley–Rousseau thoughts seeking in Nature 'the manifestation of something beyond'[1] and passing through 'the Universal system of things'[2] to the 'great Being'—the One.

[1] Cf. Ch. 12, p. 214, and *passim*.
[2] With 'the motes . . . / Rolling like worlds . . .' (line 60 of the poem). Cf. *Hellas*, 'Worlds on worlds are rolling ever . . .', quoted above in Ch. 16, p. 297.

APPENDIX IV

Henry Reveley: later achievements of Shelley's engineer
(Ch. 6, pp. 93–96)

S o m e time after Shelley's death in 1822 Reveley, who had returned to England in the previous year, became unsettled and we next hear of him at Cape Colony when H.M.S. *Parmelia*, under the command of Captain Stirling and carrying the first settlers for Western Australia, called there for stores. Reveley signed on as an engineer and he was therefore amongst those who landed at Garden Island in 1829 and he became the first civil engineer of what was then known as 'the Swan River Settlement'. He was responsible for the building of the Round House at Fremantle, the Agricultural Department, and the old Court House in the Government Gardens at Perth. He also foreshadowed the work of C. Y. O'Connor in the preparation of plans for the construction of the harbour at Fremantle. On the site of the present Technical College he received a grant of land where he erected the first mill in Perth. An inscription on the College reads

> The first mill in Perth was erected by Henry William Reveley, First Civil Engineer of the Colony. Springs at the top of the allotment were dammed to make a reservoir and the water was led down to a race to turn an upright wheel. Grinding commenced in February 1833. Reveley was a friend of Shelley the poet whose life he once saved.

The last sentence refers, of course, to the incident on 16 April 1821 which is mentioned in this book in connexion with Shelley's so-called 'last notebook'. [See above, Ch. 1, pp. 11–13, and Ch. 15, pp. 261–2.]

In 1838 Reveley again went wandering and left Western Australia for Cape Colony, after which no more seems to be known of him.[1]

[1] The information in this note I owe to Mr. Shelley Garner of Perth, Western Australia.

APPENDIX V

(a) Shelley's memoranda on Dante's *Convito* (Ch. 13, pp. 235–6)
[Bod. MS. Shelley adds. e. 8, pp. 168 rev.–167 rev.]

THE text used by Shelley was DELLE OPERE DI DANTE ALIGHIERI / TOMO PRIMO / CONTENENTE IL CONVITO / E LA VITA NUOVA / CON LE ANNOTAZIONI DEL DOTTORE ANTON MARIA BISCIONI / FIORENTINO / IN VENEZIA / MDCCXCIII / DALLE STAMPE DI PIETRO Q. GIOGATTI / CON LICENZA DE' SUPERIORI. Identification of it was simplified by his use of the title *Convito*. This title was not generally used until its introduction by Biscioni in his original edition of 1723: other editors followed him but *Convito* went out of use after 1879 when Karl Witte [*Dante-Forschungen*, Heilbronn, ii. 574–80] showed the best manuscript authority to be in favour of *Convivio*.

His memoranda run as follows—references in the text are to the 1793 Biscioni edition; these are collated in the margin with the corresponding references in Moore and Toynbee, *Le Opere di Dante Alighieri*, 4th edn., Oxford, 1924.

**O voi che intendendo—p. 40—of the explanatory discussion II. i. I which follows it—a remarkable [? mess] of Xtianity and Aristoteleanism—General reasonings as to the probability of spirits inferior to the great Spirit employed in the government of the universe—50.   ii. v. 75

Quando l'huomo riceve beneficio ovvero ingiuria prima dee ii. vii. 32 quello retraere a chi gliele fa, se può, che ad altri — acciocchè se egli è beneficiato esso che lo riceve si mostri conoscente vêr lo benefattore, e se la injuria ⟨*sic*⟩ induca lo fattore a buona misericordia colle dolci parole (This never the effect of retaliation) 57.

An argument for the immortality of the soul (61 towards the bottom) an argument from the reason of man—how false! yet founded on a deep view of things.

Ma pietade non è passione, anzi una nobile disposizione II. xi. 43 d'animo, apparecchiata di ricevere amore, e altre caritative passioni. 65.

Albumassar[1] says that the inflammation of the vapours of II. xiv. 170 Mars foretells the death of Kings 72.

In Florence ⟨*sic*⟩ nel principio della sua destruzione ⟨*sic*⟩ II. xiv. 176 veduta fu nel aire in figura d'una croce gran quantità di questi vapori seguaci della stella di Marte. 72.

E così in fine di questo secondo trattato dico e affermo che la II. xvi. 98 donna di cui io mi innamorai appresso lo primo Amore fu la

---

[1] An Arab astrologer referred to by Albertus Magnus.

bellissima e onestissima figlia dello imperadore dell'Universo,
alla quale Pittagora pose nome Filosofia . . . 79.
Amore . . . non è altro che unimento spirituale dell'anima e III. ii. 16
della cosa amata; nel quale unimento di propia sua natura
l'anima corre tosto e tardi, secondo che è libera o impedita.**

(*b*) Shelley's Italian Letters to Emilia Viviani (Ch. 13, pp. 238–41)

The following Italian text of the five fragments translated in Chapter 13
represents what Shelley finally intended to say so far as this can be
gleaned from his tortured drafting; textual commentary would run to
disproportionate lengths and is here avoided. Grammatical glosses
likewise have been avoided as far as possible: Shelley's uncorrected
errors, balanced against his fluency, will in themselves show something
of his strength and his weakness as a linguist. (On the subject of his
Italian cf. Medwin:[1] 'He had not made a study of the language which,
like Spanish, he had acquired without a grammar, trusting to his fine
ear and memory rather than the rules.')

I

[Bod. MS. Shelley adds. e. 8, p. 44a]

**] influenza veruna [coi ricchi e nobili], — avendo ⟨*sic*⟩ stato io nemico
aperto di ogni tirannia politica e domestica, io ho tutti i tiranni contro di
me — e non è il mondo dominato dai tiranni? Io ti offerio ⟨*sic*⟩ quel che ne
ho e quel che posso — o che io avessi più.
Pensi a tutti, di ogni cosa che ti vieni ⟨?vengano⟩ in mente punti e ragioni,
e mai non disperi e piu tosto creda che io non avrò riguardo a pericolo a
patria mia, ma solamente al tuo bene in ogni consiglio o ajuto che ti posso
dare.**

2

[Bod. MS. Shelley adds. e. 9, p. 32]

**] ho parlato di te ad una mia amica, e per interessarla più nella tua in-
felicissima sorte ho fattol leggere la tua ultima lettera (perdona la traduzione
per la quale i miei motivi devono recarmi la tua scusa) finalmente essa m'ha
promessa scrivere al padre priore di San Niccola a Pisa per avisargli ⟨*sic*⟩
della tua infelicità e per pregargli venire visitarti

[Ibid., p. 33]

e fare tutto il suo possibile mettendosi ⟨? ? ?⟩ di mezzo per istigar il tuo
padre a darti un ⟨*sic*⟩ sposo.**

3

[Bod. MS. Shelley adds. e. 8, p. 43b]

**] Eccoci dunque, tu e noi, che siamo legati da ⟨? nra *for* nostra⟩
amicizia di pochi giorni e accolti da qualche fortuna strana dalle estremità

[1] H. B. Forman, *Revised Life*, p. 351.

della terra per essere forse un reciproco sollievo. Mio voto per te e noi sia fatto ⟨??⟩ nelle parole di Dante—oh che

> Fossimo presi per incantamento
> E messi ad un vascel, che ad ogni vento
> Per mare andasse a voler vostro e mio
> Sicche fortuna od . . .

> ed aggiungeriei ⟨*sic*⟩ anche questo
> Che ciascuno di loro fosse contento
> Siccome io credo che sariamo noi**

4

[Bod. MS. Shelley adds. e. 8, p. 21 rev.]

**] Tu Emilia ch'era ⟨*sic*⟩ più bella a vedere Che il giglio bianco sul verde stelo E più fresca che la Maia quando [**

5

[Ibid., p. 20]

**] La tua forma visibile al occhio della mente mi circonda colla soave ombra di sua divina bellezza. Molte volte cosi mi ⟨???⟩ Tui neri occhi sempre bellissimi sopra di me mi sembra che io sento tua mano sopra la mia, che le tue labbra—ma allora io chiudo gli occhi ⟨*MS. continues in a different ink*⟩ finche tu cessi d'amarla—allora si spengerà ⟨*sic*⟩ come fiamma a chi nutrimento manca.[1] Io ho sofferto molto nella salute oggi; mai più sono stato felicissimo. Tui ⟨*sic*⟩ dolci occhi sorridono dentro di me. Io non penso più alla morte: credo che l'anima che tu ami non può [**

(c) Shelley's Italian versions of his own poetry

The two specimens here given will illustrate the instruction of Emilia Viviani, first in Platonic love and the meaning of light-symbolism, and secondly in the subject of Liberty. The text is transcribed without comment from the manuscript. Such grammatical mistakes as *nel aere* for 'nell'aere' and *mia anima* for 'la mia anima' are characteristic: so too are *videre* for 'verdere' and *flamma* for 'fiamma'—Shelley's Italian is quite apt, now and then, to slide into Latin, in which he was so much more proficient.

[1] An echo of Petrarch, *Trionfo della Morte*, 157–162.

> Poi che, deposto il pianto e la paura,
> pur al bel volto era ciascuna intenta,
> per desperazïon fatta sicura,
> non come fiamma che per forza è spenta,
> ma che per sè medesma si consume,
> se n'andò in pace l'anima contenta,
> a guisa d'un soave e chiaro lume
> cui nutrimento a poco a poco manca,
> tenendo al fine il suo usato costume.

Here is his version of the lyric 'Life of Life, thy lips enkindle . . .' from *Prometheus Unbound*, II. v. 48–71 [MS. Shelley, d. 1, f. 109 rev.]. It is prefaced by the direction 'Una voce nel aere'.

**Vita della vita! tue labbra accendano
        Il fiato fra di loro, col suo amore;
    E tuoi sorrisi innanzi che si dileguano
        Infocano il freddo aere, allora si nascondano
    In quei sguardi, dove nessuno guata
    Che non svenni, intrecciato fra loro laberinti.

Figlia della luce! tue membra ardono
        Per la veste che le celasse
    Come le radianti striscie della alba
        A traverso delle nuvole, prima che le spezzano
    E questa atmosfera divinissima
    Ti involge, dovunque tu risplendi.

Altre sieno bella — nessun ti può videre —
        Ma tua voce è tenera e dolce
    Come quella della più bella — perchè t'inviluppa
        Dalla vista, quel aerio splendore
    E tutti sentono senza mai vederti,
    Come io sento ora, perduto per giammai.

Lampa della terra! dovunque tu ti movi
        Sue oscure forme son vestite da raggi;
    Le anime di loro che tu ami
        Camminano sopra al vento con legereza
    Finche cadono, come io cado
    Vertiginoso, perduto, — mai senza guai.**

And here, in Shelley's Italian, is the first stanza of his 'Ode to Liberty' [Bod. MS. Shelley adds. c. 4, f. 84]:

**Un popolo glorioso vibrava di nuovo
        Il fulmine delle nazioni. Libertà
    Da core a core, da torre a torre a traverso la Spagna
        Spargendo per l'aere contagiosa luce,
    Balenò — Mia anima spezzava i ceppi del suo timore,
        E si vesti esultante e fiera
    Colle piume rapide di armonia
    Battendo l'ale in canto sopra l'usata preda
    Come una aquila se ruota ⟨*sic*⟩ fra le mattutine nuvole.
    Finche dal suo posto nel cielo della fama
    Della più remota sfera di vivente flamma
    Le turbine dello Spirito lo rapiva, coi raggi
    Che strisciavano il vano, erano spiriti dietro a lei
    Come spuma d'una rapida prora — quando venne
    Una voce dal profundo — Io la canterò.**

INDEX

Abinger, Lord, his Shelley MSS., v, viii, xv, 79, 213.

Aeschylus, 67, 151, 154, 161; ghost of, 66; influence of, 19, 212; in Shelley's memoranda for *Adonais*, 264; lost play of, 54; quoted, 63. *Agamemnon*, 173; *Persae*, 70, 291; *Prometheus Vinctus*, 150.

Agathon (in Plato's *Symposium*), 48, 51 ff., 54 f., 57 f., 232.

Ahasuerus, the Wandering Jew: in *Hellas*, 291–6, 298 f.; in *Queen Mab*, 318.

Alfieri, V., affinities with Shelley, 312 n. 4, 313.

Amphitryon (in Euripides' *Hercules Furens*), 19, 224.

Anacreon, in Shelley's memoranda for *Adonais*, 264.

Apocrypha, the, and *Adonais*, 266, 270.

Apollo, 100, 115 f., 165.

Apollonius Rhodius, in Shelley's memoranda for *Adonais*, 264.

Apuleius, 40.

'Ariel', *see* Maurois, André.

Aristotle, *Nicomachean Ethics*, 63, 75, n. 1.

Arnold, Matthew, his judgement of Shelley, vi.

Asia (*Prometheus Unbound*), 99, 102, 114, 128–34, 139, 156–66, 279.

Asia's song, 57, 98, 204, 242.

Aster, Plato's epigram to, 269, 282 f.

atheism: Shelley's, 58, 60, 63, 276, 278, 307, 315; Diotima's, in Plato's *Symposium*, 58 ff.; *see* Shelley, ideas, religion.

Athenaeus, 8; Shelley's memorandum from *Deipnosophistae*, 169 f.

Bacon, Lord, and Futurity, quoted by Shelley, 145, 166 f., 184, 192 f., 289, 321.

Barrett, Elizabeth, 66 n. 6.

Baxter (later Booth), Isobel, Mary Shelley's friend, 46.

Beatitudes from St. Matthew, and *Adonais*, 265; *see* Shelley, ideas, religion.

Beatrice, Dante's, 80, 234, 239, 304.

Berkeley, Bishop C., Shelley and philosophy of, 122.

Biblical study, and allusions, Shelley's, 69, 126, 225 n. 1, 265, 278, 296 n. 1; *see also* Shelley, ideas, religion.

Bion, and *Adonais*, 262.

Bixby-Huntington Notebooks, xv n. 2, 3 n. 2, 15 n. 4, 65 n. 2.

'Blackwood', 77.

Blake, W., affinity with Shelley, 309, 315.

Blunden, Edmund, viii, 334; quoted, 53, 206, 273, 280, 301, 303.

Bodleian Library, Shelley MSS. and notebooks, &c., v, vii, 10, 12 n. 5, 16, 44, 71, 75, 78, 135 n., 196 f., 201, 242, 259, 273.

Bonaparte, *see* Napoleon.

Booth, David, husband of Mary Shelley's friend Isobel Baxter, 46.

'Boscombe collection' of Shelley papers, v.

Bosis, Adolfo de (Italian translator of Shelley), 236 n. 2.

Bosis, Lauro de, *Icaro*, viii, 321 ff.

Bowra, Sir Maurice, viii, 55 n. 2, quoted, 308 f.

Bridges, Robert, 134, 135; *The Spirit of Man*, 134, 146, 166; *The Testament of Beauty*, 134.

British Museum MSS., xv, 200.

Bucolic Poets, the Greek, in *Adonais*, 25, 262 f.

Butters, Paul, xix, 301.

Byron, Lord, 13, 45, 58, 79, 97 n. 1, 219 n. 1, 260 f., 267, 311 f.; *Childe Harold*, 303, 304 n.; *Manfred*, 74.

Calderón, 23, 50, 77, 79, 94, 172 f., 177, 214, 223, 226, 233, 256, 264 f., 286, 294 f., 306 f., 334; *El mágico prodigioso*, 7, 79, 81–90, 287, 307, Shelley's translation quoted, 329–33; *El Príncipe Constante*, 220; *La vida es sueño*, 176–94, in Shelley's memoranda for *Adonais*, 264.

Cameron, Kenneth Neill, *Shelley and His Circle*, xvii, 63.

Carlile, the printer, legal defence of, 228.

Cascine, the, and Shelley's 'Ode to the West Wind', 174, 211, 219, 272, 316.

Castlereagh, Lord, Shelley's hatred of, 197 ff., 215, 281, 316.

Cavalcanti, Guido, read and translated by Shelley, 239; *Canzone d'Amore*, 52 n. 3, 237; Dante's sonnet to, 232, 239; sonnet to Dante, 232, 233 n. 1.

Cave, *see* Plato *and* Shelley, symbols, cave.

Cenci, Beatrice, 202.

Charles I, Shelley's abandoned play about, 275.

Charlotte, Princess, her death and its consequences seen in relation to Shelley, 316–17.

Chartists, the, and *Queen Mab*, 324.

Christ, Jesus, 276–9, 302 f., 318 f.; Shelley's divided opinion on, 70 f.

Christian ἀγάπη, 53, 57, 126, 128, 212, 285, 296 n. 1.

— belief in immortality, 284.

— Church, 278, 315, 318 f.

— miracles, 67, 287.

— *see* Shelley, ideas, religion.

Christianity, 55, 72–73, 81, 87, 90, 279, 284, 313, 323; medieval, 320. *See* Shelley, ideas, religion.

Clairmont, Charles, visits Shelley, 179, 226 n. 3.

Clairmont, Claire, 78, 128, 142, 250 f., 259; singing of, 97 f., 203 f., 306; unpublished journal of, xv, 11.

Coleridge, S. T.: fear of ineffectuality, 302; his influence on Shelley, 64, 77, 110–14, 119, 127, 196, 205, 268, 307, 309, 312–15; on 'the mystery of genius in the fine arts', 25, 205, 307; Shelley's verses in mockery of, 217. *Biographia Literaria*, 24 f., 111 ff., 196, 268; *Christabel*, 70 n. 4, 110 n. 1; *Kubla Khan*, 110.

Comet, Winnecke's, seen by Shelley, 205.

Congress, Library of, viii, ix, xv.

Cornford, F. M., viii, 88.

Courier, The (1822), on Shelley's death, 227 n. 2.

Cromwell, Oliver (Shelley's revulsion against a liberator become tyrant), 275.

Dante, 8 f., 23, 57, 80, 232–6, 264 f., 303; in Shelley's memoranda for *Adonais*, 264; sonnet to Cavalcanti, 232, 239. *Convito*, 233 f., 236, 240, 244–7, 304, 340; *Divina Commedia*, 234, 236, 304; *Purgatorio*, 304; *Vita Nuova*, 234, 236.

Davy, Sir Humphry, 303; *Elements of Agricultural Chemistry*, 8, 201.

Demogorgon (character in *Prom. Unbound*), 56, 129, 156–61, 164 f., 167, 279, 292; cave of, 137 n. 2, 147, 150, 155 ff., 160.

Diderot and Shelley's ideas about priests, 318.

Diogenes Laertius, Shelley translates Greek epigrams from, 258.

Dion, tyrant of Syracuse, 304.

Dionysius I, tyrant of Syracuse, 304.

Dionysius II, tyrant of Syracuse, 304.

Diotima (in Plato's *Symposium*), 20 f., 39, 57 n. 1, 58 f., 61 f., 68, 73, 136 f., 140, 170, 232; Hölderlin's poems to, 313.

'Don Juan' (boat), 12, 104.

Dowden, Edward, 312.

Draper, Ruth, 321 n. 2.

drawings, Shelley's, *see under* Shelley.

Drummond, Sir William, *Academical Questions* (1805), quoted, 64 ff., 81 n. 4, 82.

Dunne, J. W., his serialism a Shelleyan notion, 321.

Earth (in *Prometheus Unbound*), 167, 280, 325; 'the shadow of some spirit lovelier still', 155; proprietress of Caves, 166.

'Eleutherarch' (Peacock's word for Shelley: its application also to others), 257, 310 f., 314, 316, 320, 323 f.

Epipsychidion, origin of word, 245.

Epipsychidion (the poem), *see* Shelley, works, poetical.

Eryximachus, speech of, in *Symposium*, 133.

'Esdaile Notebook', 1, 38; quoted, 28–29, 91–92, 113, 120, 121, 171.

Espronceda, Spanish poet, affinities with Shelley, 314.

Euripides, 8 f., 52, 62, 76, 174, 227 n. 2, 228; *Hercules Furens*, 19 f., 56, 75, 224; *Bacchae*, 75, 272.

Faraday, Michael, his discoveries in electricity, 319.
Fascism opposed on Shelleyan lines by Lauro de Bosis, 322.
Faust, 77–81, 84, 176, 286, 288, 307, 336 f.
Fichte, 313.
Finch, Colonel, 259 f.; papers bequeathed to the Bodleian Library by, xv, 259.
Forman, Harry Buxton, viii, 213 n. 2, 223 n. 1, 334.
Forman, Maurice Buxton, viii, 2 n. 2.
Frederic of Prussia, a type of 'legal murderer', 28; in 'The Triumph of Life', 296, 300.
French, 2, 10; memorandum in, 196 f.
— literature, Shelley's study of, *see* Rousseau, Voltaire, &c.
— Revolution, 151, 197, 278, 302.

Garnett, Richard, xv n. 2, 200 ff., 237, 257.
Garrod, H. W., viii, 135 n.
Gavita, Vincenzo, coachman to Shelley 64.
Geneva, Shelley at, 44, 74, 78, 288.
German literature: Shelley's studies in, 2, 77 ff., 232, 329; *see* Goethe, Wieland, &c.
— Revolution (1848), leaders of, 324.
— romantic writers, affinity to Shelley, 312–13.
Gifford, W., editor of the *Quarterly*, 256 f.
Gisborne, John, 90, 259; letters to (1822), 77, 79, 81, 253, 286, 303.
Gisborne, Maria, 179; Mary Shelley's letters to, 11, 180, 260, 329 n. 2; Shelley's verse-letter to, 93.
Gisbornes, the, letter to, 262 n. 2.
God: a Voltairean conception of, 27; a pervading Spirit . . ., 31; Plato and 'the possibility of a right opinion', 60; in *El mágico prodigioso*, discussed, 21–22; is triumphant, 85–87; as creator, like a poet, 94 ff., 115; a Plotinian definition, 111; in *Prom. Unbound*, 157 f.; Shelley's need for prayer to, 225; Shelley quotes the Apocrypha concerning, 266, 271; defined by Shelley in 1814 or 1815, 95. *See* Shelley, ideas, religion.

Godwin, Fanny, 26, 89.
Godwin, Mary, *see* Shelley, Mary.
Godwin, W., and his influence on Shelley, 24, 36, 42 f., 112, 112 n. 4, 151, 164, 212, 228, 265, 311.
Goethe, Shelley and, 23, 77–81, 89, 233, 265, 302, 303, 310, 334, 336 f.; see also *Faust*.
Grabo, Carl, vi, vii, xviii, 26, 56, 96, 133, 156, 163.
Greece, ancient, its symbolical meaning to Shelley, 285, 292, 299, 301 f.
Greek language and literature, Shelley's studies in, 2 f., 8, 10, 14, 16, 18 f., 43, 95, 100, 111, 115, 245, 252, 256. *See also* Aeschylus, Plato, &c.; Shelley, Greek concepts; Shelley, translations.
Gretchen in Goethe's *Faust*, 77, 80, 87.
Grove, Harriet, 37.

Harvard MS. Fair Copy Book, 11, 197, 200, 208, 210.
— Notebooks, 206.
Harvard University Library, vii, ix, xv, 1.
Hegel, 313.
Hellenism, German, and Shelley, 231 n. 2, 313 f.
Heracles (Euripides' *Hercules Furens*), a symbol for Shelley, 19, 129, 166.
Hermes Trismegistus, 69.
Hewlett, Dorothy: *Elizabeth Barrett Browning*, 66 n. 1; ed. *The Keats–Shelley Bulletin*, 12 n. 5, 98 n. 4, 204 n. 7, 146, 236 n. 2, 302.
Hitchener, Miss, 22, 27, 30, 39, 62.
— correspondence, 31, 52, 60 n. 1.
Hobhouse, J. C., *Historical Illustrations of the Fourth Canto of Childe Harold* (Shelley's source for a Tasso reference), 96 n. 1.
Hogg, T. J., 43, 117 n. 2, 174, 247 f., 302; his novel *Alexy Haimatoff*, 311.
Hölderlin, F., affinities with Shelley, 313 f.
Holy Alliance, the, 319.
Homer, in Shelley's memoranda for *Adonais*, 264.
Horace, source of a quotation of Shelley, 247.
Houghton Library, Harvard University, ix.

348 *Index*

Hours, the, in *Prom. Unbound*, 162, 165 ff.
Hughes, A. M. D., 337; records Shelley's echoes of Aeschylean phrases, 151 n. 2.; on Rousseau's influence on Shelley, 337; on 'The Triumph of Life,' xix, 301, 302 n. 1.
Hugo, Victor, affinities with Shelley, 314.
Hume, David, studied by Shelley on the subject of Charles I, 275.
Hunt, Leigh, 79, 217, 219, 228, 245, 267, 286, 288.
Hunt, Mrs., 256.
Hunt, Thornton, 67, 74.
Huntington Library, viii, xv, 334.

Ingpen, R. W., 204, 240, 241 n. 4; and Peck, W. E., 12.
Irish, the: Shelley's concern for, in his last weeks, 274; Shelley's experiences among, 212.
Isaiah, quoted among Shelley's memoranda for *Adonais*, 265.
Italian, Shelley's letters to Emilia Viviani in, 238–41, 340–3.
— language and literature: Shelley's studies in, 2, 10, 12, 329; their effect upon *Epipsychidion*, 230–48; their effect upon 'Ode to the West Wind', 220, 226.

Jones, Frederick L., viii f.; *Maria Gisborne and Edward E. Williams, their Journals and Letters*, xvii, 7 n. 3, 97 n. 1, 287 n. 2, 288 n. 2; *Mary Shelley's Journal*, xvii, 10 n. 2, 11 n. 5, 11 n. 7, 11 n. 8, 24 n. 2, 45 n. 5, 46 n. 1, 105 n. 3, 110 n. 1, 141 n. 3, 147 n. 1, 150 n. 1, 179 n. 1, 215 n. 3, 216 n. 3, 226 n. 3, 250 n. 1, 255 n. 3, 259 n. 6, 261 n. 3; *The Letters of Mary W. Shelley*, xvii, 10 n. 4, 11 n. 2, 46 n. 3, 160 n. 1, 260 n. 1, 287 n. 1; in *Studies in Philology*, 67 n. 2, 329. *See also under* 'Shelley, Letters'.
Journal, Shelley's, at Geneva, 45.
Julie (*La Nouvelle Héloïse*), 40, 45, 302.
Jung, C. G., his theory of the Collective Unconscious related to Shelley's poetic vision, 320.
Jupiter, ancient god: his morality

discussed in Calderón, 82; in *Prometheus Unbound*—symbolical significance of his overthrow, 155 f.; compared as a tyrant with Mahmud in *Hellas*, 299; joined in Shelley's mind with contemporary priests, 318; appearance of his phantasm, similar to that of Justina's in Calderón, 87.
Justina, in Calderón's *El mágico prodigioso*, 81, 84–88.

kaleidoscope, popularity of: a possible source of Shelleyan imagery, 117 n. 2, 270.
Kant, his influence on Shelley satirized by Peacock, 312.
Keats, John: shrewd comment on Shelley as an artist, 2, 214–15; and *Adonais*, 12 f., 51, 115, 174, 251–72, 301, 306; fear of ineffectuality, 302; his conceptions, sometimes akin to Shelley's, 174, 195, 285, 309, 315; views on religion compared with Shelley's, 278; *Endymion*, 256; *Eve of St. Agnes*, 257, 263; *Hyperion*, 255, 257, 259; *Isabella*, 257, 263; *Lamia*, 70 n. 4., 255, 257; *Ode on a Grecian Urn*, 263.
Keats–Shelley Journal of America, see Steele, Mabel A. E.
Keats–Shelley Memorial Bulletin, The, see Hewlett, Dorothy.
King-Hele, Desmond, xix, 119, 210 n.
Koszul, A. H., 276.

Lapo, Gianni, friend of Dante, 239.
Lastri, M., *L,Osservatore Fiorentino*, source of 'Ginevra', 249 ff.
Latin language and literature: Shelley's proficiency in, 2, 10, 342; Shelley quotes, 66, 247. *See* Horace, Lucretius, &c.
Latini, Brunetto, *Tesoretto*, among the sources of *Epipsychidion*, 237.
Laud, Archbishop, in 'Charles I', 281.
Lawrence, T. E., 323 n. 1.
Leishman, J. B., *Selected Poems of Hölderlin*, xx, 313.
Leman, Lake, Shelley and Byron in danger on, 45, 58.
Lerici, Shelley's moods and thoughts at, 45, 58, 81, 84, 90, 145, 175, 177, 276. 280, 285, 286 f., 294, 298, 303, 312.

Lewis, 'Monk', discusses the supernatural with Shelley, 45, 78.
Liberal, The, Shelley's projected paper, 79, 88.
Liberalism, Shelley in relation to its beginnings, 314, 319.
Lind, Dr., at Eton, introduces Shelley to Plato's *Symposium*, 43.
'Lionel' (Shelley's name for himself in poems and memoranda), 16, 21 f., 24, 74, 101, 168, 256 f., 262, 271, 289, 304.
Locke, J., the philosopher, 265; his notion of poetry not Shelley's, 18, 306 f.
Locock, C. D., 135 n., 162, 244, 246, 301.
Lord Chancellor, Shelley's Promethean struggles against the, 150, 212, 263.
Lowes, Livingston, *The Road to Xanadu*, 111 n. 2.
Lucretius: influence on Shelley, 33 f.; in Shelley's memoranda for *Adonais*, 264; lends colour to a speech in *Hellas*, 294.
Madariaga, S. de, *Shelley and Calderón*, 226.
Mahmud (in *Hellas*), 291–5, 298 ff., 304.
Mahomet, in *Hellas*, 299 f., 304.
Malesherbes, Rousseau's letter of 1762, to, 337.
Malthus, 32.
'Manchester Massacre', The, and *The Mask of Anarchy*, 198 f., 214, 216, 306.
Mantinean woman, the, *see* Diotima.
Marchand, Leslie, 'Trelawny on Death of Shelley', 12 n. 5.
Margaret, *see* Gretchen.
Materialists of the eighteenth century, Shelley and, 27, 32, 122, 145.
Matthews, G. M., xix, 301 f.
Maurois, André, 'Ariel', vi, 194.
Medwin, Thomas, 1 f., 11, 196, 241 f., 244.
Milton, John, 224; in Shelley's memoranda for *Adonais*, 264; *Comus*, 192; *Paradise Lost*, 264.
Monboddo, Lord, *Of the Origin and Progress of Language*, 69.
Mont Blanc, as a symbol of Intellectual Beauty, 41, 111.
Montesquieu, ideas akin to Shelley's, 27.

Moore, Thomas, mentioned in *Adonais*, 267.
Morris, William, his socialism and Shelley's, 323 f.
Moschus, echoed and translated in *Adonais*, 262.
Mountcashell, Lady, 79, 239.
Mozart, *La clemenza di Tito*, 204.
Mure, Geoffrey, 'Oxford and Philosophy' in *Philosophy*, 43.
Murray, Gilbert, 75 n. 1, 321 n. 2.
Music, 116, 133, 162; effect on Shelley, 97 f., 285; Shelley composes a lyric to, 203 f.

Naples, Shelley's dejection at, 26, 285.
Napoleon Bonaparte, 28, 197 f., 265, 277, 280, 296, 302, 303.
Narcissus, the legend of, seen by Shelley as an allegory of himself, 219 ff.
Nelson, Lord, 28.
Neoplatonic ideas (Neoplatonism), 65, 69, 96 f., 112, 163, 262.
Nitchie, Elizabeth, *The Reverend Colonel Finch*, 259.
Norman, Sylva, *Flight of the Skylark*, vi n. 1, ix, xviii, 227 n. 2.
notebooks, Shelley's, *see under* Shelley.
Notopoulos, J. A., *The Platonism of Shelley*, ix, xviii, 27 n. 3, 39, 41, 42 n. 2, 69 n. 1, 78 n. 2, 112, 130, 134, 151, 243, 269.
Novalis, 309, 312.

Ollier, Charles (Shelley's publisher), 217, 219, 227, 259; letter to, 262 n. 2.
Orwell, George: his affinities with Shelley, 323 f.; *Nineteen-Eighty-Four*, 324 f.
Owen, Robert, his Socialism and Shelley's, 323 f.

Paley, W., 276, 279.
Panthea (*Prometheus Unbound*), 114, 156 f.
Paul, St., 296 n. 1, *see also* Christian ἀγάπη.
Paul I of Russia, in 'The Triumph of Life', 296, 300.
Peacock, Thomas Love, xx, 11, 12, 17, 43, 45 n. 3, 65, 68, 70, 90, 104, 122, 205, 214, 257 f., 264, 302, 311 f.; *The Four Ages of Poetry*, 12, 257, 259; *Nightmare Abbey*, 257, 310 ff.

Peck, W. E., *see* Ingpen, R. W.

'Peterloo', *see* 'Manchester Massacre'.

Petrarch: in Shelley's memoranda for *Adonais*, 264; influence on *Adonais*, 263; influence on 'The Triumph of Life', 279, 303.

Pforzheimer, Carl, notebook, 211 n. 2.

Pindar, 100, 246, 252 f., 260 f.; quoted, 95, 100 f.

Pisa canal, Shelley's accident in, 13, 261.

Plato, 22 f., 43, 117, 145, 148, 151, 153 f., 161, 166, 172, 184, 193, 230, 256, 282 f., 285, 289, 321, 334; epigram, 107, 112; parable of Cave, 111 n. 2, 123, 132, 148 f., 151 f., 156 f., 159, 163, 263; *Apology*, 4, 73; *Gorgias*, 174; *Ion*, 136; *Phaedo*, 11, 145, 154, 263, 270, 272; *Phaedrus*, 41, 136, 141 ff., 146 f., 151 ff., 163, 170, 181, 246, 270; *Republic*, 21 f., 27, 88, 132, 136, 147 f., 151 ff., 154, 156, 159 f., 163, 175 f., 263; *Symposium*, 8, 20, 39, 41, 43 f., 46 ff., 52, 54, 63, 68, 72 f., 75 f., 78, 85 n. 1, 99, 103, 109, 114, 120, 130, 133, 136, 139 ff., 143 f., 146 f., 151 ff., 157, 161, 163, 170, 175, 205, 231 n. 1, 242 f., 258, 269, 328; *Timaeus*, 31, 75 f., 234 n. 2, 246; Bipont edition (1781-7), 47 ff., 50 f., 53, 55, 61, 140 n. 1, 258, 328.

Platonic ideas (Platonism), 19, 23, 27, 31 ff., 36 f., 39-43, 47, 51, 63, 65, 67 f., 77, 85, 90, 103, 107 n. 5, 110, 112 f., 119 ff., 122, 124, 130 f., 134, 137 ff., 145 f., 150, 160, 164, 170, 173 f., 192, 212, 214, 216, 233 ff., 240, 243, 261, 263, 265 f., 269, 271, 278, 289, 292, 294, 296, 298, 304 f., 313, 315.

Pliny, *Hist. Nat.*, 81 f., 90.

Plotinus, 41 n. 1, 111, 112, 133.

Polidori, Byron's physician, 45.

priests, Shelley and, 28, 317 f.; *see* Shelley, ideas, religion.

Prince Regent, the, 315.

Prometheus (in *Prom. Unbound*), 19 f., 54, 56, 72, 80, 89, 129 ff., 132 f., 134, 138 f., 145, 156, 159 ff., 212, 277, 291, 299; Cave of, 136 f., 139, 147, 150, 160; gifts of, 158; identified with Mind, 157, 160.

Proteus, Shelley likens the Lake Poets to, 217.

Quarterly, the, *see* reviewers, Shelley and.

'Queen', synonymous with 'Liberty', 316.

Red Cross Knight (*The Faerie Queene*), a type of Shelleyan hero, 120.

Reiman, Donald, H., xix, 301 f.

Retzsch, Moritz (1799-1857), illustrator of *Faust*, 77.

Reveley, Henry, son of Mrs. Gisborne, 13, 93 ff., 96, 98, 100, 228, 259 ff., 321; later achievements of, 339.

reviewers, Shelley and, 17-18, 217 ff., 223, 227, 255 f., 258, 262 f.

Rimbaud, Arthur, his 'Bateau Ivre' and Shelley's boat-symbol, 98.

Risorgimento, the, 319.

Roberts, Captain, 12, 272.

Rogers, Neville: in *The Keats–Shelley Journal of America*, 'Four Missing Pages from the Shelley Notebook in the Harvard College Library', 10 n.1; in *The Keats–Shelley Memorial Bulletin*, 'Music at Marlow', 204 n. 7; in the *Times Literary Supplement*, 'A Shelley Letter', 174 n. 2; 'Ginevra', 249 n. 5, 250 n. 3; 'Shelleys Last Notebook', 12 n. 5; *The Esdaile Poems*, xvii, 28-29, 37-38, 91-92, 120, 121, 146, 171, 302.

Romantic Poets, English and German compared, 308 f., 311.

Romanticism, French, its Liberal ideals akin to Shelley's, 314.

Rome, Shelley's sensitivity to, 26, 64, 212, 214, 263.

Rousseau, J. J.: Shelley shares his belief in the inherent goodness of man, 27, 92; Shelley follows his pattern for idealized love, 40-41; Shelley quotes a reference to him as 'the cause of the revolution', 197; in 'The Triumph of Life', 277, 292, 295, 301 ff.; quoted, 337.

St. Augustine, motto from, attached by Shelley to two poems, 120; quoted, 38.

Salvemini, G., 322, n. 2.

Schelling, 313.

Schiller, F., 'Ode to Joy', affinity with *Prom. Unbound*, 313.

Scriptures, *see* Biblical study.

Scythrop, in Peacock's *Nightmare Abbey*, a satirical representation of Shelley, 257, 310, 312.

Shakespeare, W., 264, 294; imagery, 173; in Shelley's memoranda for *Adonais*, 264; sonnets, a clue to *Epipsychidion*, 232, 233, 234; *The Tempest*, 185, 294; *Hamlet*, 302 n. 5.

Shelley, Charles, 47.

Shelley, Clara, 213.

Shelley, Harriet, 22, 38 ff., 90, 127 f., 131, 138, 157, 240, 310 f.; children of, 46, 212.

Shelley, Hellen, 67.

Shelley, Ianthe, 47.

Shelley, Lady, 200; and Shelley MSS. and notebooks, v, xv n. 2, 242.

Shelley, Mary, 79, 88 ff., 128, 157, 206, 216, 247, 250, 286, 302–3, 310 f.; and Shelley's notebooks, 1 f., 4, 7, 10 f., 45, 71, 197, 203; children of, 212 f., 227; comments on Shelley and his poetry, 16, 24, 55, 65, 88, 99 n. 4, 105, 192, 216 n. 3, 223 n. 1, 226 n. 3, 249, 261, 285 f.; errs in dating *A Wanderer*, 173, *Woodman and Nightingale*, 263; her novel, *Frankenstein*, 46; *Journal* of, *see* Jones, Fredk. L., ed.; *Laon and Cythna* dedicated to, 107 f.; *Letters* of, *see* Jones, Fredk. L., ed.; note on *Alastor*, 69, on *Prometheus Unbound*, 15, 51, 69, 72, 126 f., 173, 306; relations with Shelley, 22, 39 f., 119, 121; transcripts, 140 n. 1, 141 n. 3, 217.

Shelley, Percy Bysshe:

CHARACTERISTICS

a 'man of his time': to be viewed also in relation to other times, 312, 317–20.

children, the loss of his, grief for, 20, 26, 46 f., 212 f., 218.

courage: moral, 211–29; physical, 45, 145.

handwriting, 3 ff., 177, 197, 238.

humanitarian instincts, 32, 53, 63, 147; *see also* Christian ἀγάπη.

imagination: creative or 'philosophic', in Coleridge and Shelley, 112, 115, 119, 268; differently conceived by Novalis, 309; as a vital power in Shelley, 308, 325; 'leap of the', a notable characteristic

of Shelley's genius, 42, 245, 267; fact and fantasy, 68, 90.

indifference to danger, 45, 145, 288.

influenced by seasons, 26, 32, 222.

intellectual control: underestimates its function in his poetry, 309.

methods of work, 2 f., 4, 9, 14, 195–210, 211–28, 235–47, 252–3, 260–6, 269 f., 305.

moods, 81, 109, 212, 227, 285 f., 334.

music, susceptibility to, 97 f., 203 f., 285.

practical good sense, 286.

punctuation, 135, 173 n. 1, 238.

revolution, fear of, 315, 318; *see also* Shelley, ideas, passive resistance.

sense of humour and of fun, 46, 66 f., 74, 101, 219, 148, 286.

'Shelley legends' unlike the real Shelley, vi, 1, 71, 229, 269, 309 f.

subtlety and complexity of mind, 16, 18, 24, 53, 114, 124.

supernatural, attraction to the, 45, 67, 74, 148, 287 f.

time, obsession with, 286, 288 f., 291, 293, 295.

two selves at Lerici, 286 f., 310; *see also* Shelley, characteristics, supernatural, attraction to the.

vegetarianism, 27; *see also* Shelley, varied interests.

DRAWINGS, 2 f., 7 f., 12, 14, 23, 26, 44, 47, 68, 74, 77, 91, 94, 105–10, 112 n. 3, 113 f., 117 n. 2, 119, 132 n. 3, 162, 205 ff., 216, 225, 240, 264, 308; *see also* Plates I and II.

GREEK CONCEPTS:

Ariadne, the quest for truth and its mortal embodiments, 17 f., 21, 23, 37, 63, 70, 74, 77, 80, 89, 93, 99, 101–4, 123, 127, 138, 170, 176 f., 230, 235, 240, 246, 253, 268, 276.

'being a mortal to aspire to immortal things' (θνητὸς ὢν μὴ θνητὰ φρονεῖν), 74–77, 234, 283, 303, 310.

daemons, 20 f., 23, 45, 52 f., 59 ff., 63 f., 67 f., 70–74, 76 ff., 80, 82, 85 ff., 90 f., 99, 110 f., 113 f., 119, 128, 147, 157, 161 f., 170, 177, 194, 234, 236, 240, 243, 263, 265 f., 287, 312, 334.

education of the Beloved, 157, 243, 248 n. 1, 310 f.

Shelley, Percy Bysshe:
GREEK CONCEPTS (*cont.*)
enlightenment through the ascent to knowledge, 153, 159, 166.
'identification with the Beautiful' in love, morals, and art, 131, 156.
'intermediate space' (μεταξὺ θεοῦ τε καὶ θνητοῦ), 68, 70, 75, 97 f., 100, 103, 123, 162, 246, 286, 312, 321.
justice (δικαιοσύνη), 138, 142.
love ("Ἔρως), 20 f., 23, 33, 37–40, 43 f., 48–63, 70, 72 f., 76, 80, 86, 89, 99, 102 f., 107, 113 f., 120, 125 f., 129, 131, 140, 144, 147, 156, 160 f., 163, 165, 167, 170, 212, 230 f., 236 f., 240, 242 ff., 246 f., 263, 266, 279, 285, 290, 300, 305, 307, 328, 337.
necessity, doctrine of (ἀνάγκη), 23, 27, 29, 31–35, 37, 51 f., 54 ff., 63, 90, 129, 145, 161, 307, 322 f.
One, the, 36, 69, 118, 126, 129 f., 133, 158, 161, 163, 235, 266, 268 f., 271, 278, 284, 338.
self-control (σωφροσύνη), 45, 55, 138, 142, 145, 198, 288.
selfless love (ἀφιλαυτία), 63.
virtue and power (ἀρετή), 17–21, 23, 30 f., 33, 52–56, 72, 77, 80, 89, 126, 128 f., 131, 138, 144, 153, 156, 171, 198, 231 n. 1, 240, 244, 255, 282, 284 f., 300, 303, 317.
See also Neoplatonic ideas (Neoplatonism); Plato, Platonic ideas (Platonism); Shelley, ideas, World-Soul.
IDEAS:
anarchy, 214, 280 f.; hatred of, 198, 315.
beauty, 22, 37, 43, 47, 52, 70, 80, 102, 104, 108, 113, 120 f., 123, 126 f., 131, 139, 143 f., 147, 152, 157, 162 f., 166, 171, 234, 242 f., 247, 258, 266, 290, 305; guide to, 85; identified with Goodness, 153 f.
— intellectual, 41 f., 47, 51, 55, 63, 73, 78, 92, 79, 99 f., 104, 112, 117, 119, 126, 137 f., 140, 142, 156, 218, 230, 245, 253 f., 258, 263, 268, 270, 282, 285, 291, 300, 302 f., 318.
corruption of men through false civilization, 27 f.

death, 104, 123 f., 145, 164, 194, 289.
effectuality, 302 f.
eternity: in *Prom. Unbound*, 133, 159, 165, 292; signified by a snake, 68 f., 118, 126.
evil: an accident, 31, 72; associated with Snake, 69; at war with the One, 69, 126, 133; conquest of, 129 f., 161, 167; identified with Veil, 125; perishable, 33, 125, 153, 281; personified in the Jupiter of *Prometheus Unbound*, 55 n. 2, 158 f.; problem of, 155; regeneration of, 291.
fate: in *Prom. Unbound*, 56, 129, 156, 161, 165; *versus* free will in Calderón, *La vida es sueño*, 184; *see also* Shelley, ideas, free will; — — predestination.
free will, and the power of the human mind, 30, 32 f., 36, 89, 158, 161 f., 191, 307, 321, 322, 325.
futurity: in *Hellas*, 295; remarks to Trelawny, 145, 289.
good, goodness, 157, 159, 161, 163, 166, 281; hidden by evil, 125; identified with the Beautiful, 138, 153 f.; regeneration of, 291; represented by a snake, 69; ultimate triumph of, 126, 130 f., 299.
— and evil: conflict between, 70; cycles of, 72 n. 3, 126, 162, 228, 321; Shelley's conception of, 261.
homosexuality, Greek, 9, 137 n. 1, 230 f.
Hour, the, in *Prom, Unbound* and 'The Tr. of Life', 279, 281, 292; *see also* Shelley, ideas, fate; — — predestination.
immortality (= reality, truth, as opposed to mutability), 76; of thought and poetic fame, 284, 290, 295, 298, 305; of Greek thought, 285; *see also* Shelley, ideas, mutability; — — reality; — — soul, immortality of; — — truth.
knowledge, 93, 96, 158, 161, 215 f., 226, 305, 325; goodness through, 152, 157; tree of, 'not that of life', 74, 76, 78, 80, 89.
liberty: the early centre of his idealism supplanted by beauty, 171; a subject on which he dis-

coursed to Emilia, 243; idealized in *Hellas*, 290 f., 300; his ideals of, in relation to his time, 316 f.

love, Christian and humanitarian (an ἀγάπη developed by Shelley out of the Platonic Ἔρως), 165, 198, 240, 296 n. 1, 300, 318; *see* Shelley, Greek concepts, Love.

Man: and the Universe, 134, 325; as Poet, 195; destiny of, 274 f., 282, 285, 289, 297 f.; perfectibility of, 127; power of his mind and will, 30 f., 33, 54, 72, 126, 158, 325.

marriage and sexual ethics, 8, 27, 201, 230, 251, 311.

mind, man's, 129, 134, 138, 157, 161 ff., 172, 201; Locke's view of, 306 f.

— universal, *see* Shelley, ideas, world soul/mind/spirit.

monarchy, 315 ff., 322.

mutability, 123–7, 146, 160, 165, 171 f., 268, 289, 295, 299 f., 323; *see* Shelley, ideas, reality.

nature and art, their interrelation in the poet, 25 ff., 220, 338.

passion, conjoined with will, among the powers of mind, 307, 325.

passive resistance: efficacy of, 55, 198, 215, 281, 322; occasional inefficacy of, 256. *See also* Spanish revolution.

poetic imagination, 308, 324–5.

poetry, not a matter of 'wit', 18; definition of, 308; didactic, Shelley's abhorrence of, 18, 275; function of, 125, 133 f., 136 f., 290 f.; immortality of, 258, 268; power of, 215, 305, 307; regenerative power of, 131, 144 f., 300; relationship to love, 55, 63, 258; source of, 1, 39, 134, 196, 244, 306.

— and poets, 144, 195, 309, 312.

political conditions in 1822, 280 f.

predestination, 27 f., 30 ff. *See also* Shelley, ideas, fate; — — free will.

priests, 28, 317 f., *see also* Shelley, ideas, religion.

reality, 22, 34, 98, 104 f., 123 f., 131, 134, 136 f., 139, 142 ff., 145, 147, 152 f., 159, 169, 172, 193, 246, 253,

266, 271, 274, 292, 294 f., 309; Cave of, 157, 160 f., 163, 166.

reason, in relation to imagination, 308 f., 325.

religion, 275–80, 303, 318 f. *See also* atheism, Beatitudes, Biblical study, Christ, Christian, Christianity, God, priests.

reviewers, 16–18, 218.

revolution, 198, 229, 315, 318.

seasons, the, *see* Shelley, ideas, spring.

soul, the: as a 'daemon', 234 n. 3; ascent of, 136 f., 164, 246; descent of, 164; immortality of, 9, 31, 65, 146, 154, 236, 278; nature of, 65, 141.

spring, regenerative power of, 20, 32–35, 156, 212, 227, 228, 317. *See also* Shelley, symbols, new birth of nature and thought.

Tätigkeit, *see above* Shelley, ideas, effectuality.

truth, 18, 22, 159 ff., 289 f. *See also* Shelley, ideas, immortality; — — mutability; — — reality.

tyranny and tyrants, 28, 36, 54, 125 f., 131, 164 ff., 198, 216, 275, 277, 296, 299 f., 322 ff.

violence: undesirability of, 198; weakness of, 54.

wisdom as a philosophical aim, 61, 270.

World-Soul (Mind Spirit), 27, 31 ff., 35, 65, 96, 129 f., 270, 278, 321. *See also* materialists of the eighteenth century.

LETTERS, xviii, 10, 11, 12, 22, 27, 30, 45, 53, 65, 77, 79, 80, 94, 174, 179, 205, 214, 217, 227, 247, 250, 253, 255, 256, 258, 259, 260, 262, 269, 273, 274, 285, 286, 302, 303.

NOTEBOOKS, 1–16, 40, 45 n. 3, 46 f., 55, 71, 88, 96, 98, 105, 115, 119, 134 n. 4, 136, 149, 173, 175 f., 195 ff., 199, 202–7, 211, 213, 215–19, 221, 223, 226, 228, 238, 241 n. 4, 242, 244, 249 f., 252, 258, 260–5, 269, 273, 305, 309, 311, 334; analysis of one of, 7 ff.; dating of, 11 ff., 46, 63, 197, 203 n. 3; memorandum from, 44, 169, 196 f.; method of investigation of, 9 ff.

Shelley, Percy Bysshe (*cont.*)
SYMBOLISM, 16 ff., 25, 32, 33 f., 58, 90,
  108 f., 121 f., 124, 131, 133, 159,
  162, 168 f., 170 f., 175 ff., 180, 193,
  195, 216, 235 f., 247, 263, 265,
  282, 291 f., 308, 315.
SYMBOLS:
Aeolian lyre, 196, 211, 215, 314.
balloons, 93.
'blood and gold', 198, 274, 280–6,
  291, 299, 301 f., 304, 316.
boat, 23, 68, 75, 91–94, 96–102,
  104 ff., 109 ff., 114, 116, 118, 121,
  132, 162 ff., 170, 172, 175, 194,
  235, 240 ff., 244, 246, 262 f., 268,
  292.
cave, 132, 147 f., 151, 153–67, 169,
  192 f., 235, 267, 292, 312.
— of thought, 23, 167 f.
— of enlightenment, 157, 160 f., 163.
cloud, 215 f., 226.
dome, 23, 108, 110, 114 ff., 119, 172,
  226 n. 4, 263, 268 f., 271, 296,
  317, 321.
dream, 169 ff., 173–7, 235, 253.
— of life, 175, 251, 294.
eagle, 69, 115.
eye, 23, 114 ff., 118.
fane *or* temple, 114, 117 f., 132, 321.
  See also Shelley, symbols, dome.
grave, 155, 223, 295.
harmony, 173.
isle, 23, 68, 75, 101–6, 109, 114, 121,
  132, 163 f., 170, 175, 235, 241, 246,
  268, 292.
leaf, 226.
light, radiance, 130, 143, 145, 147,
  152, 156, 165 ff., 172 f., 193, 218,
  225 f., 245, 255, 259, 261, 265,
  268 f., 271, 291, 301.
moon, 128, 167, 259.
new birth of nature and thought, 20,
  23, 26 f., 29, 33, 35, 62 f., 65, 124,
  164, 214, 220 f., 227, 228, 235,
  258, 263, 284, 295.
shadow, darkness, 130, 147, 152, 155,
  259, 265, 269, 291, 301.
sleep, 155, 169–72.
snake, serpent, 111; as eternity, 68 f.,
  118, 126; as the One, 69; as the
  Good, 69.
stars, 115 f., 118, 128, 205.
steps, 109.

trees, 68, 75.
veil, 63, 78, 92, 104, 120–5, 127 ff.,
  131 f., 134, 136 f., 139 f., 142–7,
  151 ff., 155 f., 164, 169, 172,
  193 f., 213, 229, 246 f., 262 f., 266,
  268, 274 f., 277, 279, 286, 289, 295,
  306, 312, 321.
water, ocean, sea, 75, 92, 97, 215,
  221, 223, 251, 268.
wave, 226.
wind, 211, 215, 272, 308.
TRANSLATIONS, vii, 2, 14; from Calderón, 78–87, 176–7, 329–33;
  from Cavalcanti, 232; from Dante,
  233, 239; from Goethe, 78–79;
  from Plato, 48–62, 136–44, 269;
  from his own poetry (into Italian),
  242 ff.
VARIED INTERESTS:
agricultural, 7 f., 201.
astronomy, modern, a source of
  imagery, 167.
pistol practice, 8 f.
political reform, 19, 93, 144, 212, 229.
reading, 2, 10, 43, 47, 64, 71, 150,
  174, 179, 285. *See also* French,
  German, Greek, Italian, Latin,
  Neoplatonic ideas, Plato, Spanish.
sailing, 285.
science: contemporary, 23, 43, 94,
  96, 97 n. 1, 117 n. 2, 145, 216, 303;
  modern development of, 319, 324 f.
  See also Davy, Sir Humphry;
  Faraday, Michael.
statistics for milk and potato production, noted by Shelley, 7.
steamboat project, 93 ff., 216, 228.
steam-power, also nautical experiments with, 97 n. 1.
WORKS, POETICAL:
'A Ghost Story', 46.
'A Lament' ('O world! O life! O
  time!), 88, 204.
'A New National Anthem', 316 f.
A Retrospect of Times of Old', 28,
  35.
'A Vision of the Sea', 3.
'A Wanderer', 173.
Adonais, 8, 12, 25, 33, 49, 51, 65 f., 69,
  95, 104, 118 f., 121, 174, 204 f., 237
  n. 2, 252 f., 255, 257–64, 266 f.,
  269, 271 f., 274 f., 278, 283, 285,
  290, 292, 294, 296, 301, 303, 308.

Alastor, 38 f., 41, 69 f., 73 f., 78, 85, 99, 108, 120, 128, 171 f., 232, 233 n. 1.

'An Allegory', 155 n. 1.

'An Exhortation' ('chameleons feed on light and air'), 218.

'Charles I', 275, 281.

early 'Mary-poems', 120, 240 n. 6.

Epipsychidion, 22, 38, 73–80, 102, 104, 109, 117, 127–30, 132, 204 f., 230, 233–9, 241, 243 f., 247, 248 n. 1, 249 f., 253, 258, 260, 266, 303, 308.

'Evening: Ponte al Mare, Pisa', 221.

'Fiordispina', 249, 303.

Fragments, 'The death-knell is ringing', 244; 'Thy beauty hangs about thee', 245; 'To one singing', 98, 203; 'To the People of England', 199.

'Fragments of an Unfinished Drama', 105, 108, 110, 175 f., 192 f.

'Ginevra', 244 n. 2, 249–53, 275, 303.

Hellas, 71, 178, 282–5, 290–301, 303, 306, 308 f., 338 n. 2.

Homer's *Hymn to Mercury*, translation of, 329 nn. 2, 3.

'Hymn of Apollo', 8, 115 f.

'Hymn of Pan', 8.

'Hymn to Intellectual Beauty', 41 ff., 45, 51, 67, 111, 113, 123, 148, 171 ff., 243.

'Indian Serenade', 204.

'Julian and Maddalo', 64.

Laon and Cythna, 105, 231 n.; *see also* Shelley, Works, Poetical, *The Revolt of Islam*.

'Life of Life' (song in *Prom. Unbound*), 128, 130, 163; (Italian version), 342 f.

'Lines to a Reviewer', 220.

'Lines written among the Euganean Hills', 102.

'Lines written during the Castle-reagh Administration', 7.

'Lines written in the Bay of Lerici', 287.

'Lines written on hearing the News of the Death of Napoleon', 198, 280.

'Marianne's Dream', 172.

'Mont Blanc', 45.

'Music' ('I pant for the music which is divine'), 203.

'Ode to Heaven', 115.

'Ode to Liberty', 7 ff., 11, 13, 125 n. 2, 201, 221, 315, 317; Italian version, 343.

'Ode to Naples', 204.

'Ode to the West Wind', 3, 8 f., 11, 13, 18–21, 26, 30 ff., 34, 36, 52 f., 62, 85 n. 3, 179, 197, 199, 208 n. 1, 211, 214 f., 221–9, 245, 249, 252, 258, 266, 284, 294, 329.

'On a Faded Violet', 50, 203 n. 3.

'Peter Bell the Third', 217, 228.

'Prince Athanase', 203.

Prometheus Unbound, 15–16, 21, 26, 30–31, 33, 36, 49, 51–57, 60, 65, 69–73, 85, 87, 96, 114, 124–46, 149–68, 171, 172–3, 179, 183, 191, 193, 199–202, 204, 212 f., 215 f., 218, 228–9, 242, 244, 245, 266, 275, 277, 279, 280, 281, 296 n. 1, 298, 307, 312, 317, 318, 325, 326.

Queen Mab, 27, 30–34, 36, 38, 51, 55 n. 4, 60, 62, 64, 68 ff., 81, 96, 104, 122, 128, 145, 251, 276, 291, 307, 311, 318, 324.

'Rosalind and Helen', 17, 46.

'Scenes from Goethe's Faust', 176, 202.

'Similes for Two Political Characters of 1819', 197.

'Song to the Men of England', 8, 199.

sonnets: 'Lift not the veil . . .', 122 f., 193 n. 1, 213 n. 4; 'To Words-worth', 233 n. 1.

'Stanzas written in Dejection near Naples', 212.

'The Boat on the Serchio', 17, 101.

The Cenci, 15, 173, 202, 212, 214.

'The Cloud', 8 f., 33.

'The Daemon of the World,' 68.

'The Fugitives', 102 n. 3, 107 ff., 244.

'The Magnetic Lady to her Patient', 287.

The Mask of Anarchy, 55, 197–200, 202, 216, 218, 228, 236 n. 2, 249, 281 f.

The Revolt of Islam, 34, 39, 64, 69, 99, 105–19, 121, 132, 172, 217, 242–3, 245, 256, 258, 268; *see also* Shelley Works, Poetical, *Laon and Cythna*.

'The Sensitive Plant', 11, 172.

Shelley, Percy Bysshe
  WORKS, POETICAL (*cont.*)
  'The Triumph of Life', 109, 175, 253, 273–304 *passim*, 319, 338.
  'The Voyage', 28 ff., 91 f., 101, 103, 121.
  'The Witch of Atlas', 9, 11, 99, 128, 231 n. 4, 329 n. 3.
  'The Woodman and the Nightingale', 263.
  'To a Skylark', 9, 11, 206–10, 242 f., 329.
  'To Constantia', 3.
  'To Constantia Singing', 97 n. 3, 116.
  'To Liberty', 171.
  'To Mary', 38, 240 n. 6.
  'To Emilia Viviani', 12.
  'To William Shelley', 46, 213, 218, 263.
  'When the Lamp is Shattered', 50.
  'With a Guitar to Jane', 194, 203.
  'Young Parson Richards', 8 n. 1, 200–1; quoted, 318.
  WORKS, PROSE:
  'A Defence of Poetry', 12, 36, 96, 115, 131, 133, 195, 211, 215, 227, 247, 257–60, 262, 272, 290, 306, 308 f., 324 f.
  WORKS, PRINTED PRIVATELY:
  'A Midsummer Night's Dream Poem', 334–8.
  A Philosophical View of Reform, 199, 228, 229 n. 6, 249, 274 f., 315.
  Address to the People on the Death of the Princess Charlotte, 316.
  'Discourse on the Manners of the Ancients Relative to the Subject of Love', 230.
  'Essay on Christianity', 167, 193.
  Refutation of Deism, 276.
  The Assassins, 292.
  The Necessity of Atheism, 276.
  'Una favola', 3, 226 n. 1, 241.
  'To St Irvyne', 37–38.
Shelley, Sir Percy Florence, 227.
Shelley, William, 46 f., 227, 264; burial of, 214, 263; death of, 26, 213; poetical laments on, 89.
Shelley Concordance, A, 7, 91, 147.
Shelley-Rolls, Sir John, 204, 240, 319; Shelley MSS. presented to the Bodleian by, v.
— Collection, 44.

— Notebook, 64, 65 n. 2, 196, 201, 206.
Shields, Amelia (Shelley's English maid), observes a comet, 205.
Sidmouth, Lord, Shelley's hatred of, 93, 197 ff., 215, 281, 316.
Silsbee, Captain, 200.
sketches, *see* Shelley, drawings.
Smith, Horace, 22, 265, 273, 282, 285 f., 298, 303.
Socialism, Shelley's, compared with that of Owen, Morris, Orwell, 323.
Socrates: and Diotima in the *Symposium*, 20, 39, 58–61; on the nature of the soul, 141; placed with Christ in 'The Triumph of Life', 277, 302; referred to in a rejected passage of *Epipsychidion*, 232; Shelley's memorandum on his daemon, 71.
Sophocles: a line about Necessity adapted by Plato, 54; memorandum by Shelley on a line from *Oedipus Tyrannus*, 15, 17, 173, 306; volume of his plays, a discredited Shelley relic, 12 n. 5.
Southey, R.: Shelley's verses in mockery of, 217; *Thalaba*, 93.
Spanish language and literature: Shelley's studies of, 177, 179 n. 3, 220, 226 n. 3, 232, 329; Shelley's translations of, 50, 141 n. 2, 81–90 *passim*, 176–7.
— revolution inspires 'Ode to Liberty', 11, 201.
Spenser, Edmund, 93, 107 n. 5, 120 f.; *The Faerie Queene*, 120, 123 n. 1.
Starkie, Enid, ix, on Rimbaud, quoted, 98.
Steele, Mabel, A. E., ed. *The Keats–Shelley Journal of America*, ix, xix, 10.
Suvoroff, a type of 'legal murderer', 28.
Symbolism, Symbols, *see under* Shelley.
Symbolists, French, Shelley's affinity with, 97.

Tan-yr-allt, Shelley's 'assailant' at, 68, 75, 90.
Tasso, quoted, 96.
Taylor, Thomas, translator of the *Timaeus*, 75 f.
Tertullian, 320.
Thompson, Francis, his judgement of Shelley, vi, 71, 269.